Scripture as
Communication

Scripture as Communication

Introducing Biblical Hermeneutics

Jeannine K. Brown

Baker Academic
Grand Rapids, Michigan

© 2007 by Jeannine K. Brown

Published by Baker Academic
a division of Baker Publishing Group
P.O. Box 6287, Grand Rapids, MI 49516–6287
www.bakeracademic.com

Printed in the United States of America

Library of Congress Cataloging-in-Publication Data
Brown, Jeannine K., 1961–
    Scripture as communication : introducing biblical hermeneutics / Jeannine K. Brown.
        p.   cm.
    Includes bibliographical references and index.
    ISBN 10: 0-8010-2788-8 (pbk.)
    ISBN 978-0-8010-2788-8 (pbk.)
    1. Bible—Hermeneutics. 2. Communication—Religious aspects—Christianity.
I. Title.
BS476.B68 2007
220.601—dc22   2006036880

To my parents,
James and Carolyn Holmen,
models of faith and faithfulness

Contents

Acknowledgments

I am deeply appreciative to my family, Tim, Kate, and Libby, for allowing me the space to go away on sabbatical to write this book. Thanks as well for the best reunion ever on Father's Day, 2005, in London!

Thank you to all who minister at Tyndale House, Cambridge, England, for a wonderful environment for scholarship and fellowship. Thank you to the Bethel Alumni Association for providing a sabbatical grant and to Bethel Seminary for granting sabbatical leave and supporting my scholarship.

Thank you to the Bethel Seminary students in my hermeneutics class who graciously read and interacted with the book in its early forms. Thanks to teaching assistants and staff who gave careful attention to reading various drafts: Alicia Gatto Petersen, Matthew Cain, Jane Spriggs, Gloria Metz, Tim Henderson, and Molly Noble.

Thank you to my Bethel colleagues who read the book and gave their invaluable feedback. Thanks to Peter Vogt, Thorsten Moritz, Mark Strauss, and DesAnne Hippe.

Thank you to Robert Stein and Kevin Vanhoozer for reading the manuscript in such careful and insightful ways. I am deeply grateful, and the book is much better for your comments.

Thank you to Baker Academic for taking on this project, particularly to Jim Kinney, who provided helpful guidance all along the way.

Finally, I would like to thank my parents, James and Carolyn Holmen, who fostered in me the conviction that the Bible is relevant to all of life. It is to you that I dedicate this book.

Introduction

Scripture as Communicative Act

> Because God reveals himself in personal categories, divine revelation is analogous to human communication.
>
> Jens Zimmermann, *Recovering Theological Hermeneutics*

> "Meaning" is the result of communicative action, of what an author has done in tending to certain words at a particular time in a specific manner.
>
> Kevin J. Vanhoozer, *First Theology*

Talking theology with my two daughters, Kate and Libby, is one of my great joys. But inevitably, their distinct personalities shape these conversations. Kate has always been an inquirer. Questions are her starting point. Questions about God, questions about the Bible, questions about people from other faith traditions—lots of questions. When she was four years old, she dropped a theological bomb that I thought I would not have to address with her until she was much older: "Mom, who did Jesus pray to when he lived on earth?" All my lofty ideals developed in seminary theological classes about not using the proverbial comparison of the Trinity with an egg went out the window as I struggled to communicate what I understand about the Triune God of Scripture to a four-year-old mind. Kate, now a teenager, continues to ask questions as she explores who God is and what the Bible means.

My other daughter, Libby, in contrast, has never been one for asking questions or advice of her parents. Most days, she lives in a world of her own making: a world in which all her creative abilities, which are considerable, are focused on joyful play and free-flowing imagination. I have discovered that Libby's way of getting at a theological conversation is to make declarative statements that, on the surface, seem to be assertions about reality but that actually are intended to invite conversation and clarification. One such conversation a few years ago went something like this:

"Mom, God doesn't exist, but we still believe in him."

I queried, "Do you mean that we can't *see* God?"

Libby responded matter-of-factly, "Yeah, God isn't real, but we believe in him anyway."

I again responded with a question, "Do you mean that God doesn't have *a body*?"

(We had recently had a conversation about John 4 and the affirmation that God is spirit.)

Libby agreed, "Yes," and then explained that she and a friend had been discussing God and Jesus and the issue of bodies came up.

When she came to our conversation, Libby was exploring the truth of the immateriality of God in contrast with other ways of expressing who God is. She was implicitly asking questions. To be more precise, she was testing ideas by making statements.

In sharing these stories, my point goes beyond expressing from the onset that I come to the tasks of theology and hermeneutics (the study of the interpretation of texts) as a parent and a confessing Christian, as well as a New Testament scholar. I certainly approach Scripture and the task of reflection on Scripture from the merging of many such vantage points. Yet my primary purpose in beginning with these stories is to illustrate the complexity of the communication process. Kate routinely asks questions that are truly questions in her exploration of the nature of God and the world around her. Libby makes statements about God and the world when she is in fact testing her ideas—an implicit sort of question-asking—although this purpose is not obvious on the surface of her sentences. The truth that Libby is requesting feedback to the ideas that she proposes is only discernable from attention to a number of factors. These include her previous patterns in communicating, the setting in which she makes these declarations, and the flow of particular conversations, past and present. But not every one of the statements she makes on a daily basis is a testing of ideas. I must discern from such rather complex contextual factors which of them function as requests. This is the nature of the task of understanding human communication—it is the task of interpretation and is often more complex than we would like to admit. But interpreting is also something we do every day of our lives, with a relatively high rate of success.

Engaging in and interpreting communication is at the heart of what we are doing when we read the Bible. Christians have a long history of describing the Bible in language that evokes its communicative nature. When we speak of the Bible as the word of God, we are affirming that God speaks and that we should listen—we are using language of communication. The phrase "word of God" occurs throughout the Bible, more often than not in reference to God's spoken word.[1] Yet there are places where its occurrence broadens to include the written word as the record of what God has spoken (e.g., Matt. 15:6; Heb. 4:12). So opening the Bible can be likened to entering into a communicative event. Or, to put it metaphorically, Scripture begins a conversation that is interpersonal and potentially life changing, because it is God who initiates the dialogue.

The movement toward a communicative model of biblical interpretation can be seen in works of a number of recent writers. Nicholas Wolterstorff, for example, has used the language of "authorial discourse" to express the communicative nature of Scripture.[2] In fact, Wolterstorff centers his discussion on how we might understand Scripture to be "divine discourse." Trevor Hart similarly expresses that the Bible is communication by emphasizing the need for readers to "presume presence." Hart introduces this phrase to indicate the presence of the human author (and, later in his essay, the divine author) in the text.[3] Other scholars have introduced the concept of "address" to focus attention on the necessity of envisioning both authors and readers within the communicative process: "language is always addressed to someone else, even if that someone is not immediately present or is actually unknown or imagined."[4]

Scripture as Communication

Such references to texts as authorial discourse or authorial presence and as addressed to readers serve to introduce the three domains of author, text, and reader. All three are implicit in the idea that Scripture is, at heart, communication. The author is the one who communicates;

1. Similar to "word of the Lord" in the OT prophetic books.
2. Nicholas Wolterstorff, *Divine Discourse: Philosophical Reflections on the Claim that God Speaks* (Cambridge: Cambridge University Press, 1995), 132.
3. Trevor Hart, "Tradition, Authority, and a Christian Approach to the Bible as Scripture," in *Between Two Horizons: Spanning New Testament Studies and Systematic Theology*, ed. Joel B. Green and Max Turner (Grand Rapids: Eerdmans, 2000), 194, 201.
4. Dick Leith and George Myerson, *The Power of Address: Explorations in Rhetoric* (London: Routledge, 1989), xii. The issue of language use as self-expression versus communication will be discussed in chap. 3. The focus here is language's communicative uses.

the text is the vehicle or act of communication; and the reader is the one who is addressed and who responds. Discussion of these three components is not new to the discussion of hermeneutics. All theories of textual interpretation must, and do, deal with author, text, and reader and their involvement and influence in the reading process. In more recent hermeneutical history these three constructs have endured an uneasy relationship. At this point, we might simply affirm that the way we understand the role of authors, texts, and readers in the task of interpretation largely depends upon our view of the nature of texts (e.g., what texts intrinsically are, whether they are communicative or expressive in nature, whether they are stable or unstable).

In this book the first two chapters will propose a communication model for interpreting the Bible. The rest of the book will then draw upon this model. In the earlier chapters, I will be elaborating the proposed communication model (chaps. 3–6), and, in the final chapters of the book, I will be applying the proposed model to various facets of the interpretive enterprise, such as genre, social setting, and issues related to contextualizing the biblical message (chaps. 7–12).

In a nutshell, the communication model I propose is this: *Scripture's meaning can be understood as the communicative act of the author that has been inscribed in the text and addressed to the intended audience for purposes of engagement*. This definition places the author's text at the forefront of the communicative act. This preliminary definition also seeks to incorporate readers in a significant way by connecting them with the audience envisioned within the text. Scripture readily addresses contemporary readers precisely as they stand in continuity with the people of God, who comprised the original audience. A commitment to the Bible as Scripture means that "we are the people of God to whom these texts are addressed."[5] Such a confessional reading of the Bible is one in which the reader identifies with God's people who were first addressed by the text, even though that original address was made to a particular cultural context, which will require our careful attention. Even as we seek the author's communicative act, we will need to be aware of the importance of our stance and responses as readers. As we will discover in chapter 3, there has been a tendency in the history of hermeneutical discussion to focus on one of the three domains of author, text, and reader, to the practical neglect of the other two. By incorporating all three more intentionally into our understanding of written communication, we hope to avoid some of the imbalances that have characterized this history.

5. "I take the claim, the Bible as Scripture, to refer to a theological stance whereby we recognize that we are the people of God to whom these texts are addressed"; Joel B. Green, "The (Re)turn to Narrative," in *Narrative Reading, Narrative Preaching*, ed. Joel B. Green and Michael Pasquarello III (Grand Rapids: Baker Academic, 2003), 23.

What are the advantages of a communication model? A few stand out as particularly helpful in the context of contemporary philosophical discussions. A major advantage of such a model is that communication is inherently interpersonal, that is, it occurs between persons. And although as readers our direct interaction is with a person's *text*, viewing textual interpretation as interpersonal, even as friendship, has some distinct advantages. "As a metaphor for the reading experience, friendship is rich in possibilities. It expresses both the emotive and the cognitive aspects of reading, and connotes the pleasures, intimacies, comforts, and discomforts of entering and living within the [literary] world for a time."[6] In this way, interpersonal categories are truer to an understanding of the Bible as Scripture and more useful than models that primarily emphasize the text as code (with the author as encoder and reader as decoder).[7] So when we speak of the text as speech, as discourse, as communication, we are affirming that it derives from a person, the author, who desires to communicate and so initiates a conversation of sorts. The same framework, I believe, also honors the experience of readers who have the sense of being personally addressed as they read texts, and the Bible more specifically. Readers are "encountered" by texts.[8]

In addition, if texts are viewed from an interpersonal perspective, we might, in the end, be able to minimize the sometimes-proposed contrast between subject and object. This contrast goes something like this: I, as subject, come to study and interpret the written text, as object. Yet communication conceived purely in terms of subject/object lacks the dialogical interplay that characterizes personal communication. I do not construe an email from my husband as an object for my scrutiny as much as I experience it as a personal address from him (person to person rather than subject to object). This is not an argument against the need for interpretation in the reading process. Instead, it is a plea for a more interpersonal model of reading and interpreting, one that lives up to the implicitly relational idea of the biblical text as communication—and therefore one that does justice to the dialogical nature of interpretation and contextualization.

6. Adele Reinhartz, *Befriending the Beloved Disciple: A Jewish Reading of the Gospel of John* (New York: Continuum, 2001), 18.

7. Gene Green argues that the code model actually eliminates the need for the author in communication, since all that is needed to interpret is found in the text, that is, in the code. "Thus the code model opens the door to the suppression of authors since texts can stand on their own and, truly, are orphaned from the moment they are given birth"; Gene Green, "Context and Communication" (paper presented at the linguistics section of the annual meeting of the SBL, Toronto, Ontario, 25 November 2002), 6. I am grateful for the permission granted by the author to use his paper.

8. Joel Green speaks of "a hermeneutic of relationship" in "(Re)turn to Narrative," 23.

There is another advantage to a communication model of the Bible and its interpretation. As communication is rarely limited to cognitive categories, so too our understanding of the text's import must move beyond cognitive categories alone. For instance, we read in Psalm 147:1 (NIV):

> How good it is to sing praises to our God,
>   How pleasant and fitting to praise him!

It would be a mistake to claim that there is no cognitive content being expressed here. The psalmist is certainly declaring the goodness and rightness of praising God. Yet the psalmist in his very words is also enacting praise to God—he is *doing something* in the offering up of his words. In addition, given the context of the whole psalm, it is difficult to ignore the idea that the psalmist is also implicitly calling his audience to praise their God in 147:1 (as he explicitly does at 147:7, 12, 20). Affirming that texts do more than contain content does not denigrate the cognitive elements of a text's message. Scripture does communicate what is often termed propositional truth. Yet we are not limited to an either/or choice between cognitive content and noncognitive purposes in texts. Noncognitive (e.g., emotive, volitional) purposes also deserve a fair representation in our discussion of textual meaning. A communication model allows for such a holistic approach. So as we explore Scripture as communication, we will find that this model helpfully expands an understanding of what the Bible is and how we interpret it.

Part 1

Theoretical Perspectives on Scripture as Communication

1

Terminology and Context for Hermeneutics

Concepts are not what we think about; they are what we think with.

Kathleen Callow, *Man and Message*

The Importance of Conceptual Clarity

A helpful starting point for exploring the idea of Scripture as an act of communication is the clarification of terminology. If, as Callow contends, we think *with* concepts, we will want to be as clear as possible about the concepts we use to engage issues of biblical interpretation. Robert Stein, in his book *A Basic Guide to Interpreting the Bible*, emphasizes the importance of definitional work for thinking clearly about hermeneutics.[1] As a beginning seminary student in Stein's hermeneutics class and as a reader of his book, I was empowered to think more clearly about issues of interpretation by working through a number of terms that formed the basis for our class discussion. Since then, I have valued the gift of

1. Robert H. Stein, *A Basic Guide to Interpreting the Bible: Playing by the Rules* (Grand Rapids: Baker Academic, 1994), 37.

definitional clarity. With the goal of passing along this gift, I will introduce a few general terms and their definitions in this chapter. In chapter 2, we will take a look at some theoretical models for interpretation and also introduce some additional terms more specifically focused on the goal of interpretation.

After seminary, I experienced firsthand the value of having ideas precisely defined when I was taking a hermeneutics course in my doctoral program. In an informal discussion outside of class one day, a fellow student and I were discussing biblical interpretation. Part of the way through the conversation, I asked my classmate how she understood the concept of meaning (that is, What do you mean by *meaning*?). She was taken aback by my question and proceeded to censure me just a bit for the attempt to define meaning. She did not give me an answer and made it clear that the question itself was essentially wrongheaded. As you might imagine, we could not proceed much further on the topic. Without at least a preliminary definition, there was no way to determine if there was any common ground between our viewpoints, or where we diverged for that matter. In fact, articulating a definition of a term, such as "meaning," is not as much about setting it in stone (mine continues to be nuanced) as it is about clarifying how a concept fits with other definitions of that same concept as well as other terms. In other words, we are best able to compare concepts and conceptual frameworks if we have adequately defined our understanding of those concepts—if we have done some basic definitional work.

Hermeneutics

To begin, what is hermeneutics? The short answer is that hermeneutics is the study of the activity of interpretation. In the realm of theory, the term is used to refer to the discipline that analyzes interpretation, specifically, how texts communicate, how meaning is derived from texts and/or their authors, and what it is that people do when they interpret a text. In practical relation to biblical interpretation, people use "hermeneutics" either to speak about the act of bringing the meaning of the text to bear in one's present context, or the study of the whole movement involved in interpreting a text's meaning and applying it today.[2] I follow the latter course. For our purposes (and to return to a shorter definition),

2. Gordon Fee and Douglas Stuart follow the former, Grant Osborne the latter. In relation to biblical hermeneutics, Osborne refers to these two stages as exegesis and contextualization (Grant R. Osborne, *The Hermeneutical Spiral: A Comprehensive Introduction to Biblical Interpretation* [Downers Grove, IL: InterVarsity, 1991], 5). See Gordon D. Fee and Douglas Stuart, *How to Read the Bible for All Its Worth*, 3rd ed. (Grand Rapids: Zondervan, 2003), 29.

hermeneutics is the analysis of what we do when we seek to understand the Bible, including its appropriation to the contemporary world. You might have noticed that in the process of defining hermeneutics we, by necessity, also defined "interpretation" (seeking to understand the Bible). When we compare these two definitions, we notice that hermeneutics is a second-order task, which means that it involves thinking about thinking. In the case of hermeneutics, thinking and reflection are focused on the act of interpreting texts (which is itself more than a thinking activity but certainly not less).

For many, this definition might beg the question: Why is interpretation needed, let alone the analysis of interpretation? (To get down to it, why this book?) This is an honest and common enough question, especially in light of reflexive assumptions that would say *reading* rather than *interpreting* is what ought to happen when we come to the Bible. I am reminded of an advertisement I came across in a Christian magazine a while ago for a new English Bible version. The slogan read, "Now No Interpretation Needed." The advertisers were implying that this particular Bible was so accurate and clear that simple reading of the text would suffice.

The matter is not so simple, however, given that all reading is interpretation. When I pick up the newspaper in the morning to read, I am, to be more accurate, an interpreter of it. I make a large number of reflexive determinations in order to read that newspaper rightly. For example, I know that I am to read the editorials differently from the front page headlines, and also from the funnies. I adjust my expectations accordingly. I also draw upon a large pool of shared assumptions with the writers of my local newspaper, such as the identities of local sports teams (Go, Vikings!) and the general political and social situation of my city, state, nation, and world. But I do so without much conscious effort, given my familiarity with my own culture's social context and literary conventions (e.g., funnies are not advertisements).

When living in England for a month, I had the experience of reading a newspaper in my own language but without fully sharing the cultural backdrop of its writers. There were many times when they referred to a name, place, or situation that would have been clearly understood by a local British resident but was obscure to me. Additionally, a turn of phrase that was commonplace for a local reader would puzzle me. I felt the culture gap, even though I share the same language and live at the same time in history.

Imagine how the task of understanding grows more complex when reading ancient texts, including the Bible. This complexity is the reason why what is usually reflexive when reading documents in our native language and from the same cultural context necessarily needs to be more

21

consciously addressed when reading ancient texts. There are significant gaps in our knowledge of the literary conventions, language, and social settings that surround and inhabit biblical texts. We live in a different time and place than the times and places in which and to which the text originally spoke. Deliberate attention to these issues and painstaking work at many junctures are required. That is the reason why interpretation is not only necessary; it is also unavoidable.[3] And that is why biblical interpretation needs second-order reflection; it needs hermeneutics.[4]

Meaning: A Preliminary Definition

Meaning is what we are trying to grasp when we interpret. That is the short answer, and one on which there is general agreement. From there, definitions diverge sharply. Is meaning to be found by attending to the author and his or her intentions? Or is meaning a property of texts apart from their authors? How do readers intersect with meaning? Do they only discover or respond to meaning, or are they in reality creators of meaning? Our answers to these kinds of questions will significantly influence our definition of meaning.[5]

At this point, with a caution that I am advancing a preliminary definition that will be expanded in chapter 2, I will refocus and briefly explain the definition of meaning already provided: meaning is the communicative intention of the author, which has been inscribed in the text and addressed to the intended audience for purposes of engagement. The author's communicative act when writing a text is an act of intention. Because the concept of "authorial intention" has been much maligned in recent years, I specify the kind of intention I mean: not simply what an author hopes to communicate (intention as wish or motive) but what an author actually does communicate by intention in a text (communicative intention).[6] The

3. Hart's words are forceful in this regard: "The idea that it is possible to . . . achieve a pure reading of the text . . . is one which must be shown up for the self-deception that it is. . . . Simple appeals to 'what the Bible says' are always the sign of (no doubt unconscious) subservience to an interpretative tradition, not liberation from it" (Trevor Hart, *Faith Thinking: The Dynamics of Christian Theology* [Downers Grove, IL: InterVarsity, 1996], 167).

4. Sometimes you may see this term in its singular form: "hermeneutic." One's particular view of hermeneutics (the specific way one thinks about interpretation) is termed a "hermeneutic." For example, my view that meaning is, at its core, an author's communicative act is part of my hermeneutic.

5. See chap. 3 for an exploration of how these questions have been answered in the recent history of hermeneutics.

6. For this terminology, I draw on Mark Brett, who distinguishes between motives and communicative intentions (Mark Brett, "Motives and Intentions in Genesis 1," *Journal of Theological Studies* 42 [1991]: 1–16, esp. 5). See also Kevin J. Vanhoozer, *First Theology: God, Scripture and Hermeneutics* (Downers Grove, IL: InterVarsity, 2002), 170.

latter is accessible to the reader of the text; the former is not. Meaning understood as an author's communicative intention avoids the pitfalls historically associated with a broader concept of authorial intentions. Once we have explored some theories of textual communication, we will be in a better position to develop this definition of meaning to express more carefully the relationship between author, text, and reader.

Exegesis

Exegesis is the task of carefully studying the Bible in order to determine as well as possible the author's meaning in the original context of writing. Or as Moisés Silva puts it, *"exegesis . . . is a fancy way of referring to interpretation."*[7] The latter definition makes it clear that our understanding and practice of exegesis are very much dependent upon our definition of meaning, since how we understand meaning inevitably works itself out in our interpretive (exegetical) practices. For example, if one understands meaning to be a property of texts divorced from their authors, interpretation will not focus on authorial meaning. So there is an organic interdependence between our definitions of meaning, interpretation, and hermeneutics. The first definition for exegesis given above, which focuses on authorial meaning within the original context, emphasizes that exegesis focuses on the *then* of the text rather than the *now* of contextualized meaning.[8]

For this reason, the exegetical process is, at its heart, a cross-cultural one. We are trying to understand the Bible in its original context. Doing so will necessarily involve bridging gaps of time and location, language and culture. Coming to study the Bible in its own context is rather like taking a trip to a foreign country. It is very exciting, but it also requires lots of energy! Even in our global age, crossing cultures is rather strenuous activity. You need to navigate a different language, different customs, differing money systems, and a location of which you may have very little firsthand knowledge.

When we come to exegete the Bible,[9] there are a number of factors to pay attention to in order to bridge the cultural gap between its setting and ours. Some of these are simply good reading habits we need to

7. Walter Kaiser Jr. and Moisés Silva, *An Introduction to Biblical Hermeneutics: The Search for Meaning* (Grand Rapids: Zondervan, 1994), 19; italics in original.

8. The use of the term "original meaning" is not particularly popular in hermeneutical circles. The idea that we can separate original meaning from our appropriation of it is often seen as both quite naïve and modernist. Nevertheless, while agreeing that in practice it is rather difficult to distinguish exegesis and contextualization, I find the distinction helpful for a theoretical exploration of interpretation. See comments under "Contextualization" below.

9. Yes, the noun can become a verb; it can also become a personal noun: the one doing exegesis is called an "exegete."

cultivate. Others are necessitated by Scripture's cultural distance. We might call all of these "guidelines for reading at a distance," and they include attention to genre, literary context, and social setting.[10]

Genre

The genre of a biblical text or book refers to its classification as a specific kind of literature. There are many types of literature in the Bible, including, but not limited to, narrative, poetry, epistle, legal texts, and apocalyptic literature. Each of these genres can, in turn, be subdivided into further generic (genre) categories. Poetry in the Old Testament, for instance, is the primary genre found in the prophetic books (e.g., Micah and Jeremiah), in wisdom literature (e.g., Proverbs and Job), and in songs (such as Psalms and Song of Songs). It is important to identify the genre of a biblical book, since we will need to familiarize ourselves with the conventions of that genre to read rightly. As modern readers, we simply do not know everything we need to know about certain conventions of the genres of the Bible. For instance, while contemporary readers often feel fairly comfortable interpreting letters (modern or biblical), none of us encounters apocalyptic literature as a genre in our own culture. It is important, then, to understand the generic categories particular to the Bible and learn the conventions and contours that come along with that genre.[11]

Literary Context

One reading skill that seems obvious for general reading, but sometimes is ignored when we approach the Bible, is reading individual texts in their literary context. Literary context is defined as the written material surrounding a text in question. Initially, it is the material immediately surrounding a proposed passage of Scripture, as well as the wider section in which that passage is located. During much of the exegetical process, the most important literary unit to attend to when reading a specific text is the book of the Bible in which it is found. For exegesis to stay true to what an author has communicated, the whole book must remain in view, even when primary focus is on a single passage (as is often the case in sermons or exegetical papers). There is a time, as well, for looking beyond the individual book to its connections within the whole of Scripture. This is called canonical context (with the canon referring to the sixty-six books that make up the Protestant Christian Bible).[12]

10. For a more complete list of exegetical guidelines for students of the English Bible, see Appendix A.
11. See chap. 7 for more on genre.
12. See chap. 10 for discussion of literary and canonical contexts.

Social Setting

The gaps that seem most obvious to us as we read Scripture are usually related to the historical and cultural distances between our world and the worlds surrounding the Bible. We experience these gaps more potently in some texts than in others. For example, my family had been reading Genesis together. Arriving at chapter 14, we read:

> Then the king of Sodom, the king of Gomorrah, the king of Admah, the king of Zeboiim, and the king of Bela (that is, Zoar) went out, and they joined battle in the Valley of Siddim with Chedorlaomer king of Elam, Tidal king of Goiim, Amraphel king of Shinar, and Arioch king of Ellasar, four kings against five. Now the Valley of Siddim was full of bitumen pits, and as the kings of Sodom and Gomorrah fled, some fell into them, and the rest fled to the hill country. (Gen. 14:8–10 ESV)

We were more than a little geographically and historically challenged by this passage, not to mention linguistically stretched. (Although we didn't know initially what a bitumen pit was, we knew it couldn't be a good thing!) This passage reemphasized in my mind that the Bible was written in a different setting than the one in which I live. This is truly a good realization. It heightens my awareness that I should be a gracious visitor in this foreign land and get to know all I can about its cultural and historical setting, what we might refer to as its social world.[13] Recognizing the "foreignness" of the biblical text can be a bit disconcerting for those of us who hold firmly to the relevance and authority of the Bible. Yet I am convinced that we can hold two truths in tension: (1) the significant distance of the social world of the Bible from our world, and (2) the nearness and relevance of the Scriptures to our lives and needs. There are times when we experience the Bible like a trip to a foreign country and times when we experience the Bible as an old and dear friend. It is my conviction that the foreign excursion will show itself to be relevant and meaningful to our contexts if we take the time to understand the gaps between the ancient and contemporary world.

Contextualization

Contextualization is the task of bringing a biblical author's meaning to bear in other times and cultures. To shift the emphasis a bit, to contextualize is to hear Scripture's meaning speak in new contexts. The assumption behind this definition is that the Bible has something

---

13. I will be using the term "social world" to refer broadly to historical, cultural, political, religious, and geographical issues that require our attention when interpreting an ancient text like the Bible.

to say to us today, because the Bible is Scripture, God's word. This is not to say that readers who do not consider the Bible to be Scripture cannot find it meaningful or helpful. It is only to affirm that issues of contextualization will be most central to those who understand the text to be authoritative.

Now, the very choice to distinguish contextualization from the exegetical process has implications for my view of hermeneutics, that is, my hermeneutic. In fact, I am tempted to include contextualization under the heading of exegesis (along with genre, context, etc.). The reason? In practice, the task of interpreting meaning will inevitably and naturally involve contextualization. The two tasks cannot easily be separated.[14] They can, however, be distinguished theoretically. In fact, to do so is helpful for conceptualizing what we do when we interpret Scripture. So, for purposes of clarifying the two tasks, they will be separated in our discussions. In chapters 7 through 10, practical matters related to exegesis will be explored. But it will not always be so easy to keep contextualization at bay. Conversely, in the final two chapters of the book, contextualization will receive our attention. But even there, we will consistently refer back to the exegetical process envisioned in earlier chapters.

Setting a Context for Our Theoretical Discussion

In chapter 2, we will be examining a number of theoretical models that either address interpretation from a communicative vantage point or include elements that help to conceptualize an aspect of the communicative process. Before we begin this discussion, I would like to outline the context for scholars' many and varied theories on the subject of hermeneutics in recent times. Why is there such disagreement on definitions of meaning and therefore of interpretation? What hermeneutical proposals have been made to make sense of issues of meaning? By scouting the theoretical landscape, we hope to understand better the nature of texts and, as a result, (1) approach texts in a way that honors their inherent nature, and (2) approach Scripture in a way that hears what God, through human authors, has communicated.

We might say that meaning is at the center of the storm. Never has there been a concept so malleable. Meaning has been defined from almost every angle, and how it is defined determines how readers go about reading—that is, interpreting—texts. Traditionally, meaning was thought

14. As Packer asserts, "Exegesis without application should not be called interpretation at all" (J. I. Packer, *Honouring the Written Word of God: The Collected Shorter Writings of J. I. Packer* [Carlisle: Paternoster, 1999], 3:27).

to rest with authors. When interpreting Scripture, readers believed they were hearing from the human or the divine author. It was not uncommon for those listening for the human author to hear something distinct from those listening for the divine author.[15] It was the case that, even when the author was the focus of interpretation, agreement was not guaranteed between interpreters on the meaning of specific biblical texts.

There came a time, however, when theorists became suspicious of the claim that authors could actually be accessed by reading their texts. Even if the interpreter could access the author's intention, some people questioned whether this would lead to successful interpretation. Consideration of texts as separate from their authors came into philosophical vogue—the text was seen as free from the author, free to impact the contemporary reader. In a more recent turn of events, it is the reader who has become the center of the interpretive process. As Hart describes, "Now we are advised that the question, What does the text mean? is insufficient, perhaps even entirely inappropriate. . . . Now the existence of meaning as in any sense an objective commodity is frequently called into question. Meaning is defined by some as what the reader creates, or brings with her to the text, or the effect the text produces in the reader, or what the reader chooses to do with the text."[16]

In the end, it comes down to the nature of texts. What are they intrinsically? If they are free-floating entities that shift and change with new readings and readers, then we will not be very concerned about authors and their intentions. But if texts are culturally located communicative acts, tied to a particular place and time (although with potential for speaking beyond that particularity), then questions of their authors and origins will be relevant for interpretation. In fact, it is meaning as communicative act that holds the most promise for doing justice to author, text, and reader, without missing the distinctive ways each contributes to the communication process.

The theories we will be exploring in the next chapter each have valuable conceptual insights to contribute to a model of Scripture as communication. We will be focusing on those insights rather than providing a comprehensive introduction to each theory. The theories we will be describing also reintroduce the author or focus on the historical particularity of communication, which almost inevitably invites a reengagement with the author. After a period of time in hermeneutical

15. Historical criticism in its early manifestations listened only for the human author and assumed all other kinds of listening to be improperly subjective. For more about historical criticism, see Appendix B. I will be arguing that we should not try to separate the two—what the human author was communicating stands in for God's communicative intent.

16. Hart, "Christian Approach to the Bible," 193–94.

history described by E. D. Hirsch as the "banishment of the author," it seems the time has arrived to welcome the author back to the hermeneutical table.[17]

So, if you're ready, take a deep breath, and we'll wax theoretical . . .

17. E. D. Hirsch, *Validity in Interpretation* (New Haven: Yale University Press, 1967), 1. Steinmetz vividly captures this notion of author banishment when he notes that "contemporary debunking of the author . . . has proceeded at such a pace that it seems at times as if literary criticism has become a jolly game of ripping out an author's shirttail and setting fire to it" (David C. Steinmetz, "The Superiority of Pre-Critical Exegesis," in *The Theological Interpretation of Scripture: Classic and Contemporary Readings*, ed. Stephen E. Fowl, Blackwell Readings in Modern Theology [Cambridge, MA: Blackwell, 1997], 36).

2

A Communication Model
of Hermeneutics

As for you, continue in what you have learned and have become convinced of, because you know those from whom you learned it, and how from infancy you have known the Holy Scriptures, which are able to make you wise for salvation through faith in Christ Jesus. All Scripture is God-breathed and is useful for teaching, rebuking, correcting and training in righteousness, so that the servant of God may be thoroughly equipped for every good work.

2 Timothy 3:14–17

There are many people who feel theory is not for them—theory is only for those inclined that way. But if one holds the view that *a theory is essentially a system of beliefs about reality*, it is difficult to think of anything more important than theory. . . .
    Our beliefs should accurately represent reality.

Ernst-August Gutt, *Relevance Theory* (italics in original)

The opening quotations seem to offer an interesting choice: the Bible or theory? Which will be our starting point when it comes to hermeneutics? Actually, I placed them both at the beginning of this chapter because both are necessary for hermeneutics. As a biblical scholar coming to hermeneutics, I am convinced that the Bible itself ought to shape our hermeneutic. My preferred starting point for conscious reflection is what the Bible communicates about itself (2 Tim. 3:14–16, in reference to the Old Testament, for example) as well as what the Bible implicitly shows itself to be.[1] Yet even as I come to the Bible with these hermeneutical questions and commitments, I already possess a theoretical framework that affects my understanding of the way Scripture communicates. We all do.

None of us is a clean slate. We have been guided, often without much conscious awareness, toward a theoretical understanding of what the Bible is and how it should be approached. Each of us has a belief system that influences our way of thinking about the Bible and its interpretation. In this chapter we will be looking at resources for thinking about Scripture and its interpretation from such disciplines as linguistic theory (the nature of language), literary theory (the nature of literary texts and how they communicate), and theology (the nature of God and God's relationship with humanity and the rest of creation). It is essential to acknowledge that each of us already has a theory (with linguistic, literary, and theological components) of how to approach Scripture. We have intuitively gleaned our theory from all sorts of sources, including family, church, education, and culture. For example, a fundamental theological assumption I have about the Bible is its unity. I believe that the messages of its different authors, although at times in tension, are not ultimately contradictory. I have inherited this conviction from my early contexts of church and family and later have come to appropriate this assumption as a conscious stance toward the Bible. It is part of my larger theoretical interpretive framework. The goal in this chapter is not to introduce theory artificially into our reflections on interpretation. Rather, our purpose is, with the help of a variety of theorists, to become more aware of our own implicit assumptions about the workings of language and written communication. We will consider how to think biblically and theologically about the task of interpretation in a more intentional fashion.

Theoretical Models of Interpretation

Theories about the nature of meaning and interpretation are abundant. Disciplines such as philosophy, theology, and linguistics, among

1. For example, the Bible shows itself to be both culturally located and deeply relevant to all cultures. This "incarnational" quality of Scripture will be explored in chap. 12.

others, examine these issues from different angles and come to differing conclusions.[2] Our goal is not to survey and evaluate in depth every existing hermeneutical theory. Instead, with communication as our standpoint, we will explore theoretical models from various disciplines. These models will help us both to conceptualize the activity of communication and to reflect productively on how interpretation of textual communication happens. When we find useful concepts and insights from different theories, we will consider whether they might be authentically integrated into a communication model of hermeneutics.[3] For each theoretical proposal introduced, I will (1) briefly summarize the theory as it relates to communication and (2) identify some of its key concepts for a communication model of texts, the Bible in particular.

Before we begin, two caveats are in order. First, I make no attempt to represent all theories, whether philosophical, theological, literary, or linguistic. For example, I do not introduce the literary theory of deconstruction, not because it lacks textual insights but because deconstruction makes different assumptions about the nature of texts than those in the communication model I propose.[4] Although the model I suggest is an eclectic one (gathering elements from different sources), it limits its eclecticism to theories that are coherent with the notion of texts as communicative acts. Second, I would like to add just a word about philosophical theories of interpretation. Philosophy reflects on concerns broader than textual interpretation but fundamentally applicable to it.[5] The influence of philosophy already is evident in the various theories we will be discussing, as I will point out along the way. In addition, some particulars of proposals by influential hermeneutical philosophers such as Hans-Georg Gadamer and Paul Ricoeur will be raised in our discussions in subsequent chapters.

2. As Hirsch notes, "Hermeneutics theory owes debts to so many fields" (*Validity*, 90).

3. I am not attempting a unique theory of communication, that is, a system of hypotheses that explain all contingencies in interpretation. Rather, in drawing on theoretical discussions, I attempt to construct a model (a simplified representation) of what seems to occur in textual communication and how such a model can assist in biblical interpretation. Stark defines a model as describing "why and how things fit together and function" (Rodney Stark, *The Rise of Christianity: A Sociologist Reconsiders History* [Princeton, NJ: Princeton University Press, 1996], 26).

4. In deconstruction theory, texts are less than stable, and they have little to do with an author's intentional communicative act. The result is that interpretation has few authorial or even, at times, textual constraints.

5. Specifically, philosophy engages issues of how we know what we know (epistemology), and what it is we are grasping to know (ontology). In relation to hermeneutics, philosophy's central question addresses human self-understanding (the nature of human "being").

Language Theory

Linguistics, the study of language, contributes significantly to a communication model of texts. Two rather recent and intriguing theories for understanding communication are speech-act theory and relevance theory. Both theories have found their way into theories of biblical interpretation. So after a brief description of each theory as it relates to written communication, I will also indicate ways that each theory has been applied to Scripture.

Speech-Act Theory

Speech-act theory has been fruitful for understanding the biblical text as communication. For this reason, I will describe it at some length. Speech-act theory was introduced by J. L. Austin, but further shaped by John Searle, William Alston, and others. The theory contends that verbal utterances not only say things; they also do things. A classic example occurs when a bride utters the words, "I do," in a marriage ceremony. She not only speaks words of affirmation to the proposed question ("Will you take X to be your husband?"); she also does something by her words. Her words commit her to her groom. By saying, "I do," she participates in a covenant, or she covenants. If the groom makes a similar statement, the person officiating will soon speak other words that both say and do something: "I now pronounce you husband and wife." These words communicate content, but in this case more importantly they change reality. Two people who were a moment ago unmarried are now in a different state. The words have enacted a marriage and formed a legal covenant.

Of course, not all words act with the same level of vigor. Nevertheless, speech-act theory rightly emphasizes the functional nature of language, which both says and does things. Austin has introduced terms to help express the ideas of speech-act theory.[6] As with any theory, the special terms can become a bit unwieldy for newcomers. So bear with me, and I will attempt to simplify as we proceed.

Let's start with an example. Let's suppose I say to my students, "You shouldn't wait until the last minute to write your research papers." The sentence I speak is what Austin calls a *locution*. A locution is *what is said*. But you may have noticed that I am *doing something* in saying, "You shouldn't wait until the last minute to write your research papers." I am warning my students. There is content to my warning (last-minute paper writing), but the content alone is insufficient to understand fully what

---

6. For the terms and basic definitions of the following discussion, see J. L. Austin, *How to Do Things with Words*, 2nd ed. (Cambridge, MA: Harvard University Press, 1975).

I said. My students need to understand *that I have warned them*. The warning in this example is what Austin calls an *illocution*. An illocution is what we verbally accomplish in what we say. It is a speech act—the force of the locution—as Austin refers to it. Illocutions, for Austin and others, are at the heart of speech as action.[7]

Another kind of action that Austin identifies belongs not primarily to the speaker but to the one who hears the speaker's utterance. What the hearer does in response to that utterance is what Austin calls a *perlocution*. According to Austin, a perlocution is what speakers *do to hearers* by saying something, that is, the responses speakers evoke from hearers. In our example, by warning students, I may deter them from the common syndrome of delayed paper writing.

Perlocutions include a whole range of what hearers do in response to utterances (although the response of the hearer is not a part of the utterance itself). First, my students may or may not *understand* (that is, grasp the import of) my utterance. Understanding is the characteristic perlocution, because it precedes and grounds all other hearer responses. If students understand my warning, the force of my words, they may be deterred from procrastinating on their research paper. That, in fact, is what I hope for and intend by saying what I said. (This speaker's intention for response by hearers has been called a *perlocutionary intention*.[8]) Some of my students, however, may not be deterred from procrastination as I had intended. They may, in response to my words, reassert (though probably not in my presence) that they are willing and able to "pull an all-nighter." They may resist or ignore my warning—not the perlocution I had intended, but an *unintended perlocution*. We could continue to imagine all sorts of unintended effects of my warning as well as various ways that students (those who cherish and trust my every word!) could heed my warning and enact my perlocutionary intention of working promptly on the assignment. The point here is that perlocutions, both intended and unintended, include a significant number of possible responses.

We have surveyed the central terminology and definitions of speech-act theory. To review, here are some simplified ways of summarizing the basic ideas. According to speech-act theory, there are three actions associated with communication: the *speaker's saying* (that is, the locution), the *speaker's verbal action* (that is, the illocution or the force of the saying), and the *hearer's response* (the perlocution) to the verbal

---

7. E.g., Wolterstorff, *Divine Discourse*, 75–76. Kinds of verbal actions or illocutions include promises, commands, requests, apologies, agreements, nominations, complaints, and reports. For a much more complete list organized into various categories, see William P. Alston, *Illocutionary Acts and Sentence Meaning* (Ithaca, NY: Cornell University Press, 2000), 34.

8. See Alston, *Illocutionary Acts*, 37.

action.[9] How are these categories relevant to a communication model of the Bible?[10]

First, speech-act theory invites us to acknowledge that the Bible not only says things with words, but it also does things with words. A number of illocutionary categories have significant overlap with actions performed in and by Scripture: confession, forgiveness, teaching, promise, blessing, pronouncing judgment, and worship.[11] When we recognize the performative nature of the Bible, its intention to do things, we see that the communicative act of Scripture should be freed from a limitation of scriptural meaning to mere propositions (statements of fact), an opinion that has too long captivated biblical studies and theology. Vanhoozer refers to this captivation as derived from "the modern obsession with information."[12] While the Bible can rightly be understood as containing propositions, its communicative message is far broader.[13] Vanhoozer expresses the performative quality of Scripture as: *"words on a mission."*[14]

Of course, understanding what is being said is essential to interpretation. Yet understanding what is accomplished in what is said (the force of what is said, or illocution) is equally essential for understanding these words on a mission.

9. Yet the hearer's response is not part of the communicative act of the speaker. In chaps. 4 and 5, we will explore the relationship between (verbal) meaning and perlocutions. For now let us simply note that what someone says includes their verbal action (locution/illocution) and also very commonly results in hearer responses (perlocutions).

10. Speech-act theory focuses on speech rather than writing, so it is a fair question to ask whether speech-act theory is helpful in shaping our understanding of written communication and specifically literature. Pratt has argued that "a speech act approach to literature offers the important possibility of integrating literary discourse into the same basic model of language as all our other communicative activities" (Mary Louise Pratt, *Toward a Speech Act Theory of Literary Discourse* [Bloomington, IN: Indiana University Press, 1977], 88). Briggs sees speech-act theory as a productive resource to be adapted for biblical interpretation and notes that "it remains largely untapped" in this field (Richard S. Briggs, *Words in Action: Speech Act Theory and Biblical Interpretation—Toward a Hermeneutic of Self-Involvement* [New York: T&T Clark, 2001], 293). See also Anthony C. Thiselton, *New Horizons in Hermeneutics: The Theory and Practice of Transforming Biblical Reading* (Grand Rapids: Zondervan, 1992), 17–18; Kevin J. Vanhoozer, *Is There a Meaning in This Text? The Bible, the Reader, and the Morality of Literary Knowledge* (Grand Rapids: Zondervan, 1998), 226–28; and Vanhoozer, *First Theology*, 164–65.

11. The first three are explored by Briggs, *Words in Action*. Thiselton catalogs the rest of these and more in *New Horizons*, 17–18. Vanhoozer includes "instructing the believing community, testifying to Christ, and perhaps most obviously, covenanting" as illocutions at the level of the whole of Scripture (*First Theology*, 195).

12. Vanhoozer, *First Theology*, 163.

13. In addition, there are certain genres that are less helpfully understood using language of "proposition." Narrative, for example, does not move along primarily by making propositions, but through the plotting of the story line.

14. Vanhoozer, *First Theology*, 179; italics in original.

Second, speech-act theory reaffirms the interpersonal nature of textual communication. Autonomous texts cut off from their authors do not warn, promise, or covenant. People warn, people promise, people covenant. This is the case even if we do not know who wrote a text. The author remains, in theory, connected to the text's communicative aims.[15] In a communicative model of texts, texts are vehicles for personal actions. Texts accomplish person-to-person communication. Speech-act theory, in this way, reintroduces the author for interpretive consideration.

Finally, speech-act theory will be of great assistance in navigating the complex waters of reader participation in the written communicative act, without requiring the conclusion that readers actively create meaning, a rather common perspective in contemporary conversations on hermeneutics. It is the concept of perlocutionary intention particularly that will help us do justice to readers in the interpretive process. Perlocutionary intention—the speaker's intent for a hearer's response—is an extension of the speaker's illocutionary act or intention. Speech-act theory will resurface as we deal with meaning and reader participation from a number of angles in subsequent chapters.

Relevance Theory

Relevance theory, which shares points of continuity with speech-act theory, can also assist in understanding communication.[16] Relevance theory at its center claims that (1) an utterance requires hearers to infer more than is provided in the linguistic features of the utterance itself, and (2) hearers will select from among a host of contextual inputs those that are most relevant for understanding a particular utterance. In fact, according to relevance theory, speakers assume these tenets of communication to be true and rely on their hearers to supply the most relevant information to interpret their utterances. An *utterance* is a speech act with a context.[17] Crucial to this definition is the idea that meaning is always contextually situated. In relevance theory, a communicative act assumes a context. Thus, we might understand an utterance as consisting of both *linguistic expression* and *assumed context*.[18]

15. On this connection, see below for discussion of the notion of the implied author.

16. See Dan Sperber and Deirdre Wilson, *Relevance: Communication and Cognition* (Cambridge, MA: Harvard University Press, 1986). While speech-act theory and relevance theory tend to emphasize different aspects of the communicative process, they are congruent and so work together well in a communicative model.

17. I am indebted to my colleague Mark Strauss for the particular phrasing of this definition.

18. While these are not actually divisible (one cannot isolate linguistic expression from context and retain the utterance), it will be helpful for a comprehensive definition of meaning to distinguish linguistic expression (the words of an utterance) from the act

Gene Green claims that "relevance theory offers a unified theory of communication which argues that the recovery of contextual information is essential for comprehension and that communication is largely an inferential process."[19] Green's statement introduces two primary insights of relevance theory that are crucial for the communication model developed in this chapter.

The role of *implications* (often called "implicatures") is conceptually important in relevance theory. The notion that communication is highly inferential means that it is important to attend to what is implicit in a speaker's meaning as well as what is explicit, since both are essential for understanding meaning. For instance, I can communicate the utterance, "I'm hungry," by stating these words explicitly. I can also communicate a virtually identical meaning given the right context by saying, "My stomach is growling." In the latter circumstance, I communicate both explicit information *and* an implication, central to my meaning, that I am indeed hungry. Both explicit and implicit meaning are essential to successful communication.[20]

Let me provide another illustration: My daughter comes to me after school and asks, "Can I watch a TV show?" I respond, "Have you finished your homework?" My meaning is entirely implicit in the question I ask. In fact, it is a multioptional answer phrased in a question. If she has finished her homework, she knows (from previous experience) she is free to watch a TV show. If she has not, I have informed her that she may not watch a show until her homework is finished. Although my meaning is completely implicit, my daughter has no problem understanding my inference or meaning because she and I share an assumed context.

Assumed context refers to the relevant presuppositions shared by speaker and hearer that make communication work. "Text and context work together in successful communication."[21] In fact, according to relevance theory, the assumed contextual information is essential for proper interpretation of utterance meaning.[22] Max Turner, who coined the term "presuppositional pools" to refer to assumed context, identifies this concept as "things that are known by speaker and hearer, writer and reader, because they are conventional to the society of the

---

of that utterance heard in its particular context. In fact, it is in the unity of the two that meaning is communicated.

19. Green, "Context and Communication," 2.

20. For this example, I would like to thank Yee-Von Koh, a PhD student I met at Tyndale House, Cambridge, England, 23 May 2005.

21. Green, "Context and Communication," 22.

22. Ernst-August Gutt, *Relevance Theory: A Guide to Successful Communication in Translation* (New York: United Bible Societies and Summer Institute of Linguistics, 1992), 34.

dialogue partners, or because they are situational elements shared by them."[23] Another example might help to illustrate. My husband says to me, "It's Friday." What does he mean (imply) by this? Much depends not only on how the utterance fits in the flow of conversation (what in textual communication is termed "literary context") but also upon assumed (background) context. If I have just asked him the day of the week, his words are an explicit answer to my question. Yet if the big thing that happens in our household on Friday is the weekly grocery trip, then he might be implying (and so I should infer) that it's time to head to the store. But in our home, "It's Friday" most regularly implies the coming of a weekend and with it a needed breather. Deciding the most probable among the various possibilities for meaning is a matter of choosing, often intuitively, which is most relevant to our context. So the "assumed context" includes *relevant* shared presuppositions for particular communication rather than all possible shared presuppositions in a social context.

What value do the concepts of implications and assumed context hold for a model of communication? In both cases, these concepts expand our definition of meaning beyond the explicit meaning of an utterance. "The coded signal . . . is only a piece of evidence about the communicator's intentions, and has to be used *inferentially* and *in a context*."[24] In the first case, we will need to make room in our definition of meaning for implications (what is to be inferred), or we will frequently misunderstand biblical writers.

Let's look at an example from Scripture. In Psalm 43 we hear the psalmist's internal dialogue:

> Why are you in despair, O my soul?
> And why are you disturbed within me?
> Hope in God, for I shall again praise Him,
> The help of my countenance, and my God. (Ps. 43:5 NASB)

We could read the two initial questions as explicitly asking for specific reasons for the soul's despairing and disturbed state. But upon reading the call to hope that follows, we quickly understand that the meaning of the first two lines is not so much a request for reasons as an admonition to the soul or self to let go of its despair and turn to God in hope. This is implied in the context of the psalm. In context, the questions function as part of the exhortation to hope in God.

---

23. Max Turner, "Theological Hermeneutics," in *Between Two Horizons: Spanning New Testament Studies and Systematic Theology*, ed. Joel B. Green and Max Turner (Grand Rapids: Eerdmans, 2000), 50.

24. Sperber and Wilson, *Relevance*, 170; italics mine.

Assumed background context also belongs to the realm of meaning. As Turner contends, "The content of 'presuppositional pools' is thus a matter of what is in the public context of a speaker's utterance, and so may be taken to count as part of the utterance meaning."[25] We might put it this way: linguistic expression + background context assumptions = meaning (i.e., utterance meaning, which includes both explicit and implicit meaning).[26] If this is the case, then careful attention to the assumed background context will be important for biblical interpretation.

Literary Theory

Literary theory is reflection on what literature is and how it should be interpreted. Historically, literary theory has had significant impact on the study of the Bible, as we will see in chapter 3. For our purposes, I will be engaging some important concepts from literary theory that assist in interpretation of textual communication, specifically from the work of Hirsch and from application of narrative theory to the Bible.

Hirsch, a literary critic who almost forty years ago argued for the return of the author to literary interpretation, developed a framework for interpretation that includes a number of helpful concepts for a communicative understanding of texts.[27] In particular, three concepts and their distinctions will be useful in sketching out a communication model. Hirsch defines "meaning," "implications," and "mental acts" in relation to one another.

Meaning, for Hirsch, is essentially the pattern of what an author intended to communicate, conveyed through the text's linguistic signs based on shareable conventions.[28] Crucial to this definition: meaning as a pattern of intention[29] and as participating in shareable conventions, thus aligning meaning with communicative intention. Two other terms,

25. Turner, "Theological Hermeneutics," 50; see also Vanhoozer, *First Theology*, 167; and Thiselton, *New Horizons*, 67.

26. It is the assumption of specific knowledge and not the knowledge itself that can be said to be a part of meaning.

27. I was introduced to Hirsch's *Validity in Interpretation* in my seminary hermeneutics course taught by Robert Stein. Stein had his students read *Validity*, a rather daunting but ultimately very rewarding requirement. Since that time, Stein has helpfully summarized some of Hirsch's significant contributions for biblical interpretation in *A Basic Guide to Interpreting the Bible: Playing by the Rules*. The definitions provided here, although based on Hirsch, owe more in their particular shaping in most cases to Stein (*Basic Guide*, 38–39, 52).

28. Hirsch, *Validity*, 31, 49–51, 66–67; Stein, *Basic Guide*, 38.

29. The concept of meaning as a pattern of intention allows Hirsch to avoid a simplistic understanding of meaning, although this has not kept some of his critics from accusing him of a simplistic perspective.

"implications" and "mental acts," provide further clarity on just these two points of Hirsch's construal of meaning.

Implications, for Hirsch, are those (sub)meanings in a text of which the author may have been unaware while writing but that nevertheless legitimately fall within the pattern of meaning he or she willed.[30] Hirsch emphasizes that there are aspects of meaning that an author may not be attending to (unattended meaning) but that will nevertheless fall into the pattern of authorial intention (intended meaning). Hirsch's definition of implications varies slightly from its definition in relevance theory; however, they are not incompatible. Hirsch's definition focuses a bit more narrowly on implicit meanings, which are not only nonexplicit but also may be unattended to by the author during the communicative act. Hirsch tries to do justice to the phenomenon that writers mean more than they give complete conscious attention to in the act of writing. A construct of meaning involving or including implications grants a greater complexity to meaning without saying that meaning is virtually open-ended.[31] For example, if I come to a Wednesday morning class and remind my students that their papers are due Friday, I could get a question like this: Does this mean that I can turn in my paper anytime on Friday? The question attempts to get at my intention in my statement that the paper is due on Friday. It may be that I imply in my statement that the paper is due at class time. Given that this is a typical expectation for work due in an academic setting, I might even expect that students will infer such an implication from my words. If I were assuming this typical academic procedure, the implication would necessarily be a part of my meaning, even if I was not consciously attending to that aspect of my meaning in my reminder to students.

Mental acts, in contrast, are authorial motives that are precisely not included in meaning. According to Hirsch, mental acts are the inaccessible experiences of the author when writing the text (e.g., an author's hidden feelings and thoughts). Hirsch's distinction between meaning and mental acts provides a way for interpretation to avoid seeking the author's mental state, while still being able to hold to the notion of authorial intention, specifically what we have described as communicative intention. As N. T. Wright has so vividly put it, "[It is] entirely correct to reject the idea . . . that criticism either could or should attempt to work out, by reading between the lines of a poem, what the author had for breakfast that morning, or whether he had just fallen in love with the housemaid."[32]

---

30. Hirsch, *Validity*, 62, 51–52; Stein, *Basic Guide*, 52.

31. We will return to the concept of implications in chaps. 4 and 5, as we explore the complexity yet determinacy (bounded nature) of meaning.

32. N. T. Wright, *The New Testament and the People of God* (Minneapolis: Fortress, 1992), 55; hereafter abbreviated as *NTPG*.

Hirsch's careful attention to the concepts of implications and mental acts contributes to a way of construing meaning that allows for its complexity (it is a pattern of intention) as well as its public nature (it participates in shareable conventions instead of addressing the psychological level of authorial motives). The goal of interpretation then will be to ascertain the author's communicative intention rather than his or her motives.[33]

In addition to Hirsch's conceptual work, another vein of literary theory that has yielded helpful concepts for thinking of texts as communication is narrative theory, that is, literary theory applied to narrative texts. Specifically, the concepts of "implied reader," "implied author," and "point of view" provide significant avenues for clarification, certainly for Scripture's narrative texts but also for its other genres.

The *implied reader* can be defined as the textually constructed "reader presupposed by the narrative" or text.[34] While many literary theorists utilize this construct, it has been called by various names, including the "ideal reader" and the "model reader." Umberto Eco, a literary critic, speaks of the "model reader" as the one foreseen by the author of a text and who is "able to deal interpretively with the expressions [of the text] in the same way as the author deals generatively with them."[35] The implied reader reflects the intended response the author envisions for the text. While actual readers may respond in all sorts of ways to a text, the implied reader responds only as the author intends.

What is the value of the concept of "implied reader" for interpreting biblical narrative and other parts of the Bible? First, the implied reader functions as the embodiment of the right response at every turn to the author's communicative intention. As a result, the concept can help us flesh out what active reception of a text is meant to look like. For example, Matthew's implied reader is implicitly encouraged to identify with various characters in the narrative who demonstrate their wholehearted trust in Jesus and his authority, such as the Roman centurion and the Canaanite woman (Matt. 8:5–13; 15:21–28). In contrast, the implied reader experiences more ambivalence with the character group of the twelve disciples. Sometimes identification is encouraged (as when the disciples

---

33. Brett, "Motives and Intentions," 5.

34. Jeannine K. Brown, *The Disciples in Narrative Perspective: The Portrayal and Function of the Matthean Disciples*, Academia Biblica 9 (Atlanta: Society of Biblical Literature, 2002), 36; for a lengthier discussion of the implied reader construct, see 123–28. Booth uses the language at one point of the "postulated reader" (Wayne Booth, *The Rhetoric of Fiction*, 2nd ed. [Chicago: University of Chicago Press, 1983], 177). This seems to me a helpful shorthand for what I describe here.

35. Umberto Eco, *The Role of the Reader: Explorations in the Semiotics of Texts* (Bloomington, IN: Indiana University Press, 1979), 7.

leave all to follow Jesus in Matt. 4:18–22). Other times the implied reader experiences a distancing effect where discernment of improper attitudes and actions is encouraged (as when the disciples misunderstand Jesus' mission and the way their discipleship is to mirror that mission in Matt. 16:21–28; 18:1; 20:20–28).[36] The implied reader "gets" what the disciples do not yet understand about Jesus' mission and about discipleship. This is one of the ways that the implied reader is encouraged to embrace who Jesus is and the ideals of discipleship expressed in Matthew.

A second value of the construct of implied reader is that it focuses attention on noncognitive as well as cognitive responses envisioned in the text. In fact, approaching the text as the implied reader helpfully balances cognitive and noncognitive intended responses, since the question is raised, How is the reader shaped by the text (in thinking, being, and doing)? Scripture is meant to shape people in all ways, not only in their thinking. For instance, Matthew, through the construction of the implied reader, intends to shape a Christian community that is drawn further into both the truth about Jesus and active trust in Jesus.

The *implied author* is a sort of mirror-image to the implied reader: the textually constructed author who communicates with and seeks to persuade the implied reader.[37] The implied author can be discerned wholly from the text itself; the construct is implied in the text. Wayne Booth, well known in literary circles for defining the textually focused implied author, describes the concept in comparison to the real author: "Just as one's personal letters imply different versions of oneself, depending on the differing relationships with each correspondent and the purpose of each letter, so the writer sets himself out with a different air depending on the needs of particular works."[38] As my textual persona in writing a personal letter to my husband will be in some (although not all) ways different from a business letter to a colleague, so the implied author of a particular work will have specific textual contours that interpreters will want to discern.

But why not simply refer to the empirical author of a biblical narrative, you might ask? Let's take the example of the Gospels. For almost two hundred years biblical scholarship spent much time and energy trying to nail down the authorship of the Gospels, at times neglecting a more holistic study of the Gospels themselves.[39] The notion of implied author allows us to move, at least preliminarily, past the introductory issues of author, date,

36. See Brown, *Disciples*, chap. 5.
37. Ibid., 36. See also Eco, *Role of the Reader*, 11.
38. Booth, *Rhetoric of Fiction*, 71.
39. The Gospels themselves (in their texts) are anonymous. The titles for each of the Gospels that ascribe them to Matthew, Mark, Luke, and John, respectively, were most probably additions to the original text, likely added very early in their history (ca. 125 CE).

and so on, and focus our initial attention on reading the Gospels. In the end, confirmed knowledge that Luke, a physician and missionary companion of Paul (Col. 4:14), was the author of the third Gospel would not, in fact, help us greatly in interpreting that Gospel. In spite of the occasional comment by interpreters about that Gospel's particular interest in healings (although all the Gospels provide numerous healings) and physicians (e.g., Luke 5:31, which, however, the Gospel of Matthew also includes at Matt. 9:12), it is far more helpful to identify the implied author of the third Gospel. It is the implied author of Luke who, for example, emphasizes the theme of wealth, its dangers and uses.[40] The implied author is fully discernable from the narrative and, I would argue, far more useful for interpreting the communicative aims of that Gospel. Tending to what the implied author is doing in a Gospel keeps us textually on target.

Point of view, our final literary term, is the perspective of the implied author, shared both explicitly and implicitly in the text. While in genres such as epistle and poetry we routinely hear the author's point of view more directly, point of view in narrative texts is primarily communicated at an indirect or implicit level.[41] Explicitly, we hear from the author of a narrative through authorial comments, which directly indicate the author's perspective. Implicitly, we hear a point of view through the implied author's appropriation (or lack of appropriation) of various characters' perspectives.

To illustrate from the book of Job, which includes both narrative and poetic elements, we sometimes directly hear the author's point of view, including its expression in the book's opening lines:

> In the land of Uz there lived a man whose name was Job. This man was blameless and upright; he feared God and shunned evil. (1:1 NIV)

This information will be crucial for understanding the book of Job, because Job's three friends, Eliphaz, Bildad, and Zophar, regularly assess the situation differently.

> If you devote your heart to [God]
>   and stretch out your hands to him,
> if you put away the sin that is in your hand
>   and allow no evil to dwell in your tent,

40. See 1:53; 6:24–25; 12:13–15, 16–21, 22–32, 33–34; 16:9–13, 19–31; 18:18–25; 19:1–10, 11–27.

41. For example, it is rare in narrative for the author to say at the end of a passage, "The moral of this story is. . . ." This may happen in Aesop's fables, but the writers of biblical narrative assume the reader (implied reader, at least!) will catch the implications of the passage for its meaning. It is the pervasiveness in narratives of implicit point of view that makes the concept particularly helpful in narrative interpretation but not irrelevant for interpretation of other genres.

> then you will lift up your face without shame;
> you will stand firm and without fear." (Zophar to Job; 11:13–15
> NIV)

It becomes clear that the perspective that Job has sinned to deserve such punishment, expressed by Job's friends, is not the implied author's point of view, since their perspective is contradicted by the author's opening assessment and by those whose point of view the author has implicitly "authorized" (that is, has shown to be fully trustworthy). God's words in the book of Job would certainly fit into this "authorized" category. So when God finally speaks, after the reader has heard the running debate between Job and his friends, it is clear that God's perspective is the right one, and that it fully coheres with the implied author's point of view (Job 38–41). The implied author's use of characters' voices both to express his point of view and to provide its contrast (what Job's friends often say) is an implicit but clear way to convey point of view.

While God's voice in Job fully aligns with the implied author's point of view, and Job's friends routinely espouse wrong points of view (although in wonderful proverbial platitudes), Job is a bit more ambiguous. While he is right in continuing to claim his innocence to his friends (1:1 confirms this) and right in what he says about God (42:7),[42] his consistent complaint before God shows a need for his picture of God to be enlarged (a powerful identification point for the implied reader!). By the end of the story, the author has shown God and God's ways often to be inscrutable from a human perspective; God is far bigger than imagined by the characters of the story, including Job: "Surely I spoke of things I did not understand, things too wonderful for me to know. . . . My ears had heard of you but now my eyes have seen you. Therefore I despise myself and repent in dust and ashes" (Job's final words; 42:3, 5–6 NIV).

Narrative Theology: "The Priority of Story"[43]

The postmodern turn has gifted the modern world with a reemphasis upon story as a resource for thinking about biblical interpretation.[44]

42. As heard in God's words to Eliphaz: "I am angry with you and your two friends, because you have not spoken of me what is right, as my servant Job has" (42:7).

43. This is Lindbeck's phrase (George Lindbeck, "The Story-Shaped Church: Critical Exegesis and Theological Interpretation," in *The Theological Interpretation of Scripture: Classic and Contemporary Readings*, ed. Stephen E. Fowl, Blackwell Readings in Modern Theology [Cambridge, MA: Blackwell, 1997], 42).

44. The use of "story" in the following discussion is not meant in any way to suggest the nonreality of story, as with the term "fiction." Instead, "story" is an all-encompassing term that includes historical accounts and all other kinds of narratives.

Postmodernism involves a movement beyond or reaction to certain tenets of modernism, such as reason used to gain absolute certainty.[45] A hermeneutical contribution of postmodernism is its emphasis on the pervasiveness and power of story in describing how humans perceive and understand their world. Stories help us configure a coherent view of ourselves and our life experiences; they are integrally related to our worldview. How I understand life is captured in a certain way of telling the story of my life by making connections between my varied experiences. This is what Wright has termed "the storied and relational nature of human consciousness."[46] And, in fact, my way of telling this story implies the reality of an overarching story (a meta-story or meta-narrative). Since I will work to bring coherence to my various beliefs and experiences by seeing them through a storied lens, this assumed meta-narrative is another way of referring to my worldview. Stories also help us recognize that we are contextual beings. We are located in the middle of a community, a certain set of stories that have been enacted and passed on to us by family, culture, and faith. These stories make sense of the world around us. When I hear someone else affirming a way of seeing the world that is different from my own, I become very aware that the two of us are assuming, at least in some respects, different meta-narratives. In fact, we may both experience the same event and interpret it in quite different ways because of our different worldviews or meta-narrative assumptions.[47]

We may have seemed in the last few paragraphs to have lost our way a bit in a maze of postmodern reflection. How does the storied nature of human existence actually help us when it comes to biblical interpretation? Here is where narrative theology steps in. Narrative theology, which incorporates the insights of story just described, is interested in at least two things. First, narrative theology, in line with the postmodern turn, wants to counter the ahistorical tendencies that sometimes accompany the doing of theology. Instead, narrative theology "attempt[s] to discern an

45. Myron B. Penner, "Christianity and the Postmodern Turn: Some Preliminary Considerations," in *Christianity and the Postmodern Turn: Six Views*, ed. Myron B. Penner (Grand Rapids: Brazos, 2005), 18–24. Penner describes postmodernism as an "ethos" rather than a set of beliefs (16–17). This volume of essays offers a critical assessment of postmodernism.

46. Wright, *NTPG*, 61: "What we need, I suggest, is a critical-realist account of the phenomenon of reading, in all its parts. . . . I suggest that we must articulate a theory which locates the entire phenomenon of text-reading within an account of the storied and relational nature of human consciousness."

47. Green, "(Re)turn to Narrative," 17: "Turning to philosophical hermeneutics since Gadamer [an influential twentieth-century philosopher], we have realized that, in the never-ending work of interpretation, we cannot jump out of our skins. We bring with us always and everywhere our selves—that is, our presuppositions and histories, our stories."

overall aim and ongoing plot in the ways of God as these are revealed in Scripture and continue to express themselves in history."[48] A way of doing theology that begins with propositions and doctrines extracted from history and culture is, according to narrative theologians, not consonant with the way the Bible reveals who God is. As George Lindbeck has put it, "The story is logically prior [to doctrinal descriptions]. It determines the meaning of images, concepts, doctrines, and theories . . . rather than being determined by them."[49] Narrative theology does not necessarily ignore the importance of doctrine. Rather, it affirms that doctrine and values must be derived from the meta-narrative of Scripture.

Narrative theology, at least in some of its expressions, also claims that Scripture's overarching narrative is *the* story that must shape Christian theology and practice. "The biblical narrative is present as an alternative framework within which to construe our lives."[50] The Bible offers a normative story or worldview by which to make sense of ourselves and our world. Worldviews are inherently normative, since they claim to make sense of all of life and reality and so provide direction for living in it. This normative claim is quite different from a postmodern perspective that emphasizes the multiplicity of stories between people and cultures. For many in our postmodern world (and some narrative theologians), we cannot affirm one worldview over others; we must instead recognize the absence of any kind of meta-narrative to explain our world.[51] Yet one significant stream of narrative theology affirms the normativity of the biblical story, because the Bible itself takes a normative stance in relation to other ways of explaining God and human existence.

What is the biblical story expounded and assumed in narrative theology? Wright has helpfully summarized its basic contours:

> Christian theology tells a story, and seeks to tell it coherently. . . . The story is about a creator and his creation, about humans made in the creator's image and given tasks to perform, about the rebellion of humans and the

48. Joel B. Green, "Practicing the Gospel in a Post-Critical World: The Promise of Theological Hermeneutics," *Journal of the Evangelical Theological Society* 47 (September 2004): 392.

49. Lindbeck, "Story-Shaped Church," 42.

50. Green, "(Re)turn to Narrative," 17. The author's italicization of the entire sentence has been removed.

51. Sugirtharajah notes that the rejection of an overarching meta-narrative by Western postmodern theorists ironically continues Western dominance: "Why is it that, at a time when previously silenced people have begun to script their own stories and speak for themselves, the West celebrates the death of the author and proclaims that the mega-stories are over" (R. S. Sugirtharajah, "Critics, Tools, and the Global Arena," in *Reading the Bible in the Global Village: Helsinki*, ed. Heikki Raisanen et al. [Atlanta: Society of Biblical Literature, 2000], 49–60, esp. 59).

dissonance of creation at every level, and particularly about the creator's acting, through Israel and climactically through Jesus, to rescue his creation from its ensuing plight. The story continues with the creator acting by his own spirit within the world to bring it towards the restoration which is his intended goal for it.[52]

It is this meta-story that must shape our worldview, that is, our thinking, being, and doing. In the task of interpretation, then, paying attention to the meta-narrative or story of the text is crucial. This means every part of Scripture participates in and projects a narrative (even non-narrative genres), since all parts of the Bible contribute to the biblical meta-narrative. As Joel Green describes, "The particular narratives related in the biblical books, together with the non-narrative portions of Scripture, participate in a more extensive, overarching narrative (or meta-narrative)."[53] The biblical authors both assume and contribute to the meta-narrative of Scripture because they are convinced that they are participants in the biblical story. One way of attending to the biblical story envisioned by the biblical authors is to focus on what has been called "the world projected by the text."[54] In fact, we may speak of entering the world of the text as a way of allowing its normative story to shape us.

Theoretical Eclecticism in Biblical Interpretation

Now that we have identified and described a number of concepts that help us understand the communicative features of the Bible, we can begin to develop a communication model of interpretation. The model I am proposing has developed organically over time as my understanding of the interpretive process has expanded. The goal has not been to take the various concepts introduced in this chapter and force them into a model regardless of their "fit." Rather, my conceptual understanding of textual communication continues to be challenged by others, inviting exploration of new theories and concepts, yet attempting to remain true to what Scripture says about itself and what it shows itself to be. Some new concepts will not fit so well in the model I propose, but others will make sense of some aspect of Scripture as communication that I have not yet explored.

52. Wright, *NTPG*, 132.
53. Green, "Practicing the Gospel," 392–93.
54. This concept employed by narrative theology is one of a number of hermeneutical contributions of philosopher Paul Ricoeur. See, for example, *Time and Narrative*, trans. Kathleen Blamey and David Pellauer (Chicago: University of Chicago Press, 1984). For an assessment of Ricoeur's theory, see Kevin J. Vanhoozer, *Biblical Narrative in the Philosophy of Paul Ricoeur* (Cambridge: Cambridge University Press, 1990).

Eclectic models such as my own are not unusual; they are in fact the norm. As the introduction to this chapter attempted to show, we all have implicit theories of language and literature, philosophy and theology. So we all have an interpretive model that is likely to be fairly complex and eclectic (though possibly unexamined). One result of reading this chapter may be that you are becoming more conscious of your own outlook on what texts are and how interpretation works. It is very possible that you have been most aware of the way you understand interpretation when you disagree with my own assessment. This is a good realization! There is nothing to be lost and everything to be gained by clarifying your own hermeneutical thinking. And our hermeneutical thinking is most easily clarified by reading what others think about interpretation and by noticing when we agree or disagree and why.[55]

A Model of Communication for Interpretation

So let's draw together the conceptual insights I have introduced to help us define and describe meaning from the vantage point of a communication model. Afterward, I will propose a way of interpreting Scripture that is coherent with this view of meaning. In the process, we will briefly revisit each of the concepts from earlier discussion, as they are brought together into a communication model for interpretation.

Meaning in Communication

Meaning in the act of communication can be understood and described in a variety of compatible ways. Within this model, we can define meaning:

- *As communicative intention in contrast to mental acts.* The author inscribes in the text what he or she wants communicated. So we do not need to read an author's mind, only the intention communicated

---

55. Two particularly influential contemporary Christian hermeneuts (people who theorize about hermeneutics) who nicely illustrate interpretive eclecticism and to whom I am indebted in my own hermeneutical work are Anthony Thiselton, a biblical scholar, and Kevin Vanhoozer, a theologian. How they envision the interpretive task is based on what they glean from a wide variety of theoretical paradigms to be coherent and consistent with the particular theory they are constructing. See Anthony C. Thiselton, *New Horizons in Hermeneutics*, and his earlier influential work, *The Two Horizons: New Testament Hermeneutics and Philosophical Description with Special Reference to Heidegger, Bultmann, Gadamer, and Wittgenstein* (Grand Rapids: Eerdmans, 1980); as well as Vanhoozer, *Meaning*; *First Theology*; and *The Drama of Doctrine: A Canonical-Linguistic Approach to Christian Theology* (Louisville: Westminster John Knox, 2005).

through and in the text. In this model, the focus of interpretation is on the implied author of the text.

- *As both locution and illocution.* The meaning of a text includes what the text says and what it intends to do, both its content and its force. As Vanhoozer puts it, "The most important thing we need to know about a text, I submit, is what kind of communicative act(s) it performs and with what content."[56]
- *As both explicit and implicit meaning.* Texts communicate both through explicit use of language and by implications, the two working together in an organic rather than an artificial fashion. Implications are included in a text's communicative meaning and often are of central importance to that meaning.
- *As linguistic expression set within background-contextual assumptions.* The linguistically derived import of a text can be understood only in light of the relevant, shared assumptions of original writer and reader. Utterance meaning (a speech act with a context) arises from language used in concert with contextual assumptions.
- *With perlocutionary intention as extension of meaning.* The author's intended response for readers is intimately linked to and can be derived from the communicative act itself.

Given these parameters, we can define meaning as *the complex pattern of what an author intends to communicate with his or her audience for purposes of engagement, which is inscribed in the text and conveyed through use of both shareable language parameters and background-contextual assumptions.*[57]

A Movement for Interpretation

Wright has asserted, "Each stage of [the reading] process becomes a *conversation*."[58] If this is a helpful image, then we might envision interpretation as a movement back and forth (a conversation) between reader and text. Based on the definition of meaning just provided, I will suggest a model for this movement of interpretation and then illustrate the model with an extended example from 1 Corinthians 8.

The reader enters "the world projected by the text" in all its complexity. What does this world look like? In visualizing the textually projected world, we will first need to visualize the textual world against its proper

56. Vanhoozer, *First Theology*, 179.
57. Presuming this definition, we can affirm that meaning as a whole is determinate, that is, it has boundaries. This notion will be discussed in chap. 4.
58. Wright, *NTPG*, 64; italics in original.

backdrop: the background-contextual assumptions shared by author and original audience, as relevance theory has helpfully pointed out. This crucial background information is not derived from the text alone, although some of it can be inferred from the text. We will need to get to know that assumed world by studying the historical setting of the work. In addition to locating the textually projected world against its proper background, we will also want to identify the normative stance of the text.[59] This is the authorial stance taken in relation to the textually projected world set within the assumed context. Discovering this normative stance is helped by listening for the implied author, point of view, and the shaping of the implied reader. In fact, we may define this goal more particularly as the normative stance of the implied author.

I would suggest, then, a threefold movement between reader and text in conversation. The three movements are not necessarily sequential or singular. In other words, they may happen in any order (and in actuality will overlap significantly) and in multiple back-and-forth movements. The model is meant to be a helpful visualization of key movements in the interpretive process and will, by necessity, simplify what is a complex and dialogical relation between reader and Scripture. (See figure 2.1 for a visual representation of this three-movement model.)

The first movement is the reader's engagement with the textually projected world. Initial exploration often focuses on what we have termed the linguistic expression of the text: locution/illocution and explicit/implicit meaning within the specific genre chosen by the author. Attention is given to what the text says, what it does in what it says, and how it says/does it. It includes both what is stated explicitly and what is implicitly communicated.[60] The reader will take this linguistically derived textual sense and will begin reflecting on the communicative act arising from it. This textually projected world includes, but is not limited to, the normative stance of the implied author. So this "first" movement will intersect more broadly with the normative stance of the text as well as the textually projected world, but with an initial focus on the whole.

The second important movement is the reader's movement toward the textual world with a particular focus on background-contextual assumptions. The reader at this juncture begins to weigh possible and then probable necessary assumptions shared by both the author and original readers with the goal of clarifying utterance meaning. This will involve historical analysis and reconstruction of the original setting of

---

59. "Normative stance" is language borrowed from Wolterstorff, *Divine Discourse*, 35. My understanding of the text's normative stance focuses on the authoritative voice of the implied author. See chaps. 11–12 for how this plays out in contextualization.

60. Much that is implicitly communicated will become clearer only as we examine the contextual assumptions of the text.

Figure 2.1: Exegesis

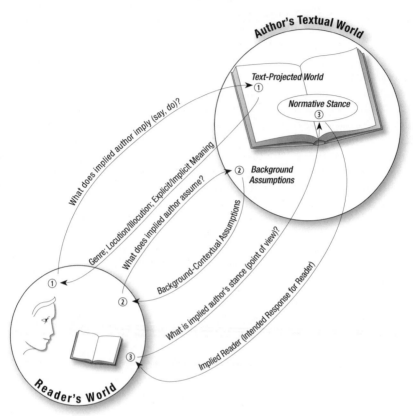

the text in question. In this second movement, implicit meaning often becomes more apparent, as the communicative act is understood more fully against its background.

In the third movement, the reader brings the conceptual tools of implied author and reader and point of view to the task of discerning the normative stance of the text. Amid potentially multiple perspectives represented in a text, what is communicated through the implied author's point of view?[61] As the reader "rounds the corner" of the third movement, the implied reader will come into focus. At this point, it is helpful to ask

61. In narrative genres, distinguishing between the implied author's point of view and the perspectives of various characters of the story is especially helpful for hearing the text's normative stance. Although the process of discerning authorial point of view in epistles and even some poetic texts is typically more direct, asking questions about point of view in these genres may help to clarify what is implicit as well as explicit in their communication.

how the implied author constructs the implied reader. What is the author communicating that the implied reader is meant to grasp, receive, and embody? The real reader of today may then be drawn into step with the implied reader discerned from the text's normative stance.

The Model Applied: 1 Corinthians 8:1–13

To illustrate this model we will apply it to a Bible passage from 1 Corinthians:[62]

> Now about food sacrificed to idols: We know that "We all possess knowledge." But knowledge puffs up while love builds up. Those who think they know something do not yet know as they ought to know. But whoever loves God is known by God.
>
> So then, about eating food sacrificed to idols: We know that "an idol is nothing at all in the world" and that "there is no God but one." For even if there are so-called gods, whether in heaven or on earth (as indeed there are many "gods" and many "lords"), yet for us there is but one God, the Father, from whom all things came and for whom we live; and there is but one Lord, Jesus Christ, through whom all things came and through whom we live.
>
> But not everyone possesses this knowledge. Some people are still so accustomed to idols that when they eat sacrificial food they think of it as having been sacrificed to a god, and since their conscience is weak, it is defiled. But food does not bring us near to God; we are no worse if we do not eat, and no better if we do.
>
> Be careful, however, that the exercise of your rights does not become a stumbling block to the weak. For if anyone with a weak conscience sees you, with all your knowledge, eating in an idol's temple, won't they be emboldened to eat what is sacrificed to idols? So this weak brother or sister, for whom Christ died, is destroyed by your knowledge. When you sin against them in this way and wound their weak conscience, you sin against Christ. Therefore, if what I eat causes my brother or sister to fall into sin, I will never eat meat again, so that I will not cause them to fall. (1 Cor. 8:1–13)

In the first movement of attending to the textually projected world, we enter a world where such a thing as food sacrificed to idols exists and whether to eat it or not is the topic at hand (8:1, 4). Given that this is an

---

62. It is always hazardous jumping into a text midpoint. I would want to qualify my discussion, then, in two ways. First, the previous literary context makes it clear that this is the second of a set of issues the Corinthians have raised in a letter sent to Paul (see 7:1; with 8:1 containing the same formula). Second, I am convinced that the argument begun in 1 Cor. 8 is not completed until 10:22, so that to halt at 8:13 as Paul's final point is misleading, even though we will be stopping there in this illustration.

epistle text in which Paul as author communicates in fairly direct fashion with the Corinthian church, there is significant overlap between the textually projected world and the normative stance of the implied author.[63] So it may not be apparent right away what the difference is between the normative stance and the whole of the textually projected world. In addition, we often hear the normative stance first when we read; it is how we are trained to read. So let's begin there for just a moment and hear some key affirmations by Paul (his point of view).[64] Paul emphasizes the supremacy of love over knowledge (8:1–3) and the dual truth that for Christians there is only one God (monotheism), while for pagans there are so-called gods (polytheism; 8:4–6).[65] He also affirms that food does not commend believers to God (8:7–8), and he admonishes his audience to prioritize care for the "weak" believer above their own freedom (8:9–13). But to what situation are his affirmations and admonitions addressed?

At this point, we need to listen for the whole of the textually projected world, not just Paul's point of view that provides the normative stance of the text. So let's enter the textual world again. In the midst of Paul's normative affirmations, we also can reconstruct a sense of the point of view of the Corinthians by listening to the counterpoint to Paul's perspective.[66] Their point of view embraces in some way the notion that eating sacrificial food *will* bring one near to God, and one *is* worse off not eating, and one *is* better off eating sacrificial food (8:8).[67] It seems that believers in the Corinthian church view the eating of sacrificial food as a means of benefit.

In addition, some of them view eating idol food (meat, see 8:13) as something they are free to do (8:9), based on their superior knowledge that idols do not exist (8:4–6, 7, 10). Paul also gives clear indication of the point of view of another group of the Corinthian Christians, whom he terms "weak" (lacking the knowledge just described). Their difficulty is in getting

63. Although there is no significant debate over Pauline authorship of 1 Cor., it is still the case that the author who ought to receive our focused attention in 1 Cor. is its implied author. The portrait of Paul derived from the text itself is the primary vehicle for determining the text's normative stance. For more on the relationship between empirical and implied authors for interpretation, see chap. 4, affirmation 1. In the following discussion, when I speak of Paul, I am referring specifically to the implied author of 1 Cor.

64. As already indicated, the three movements I suggest do not have a necessary sequence.

65. We can hear in 8:4–6 the pagan affirmation of polytheism (the pagan point of view) in "there are many 'gods' and many 'lords'" but with Paul's point of view overlaid: they are not really gods; they are only so named.

66. Since Paul is answering questions they have raised in a previous letter (see 7:1; 8:1), we will sometimes be able to hear echoes of their letter (and so their point of view) in Paul's responses.

67. Reversing Paul's affirmations at 8:8 helps us to hear the likely arguments he is countering.

over their former polytheistic worldview and practices. They cannot quite break from their formerly held conviction that idols are or represent real deities. By eating meat offered to the idols that they used to worship, these weak believers are being harmed in their consciences (8:7, 12).

Now that we have viewed the lay of the land in the textually projected world, especially attending to the points of view Paul wants to counter, let's attend to relevant background-contextual assumptions. Some of this can be deduced from the text itself; some will be derived from the assumed context, in this case, of religious practices current at Corinth. Paul, in 8:10, gives fairly clear evidence that the kind of eating being addressed takes place in pagan temples.[68] So what is going on in the Corinthian church in its setting?

In the Greco-Roman world, and specifically its religious worship, some of the meat sacrificed at the altar of a god would then be served in a type of restaurant area adjoining the temple. It would be quite commonplace for those worshiping at a pagan temple to participate in a sacrifice and then eat the fruits of that sacrifice in celebration of the god.[69] Thus, eating, in this context, does commend one to the pagan god (as suggested at 8:8), according to pagan thinking. One would be better off eating, because eating in this context had religious as well as social payoffs. What Paul seems to be addressing then is the issue of whether Christians may eat at these temple dinners, with the main course having just recently been sacrificed to a pagan god. This background contextual information helps us to pull together the alternate points of view echoed in the text, so that we can hear Paul's normative stance in relation to the issue more clearly.

Let's draw together what we have explored. Newly converted Christians from pagan backgrounds are faced with the issue of whether to continue participating in celebratory dinners at idol temples. Paul had probably made it clear in his early preaching at Corinth that any direct participation in idol sacrifice was completely off limits. (See Acts 18 for the story of Paul's founding of the Corinthian church.) Yet cutting oneself off from the social connections and benefits associated with eating after the sacrificial ceremony (think of power lunches) would be behavior difficult to maintain in that culture. So some Christians in the Corinthian church are reasoning that, since the gods represented by idols do not exist (and Paul

---

68. Paul will eventually address the issue of whether or not to eat idol meat that is sold in the marketplace after being used in sacrifices (10:23–11:1). This is not, however, his topic in 1 Cor. 8:1–10:22.

69. Gordon D. Fee, *The First Epistle to the Corinthians,* New International Commentary on the New Testament (Grand Rapids: Eerdmans, 1987), 357–63. Contextual information such as this can be gleaned from Greco-Roman and Jewish writings contemporary with the New Testament as well as archaeological discoveries. For how to go about historical work, see chap. 9.

had surely taught them this fundamental monotheistic truth), there is no compelling motive for avoiding these meals. They are benefited; no harm is done. What could be wrong with this scenario? The harm, however, is to their fellow believers who cannot quite get over the idea that the meal is attached to a pagan reality. For them, given their weak conscience, to eat at a temple is devastating to their spiritual lives.

If this is a close approximation of the assumed context and the various points of view represented in the Corinthian church, then we can now return to the normative stance that Paul takes in response to the situation. Paul begins by addressing the Corinthians' reasoning that right knowledge (gods represented by idols are nonexistent) gives them freedom to eat temple meals. His first counterargument is that knowledge is less important than love.[70] This sets up his later admonition that Christians should be more concerned about their weak brother or sister than with their knowledge and the supposed freedom that comes with it. Paul goes on to agree with the content of their knowledge: that there is only one God and therefore idols are nothing (8:4–6). But he then qualifies the applicability of this truth, since not every believer at Corinth fully "gets" this. Instead, weak believers are compromised in their faith when they eat temple meals (8:7–8). Paul then argues that there is really no need to participate in these temple meals, since they do not result in commendation from God, which is the only commendation that ultimately matters. Implicit here is that social-cultural pressures to eat these meals are not to motivate the behavior of the Corinthian believers.

Finally, Paul warns believers who think they have knowledge enough to eat temple meals with impunity (8:9–13). There is great harm to weak fellow Christians, who will actually be emboldened to join in the meal by the presence of other Christian believers there. The harm is ultimate, according to Paul: destruction of the weak believer. If that potential damage were not deterrent enough to disassociate Christians from temple meals, Paul argues that sinning against a fellow believer is tantamount to sinning against Christ. Paul's final move is to become autobiographical to provide another motive—Paul's own choice in the same situation. Paul would never, ever eat meat of any kind if it caused a brother or sister to stumble.[71]

70. Notice that Paul does not contradict their knowledge claim; instead he qualifies it. Fee thinks that the words "We know that . . ." (8:1, 4) introduce quotations from the Corinthian letter (*Corinthians*, 362n20).

71. The language of 8:13 is triply emphatic. First, he widens his scope to include meat in general (*krea*) rather than sacrificial food/meat (*eidōlothyton*). Second, he uses a kind of verb ("eat" in the subjunctive mood) and its negation that provides the strongest way of negating an action in Greek: "I will *never* eat meat." Finally, he uses an idiomatic expression, which in English is usually translated "forever" to describe the never eating meat idea:

This rehearsal of the normative stance of the text should make it rather clear who the implied reader is in 1 Corinthians 8. The implied reader is the believer who gives up perceived rights for the sake of Christians who are more vulnerable in the body. Such a believer finds every aspect of his or her life in God through Christ, and so is constantly attentive to steering clear of idolatrous practice at every level. The implied reader understands that love, with its great power to build up rather than destroy, trumps knowledge and freedom at every turn and is the higher value of the Christian community.

Conclusion

In this chapter, we have been on a whirlwind tour of linguistic, literary, and theological formulations about communication and its interpretation. After proposing some particularly fruitful conceptual terms from various theories for integration into a communication model of hermeneutics, I have practiced this model on a particular Scripture text in 1 Corinthians. In the process, I have made some definitional statements about the nature of meaning in this communicative framework, statements that attempt to address the place of authors, texts, and readers in communication. The next chapter will explore the ways in which authors, texts, and readers have been understood in hermeneutical theory in the span of the past two hundred years.

Suggestions for Further Reading (for Chapters 1 and 2)

Alston, William P. *Illocutionary Acts and Sentence Meaning*. Ithaca, NY: Cornell University Press, 2000.

Austin, J. L. *How to Do Things with Words*. 2nd ed. Cambridge, MA: Harvard University Press, 1975.

Sperber, Dan, and Deirdre Wilson. *Relevance: Communication and Cognition*. Cambridge, MA: Harvard University Press, 1986.

Thiselton, Anthony. *New Horizons in Hermeneutics: The Theory and Practice of Transforming Biblical Reading*. Grand Rapids: Zondervan, 1992.

"I will *never, ever* eat meat." This is strong language to make his point. I would mention here as well that I believe Paul will in the course of 1 Corinthians 9–10 argue that no one in the Corinthian church should eat meals in a pagan temple at any point. But this lies outside the scope of this illustration.

Vanhoozer, Kevin J. *Is There a Meaning in This Text? The Bible, the Reader, and the Morality of Literary Knowledge.* Grand Rapids: Zondervan, 1998.

Wright, N. T. *The New Testament and the People of God.* Minneapolis: Fortress, 1992.

3

Authors, Texts, Readers

Historical Movements and Reactions

> Modern biblical interpretation is shaped in a thousand ways by philoso-
> phy. . . . We have to attend to this shaping if we are to understand where
> we are and where we should move.
>
> Craig G. Bartholomew, "Philosophy, Theology and the Crisis in Biblical
> Interpretation," in *Renewing Biblical Interpretation*

It has always been recognized that authors, texts, and readers are "part of
the equation" in written communication. What has been and continues
to be debated is the role of each in producing communicative meaning.
For some, the author has no part in the meaning of a text because the
text is "free floating" as soon as it is written. Others argue that *readers*
essentially create meaning given their place, time, and life experience.
Traditionally, it was assumed that *authors* determined the meaning of
their texts (and so Hirsch speaks of "the sensible belief that a text means
what its author meant").[1] Why such different viewpoints? And where

---

1. Hirsch, *Validity*, 1. Though we will be examining post-Enlightenment history of
hermeneutics, there has also been much ink spilled on pre-Enlightenment hermeneutics.
For a helpful look at Reformation and pietistic hermeneutics, with the argument that they
both exhibit "a relational concept of epistemology" that can inform modern attempts to

have these various perspectives come from? A brief look at the last two hundred years of hermeneutics discussion not only clarifies these various viewpoints but also gives us a sense of the rationale for specific views at particular moments in history.[2]

For every action there is an equal and opposite reaction: One way of understanding theoretical discussions of author, text, and reader is by their patterns of action and reaction. From this perspective, the nineteenth century was the century of the author. In the early part of the twentieth century, reaction against the author as central to the hermeneutical task resulted in an understanding of the text as entirely disengaged from its author. Toward the end of the twentieth century, the reader became the focal point of hermeneutical discussion. Recently, there has also been a growing interest in more holistic models that welcome the author back to textual meaning, while acknowledging the reader in significant ways. Let's take a closer look at these four historical moments.

The Century of the Author

There are at least two philosophical currents we should be aware of if we want to understand the shape of nineteenth-century hermeneutics and its twentieth-century reaction. The first has to do with the development of a theory of hermeneutics, the second with the overall tone of nineteenth-century theological endeavors.

Friedrich Schleiermacher (1768–1834) has been cast as the "father of modern hermeneutics." He developed a theory of hermeneutics that set the foundation for much of the discussion that followed. Schleiermacher was interested in providing a basis in philosophy for theological hermeneutics. He identified two aspects of interpretation: the technical aspect, which focused on grammatical analysis, and the psychological dimension. The latter, which is perceived by a divinatory method, has to do with accessing the mind of the author that gave rise to writing. "The divinatory method is the one in which one, so to speak, transforms oneself into the other person and tries to understand the individual element directly."[3] The goal of interpretation for Schleiermacher was

---

move in this direction, see Jens Zimmermann, *Recovering Theological Hermeneutics: An Incarnational-Trinitarian Theory of Interpretation* (Grand Rapids: Baker, 2004), 88.

2. The rise of modern hermeneutical theory is usually traced back to the early nineteenth century, and Friedrich Schleiermacher particularly.

3. Friedrich Schleiermacher, *Hermeneutics and Criticism and Other Writings*, trans. and ed. Andrew Bowie, *Cambridge Texts in the History of Philosophy* (Cambridge: Cambridge University Press, 1998), 92.

to reach through the text to the personhood of the author as he wrote. In Schleiermacher's thought, "the technical aspect of hermeneutics serves as a conductor to the spiritual-psychological 'pulse' of the author. . . . Therefore, careful grammatical exegesis is required to get to the point at which we resonate with the author's expression of immediate self-consciousness."[4]

To put it another way, the interpreter seeks to grasp the meaning of the text as well as, and then better than, the author did by putting himself or herself in the position of the author.[5] To do this, the interpreter "must look behind the text to the situations, experiences, and intentions that gave rise to the text, some of which may not even have entered the author's awareness."[6] In the end, the interpreter is trying to access a sort of universal unity of consciousness that lies behind all human expression.[7] Schleiermacher's interpretive goal of understanding and "connecting" with authors at this universal level set the stage for discussion of hermeneutics in the nineteenth century and beyond.

The philosopher Wilhelm Dilthey (1833–1911) popularized Schleiermacher's ideas and elaborated them for his own context. For Dilthey, the hermeneutical goal became to understand the *author* better than the author understood himself.[8] This could be accomplished by attempting to "transpose" oneself into the author's circumstances.[9] Dilthey speaks of the importance of historically reconstructing human experience and re-creating in the reader's mind the experience of the author.[10] Notice that, with Dilthey, there is an increased shift of focus from text to author. His ambitious goal was assumed to be possible because the modern

---

4. Zimmermann, *Theological Hermeneutics*, 149.

5. Schleiermacher, *Hermeneutics and Criticism*, 23. Schleiermacher goes on to explain: "For because we have no immediate knowledge of what is in [the author], we must seek to bring much to consciousness that can remain unconscious to him" (23). Thiselton also notes that "within this framework Schleiermacher formulates his version of the hermeneutical circle," that continual return to the text to understand it better (Thiselton, *New Horizons*, 221).

6. Thiselton, *New Horizons*, 59.

7. We may illustrate this romanticist notion of texts as expressions of a unitary consciousness in Hazlitt, a writer of Schleiermacher's time, who comments on his own collection of "classic" literary works. He refers to them as "standard productions . . . links in the chain of our conscious being [that] bind together the different scattered divisions of our personal identity" (William Hazlitt, "On Reading Old Books," in *The Plain Speaker* [London: Henry Colburn, 1826], quoted in William St. Clair, *The Reading Nation in the Romantic Period* [Cambridge: Cambridge University Press, 2004], 395).

8. Wilhelm Dilthey, *Hermeneutics and the Study of History*, vol. 4, *Selected Works*, ed. R. Makkreel and F. Rodi (Princeton, NJ: Princeton University Press, 1996), 232. This idea emerges in Dilthey's lecture "On Understanding and Hermeneutics" (1867–68).

9. Thiselton, *New Horizons*, 248.

10. Dilthey, "On Understanding and Hermeneutics," in *Hermeneutics*, 229–30.

interpreter had a bird's-eye view of the author's time and place, and so was able to understand the text better than the author, who was locked in his own historical location and so unable to understand his own times completely. Dilthey comes to epitomize the nineteenth-century preoccupation with the author. The thought world of the author, the focus of this preoccupation, is quite often referred to as authorial intention. Another way of speaking of the goal of interpretation in this model is accessing "the world behind the text."

Beyond the theoretical discussion of hermeneutics, there was a highly optimistic tone to biblical and theological studies of the nineteenth century, which contributed to the general tenor of biblical inquiry, hermeneutics included. Many theologians embraced the sciences, historical analysis in particular, as keys to answering the most significant religious questions. Historical investigation of the life of Jesus, for example, was a major area of inquiry in nineteenth-century New Testament studies. In Old Testament inquiry, investigation of the apparent sources of the early narratives (Genesis–Deuteronomy) was prominent. There was a sense in both these endeavors that, with enough time and the right investigative tools, results were assured. This extreme optimism colored (we might say, "rose-colored") theology in general, and thus hermeneutic theory as well. Historical reconstruction was the goal; the possibility of reaching it was virtually guaranteed.

When attempts to get at the mind of the author were coupled with such widespread historical positivism, there was a combination ripe for strong reaction. In hermeneutics, there was a reactive critique of the preoccupation with the author and a corresponding stress on an autonomous text. There came a questioning of whether interpreters are really able to "get into the heads" of authors, as Dilthey and others seemed to suggest. Instead, the text was viewed as independent from its author, whose influence was no longer decisive for interpretation. Before we look at this movement away from the author, it might be helpful to ask the question of relevance in relation to nineteenth-century hermeneutics. How are we helped by knowing what went on two hundred years ago?

So What?

Today when an interpreter speaks of getting at authorial intention, reactions typically include corresponding claims of presumption and inaccessibility, such as, "We simply cannot presume to know an author's thoughts or intentions." This reasoning makes sense if authorial intention refers to the interior world and motives of an author as he or she writes a text. Unless authors make their motivations clear in their texts, it is quite unlikely that readers will be able to identify them correctly.

The term "authorial intention" has, however, been used in at least a couple of ways in contemporary discussion. It certainly has been used in a manner more representative of the nineteenth-century viewpoint epitomized first by Schleiermacher, then by Dilthey. It is also used by others to express a more text-centered perspective: what the author intended to communicate through use of shareable linguistic conventions. This outlook places a concerted focus on the text itself.[11]

Some contemporary interpreters have proposed alternative terms to more clearly communicate that readers can access an author's intentions discernable within the discourse of a text, without having to read an author's mind. This interpretive goal has been termed "communicative intention" or "embodied intention."[12] The more modest goal in this case is to access only those authorial intentions that are communicated via the text in its setting, not to re-create the motives of the author that lie outside the boundaries of textual meaning. In either case, whether in reaction against it or modification of it, the legacy of "authorial intention" remains influential in contemporary discussions of hermeneutics.

The Text Stands Alone

Reaction against the Author

There was understandably a strong reactive move away from the overly optimistic goal of "getting into the head of an author," that is, sharing the author's mental world. The reaction occurred at a number of levels. First, there was a general reaction against the extreme intellectual optimism of the nineteenth century. Especially following World War I, such optimism seemed misguided at best. A more chastened perspective was called for in the aftermath of such widespread human atrocity and suffering.

In addition, there was growing dissatisfaction with the results of nineteenth-century methods. Because nineteenth-century scholars had been deeply involved in reconstructions of the "world behind the text," they had generally given less attention to the study of the text's message.

11. This is true of both Hirsch and Stein in their formulation of authorial intention when they refer to meaning as shareable; Hirsch, *Validity*, 31, 66; Stein, *Basic Guide*, 38.
12. "Communicative intention" is language from Brett, "Motives and Intentions," 5. Authorial motives as distinct from meaning, at least in some of its uses, derives from Quentin Skinner, "Motives, Intentions and the Interpretation of Texts," *New Literary History* 3 (Winter 1971): 393–408. Sternberg has coined "embodied intention" (Meir Sternberg, *The Poetics of Biblical Narrative: Ideological Literature and the Drama of Reading* [Bloomington, IN: Indiana University Press, 1987], 9).

Often historical reconstruction all but replaced exegesis. This certainly was the case in studies of the Gospels, which often were mined for evidence about who Jesus was rather than for their messages to the faith communities addressed by the Gospels.

Approaching the text as a means for reconstructing history tended toward results that were often irrelevant for contemporary faith and at times antithetical to it. There was a developing desire to move away from the author's meaning, which was presumed to be locked in the past with the author. Existential philosophy, undergirding the work of theologians such as Rudolf Bultmann, provided compelling reasons for freeing meaning from its chains to the author, at least the chains of a positivistic perspective on the accessibility of authors that produced results antithetical to Christian faith.[13] The time was ripe for asserting the continuing relevance of the biblical text. As Bultmann wrote, "The understanding of the text is never a definitive one, but rather remains open because the meaning of the Scriptures discloses itself anew in every future."[14] Finally, currents in the field of literary analysis, especially the literary critique of "authorial intention," prompted reassessment of hermeneutic theory in biblical interpretation. In fact, an understanding of the movement away from authors in literary criticism is crucial for understanding similar and partially dependent reactions in biblical hermeneutics.

Textual Autonomy in Literary Criticism

"New Criticism" arose in literary circles in the 1920s–1940s in reaction to a type of literary analysis that focused on retrieving the author's psychological motives for writing. New critics claimed that the search for this interior world of the author was doomed from the start and irrelevant for textual interpretation in the end. Representative of this perspective are W. K. Wimsatt and Monroe Beardsley, who coined the term "intentional fallacy" to refer to the misguided search for authorial intention. For Wimsatt and Beardsley, authorial intention is both

13. Existentialism, as worked out by Martin Heidegger for example, disassociates truth from "objective" knowing (defined in the scientific, positivist model as the only "right kind of knowing"). "Heidegger argues that human beings know primarily existentially or interpretively" (Zimmermann, *Theological Hermeneutics*, 162). The goal was to reclaim knowledge by asserting human subjectivity in relation to knowing, what Gadamer later would conceive of as participatory knowledge (ibid., 173). This central tenet of Heideggerian hermeneutics does not necessitate a slide into relativism, although existentialism has generally lent itself to relativistic interpretation and uses.

14. Rudolf Bultmann, "Is Exegesis without Presuppositions Possible?" in *Existence and Faith*, trans. Schubert M. Ogden (London: Hodder and Stoughton, 1960), 295.

inaccessible and undesirable for interpretation.[15] In New Criticism, the focus decidedly shifted to the text as the sole vehicle of meaning, since in previous literary interpretation "the work itself hardly needed to be mentioned."[16] In fact, because the search for the author had so long tended to obscure the text itself, New Criticism established the autonomous text as one of its highest values.

That the text is autonomous means it is divorced from its author. In this view, the author no longer controls interpretation of the text and so cannot determine meaning. In fact, the author is irrelevant to textual meaning, since once the text is written it becomes a free-floating entity with a life of its own. It is no longer bound to the author or the original setting of its composition. T. S. Eliot, a poet and proponent of New Criticism, commends an "impersonal theory of poetry" in which the poet strives for "a continual extinction of personality," so that the author's intentions become irrelevant for interpretation.[17] In addition, New Criticism tended to foster the attitude that literature is by nature distinct and superior to ordinary communication (oral or written).[18]

There was a noble rationale for this viewpoint. Part of the reasoning behind this divorce between text and author was the desire to protect the contemporary relevance of the text. For literary critics, this meant affirming the unique and life-changing nature of literature. If literature was freed from the author and an obsession with the world behind the text, then it could vividly influence readers by inviting them into the "world projected by the text." Literature could be resurrected to a living significance.

Textual Autonomy in Biblical Hermeneutics

Following in the footsteps of their literary counterparts, many interpreters of the Bible advocated the autonomous text as the way forward out of an authorial quagmire. This movement in biblical hermeneutics, however, developed later and a bit more gradually than in literary criti-

---

15. W. K. Wimsatt and Monroe C. Beardsley, "The Intentional Fallacy," in *On Literary Intention*, ed. David Newton-de Molina (Edinburgh: University Press, 1976), 1–13.

16. Mary Ann Tolbert, *Sowing the Gospel: Mark's World in Literary-Historical Perspective* (Minneapolis: Fortress, 1989), 12.

17. T. S. Eliot, "Tradition and the Individual Talent," in *Selected Essays* (London: Faber & Faber, 1932), 17–18. Note also Gadamer's philosophical stance that "what is fixed in writing has detached itself from the contingency of its origin and its author and made itself free for new relationships" (Hans-Georg Gadamer, *Truth and Method*, 2nd rev. ed., trans. Joel Weinsheimer and Donald G. Marshall [New York: Continuum, 2004], 395).

18. Pratt, *Literary Discourse*, xiv–xvi. Pratt's work argues (successfully, to my mind) that such a distinction cannot be maintained, so that a linguistics of human communication can properly be applied to literature of all kinds.

cism. Though the seeds of change were sown in the early to middle part of the twentieth century, the text as independent of the author did not, in fact, gain significant ground until the 1960s and 1970s. A leading figure in the development of the theory of semantic autonomy for the interpretation of the Bible was Paul Ricoeur, whose writing in this area has had significant influence.

Ricoeur has provided philosophical underpinnings for a biblical hermeneutic of textual autonomy. First, he emphasizes the metaphorical nature of biblical language. Metaphorical language results in a "surplus of meaning" that cannot be limited to the author's meaning.[19] Second, an important basis for the divorce of the text from its author is a radical distinction between spoken and written communication. Ricoeur frames it like this: "With writing, the verbal meaning of the text no longer coincides with the mental meaning or intention of the text."[20] At least part of his purpose in this configuration of meaning is his interest in "the poetic dimension of texts," that is, the ability of texts to speak to contemporary readers.[21]

Both these ideas, the radical openness of metaphor and the uniqueness of written communication, support the notion that meaning is polyvalent. In other words, there are multiple, potentially conflicting, meanings for any given text because language allows for multiple possibilities, and an absent author cannot arbitrate between these possibilities. In this view, it is the text rather than the author that provides a measure of interpretive constraint, although the text cannot provide determinate limits. Therefore, in this view, meaning does not have such clear boundaries between what it is and what it is not. Meaning is not determinate, that is, bounded; rather, it is indeterminate and polyvalent.

So What?

Emphasis on an autonomous text still exerts significant influence in biblical hermeneutics. This can be seen in such commonplace phrases in hermeneutics and biblical studies as "semantic autonomy," "textual polyvalency," and "the indeterminacy of the text." On a deeper level, the autonomous text reveals itself in affirmations of the legitimacy of conflicting interpretations of a text. The claim for a unified, coherent perspective on a text receives immediate criticism in many circles. If the

19. The impetus for Ricoeur's emphasis on a "surplus of meaning" is his affirmation of human possibility in the face of philosophies that conclude that human existence is meaningless. See Vanhoozer, *Philosophy of Paul Ricoeur*, 6–9.

20. Paul Ricoeur, *Interpretation Theory: Discourse and the Surplus of Meaning* (Fort Worth: Texas Christian University Press, 1976), 75.

21. Vanhoozer, *Philosophy of Paul Ricoeur*, 276.

text allows for alternate readings, then each of these interpretations is held to be legitimate. Notice here that the autonomous text is the arbitrator of meaning. Standards for determining what is or is not a legitimate interpretation come from the text itself quite apart from its author.

As I will argue at the close of this chapter, the move to divorce the author from his or her text was an overreaction to earlier attempts to re-create fully the author's writing experiences by means of the text. At that point, I will suggest that we bring the author back into definitions of textual meaning, albeit in a more modest way.

Yet overall, in spite of an overreaction against the author, New Criticism's textual focus has made some helpful contributions to biblical interpretation. As a first contribution, emphasis on the text itself rather than the author's psychology or the world behind the text has promoted a textually centered interpretation that was often missing in earlier authorial approaches. Second, literary approaches to the text (centered on the final form of the text) have been hailed by many for emphasizing an appreciation for the artistry of the text. Finally, literary methods also have the capacity to bridge to theological readings of the Bible.

Textual autonomy in its more rigid forms, however, set the stage for another significant reaction, emphasizing the reader in interpretation.[22] Structuralism, for example, which is based on the philosophy of the autonomous text, objectified the text to such an extent that it came to be viewed more as code than as communication.[23] In turn, reaction against this type of more extreme objectification of the text moved hermeneutical reflection toward a reader-centered perspective.

The Reign of the Reader

Reaction to an objectified text was one of a number of influences that moved hermeneutical theory to stress the reader as generator of meaning, in part or whole. Other influences included philosophical currents that took seriously the impact of presuppositions in interpretation as well as the explosion of methods beyond historical criticism in biblical studies.[24]

22. This was a reaction to but also continuation of previous thinking. For example, the autonomous text began the movement toward polyvalency (many potential meanings of a text). Affirmation of polyvalency continues with reader perspectives. Yet reader approaches reacted against an autonomous, impersonal text. Instead, in reader-centered viewpoints, readers bring all that they are to the text to create meaning.

23. Structuralism is a method of interpretation that examines the dual structures of a text to discover meaning at the superficial and deeper levels of the text. The deeper level provides access to the text's universal nature.

24. This multiplication can rightly be perceived as a result of openness to readers and their vantage points as well. My sense is that the introduction of literary criticism (which

The philosophical and theological move away from extreme historicism had really begun early in the twentieth century with the work of the influential German philosopher Martin Heidegger (1889–1926).[25] Heidegger emphasized the importance of the interpreter's presuppositions in textual interpretation. For Heidegger, these presuppositions precluded any kind of objectified knowledge of the text. Instead, interpreters bring their own interests, foresight, and pre-understandings to the text. Their understanding of the text is structured by their own presuppositions. According to Heidegger, the interpreter's presuppositions are challenged by the text; the text is then challenged by other assumptions of the interpreter, and so on. This hermeneutical circle is a necessary part of all textual understanding. Only in the circle's dialogue between text and interpreter does the possibility of true understanding exist. As Wilkinson notes, one of Heidegger's key contributions was to put this hermeneutical circle at the center of interpretation.[26]

Heidegger's work on the contextual nature of understanding influenced his student Hans-Georg Gadamer (1900–2002), another important twentieth-century hermeneutical philosopher. Gadamer's "foundational insight . . . is the universality of hermeneutics," that is, the truth that all human knowing is mediated.[27] This leads Gadamer to conceptualize the relationship of interpreter to text by speaking of the horizon of each. For Gadamer, understanding occurs in the fusion of the horizon of the text with the horizon of the interpreter: "All reading involves application, so that a person reading a text is himself part of the meaning he apprehends. He belongs to the text that he is reading."[28] For Gadamer, this "blurring of the boundaries" between text and reader is balanced by universal human participation in reason (what he means by "tradition") and language.[29]

---

focuses exclusive attention on the final form of the text) into biblical studies, which had been dominated up to that point by historical criticism, facilitated discussion in biblical studies of the role of readers and so precipitated the proliferation of methodologies that followed early application of literary criticism to the Bible. For a description of historical criticism, see Appendix B.

25. Wilkinson refers to Heidegger's *Being and Time* (originally published in 1927 as *Sein und Zeit*) as "arguably the most influential work in twentieth-century philosophy" (Loren Wilkinson, "Hermeneutics and the Postmodern Reaction against 'Truth,'" in *The Act of Bible Reading: A Multidisciplinary Approach to Biblical Interpretation,*" ed. Elmer Dyck [Downers Grove, IL: InterVarsity, 1996], 119).

26. Wilkinson, "Hermeneutics," 120.

27. Zimmermann, *Theological Hermeneutics*, 161.

28. Gadamer, *Truth and Method*, 340.

29. Zimmermann, *Theological Hermeneutics*, 167–69. Zimmermann's critique of Gadamer (and Schleiermacher for that matter; see 190) is that his confidence that language and reason "can be trusted to reveal true aspects of human existence" falters on his naturalistic worldview (177). Gadamer, in the end, collapses the distinction between transcendence

Some theorists, while convinced by Gadamer's (and Heidegger's) notion of the contextualized nature of human knowledge, are not so confident in any kind of universality that allows for mutual understanding. They instead see in the work of Gadamer the potential for radical contextualization apart from confidence in mutual understanding. We might refer to this viewpoint as a reader-centered perspective, by which I mean an almost exclusive focus on the reader as contextualized as the basis for interpretive theory.[30] In fact, part of the impact of Heidegger and Gadamer can be seen in the current prominence of reader-centered perspectives within literary criticism, theology, and biblical studies.

In recent years, the birth of a wide variety of new methodologies in biblical studies and the emergence in theology of multiple "contextual" theologies have emphasized how diverse the interpretation of a single text can be. When historical methods were privileged in biblical studies, this diversity was not quite so obvious. But a plurality of interpretations needs to be taken seriously given the rise of literary criticism, socioscientific criticism, feminist criticism, rhetorical criticism, and more, in addition to interpretive voices from non-Western cultures. One way of doing this is to tie meaning to the reader in a thoroughgoing way.

A number of features are typical of a consistently reader-oriented perspective. Meaning, in this view, is inevitably determined by the reader of the text. For instance, David Gunn and Danna Fewell hold that "texts are multivalent and their meanings radically contextual, inescapably bound up with their interpreters."[31] It follows from this perspective that a wide variety of interpretations, whether they are in agreement or not, are affirmed as legitimate readings of the text. In fact, for some who subscribe to a reader-controlled hermeneutic, meanings are as numerous as readers. Others would affirm a multiplicity of potentially conflicting, legitimate interpretations, while acknowledging the possibility of illegitimate readings that go beyond the horizon of the text. In the end, the primary criterion for determining whether an interpretation is legitimate comes from "reading communities." In this view, reading com-

---

and immanence, that is, the text as other and the text as accessible. Zimmermann's claim is that it is possible to maintain the distinction between transcendence and immanence only by grounding it in the theological truth of the incarnation (184–85). Others focus their critique on Gadamer's view that tradition rather than the text itself is the arbitrator of meaning. Hirsch, Osborne, and others argue that tradition as arbitrator is an inadequate hermeneutical control (Hirsch, *Validity*, 250; Osborne, *Hermeneutical Spiral*, 371).

30. Since I accept the argument that readers are contextualized, I refer here to a view (in distinction to my own) that emphasizes contextualization to the point of questioning the human ability to understand other human beings or their writings.

31. David M. Gunn and Danna Nolan Fewell, *Narrative in the Hebrew Bible*, Oxford Bible Series (Oxford: Oxford University Press, 1993), 9.

munities determine the proper boundaries of interpretation rather—or more—than the text.

What is a reading community, and how might it provide controls on interpretation? Each of us is a part of a reading community. In fact, most of us are part of a number of communities that influence how we interpret the Bible, including our faith community, our family, and our particular subcultures. These communities, through their communal values and norms, set up implicit and explicit boundaries for their members. Individuals who move outside the interpretive parameters of the group are censured, sometimes formally but more often informally and indirectly. In this way, the reading community restrains the interpretations of its members. If individuals go too far outside the boundaries, they will often find it difficult to remain in that particular community. A thoroughgoing reader perspective understands reading communities rather than texts as the "check and balance" of interpretation. A prominent proponent of this perspective is Stanley Fish. His view of interpretive boundaries has been summarized aptly by Robert Fowler: "Readers may control texts, but that does not lead to anarchy, because interpretive communities control readers."[32]

Another feature that often, though not always, attends reader-centered approaches is the notion of the instability of language and texts. Gunn and Fewell express this textual quality when they write, "We understand texts to be inherently unstable, since they contain within themselves the threads of their own unraveling."[33] According to this view, textual instability necessitates the indeterminacy of texts, so texts lack boundaries. In its more extreme forms, as in deconstructionist models, language itself is understood as not only unstable but also random and lacking in meaning.[34] If the text with all its linguistic ambiguities is not the arbitrator of meaning, then readers create meaning as they come to unstable texts.

32. Robert M. Fowler, "Who Is 'the Reader' in Reader Response Criticism?" *Semeia* 31 (1985): 14. See Stanley Fish, *Is There a Text in This Class? The Authority of Interpretive Communities* (Cambridge, MA: Harvard University Press, 1980).

33. They go on to describe their method of deconstructive criticism as "seek[ing] to expound the gaps, the silences, the contradictions, which inhabit all texts, like loose threads in a sweater, waiting to be pulled" (Gunn and Fewell, *Narrative*, 10).

34. Craig Bartholomew, "Before Babel and after Pentecost: Language, Literature and Biblical Interpretation," in *After Pentecost: Language and Biblical Interpretation*, Scripture and Hermeneutics Series 2, ed. C. Bartholomew, C. Greene, and K. Möller (Grand Rapids: Zondervan, 2001), 143. In chap. 8, we will address views on language and seek to define a biblical understanding of language's role in communication. If this view of language and texts seems extreme, there is comfort in Wright's observation that "the way is hard that leads to genuine deconstructionism, and those who follow it consistently are few" (Wright, *NTPG*, 60).

So What?

Reader-centered viewpoints have caused hermeneutical theorists and theologians alike to take more seriously the role of the reader in interpretation. Every reader has an interpretive "location" that influences his or her understanding of the biblical text. This location includes the reader's theological tradition, cultural and social location, and pre-understandings brought to specific texts and Scripture in general. To claim that the reader's location does not significantly influence interpretation is no longer possible, given the work of Heidegger, Gadamer, and others. In addition, the idea that meaning occurs in the interplay of text and reader is now a standard one in hermeneutics. Whether the image is one of the hermeneutical circle (Heidegger) or the fusion of the horizons (Gadamer), this idea exerts significant influence in contemporary conceptions of interpretation.

Summary

We might summarize the three movements discussed so far by drawing on a frequently used analogy. The search for authorial intention as defined in the nineteenth century might be compared to approaching the text as a window. The text was understood as a means to understanding the world of the author (history) and the mind of the author (personality or psychology). Textual autonomy, however, understands the text to be a picture, a work of art to be studied and appreciated in its own right, rather than for what it can reveal about the situation or intention of the author. Finally, a singular focus on the reader's role has been likened to the text as mirror. In the end, the interpreter does not see a pristine text, but the reader's own reflection in relation to the text.

A Contemporary Movement: The Return of the Author to Textual Meaning

We have seen that the twists and turns that located meaning first in the author, then in the autonomous text, and finally in the reader, closely followed philosophical currents of the past two hundred years. After primary stress first on the author, then the text, and finally the reader, it is not surprising to see a movement toward a mediating position that embraces all three,[35] and particularly a return of the author as important for inter-

---

35. A. C. Thiselton terms this position an "integrated" hermeneutics in "'Behind' and 'In Front Of' the Text: Language, Reference and Indeterminacy," in *After Pentecost: Language*

pretation. This is the case for a number of prominent voices in contemporary hermeneutics. For example, Anthony Thiselton, respected for his long-standing and wide-ranging work in hermeneutical discussions, argues against "sweeping, wholesale attempts to strip *all* written texts and certainly all biblical texts, from authors and from situations in life."[36] For Thiselton, some texts continue to invite more pointed questions about authors.

Chastened Notions of Authors in Communication

We might, along with Stephen Fowl, refer to this renewed interest in authors as the formulation of a "chastened notion of authorial intention."[37] But the nature of the chastening varies from theorist to theorist. Thiselton constrains the importance of authors by genres, arguing for distinct theories of interpretation applied to different genres. Fowl limits authorial intention to the author's "communicative intention" and then argues against limiting meaning to an author's communicative intention.[38] Alternately, Vanhoozer, while embracing the notion of communicative intention as Fowl does, contends that meaning is coextensive with communicative intention and therefore that meaning is determinate. For Vanhoozer, meaning arises from, and is to be identified with, the communicative act of a personal agent.[39]

Vanhoozer's construction is a compelling one, because his view of authors and meaning is set within a general theory of textual meaning based on communication. He argues for communication as an overarching construct in understanding texts (although he focuses in the end on biblical texts particularly).[40] And I am convinced that communication as a textual model is sufficient for this task for at least three reasons.

---

and Biblical Interpretation, Scripture and Hermeneutics Series 2, ed. C. Bartholomew, C. Greene, K. Möller (Grand Rapids: Zondervan, 2001), 108.

36. Thiselton, *New Horizons*, 20.

37. Fowl, "Authorial Intention," 73.

38. Ibid., 77–82.

39. Vanhoozer, *Meaning*, 201–80; see also *First Theology*, 164n12.

40. Vanhoozer in his theoretical discussions of hermeneutics casts a wide net for theoretical resources as he develops an explicitly theological model of communication for interpreting Scripture. He draws from linguistics (speech-act and relevance theories) and literary theory, as well as drawing carefully from a variety of hermeneutical philosophers (most notably Ricoeur) and theologians. One of Vanhoozer's significant contributions is to construct a theological paradigm of communication that is trinitarian, explicitly utilizing the resources of speech-act theory. "Speech-act theory serves as handmaiden to a trinitarian theology of communication. If the Father is the locutor, the Son is his preeminent illocution. Christ is God's definitive Word, the substantive content of his message. And the Holy Spirit—the condition and power of receiving the sender's message—is God the perlocutor, the reason that his words do not return to him empty (Isa. 55:11). The triune God is therefore the epitome of communicative agency" (*Meaning*, 457).

First, even though different kinds of genres communicate in different ways and to differing degrees, the rubric of communication still fits the nature of literary texts on the whole. A communication model of authors, texts, and readers can avoid the tendency toward trichotomizing (dividing in three) that is prevalent in some discussions of textual interpretation, which seems to be rooted in the supposed distinction between literature and ordinary communication. With this distinction came the elevation of poetry over other literature as superior in its impersonal detachment from authors and contexts. After a time, literary prose joined the ranks of textual autonomy, so that novels and other narratives no longer required their authors for proper interpretation.

Yet the basic assumption that ordinary communication differs dramatically from literary "communication" has never been substantially proven. In fact, Mary Pratt's work comparing literary narrative with ordinary, spoken narratives points in the opposite direction. As she concludes:

> Even . . . rudimentary similarities between literature and other speaker/audience situations are enough to tell us that speaker and audience are present in the literary speech situation, that their existence is presupposed by literary works, that they have commitments to one another as they do everywhere else, and that those commitments are presupposed by both the creator and the receivers of the work. Far from being autonomous, self-contained, self-motivating, context-free objects which exist independently from the "pragmatic" concerns of "everyday" discourse, literary works take place in a context, and like any other utterance they cannot be described apart from that context. . . . A theory of literary discourse must [acknowledge this fact].[41]

Texts across a wide variety of genres have a basic communicative commonality. This basic communicative aspect of texts holds across genres. If this is the case, then the quite correct impulse to read a poetic text differently from an epistle arises from the observation that some textual features come to the fore in certain genres more than others. If the author's point of view in an epistle is more explicit than in a narrative text, this difference is not an argument for the unimportance of the author in a narrative text. Instead, it would seem to invite the interpreter to pay close attention to the author's way of communicating point of view narratively, that is, implicitly within the movement of the plot. A variety of conceptual tools should be in the interpreter's toolbox so that various genres can be helpfully engaged, without the interpreter needing a different toolbox for each genre.

A second observation in support of the adequacy of a communication model in reviving authors without exiling readers returns to the theme

41. Pratt, *Literary Discourse*, 115.

of story from chapter 2. Authors and their communicative intentions cannot be understood apart from the larger stories that map their intentions. This is precisely a quality of communication, that it is based in story. The worldviews of biblical authors, their assumed stories, need to be illuminated in order to hear the normative stance or story that authors communicate in Scripture. Authors' intentions can make sense only within these assumed and projected stories. This story model is exemplified by Wright in "his pursuit of historical research within an intentionality framework, a framework which consists primarily of the triangle . . . [of] knowledge-story-worldview."[42] For instance, the Old Testament prophets assume a worldview where people and nations worship multiple deities (polytheism), while asserting with all their might the normative story that Israel's God, Yahweh, is the creator God, who is utterly unique. This was quite a subversive story within such a wider worldview, and certainly a normative one according to the prophets. In addition to a storied way of understanding the Bible, we ought to foster an awareness of our own storied location—the stories we assume and are shaped by—as we come to appropriate the normative story of the Bible. It seems to me that attending to both sets of stories (the text's and our own) is what Thorsten Moritz means by taking "the story dimension of knowledge and interpretation seriously."[43]

Third, as discussed in chapter 1, a communication model adequately attends to the interpersonal nature of texts. An understanding of meaning that attends to texts as expressions of personal interfacing rather than impersonal objects will help us adequately attend to authors, texts, and readers, while keeping each in proper focus. It is my belief that this interpersonal quality of communication can be of particular help in navigating the tensions between various ways that reader involvement in texts and meaning has been construed.

The Chastened Reader

The challenge will be to give due attention and proper place to readers in the act of communication without going to either of two extremes:

42. As assessed by Thorsten Moritz, "Critical but Real: Reflecting on N. T. Wright's Tools for the Task," in *Renewing Biblical Interpretation*, Scripture and Hermeneutics Series 1, ed. C. Bartholomew, C. Greene, and K. Möller (Grand Rapids: Zondervan, 2000), 172–97, esp. 192.

43. Moritz, "Critical but Real," 194. Steiner claims that the move in New Criticism to dehistoricize texts was "a useful pedagogic trick . . . nothing more." For Steiner, texts and other works of art "are grounded in historical temporality." In our terms, they are storied. George Steiner, *Real Presences: Is There Anything in What We Say?* (London: Faber & Faber, 1989), 166–67.

making readers into authors or claiming that readers reach complete objectivity in their interpretations. Let's look at these two polarities more closely in our effort to steer a course between them.

More extreme reader-centered approaches end up making an author of the reader. My husband, Tim, while taking a university literature class, was told that readers create the meaning of texts. Readers, supposedly, become authors of the texts they read. We have already discussed how this viewpoint developed. But how might it be effectively addressed from the standpoint of a communication model of texts? The interpersonal nature of communication reminds us that the conversation we are hearing in a text is ultimately between the author and the reader, not an autonomous text and the reader.[44] The author known through the text, if viewed from a communicative perspective, cannot be collapsed into the identity of the reader. To collapse the distinction between the two would be to privilege the reader over the author, doing harm to the "otherness" of the author and his or her text in the process. Drawing on Emmanuel Levinas's notion of "the irreducible otherness of the personal," the author should be conceived of as a personal "other" to be encountered through the text rather than as absent author who has simply left a faceless text.[45] Levinas's concept of "the other," as Zimmermann says, "grounds understanding [that is, hermeneutics] in the radical difference of ethical transcendence."[46] Conceiving of the author as well as the reader in personal categories helps to honor the difference between the two. We can best hear from the author if we respect the author and authorial communication as distinct from us yet personally related or addressed to us.

As mentioned, the second extreme to avoid is making the claim that readers are objective in their readings. This posture, which ignores the significant insights of twentieth-century philosophy,[47] inherently assumes that the purpose of interpretation is mastery over the text. Again, conceiving of texts as communication can help us here. My goal when participating in communication with a friend is not to master what is communicated, or the person communicating it for that matter. Instead, I want to really hear and thereby know the other person more fully.

44. Yet it is primarily the author we come to know from the shape of the text itself (the implied author). See chap. 2.

45. Zimmermann's phrase summarizing Levinas's work (*Theological Hermeneutics*, 225). For Levinas's discussion of the "other" and its ethical correlate, see Emmanuel Levinas, *Totality and Infinity*, trans. Alphonso Lingis (Pittsburgh: Duquesne University Press, 1969), 194–219. See also Vanhoozer, *Meaning*, 459–62.

46. Zimmermann, *Theological Hermeneutics*, 227.

47. This posture also ignores the biblical perspective of human finitude, as we will see in chap. 4.

Analogously, our goal in textual interpretation involves, at its heart, listening in order to hear well. This listening is attentive to what is being communicated, without requiring the assurance that I can reach some sort of pure objectivity. Instead, listening seeks relationship.

It is an interesting observation that both these extremes—making readers of texts into authors and claiming full objectivity for readers—assert the reader as all-powerful. The reader becomes god of the text, whether through assimilation or mastery.[48] Somewhere in between these two extremes is a balance of respect for the text and awareness of one's own contextualization.[49]

A strength of reader-centered approaches to hermeneutics is their willingness to wrestle with the contextual nature of human existence, as emphasized by Heidegger and Gadamer. Heidegger observes that the reader's own perspective is the starting point of interpretation; there is no immediate access to a text: "An interpretation is never a presuppositionless apprehending of something presented to us. If . . . one likes to appeal to what 'stands there,' then one finds that what 'stands there' in the first instance is nothing other than the obvious undiscussed assumption of the person who does the interpreting."[50] This realization is a good one, though it does not mean the reader is forever locked in his or her perspective. Repeated interaction with a text—particularly with the awareness of one's own presuppositions, the otherness of the text, and the storied nature of the whole—can move one productively toward textual understanding. For Heidegger, this is the nature of the hermeneutical process: its circle. We might even expand the image to talk about a hermeneutical spiral, which moves toward greater and greater understanding.[51] Yet this movement toward understanding must never be conceived in absolute terms, as if we can attain the perfect reading and then close the book. "Every time one goes around the spiral the lenses of the telescope have altered, but every time there are still lenses."[52] At its heart, the hermeneutical process is open-ended, never fully completed. Maybe this should not surprise us, since an interpersonal view of hermeneutics invites the analogy of relationship or friendship, whose goal is not completion for its own sake but continual longing to know and be known.

---

48. Zimmermann points this out: "Human knowledge is finite and perspectival and . . . forgetting this amounts to claiming the status of a god" (*Theological Hermeneutics*, 162).

49. Chap. 6 will address these issues in more depth.

50. Martin Heidegger, *Being and Time*, trans. J. Macquarrie and E. Robinson (Oxford: Blackwell, 1978), 191–92.

51. A now commonplace way of describing the circle in progress; see Osborne, *Hermeneutical Spiral*.

52. Moritz, "Critical but Real," 193.

Figure 3.1: Communicative Spectrum of Intentionality Types

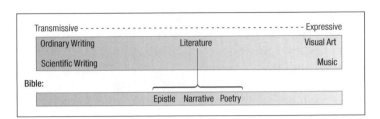

Postscript: A Communicative Spectrum of the Biblical Writings

In order to take seriously the communicative nature of all texts without embracing a simplistic one-size-fits-all method of textual interpretation, we might helpfully conceptualize texts as resting on a spectrum of types of intentionality. The spectrum I suggest would have what we might call "transmissive" communication on one end and "expressive" communication on the other.[53] In transmissive communication, the personal, transactional nature of the communicative act is emphasized (as in a letter). In such communication, the author may speak in first person in a fairly direct fashion with the intended audience. In expressive communication, on the other hand, the author generates a textual world, inviting readers to experience it with their mind's eye (as in a narrative or poem). Characters in narrative and images in poetry produce vivid visual worlds that beckon readers into an encounter. Understandably, authors tend to be more prominently featured in transmissive than in expressive communication. (See figure 3.1.)

The idea is to determine where along this spectrum from transmissive to expressive intention a particular kind of text fits. On the far transmissive end, we would likely place ordinary texts such as certain personal letters, textbooks, and instruction manuals (e.g., a recipe card). On the expressive end of the spectrum, certain kinds of poetic texts would find their place. In fact, if our spectrum were to include nontextual forms of communication, music and visual arts would occupy that far end, being expressive creations *par excellence*.[54]

---

53. Eco speaks of transmissive and productive texts (cited in Thiselton, *New Horizons*, 131).

54. Having been a music major in college, I am intrigued by the idea sometimes proposed that, when it comes to music, the intentions of composers are of little or no importance. (See, for example, Thiselton, *New Horizons*, 129: "Music can be endlessly played and enjoyed, without our necessarily asking about the conscious horizons and situation of the composer.") This has not been my experience. It is true that the choice to write a

Somewhere in between the ends of the spectrum, however, we could locate the literature, that is, the various genres, of the Bible. Much biblical poetry would fit on the more expressive side of the spectrum of biblical writings.[55] On the transmissive side, we would find the New Testament epistles.[56] Narratives would fit somewhere in between. You get the idea. By doing this exercise of placing various genres on a communicative spectrum, we get a sense of types of textual intentionality. The first thing to note is that authors by their genre choices dictate the kind of importance due themselves in interpretation. By choosing certain genres where expression rather than transmission is primary, authors submit their intentions to the particularities generated by that genre.[57] To choose to communicate through narrative, for example, means that you choose to communicate primarily in indirect fashion through plot and theme rather than through direct voice. The interpreter of narrative, then, is guided by the author's genre choice to focus primarily on indirect communication, since the author's direct voice is less utilized and so less accessible.

This attention to genre does not, however, invite interpreters to ignore the author's intention embodied in texts. Communicative intention matters in any genre. Rather, the argument here is that the level of at-

---

musical composition does place a self-imposed limit on the composer in terms of how his or her intentions are attended to by performers. Yet there is no way we could speak of Beethoven turning over in his grave at a particular rendering of one of his sonatas if intention was not at least part of what we are attempting to actualize in performance (with attention to dynamics and other markings, in addition to actual note accuracy). Orchestral arrangements are routinely made to approximate the size and instrument make-up of a composer's particular historical situation. As Eco notes, "a classical composition, whether it be a Bach fugue, Verdi's *Aïda*, or Stravinsky's *Rite of Spring*, posits an assemblage of sound units which the composer arranged in a closed, well-defined manner before presenting it to the listener. He converted his idea into conventional symbols which more or less oblige the eventual performer to reproduce the format devised by the composer himself" (*Role of the Reader*, 480).

55. In spite of the variety of ways poetry is used in the Bible, I believe we can make the generalization that biblical poetry is not purely expressive. Even some of the most personal and poignant of lament psalms, for example, are still, at least by virtue of their inclusion in the Psalter, meant for communication as well as expression.

56. Adolf Deissmann, a biblical scholar writing in the late nineteenth and early twentieth centuries, categorized New Testament letters as either letters (nonliterary and personal) or epistles (artistic literature meant for public consumption). See Fee and Stuart, *How to Read the Bible*, 56. Deissmann may have overplayed this distinction by placing the issue in terms of either/or categories. Instead, it is more helpful to think of a spectrum even within the category of New Testament letters/epistles. For example, Philemon is more personally focused than, for instance, the Epistle to the Hebrews.

57. By choosing particular genres, authors also make accompanying (implicit) choices about referentiality. See Thiselton, *New Horizons*, 130. On the related poles of referential and emotive language, see Pratt, *Literary Discourse*, 27.

tention appropriate to various modes of communicative intention (e.g., direct/indirect) is already implicit in an author's communicative intention when making genre choices. Since choosing to use an expressive textual medium is a communicative choice, it will not do to argue that in expressive-type texts we can ignore the author. We have just respected the author by choosing to interpret expressive texts as they were intended to be interpreted. If this means not focusing on the author in the same way as one would in a transmissive text, then the author's intent has still been honored!

All this is to say that genre provides clear and adequate indication of the appropriate level of prominence afforded an author in the interpretive task. It is important then to determine the genre of a particular text. But in addition, it will also be important to ask the accompanying question, How does this particular genre communicate? This question will guide our discussion of genre in chapter 7.

We can illustrate the value of this spectrum by looking at two Scripture texts. Paul's correspondence to Philemon is a New Testament letter on the transmissive end of biblical writings. Other than a more general blessing and thanksgiving (Philem. 3–7), the contents of this letter are very personally oriented and specifically aimed at persuading Philemon to receive his runaway slave, Onesimus, back with the very welcome Philemon would give to Paul himself. In the range of biblical books and even of New Testament letters, the author is "present" in a particularly personal way in this letter. We very much get the sense that we are hearing one end of a conversation, even more so than in, say, 1 Peter—a letter with a more general audience. Of course, we are speaking in a matter of degrees, which is precisely the value of a spectrum.

Toward the other end of the spectrum is Proverbs, an Old Testament poetic book that is part of the genre of wisdom literature. Let's choose a particular proverb:

> A gentle answer turns away anger,
>   but a harsh word stirs up wrath. (Prov. 15:1 HCSB)

Notice the general nature of the proverb. In fact, one definitional feature of the genre of proverb is its expression of a general truth.[58] The general nature of this proverb does not encourage highly specific contextual questions, about when, where, and to what audience an author crafted the proverb. We cannot say, however, that information about setting is not helpful in interpretation of proverbs. Comparatively, though,

---

58. A modern proverbial example, "The early bird gets the worm," is a generality expressing the advisability of getting at things early. It is no guarantee, however, that being early will always produce favorable results.

authors fade into the background more in proverbs than in New Testament letters.

To sum up this chapter, we have toured about two hundred years of the history of hermeneutical philosophy. Our purpose has been to show how authors, texts, and readers have been at the forefront at various points in this history. I then described the recent return of the author to hermeneutical deliberation and placed my communication model of interpretation within this movement, drawing together themes from chapters 1 and 2 in the process. I have concluded the chapter by proposing to understand different genres along a spectrum of types of intentionality in order to further a communicative model of textual interpretation. Our next chapter will draw together insights from the first three chapters in a series of affirmations about meaning within this communication model.

Suggestions for Further Reading (for Chapters 3–5)

Bartholomew, Craig G., Colin Greene, and Karl Möller, eds. *Renewing Biblical Interpretation*. Scripture and Hermeneutics Series 1. Grand Rapids: Zondervan, 2000.

Hirsch, E. D. "Transhistorical Intentions and the Persistence of Allegory." *New Literary History* 25 (1994): 549–67.

———. *Validity in Interpretation*. New Haven: Yale University Press, 1967.

Jeanrond, Werner G. *Text and Interpretation as Categories of Theological Thinking*. Translated by T. Wilson. Dublin: Gill and Macmillan, 1988.

Pratt, Mary Louise. *Toward a Speech Act Theory of Literary Discourse*. Bloomington, IN: Indiana University Press, 1977.

Stein, Robert H. *A Basic Guide to Interpreting the Bible: Playing by the Rules*. Grand Rapids: Baker Academic, 1994.

Zimmermann, Jens. *Recovering Theological Hermeneutics: An Incarnational-Trinitarian Theory of Interpretation*. Grand Rapids: Baker Academic, 2004.

4

Some Affirmations about *Meaning* from a Communication Model

Humpty Dumpty: "There's glory for you!" "I don't know what you mean by 'glory,'" Alice said. Humpty Dumpty smiled contemptuously. "Of course you don't—till I tell you. I meant 'there's a nice knockdown argument for you!'" "But 'glory' doesn't mean 'a nice knockdown argument,'" Alice objected. "When I use a word," Humpty Dumpty said, in a rather scornful tone, "it means just what I choose it to mean—neither more nor less." "The question is," said Alice, "whether you can *make* words mean so many different things." "The question is," said Humpty Dumpty, "which is to be master—that's all."

Lewis Carroll, *Alice in Wonderland*

Meaning—according to Humpty Dumpty: you can make it into anything you want it to be. But of course this kind of mastery, as he puts it, doesn't enable communication to succeed. Luckily, those who spend their lives exploring hermeneutics do not produce theories of meaning that much resemble Humpty Dumpty's way of doing things with words. Yet, Carroll helps us raise the issue of what meaning might *mean* within a communication model that takes authors seriously. Doesn't placing meaning in the domain of authors move meaning outside the public sphere (like Humpty Dumpty making "glory" to mean "a nice knockdown argument")? My discussion in this chapter will attempt to both summarize and nuance what I have already set forth about textual communication, defined in chapter 2 as "the complex pattern of what an author intends to communicate with his or her audience for purposes of engagement, which is inscribed in the text and conveyed through use of both shareable language parameters and background-contextual assumptions."

I must confess that I come to this chapter, which is devoted to affirmations about meaning, with no small amount of fear and trepidation. Vanhoozer indicates that he has avoided as much as possible using the term "meaning" in his chapter on Scripture in *First Theology*, preferring instead to refer to communication and communicative acts.[1] There is wisdom in this avoidance. People define meaning so variously in hermeneutical discussions that it may seem futile to attempt a one-size-fits-all definition. My goal is not so lofty. I do not expect that the definitional work I do in this chapter will build a consensus around a definition of meaning. But as I have already mentioned in chapter 1, we tend to think more clearly when we have our own definitions clarified. So to clarify the communication model I am proposing, I will offer a number of affirmations about meaning in this chapter. The affirmations that follow are not particularly idiosyncratic with me, since they have been worked out in conversation with a great many hermeneutical thinkers. These affirmations do, however, go to the heart of what I have been saying in the initial chapters about meaning in relation to interpretive goals.

Six Affirmations about Meaning

Meaning is author-derived but textually communicated. Meaning can be helpfully understood as communicative intention.[2]

As much recent work in hermeneutics has concluded, there is no need to excise the author from meaning. The divorce of the author from the text may have been a needed corrective to hermeneutical approaches that attempted to "get into the author's head," which in the end were more concerned with reconstructing the world of the author than hearing the textual message. For some, the author's mind and contextual world had become the purpose of the interpretive task. But the author and the text

---

1. Vanhoozer, *First Theology*, 163n11.
2. "Communicative intention" is Brett's term ("Motives and Intentions," 5). See chaps. 1–2.

need not be divorced from each other to restore a proper focus on the text itself, as was claimed by proponents of textual autonomy.

My first affirmation raises the question, What is the relationship between author and text in a communication model of meaning? First, we have already discussed in chapter 2 what we are *not* saying about this relationship. Meaning is not the retrieval of the author's mental acts or the motives behind writing. Psychological musings about Paul's sense of self-esteem when writing 2 Corinthians are not only somewhat anachronistic, they are also fairly irrelevant for determining the author's communicative intention. In chapter 3, we heard that the term "authorial intention" has often been understood as including an author's mental acts. Given the ambiguity of this term, it is more helpful to speak of the "communicative intention" of the author. Other similar terms, such as "embodied intention" and "inscribed intention," also do not divide the author from the text and so can helpfully express the coherence of author and text for an understanding of meaning.

Second, focusing on communicative intention helpfully implies that we take our primary interpretive cues from the author that we learn about from the text itself. The notion of an implied author is helpful not only for anonymous books of the Bible but also for books for which we know the author by name, since everything we can affirm about the implied author can contribute to an understanding of the real, or empirical, author. Typically what authors want audiences to know about themselves is inscribed by them in their texts. While information about the author gleaned from outside sources may further assist the interpreter, such information should not be used to trump the portrait of the implied author derived from the text itself. There is a tendency to assemble ad hoc material about empirical authors and allow it much greater weight than the textual testimony about the author. (Remember our example of "doctor" Luke from chapter 2.) This can lead to skewed interpretations. We should take our cues about the author first and foremost from the text itself.[3]

Finally, holding the author and text together allows for the relevance of information about the social world of the text. A communicative model

---

3. You may have noted that this is a clarification of our discussion in chap. 2. The implied author construct can helpfully be supplemented by contextual information about the real author in biblical books that are not anonymous, with what we learn about the author from the book itself being the primary data to consider. Lundin, Thiselton, and Walhout suggest that "the narrative voice of the text may be considered in relation to the real author" (Roger Lundin, Anthony C. Thiselton, and Clarence Walhout, *The Responsibility of Hermeneutics* [Grand Rapids: Eerdmans, 1985], 49). Vanhoozer argues that "the implied author . . . need not exclude the notion of the historical author as communicative agent" (*Meaning*, 239).

emphasizes the artificiality of separating authors from their texts. The historical contexts of author and original audience set the parameters for what the reader needs to know about the communicative setting. What was assumed between them may be alluded to in the text but will most often require further historical investigation. Certain information will be only partially inscribed in the text, given that the author could assume that the audience had adequate shared knowledge to fill in the rest. Our task will be to ascertain the shared knowledge that is assumed. This is not a reversion to the author's mental acts, because the assumed context is information common to both author and original audience. While today's readers of the New Testament, for example, may not be able to access every relevant detail of the assumed context, there is much that can be gleaned from texts themselves and from historical study of the Jewish and Greco-Roman world of the first century.

Here's an example. In 1 Corinthians 14:40, Paul tells the Corinthian church that "all things should be done decently and in order" (ESV). The literary context of Paul's instruction is set within exhortations for proper conduct in corporate worship (chaps. 11–14). Much of the background context assumed by Paul is referred or alluded to in the text of 1 Corinthians itself. For instance, worship in the Corinthian church involves prayer and prophecy by members of the church (both men and women, 11:2–16); the Lord's Supper shared in the context of a meal (11:17–34); and varieties of gifts being used in both corporate worship and church life, including wisdom, knowledge, faith, healing and other miraculous powers, prophecy, discernment, tongues, interpretation of tongues, apostleship, helping others, and administration (12:8–10, 28). Many of these gifts are included in Corinthian worship, where every member has the opportunity to share a gift within the corporate gathering, such as "a hymn, a lesson, a revelation, a tongue or an interpretation" (14:26). So we find in the worship of the Corinthian church a high degree of involvement by individual members. In fact, we have indications that this level of personal involvement is resulting in disorder, so that multiple tongues and prophecies are occurring simultaneously (14:23–24, 27); tongues are not being followed by interpretation as they ought (14:6–7); and the communion meal is leaving hungry the poorest among the church (11:21). On top of all this, some gifts (tongues) are being touted as "the best" ones (12:12–30); women are prophesying and praying without the appropriate head covers (11:2–16); and, in general, love for others is being ignored (13:1–13).

If this kind of worship environment is difficult for us to fathom, it may be helpful to attend to information about the social setting gleaned from resources besides 1 Corinthians. From this contextual information, we learn that the Corinthian church met and worshiped in a quite different social and physical context from the ones we are probably accustomed to in the contemporary Western church. It is quite likely that the Corinthian church met in a home belonging to a wealthier member of the church.[4] The home setting renders the various worship abuses of the Corinthian church more understandable. For example, divisions at the Lord's Supper and accompanying meal might have been exacerbated by separation of wealthier and poorer members into the "formal" dining room and a less comfortable atrium.[5]

Once the stage is set with the assumed context drawn from both the text itself and outside sources, Paul's words, "But all things should be done decently and in order," take on their proper sense. Corinthian worship, in contrast to many modern worship contexts, had gotten out of hand. As I tell my students, Corinthian believers are not sitting primly in their pews facing forward and remaining silent except while singing. For the Corinthians, worship is much less like what some of us might be used to and more like swinging from the chandeliers! Speaking into this context, Paul admonishes the church that worship must be decent and orderly. His words sum up much of his instruction to the church woven already into 1 Corinthians 11–14 and make much practical sense in this context.[6]

Meaning is complex and determinate.

Meaning can and most often does involve cognitive, emotive, volitional, and, in general, persuasive purposes on the part of the writer, whose intentions include but go beyond cognition for the reader. Affirming the complexity of meaning in this fashion in no way argues against the "determinacy" of meaning. The claim that meaning is determinate affirms its bounded, though not simplistic, nature. As Hirsch writes, "To say that verbal meaning is determinate is not to exclude complexities of meaning but only to insist that a text's meaning is what it is and not a hundred other things."[7] Or as Vanhoozer has stated, "It is important to acknowledge that authors may intend to communicate complex, multilayered intentions."[8]

4. David E. Garland, *1 Corinthians*, Baker Exegetical Commentary on the New Testament (Grand Rapids: Baker Academic, 2003), 536.

5. Ibid.

6. It would be a mistake to import Paul's admonition for order into contemporary settings without this kind of close contextual investigation. Doing so might have a quite different result than Paul intended, given the different settings. Paul's call to order may not be what is needed in some contemporary corporate worship settings where disorder is hardly an issue, since the schedule of worship is predetermined and led by only a few from among the church body. In this context, it may be more timely to hear Paul's words from 1 Thess.: "Do not quench the Spirit" (5:19).

7. Hirsch, *Validity*, 230.

8. Vanhoozer, *First Theology*, 178.

It is rather popular in current hermeneutical discussion to affirm the "indeterminacy" of meaning. In fact, the text's indeterminacy is often spoken of as self-evident. Why? I believe the idea derives from the tendency to assume that meaning either is multifaceted or is determinate and therefore singular. The latter two terms are often unhelpfully wedded together. Whether arguing for or against singular meaning, scholars seem bound and determined (pun intended) to link "determinate" and "singular." William Larkin combines the two ideas when he affirms as legitimate only "meaning that is single, definite, and fixed."[9] Hart, in commenting on this view, defines determinate readings (approaches to Scripture that claim objectivity) as "those which suppose that a single fixed and authoritative meaning is there to be had."[10] Single and determinate—how might we disentangle these two terms?

"Single meaning" inadequately describes meaning, since singularity implies, for most, a simplistic construal of meaning. It conjures up an image of a single point at the end of a trajectory. We work to get at meaning, and, voilà, we arrive at a fixed point that is the text's meaning. Isn't this process simple? For many like Hart, I imagine the whole thing smacks of the positivistic, historical-critical claims of the nineteenth century all over again.[11] In retrospect, my guess is that the fellow student in hermeneutics class I mentioned in chapter 1 was resistant to defining meaning because a definition might oversimplify the complexity of meaning.

So the language of "singular" meaning is problematic, even though I am utterly sympathetic with its corollary that meaning has boundaries. Meaning is determinate.[12] It seems to me that we can legitimately avoid the term "single meaning" and still affirm determinate meaning,

9. William J. Larkin Jr., *Biblical Theology of Hermeneutics and Culture: Interpreting and Applying the Authoritative Word in a Relativistic Age* (Grand Rapids: Baker Academic, 1988), 303. "Fixed" is another way of describing determinacy.

10. Hart, "Christian Approach to the Bible," 194. See also Steinmetz who argues rigorously against what he terms "the single meaning theory" ("The Superiority of Pre-Critical Exegesis," 37).

11. In addition, for those who refer to a single meaning, what is often not specified is whether the single meaning arises from a single passage or a whole book. It seems to me that we should speak of meaning primarily at the level of an entire book, since it is not clear that a biblical author would want us to isolate individual passages and garner a single meaning from each. Instead, if our focus is on a book as a whole, it becomes much more difficult to maintain the language of single meaning, since it is hard to fathom that the author of Jeremiah, for instance, is concerned to communicate a single meaning! I would affirm wholeheartedly, however, that the author of Jeremiah communicated meaning that is determinate.

12. Alston affirms determinate meaning without implying that it is singular: "I avoid any suggestion that each expression has only one meaning. That is why I ask what it is for an expression to have a *certain meaning*" (*Illocutionary Acts*, 148; italics mine).

by recognizing meaning as multifaceted yet bounded.[13] The analogy of a sphere is potentially helpful. Instead of meaning as a single point, why not envision meaning as a sphere—a complex entity that still may rightly be described as having boundaries? "Meaning" in this construal has a richness that adequately addresses our experience of texts as speaking to us in fresh ways. Yet this way of thinking about meaning does not negate the need to ask ourselves if our interpretations truly reflect what lies within the boundaries of meaning.[14] As Mark Brett has affirmed, "The complexity of authorial [communicative] intention is not a sufficient reason for disposing of it as an interpretive goal."[15]

Let's explore a little what this richness of meaning entails. Under the rubric of meaning we can speak of a number of elements. Initially, we may seek to identify a text's primary point or thrust. Clearly, this would be a crucial aspect of meaning to discern, yet its discernment would not exhaust the meaning of that text. For example, take this passage from Matthew:

> When they saw him, they worshiped him; but some doubted. And Jesus came and said to them, "All authority in heaven and on earth has been given to me. Go therefore and make disciples of all nations, baptizing them in the name of the Father and of the Son and of the Holy Spirit, and teaching them to obey everything that I have commanded you. And remember, I am with you always, to the end of the age." (Matt. 28:17–20 NRSV)

We might come to the conclusion that the main point of this particular passage is that disciples are to make other disciples.[16] Discerning this key point is not, of course, to have exhausted the meaning of this text. So why bother looking for the passage's main idea? The main point helps to guide us further in our understanding and contextualization of a text. If we come to an interpretive decision as we study a text that does not agree with the main point we have discerned, it is time either

---

13. Vanhoozer, who uses the term "singular" at just a few points, concedes that it may not be all that helpful. "If need be, I would be prepared to abandon the term 'single,' though I think it is still implied in the really important qualifying term 'determinate'" (*First Theology*, 178). I agree that "single" is implied in "determinate" if by "single" we mean "single entity" (a single complex). Yet the term hardly connotes that for most people. That is why I think the term has outlived its usefulness.

14. This is the issue of determining the validity of interpretations. Doing so makes sense only from the perspective of meaning that is determinate. See Hirsch for an explanation of four criteria for validation: legitimacy, correspondence, generic appropriateness, and coherence (*Validity*, 236).

15. Brett, "Motives and Intentions," 5.

16. Main points of texts will very much depend on how large a section of text is chosen for study. I readily acknowledge that I have chosen a rather brief text in order to make the illustration manageable.

to revise that interpretive decision or rethink the way we have framed the main point. In fact, the nature of the hermeneutical circle or spiral is just such a back-and-forth between a text's main point, its subpoints, its implications, and so on. The circle moves from the parts to the whole and back again.

A text's secondary ideas are those that support the main point. These are also part of meaning. In Matthew 28:17–20, we might note the secondary ideas that flesh out *how* disciples are to reproduce themselves—by baptizing and teaching obedience to Jesus' commands. Another important supporting idea is that the basis for the discipleship mission is rooted in the authority of Jesus through his presence with his followers. In fact, in the wider perspective of Matthew's whole Gospel, the theme of Jesus' presence is a major stress of this text, since the Gospel really begins and ends on this theme (1:23; 28:20).

This raises the notion that the placement of a particular passage affects its meaning. In this case, 28:17–20 is the culmination of the entire Gospel of Matthew. What difference does this make for meaning? Well, for one thing, the reader hears in this text the final word about the twelve (now eleven) disciples who have struggled throughout the narrative to understand what Jesus is about and to adequately trust in him. "Those of little faith" describes the disciples at five occurrences earlier in Matthew (note especially 14:31, where little faith is tied to vacillation or doubt). Now in 28:17, we hear that they continue in their vacillation: "They worshiped him; but some doubted." Yet we also hear the already emphasized guarantee of the disciples' success for the mission Jesus calls them to in Matthew—the presence of Jesus with his followers (28:20; see 18:20).[17] If we are paying attention to the narrative flow of the Gospel, we will see in this culminating passage various resolutions to the plot. These resolutions may often be implicit aspects of meaning.

Are there other implications of this text, that is, nonexplicit meanings, to address? If so, these are also part of its meaning. In Matthew 28:20, we read that part of making disciples is teaching obedience to "everything" that Jesus has commanded. The reference point for "everything" commanded by Jesus is not made explicit in this passage or even in Matthew elsewhere. Yet the implied reader of Matthew is fairly sure that "everything" primarily focuses on the five great teaching discourses of Matthew's Gospel. Matthew organizes most of Jesus' teaching into these five discourses (chaps. 5–7, 10, 13, 18, and 24–25). Together these discourses build to the climactic ending of the fifth and final discourse (25:31–46). In 28:17–20, the content implied in "everything" seems focused in this direction.

17. Brown, *Disciples*, 115–20.

But even by paying attention to the main point, subpoints, and the author's placement of a passage and its implications, we have not exhausted its meaning. Up to this point, we have been referring to only cognitive aspects of the meaning of Matthew 28:17–20 (and have not exhausted even its cognitive meaning). Clearly, Matthew is interested in more than simply having his audience understand Jesus' command to the eleven disciples and its implications. He has volitional goals for his audience that are made clear in the command to engage in making disciples, and probably emotive/relational goals, such as the comfort that comes from understanding Jesus' presence with them. Are these a part of meaning? In the language of speech-act theory we would call these perlocutionary intentions, which cohere with meaning and are, at minimum, appropriate extensions of the meaning of Matthew 28:17–20.[18]

If meaning is as complex as this, then not surprisingly there is no single, correct way to describe a text. Interpretation, in other words, can be wonderfully varied. You may describe the meaning of a text in one way, while I choose other words to describe meaning. Or I may describe other aspects of meaning that you have not addressed. Or you may bring together its various parts into a holistic expression of meaning. As long as the interpretations we make are not mutually exclusive, we both may be describing faithfully communicative intention or meaning. If meaning is determinate, however, our interpretations cannot be directly conflicting and yet accurate in their representation of meaning. Vanhoozer brings interpretation and determinate meaning together when he writes, "It does not follow from the fact that a text is a determinate communicative action that there is only one correct way to describe it. Opinions as to what an author did may, and should, change as we come to a deeper understanding of the author's language and circumstances. But this is not to say that the author did something that she had not done before."[19]

So let's make a final clarification about what determinacy of meaning means and what it does not mean. Determinacy means that interpretations can be weighed on the basis of their alignment and coherence with an author's communicative intention. It means that, in *interpretive theory*, we can describe and explore the limits of meaning (we can affirm its bounded nature). Yet determinacy does not mean that we will be able to exhaust the meaning of a text (especially on the book level) in *interpretive practice*. As Wright puts it, "A complete account of intention

18. We will be discussing the relationship of perlocutionary intentions to meaning in chap. 5.
19. Vanhoozer, *First Theology*, 178.

is of course impossible."[20] Hart defends the importance of "recognizing the partial and provisional nature of all . . . readings."[21]

So, can we ever finish reading the text? We can answer "no" to this question for at least two reasons. First, meaning provides a rich and complex world to explore, and in practice it is not exhaustible. Second, the world around us and we ourselves are constantly changing in relation to the Scriptures. Each time we return to the text we are different: we ask different questions, we bring different issues, we arrive at different insights. Our contextualizing of the text occurs between the textual world and our world, and this interaction helps to explain our experience of flux in relation to meaning. In reality, what is in flux is contextualization, our experience of the text and its meaning. Yet the text's meaning remains a stable reality with determinate meaning.

Take the book of Judges. We can rightly speak of the multidimensional meaning of this book. There are numerous purposes in the book of Judges. We can discern any number of themes that indicate the author's point of view, one being the futility and destruction arising from "everyone doing what was right in their own eyes." Judges consists of many parts that have main ideas that cohere with the whole but that also have secondary ideas. We must also pay attention to the overarching movement of the narrative and how that structure impacts the messages and themes of the book. Judges moves along primarily through the repeated cycle of disobedience, subjugation, rescue via a judge, and rest for the land. The narrative of Judges is a complex of meaning that remains determinate, although not reducible to simplistic generalizations. Yet we are still able to ask, "Does a particular interpretation fit the communicative intention of the author?" And we can assess such interpretations by means of their fit within the whole of the text within its historical context and our understanding of the coherence of its parts.

Meaning is imperfectly accessed by readers, both individual readers and readers in community.

The complexity of meaning implies that readers will struggle to "get it right" and will fall short of "getting it fully." Yet even as we acknowledge that readers access meaning imperfectly, we need not give up on the goal of reaching meaning. It will be helpful, in this regard, to distinguish carefully between truth and knowledge as we speak of accessing meaning. The argument often goes that, since human beings cannot know truth

---

20. Wright balances this with a previous statement: "This does not mean that authorial intention is unimportant, or, in the last resort, indiscoverable" (*NTPG*, 58).

21. Hart, "Christian Approach to the Bible," 196.

in any kind of objective fashion, then truth itself is relative (it differs from person to person). On the other side of the argument, those who want to preserve the objectivity of truth sometimes do so with the additional claim of objective knowledge of that truth—as if we ourselves see reality, the Bible included, from an objective vantage point. But we need not fall into either extreme in our hermeneutic, if we clearly distinguish between objective truth or reality and the always-subjective human appropriation of truth.[22]

We can access reality only through subjective appropriation. This subjective access affects how we approach texts and Scripture specifically. The goal of reading is the approximation of the communicative intention, and communicative intention is a reality apart from readers' perspectives on it. Readers, however, approach the text from their particular subjective vantage points. So our knowledge of meaning is not objective, since human beings are not objective. We will only partially access meaning, in the end. We "see in a mirror dimly," as Paul would put it.

Why is this the case? Fundamentally, we are subjective beings because God has created us this way. Even before the entry of sin into the human condition, our creaturely identity was established. We are finite, Scripture reaffirms time and again; God alone is infinite.[23] Our finitude means we are contextually located and our way of knowing truth is mediated. "To be human is to interpret. This is not a flaw but a gift; it is part of who we are."[24] Finitude is a gift, but what a difficult gift to receive gladly! The human sinful condition rebels against the gift of finitude. It is the desire for infinity, the desire to be godlike, that got us into trouble in the first place (see Gen. 3). Yet finitude is part of our creaturely, pre-fall condition, and so is a gift from our good Creator. Our finitude means that "however close the reader gets to understanding the text, the reading will still be peculiarly that reader's reading: the subjective is never lost, nor is it necessary or desirable that it should be."[25]

It is also true, however, that we have been impacted in our interpretation by sin. The distortion of sin impacts all our faculties, and so our abilities to understand Scripture as well. As Zimmermann notes, "All human endeavors of interpretation are marred by sin and require

22. See Clark's distinction between God's absolute knowledge and human perspectival knowledge (David K. Clark, *To Know and Love God* [Wheaton: Crossway Books, 2003], 147).

23. See for example, Pss. 102; 103:13–19. My understanding of the relationship of human finitude and hermeneutics has been enriched by numerous conversations with my colleagues Thorsten Moritz and Peter Vogt.

24. Zimmermann, *Theological Hermeneutics*, 165; see 272 for the notion of mediated knowledge.

25. Wright, *NTPG*, 64.

restoration. Human interpretation is not limited by finitude alone. . . . What theological hermeneutics for our time must retain is the 'veil' that covers and distorts our view of reality."[26] Just how and at what points sin adversely affects our interpretation are rather broad questions. We might note, however, that sin may show itself in an unwillingness to hear Scripture when it confronts our idolatries, our prized ideas, or our cherished ways of life. Sin's effect on interpretation might also show itself in an arrogant stance that privileges our particular readings of the text above all others. In each of these cases, the good news is that God is in the business of restoring sinful humanity, including our faulty ways of appropriating the Bible.

If it is the case that we lack the ability to access Scripture perfectly because of both our inherent finitude and our sinful condition, how should we proceed in interpretation? An important initial response would be to acknowledge our creaturely status and sinful tendencies. Humility would be the order of the day, given these truths. Yet our limited perspective does not necessitate that we give up the goal of understanding the text. If God has chosen to speak through Scripture, we can trust that the capacity to understand has been built into us, however finitely and imperfectly. If the author is not obsolete or lost forever but has communicated in and through the text, then meaning is *in theory* attainable. What we ought always to remember, however, is that when we do access textual meaning, we do so in partial ways. This condition provides great encouragement to read carefully, with an awareness of what we bring to the hermeneutical process, and to read in community. For if my access to meaning is partial at best, then I need you to read with me. I can learn from what others see when reading Scripture. Reading with and across communities, intentionally and humbly, is one way of expanding our limited horizons. Hearing from those with whom we do not initially agree enables us to perceive better our own interpretive blind spots.[27]

Ambiguity can and often does attend meaning.

Although we have just emphasized that readers do not access meaning perfectly, that reality bears repeating from another angle: ambiguity can and often does attend meaning. The focus of this fourth affirmation is directed not so much toward readers (in their finite and sinful condition) but on problems in accessing meaning from the vantage point of authors and what they do in communication.

26. Zimmermann, *Theological Hermeneutics*, 272.
27. The role of the Spirit in interpretation could also be raised here. We will be focusing attention on the Spirit's role in interpretation in chap. 6.

Ambiguity is one issue in this regard. Let's suppose you say to me, "You're being ambiguous." What might be the problem in our communication? Well, first, it might be that I am simply not being clear in my use of language, perhaps unintentionally. I may have communicated poorly, or the language I have used may lack the precision necessary to remove all ambiguity. As Dan Stiver points out in relation to language, "Words are both fixed enough to convey a surprising amount of stable meaning without being specifiable enough to overcome imprecision and rough edges."[28] On the other hand, I may have intended to be ambiguous; perhaps I was being ironic, and you did not grasp my intent.

The problem might alternately be that I have not provided key contextual information for you. In other words, I am assuming too much shared context, part of which you simply do not have access to for some reason. This lack of context is particularly helpful for understanding what I will refer to as gaps between biblical authors and today's contemporary readers. Let's look at an everyday example. In families, communication can be done in shorthand much of the time, given the large amounts of shared context among family members. For example, it would not be unusual in my family for my husband, Tim, to arrive home from work after I have and call out as he enters the house, "Heidi?" Although this is the name of our dog, Tim is not directly addressing her. Instead, he is asking me in significant shorthand if I have fed our dog her evening meal yet. Since Heidi will pretend that she has not been fed either way, it is an important question to ask each evening if we want to keep her from getting overfed. Over time, we have developed a communicative shorthand to facilitate this exchange. "Heidi?" is all that is necessary.

Unfortunately for someone outside our family circle, the shorthand would probably provide too little information for understanding to occur. Similarly, the biblical writers often assume and therefore leave out, or only allude to, information familiar to their original audience. Our task as responsible readers will be to acquire, as much as possible, that assumed information. This is why an important interpretive question is, "What would the original audience have understood when hearing this text?" It is not the case that the original audience could not have misunderstood the biblical writer. It is true, however, that they would have been in a better situation to understand what is assumed by the author and so implicit in the communication. So let's take a brief look at these two categories of possible ambiguity: an author's communicative acts and the gaps between authors and readers.

28. Dan R. Stiver, *The Philosophy of Religious Language: Sign, Symbol, and Story* (Malden, MA: Blackwell, 1996), 196.

It is certainly the case that human authors, even with the best of intentions, do not always communicate clearly; they can be, in some cases, inadvertently ambiguous. Many times, those who argue against the possibility of accessing authorial intention use this truism to support their contention. My guess is that their argument is overdrawn. While we as human authors are not always perfectly clear, most authors can communicate their intentions so that adequate and even successful communication happens. In addition, if we affirm the Christian claim that Scripture is God's word for the people of God, we may assume this to be especially the case for the Bible. God has inspired Scripture in such a way as to ensure that what God wanted to communicate was communicated by the human authors.[29]

But what happens when authors use ambiguity intentionally? Ambiguity is intentional when an author chooses to use a pun or wordplay.[30] Fortunately, within the conventional parameters of language, this kind of ambiguity requires some sort of linguistic or literary signal to the reader. In other words, the author is required to let the reader know in some way that ambiguity is being exploited. I saw a billboard recently for a hotel chain: "Quiet Nights. Rest Assured." Since advertisements do use wordplay rather frequently, I was not surprised to see a wordplay in this case. Either *rest* or *assured* may be the verbal component in the second word pair, so that the reader can construe the meaning either as, "You can be assured that your nights will be quiet at this hotel," or "Your rest is assured when you stay with us." In this case, the genre of advertisement provides an interpretive pointer toward pun.

In John 1:5, we read that the light shines in the darkness yet the darkness has not . . . *understood* it. Or is it that the darkness has not *overcome* the light? The Greek word *katalambanō* can be translated by either English word. As with decisions of translation in general, the literary context will let us know which is more appropriate in John 1:5. But there are reasons to suspect that the Gospel writer is using a wordplay here. We need to recognize first that either translation makes a good deal of sense in the context of John's Gospel. In John, darkness seeks to overcome the light (12:35). It is also true that darkness does not understand the light in John's Gospel; misunderstanding is a significant Johannine motif (e.g., 8:27). If either makes good sense, might John be playing on both aspects of *katalambanō*? Although assuming wordplay is not at all a first step in determining the meaning of a particular word in context, it is not such a bold move in John's Gospel. John seems to appreciate good plays on words more than most. For example, we see the author playing on the

---

29. For the interplay of the divine and human in Scripture, see chap. 12.

30. The use of metaphor fits here as well. Vanhoozer also includes allusion and irony as examples of intentional ambiguity (*Meaning*, 256–58).

word *anōthen* in the narration of Jesus' conversation with Nicodemus in John 3. The progression of the dialogue comes to life when we realize that to be born *anōthen* can be rendered either "from above" or "again." Jesus says a person must be born from above (3:3; see confirmation at 3:12–13), while Nicodemus misunderstands and gets preoccupied by the literal notion of being born again (3:4). We also see a probable wordplay in the dialogue between Jesus and the Samaritan woman. When Jesus offers "living water," she apparently hears "running water"—another possible meaning of *zōn* (4:10–11). This cumulative evidence makes it plausible that a wordplay is being communicated at 1:5 as well.

Beyond the ambiguity of authors, whether intentional or unintentional, it is also the case that ambiguity occurs because of the potential distance of time and space between the authors and their readers. This is certainly the case for the Bible, since its various books were written thousands of years ago, in quite different settings from those of today's readers. The distance between the biblical authors and contemporary readers has to do with linguistic, cultural, and worldview gaps between them. Since the Bible was written in Hebrew (most of the Old Testament), Aramaic (parts of Daniel and Ezra), and Greek (the New Testament), there is a *linguistic gap* between the original texts and English-speaking readers.

There are also many *cultural gaps* that readers need to bridge as they come to the Bible. I grew up hearing the story of Jonah every year in Sunday school, where we would revisit this familiar story from the Old Testament. I became convinced from those Sunday school lessons that Jonah ran away from God's call to preach at Nineveh because he was afraid. This idea made for a great application to kids (don't be afraid to do what God commands) but it does not come from the text of Jonah.[31] The real reason for Jonah's flight is immediately apparent from a look at the social world of his day. Jonah was from the land of Israel, and Nineveh was the capital city of Israel's archenemy, Assyria. Assyria sat to the northeast of Israel and was the dominant world power during the eighth century BCE. This historical information goes a long way in explaining why Jonah refuses to preach at Nineveh. The book of Jonah confirms the prophet's motive:

> But it [Nineveh's repentance and God's forgiveness] displeased Jonah exceedingly, and he was angry. And he prayed to the LORD and said, "O LORD, is not this what I said when I was yet in my country? That is why I made haste to flee to Tarshish; for I knew that you are a gracious God and merciful, slow to anger and abounding in steadfast love, and relenting from disaster." (Jon. 4:1–3 ESV)

31. Even though Jonah's fear of the Lord is mentioned (1:9), it is clear that this refers to Jonah's identification of himself as a Jew (one who fears Yahweh).

Jonah's motive for fleeing God's command was hatred of his enemies, the Ninevites, coupled with his knowledge that God would demonstrate grace and compassion even to Israel's enemies if they repented. As in this example, the cultural gap between then and now can usually be bridged by careful historical work.

Finally, there are significant *worldview gaps* between the biblical authors and original readers and today's contemporary readers that will need attention in order to move beyond the ambiguity that contemporary readers will otherwise necessarily experience. An example that surfaces every time I teach New Testament Greek is the difference between the essentially individualistic worldview of the twenty-first century Western world and the communal worldview of ancient cultures. Beginning Greek students quickly discover that, while we are not able to distinguish the singular "you" from the plural "you" in English, the Greek language has different forms for the singular and plural second-person pronoun. In reading 1 Corinthians 3:16, the majority of English readers from a Western vantage point will hear the singular "you." "Do you not know that you are a temple of God and that the Spirit of God dwells in you?" (NASB). The surprise for most of us will be that Paul is referring to the corporate church as God's temple and the dwelling place for God's Spirit. This is clear from his use of the second-person plural form ("you") in the Greek. Our worldview tendency is to read many Scripture texts individualistically, when more often than not the biblical authors used plural language to express corporate values.

In the end, these gaps reflecting the distance between the Bible and ourselves are not insurmountable. They will require, however, careful attention to the social world of the Bible.[32] By attending to these issues, we will have a much better vantage point for understanding the communicative intention of Scripture. Yet these temporal and cultural gaps do bring to the fore the issue of how readers might appropriate the biblical messages in their own contexts. How do readers not only bridge the gap to understand Scripture within its original contexts but also hear the biblical messages speak into the contemporary contexts these thousands of years later?

Contextualization involves readers attending to the original biblical context and to their contemporary contexts, so that meaning can be appropriated in ways that acknowledge Scripture as both culturally located and powerfully relevant.

We have spent the first four chapters developing a communication model for biblical interpretation. In the process, we have talked a lot

---

32. We will delve into this topic more thoroughly in chap. 9.

about meaning. Yet we have not looked much at contextualization—the task of appropriating meaning for other times and cultures, and specifically for our own context. We have, however, attempted to sketch a way of discerning the normative stance of the text in the process of interpretation (see chap. 2). To contextualize meaning involves hearing the normative stance of the text in one's own cultural and personal contexts.

As we have just seen, there are gaps between our world and the biblical world. Scripture was written within particular times in history and to specific historical audiences. The Old Testament addresses the ancient Hebrew people who lived within broader ancient Near Eastern cultures. The New Testament addresses early Christian communities within the first-century Jewish and Greco-Roman contexts. Understanding these social contexts is crucial as we come to the task of contextualization.[33] For, as we saw in chapter 2, the author's normative stance becomes clear as it is illuminated by the assumed background context. This normative stance may need to be transposed as it enters a different cultural context in order to fulfill its purposes. To use a musical metaphor, the same melody might need to be transposed into a different key.

Is this transposing really necessary, however? Why not the same song in the same key? In fact, does not Scripture speak the same message to all times and places? In response to such questions, I believe we can heartily affirm the relevance of all Scripture, even while acknowledging that it is culturally located. I prefer this term to the frequently used term "culturally conditioned." The latter term is used to distinguish "universal" messages in Scripture from those that need some sort of transposition for application to occur. I find this dichotomy not fully adequate in its assumptions or particularly helpful in its application.[34] Instead, if we recognize that all the Bible is culturally located, and that all the Bible is relevant to all times and cultures, we will ask a different set of questions when our purpose is contextualization. Rather than asking which parts of Scripture are universal and which are culturally conditioned, we will ask, how is this particular Scripture text relevant to my cultural context? In other words, what is the author's normative stance in relation to my context?

In the end, the Bible's "cultural locatedness" actually helps us take seriously its cross-cultural relevance, that is, its relevance to all times and places. And to take its relevance seriously, we will need to be prepared to

33. In chap. 11, I will introduce the idea that contextualization, like exegesis, is more a movement than a single-stage task.

34. Its inadequacy arises from (1) the assumption that we can easily divide the Bible into these two categories, and (2) a methodology that tends toward a one-size-fits-all assessment of the way cultural conditioning of texts impacts the contextualization process. See chap. 12 for more on this subject.

transpose the same song into a different key. At the end of chapter 2, we spent some time with 1 Corinthians 8, exploring the world of the text in relation to its assumed context and Paul's normative stance on the issue of eating idol meat at temple feasts. Although in contemporary Western culture we do not face this same issue, we are called to remain true to the normative stance Paul takes toward his cultural situation by transposing that stance to our own context. In my reading, Paul's central concern in 1 Corinthians 8 is the Corinthians' participation in idolatry as they join in temple feasts. The root problem is idolatry, specifically, attempting to affirm one's allegiance to the one true God, while playing at the edges of idolatrous practice, when the call of God is to exclusive allegiance. This normative stance seems quite transferable to my cultural context, since today's contemporary church struggles with compromised allegiance, as did the Corinthian church, although not in relation to temple feasts. For instance, the siren song of materialism woos us from wholehearted allegiance to God toward placing possessions, money, and comfort at the center of our existence. The normative song of resistance to idolatrous temptations resonates well in this different key.

Even texts that are less obviously culturally located than 1 Corinthians 8, with its temple feast setting, are still helpfully understood in terms of their cultural locatedness. We read at the beginning of the Ten Commandments:

> And God spoke all these words, saying: "I am the LORD[35] your God, who brought you out of the land of Egypt, out of the house of bondage. You shall have no other gods before Me." (Exod. 20:1–3 NKJV)

Now if any Old Testament passage has been understood as universally applicable, I would imagine it would be the Ten Commandments. Yet to uphold the crucial relevance of the Ten Commandments, and this first one in particular, it is unnecessary to claim that they are *not* culturally located.[36] We hear clearly the text's cultural location in Exodus 20:2, which makes it apparent that God is speaking to the people of Israel after they have been led out of Egypt and their slavery. The words that follow this verse have a very particular cultural and historical shaping. Does Exodus 20:2 preclude contemporary readers from appropriating the following commands from God? Of course not. God's people

---

35. The use of LORD with small caps is the way English editors uniformly signal that the Hebrew word being translated is the divine name Yahweh (see Exod. 3:14), rather than the more generic *Adonai*, which can be rendered "Lord" or "master" and can be used to refer to human beings as well as to God.

36. Harvie M. Conn, "Normativity, Relevance, and Relativism," in *Inerrancy and Hermeneutic: A Tradition, a Challenge, a Debate* (Grand Rapids: Baker Academic, 1988), 196.

throughout history have rightly heard and continue to hear these words addressed to them. The fact of their cultural location does not inhibit their relevance. The fact of their cultural location does, however, ask the readers to listen closely to the text against its own cultural context, so that the resulting contextualization is true to Scripture's normative stance. In this case, hearing the call to exclusive worship of the Lord is powerfully intensified by the knowledge that God's great act of deliverance from Egypt grounds God's right to their wholehearted allegiance. In addition, knowing that Israel is called to this exclusive worship in a social context where polytheism is the reigning worldview sharpens our picture of what is at stake in this first command. Hearing how we ought to respond to such an exclusivist and countercultural call is the task of contextualization.

The entire communicative event cannot be completed without a reader or hearer.

Our final affirmation continues to focus on readers in relation to communication. As readers contextualize the messages of Scripture, how might we conceive of their involvement in the communicative process? Communication viewed holistically takes at least two people to be successful. We might speak of this success as the "actualized communicative event," as distinct from meaning proper, that is, the communicative intention of the speaker or author. Meaning (as communicative intention) can exist without a reader, but the communicative event viewed in its entirety cannot. We can therefore define the actualized communicative event as the fulfillment of an author's communicative intention in all its parts.[37] It is possible to incorporate "the reader's reception of the message into one's definition of 'communicative act.'"[38] To use our speech-act categories, meaning as communicative intention would include the author's locution and illocution. The actualized communicative event would include meaning as well as the reader's perlocutions (responses to meaning). The actualized communicative event includes the reader's response. That response involves understanding as well as other possible intended effects.[39]

---

37. Eco, *Reader*, 11. Thiselton asserts his thesis that a Christian emphasis on the text's givenness does not preclude "the [reader's] actualization of the text as a particular act of communication" (*New Horizons*, 64).

38. Vanhoozer, *First Theology*, 195.

39. The distinction between meaning and actualized communicative event helps to secure meaning as a speech act that does not require hearer action for its existence. Alston comments on this stand-alone quality of meaning with an example: "Whether I told you that the dean is coming to dinner or asked you to bring me a towel does not hang on

Readers play a part in the realization of meaning, but all the elements of that potential realization are bounded or included within the communicative intention of the text.[40]

Let's suppose I say to my daughter, "Kate, please come and clean your room." If I receive no response, I may ask, "Did you hear me?" Now if Kate responds, "Yes," then my command would be, in Austin's terminology, a "happy illocution."[41] A happy illocution occurs when the illocutionary act is completed and is understood. But is there more to this communicative exchange? Of course there is. There is a response I intend from Kate beyond understanding. To be quite honest, I will not be happy with our communication (even if my illocution is deemed "happy"!) until Kate moves from understanding to compliance. The intended perlocution or the intended response by the hearer to a command is typically compliance. This is what I intend Kate to do in issuing my command. Now, she cannot obey if she does not understand the command. But the actualized communicative event is not complete until she has both understood and obeyed.[42]

Actualized communicative events involve appropriation by the reader, because meaning calls for actualization. Understanding, although the first and essential perlocutionary act, is not usually the final reader's response intended by the biblical authors. I would not want to be misunderstood on this point, so allow me to reiterate. Understanding on the part of the reader is crucial for meaning to be actualized. There is propositional content and illocutionary force to be understood in the text. Nevertheless, I am hard pressed to imagine that Paul would be satisfied if his audience rightly understood his command to "practice hospitality" (Rom. 12:13), but then *chose not* to practice hospitality! Paul intends for readers to respond to his illocution—his command (this is his perlocutionary intent in illocuting!). The intended perlocution or effect envisioned is the practice of hospitality by his audience. As we come to Scripture, it is important to realize that "every text contains not merely information but an implicit call, 'Follow me.'"[43]

Here is a rehearsal of the six affirmations we have been discussing.

---

whether you heard or understood me. If you didn't, my communicative purpose has been frustrated. But it doesn't follow that I didn't tell you or ask you" (*Illocutionary Acts*, 24).

40. It is also true that readers may respond to communicative intention, perlocutionary intentions included, in ways that counter these very intentions. In other words, readers may and often do respond in unintended ways to meaning.

41. If you recall, Austin introduced speech-act theory; see *How to Do Things with Words*, 116.

42. If she chooses to ignore the command, this leaves my perlocutionary intention (that she comply) and thus the intended perlocution of obedience unfulfilled.

43. Vanhoozer, *First Theology*, 202.

1. Meaning is author-derived but textually communicated. Meaning can be helpfully understood as communicative intention.
2. Meaning is complex and determinate.
3. Meaning is imperfectly accessed by readers, both individual readers and readers in community.
4. Ambiguity can and often does attend meaning.
5. Contextualization involves readers attending to the original biblical context and to their contemporary contexts, so that meaning can be appropriated in ways that acknowledge Scripture as both culturally located and powerfully relevant.
6. The entire communicative event cannot be completed without a reader or hearer.

These affirmations focus on author, text, and reader and elaborate the complexity of meaning presupposed in a communication model. Complexity of meaning, potential for misunderstanding, ambiguity, contextual gaps, and readerly involvement all help to assure that interpretation will be no easy task. From a theoretical vantage point, how is it that we might understand meaning at its points of greatest complexity? Chapter 5 will explore this question with further help from literary and linguistic theory, especially from conceptual work around the notions of textual implications and effects. We will also explore more deeply issues surrounding contextualization.

5

Developing Textual Meaning

Implications, Effects, and Other Ways of Going "Beyond"

> Most of the practical problems of interpretation are problems of implication.
>
> E. D. Hirsch, *Validity in Interpretation*

There is virtually no end to the difficult questions that get asked when people read the Bible.[1] At least some of these questions have to do with the complexity of meaning—questions that push at the boundaries of what authors might mean in particular instances. Here are a few examples:

- Does the author of Genesis have anything to say to a post-Darwinian world? In other words, how does Genesis 1 speak to issues of human origin?

1. Judging from the number of books on difficult texts, passages, and sayings of the Bible, such questions are perennial. For a helpful example, see Robert H. Stein, *Difficult Passages in the New Testament: Interpreting Puzzling Texts in the Gospels and Epistles* (Grand Rapids: Baker Academic, 1990).

- When Zechariah proclaims the coming of Israel's king "gentle and riding on a donkey," did he specifically envision Jesus' ride into Jerusalem (Zech. 9:9; see John 12:15)?
- When Matthew included four Old Testament women (Tamar, Ruth, Rahab, and the wife of Uriah) in his genealogy (Matt. 1:1–17), was he saying something by this? If so, what?
- Does Paul in Philemon provide the impetus for the abolition of slavery (Philem. 15–16)?

These sample questions are intentionally phrased in a variety of ways and with rather imprecise language in some cases,[2] but they all focus on the issue of meaning near its boundaries.

In chapter 4, I affirmed the determinate nature of meaning—that it has boundaries. It is often the case that the thorniest interpretive problems do not rest at what we might call the center of meaning, such as, an author's central ideas or speech acts. Interpretive difficulty frequently arises from what rests at the "edges" of meaning. Ludwig Wittgenstein, for his part, refers to these edges as "blurred."[3] It is sometimes difficult to decipher what is a part of meaning and what is not, especially at meaning's "edges." To help us do so, we will be returning to some of the concepts introduced in chapters 1 and 2: implications, perlocutions, and contextualization. Our goal will be to explore the edges of meaning and "beyond."

Probing Meaning: Implications

The concept of implications has already been introduced in chapter 2 as a fruitful contribution from relevance and literary theories. At the simplest level, we may define an "implication" as that which is not explicit in communication. An author may assume something in his or her writing that is not explicitly stated. If the author provides adequate contextual clues,[4] her reader will usually have no difficulty inferring her implication. This kind of implication is routine in communication and fits well

2. I do this because that is how most questions are raised. Although we are developing a more precise terminology to assist in interpretation (such as distinctions between implications and contextualization), we will not necessarily "convert" others to our terminology and it is not important that we do so. What we need to do is decipher what people are asking, whatever terminology they use.
3. Wittgenstein contends that "some language-uses operate with blurred edges; others, not" (as cited in Thiselton, *New Horizons*, 131).
4. I.e., if the author and his or her audience clearly share common assumptions on which the implication is based.

the way relevance theory has described implications, or implicatures. It is also possible for an author to imply something that he or she is not fully aware of or attending to. We have not yet examined closely this type of implication. Yet as we examine the edges of meaning, it would be helpful to explore the notion that various kinds of implications are part of communicative intention.

The Role of Implicit Meaning in Communication

It is fairly self-evident that explicit meaning, what is linguistically expressed, does not exhaust communicative intention.[5] Authors often rely on readers to infer intentions that go beyond what is explicitly written. In fact, it is not uncommon for an author to communicate primary aspects of meaning implicitly rather than explicitly. We looked at a number of examples of this in chapter 2.

Let's take another biblical example. In Philippians 4:10–19, Paul thanks the Philippians for their monetary gift. At least this is what most Bible editors and the majority of commentators tell us.[6] And I think they are right. The problem is that Paul nowhere explicitly includes the words, "Thank you." He doesn't even use the verb for thanks. He does, however, make the following explicit statements: "It was good of you to share in my troubles. . . . Not one church shared with me in the matter of giving and receiving, except you only. . . . When I was in Thessalonica, you sent me aid again and again. . . . I am amply supplied, now that I have received from Epaphroditus [their messenger] the gifts you sent" (NIV). How then is it that there is almost universal claim that Paul is thanking them for their gift in this passage? It is because the act of gratitude, though only implicit in the acknowledgment, is a primary message of 4:10–19. In other words, though implicit, the meaning is quite clear.[7]

This is not always the case with implications, however. Pratt notes, "In many cases of implicatures, more than one explanation is possible, a fact that is exploited a great deal by [those] interested in multiple meanings."[8] So does the concept of implications move us beyond authorial intention, to a place outside of determinate meaning? What should we

5. Pratt defines "implicit meaning" as "the various kinds of calculations by which we make sense of what we [read]," as distinct from "the literal and conventional meanings of the words [one] uses" (explicit meaning). For Pratt, as for relevance theorists, meaning is formed by explicatures and implicatures together (*Literary Discourse*, 154).

6. The heading for 4:10–19 in the NIV says, "Thanks for Their Gifts."

7. This example fits the definition of implication from relevance theory, which emphasizes the implicit assumptions that exist between speaker and hearer (author and reader).

8. Pratt, *Literary Discourse*, 155.

do with Wright's statement, "It does not take much thought to see that criticism cannot shut the door on [the possibility of meaning that goes beyond authorial intention], even though it may find it hard to handle either descriptively or hermeneutically"?[9]

It seems to me that the concept of implications actually allows us to explore what I have called the "edges" of communicative intention without losing the notion of the determinacy of meaning in the process. For help in this endeavor, we will explore more closely Hirsch's understanding of implications, one of his important contributions to hermeneutical discussion.[10]

Implications within the Pattern of Meaning

It is not uncommon to encounter focused attention placed on the conscious intentions of biblical authors in definitions of meaning or guidelines for interpretation. For example, the first of four principles of an evangelical hermeneutic, according to J. I. Packer, is that "biblical passages must be taken to mean *what their human writers were consciously expressing.*"[11] While what biblical authors consciously expressed is central to the goals of interpretation, Hirsch provides a broader definition of meaning through his exploration of implications.

Listen again to the definition of implications given in chapter 2, derived from Hirsch in *Validity in Interpretation*: implications are the (sub)meanings in a text of which the author may have been unaware while writing but which nevertheless legitimately fall within the pattern of meaning he or she willed. Hirsch allows for what he initially terms "unconscious meanings" within the concept of implications. From the less precise "unconscious meanings" he narrows the idea to "unattended meanings," which the author was not fully attending to but which nevertheless fit meaning as a whole. "An author always means more than he is aware of meaning, since he cannot explicitly pay attention to all the aspects of his meaning."[12]

Hirsch affirms that this expansive concept of meaning is still determinate, since the meaning as a whole entity is willed by the author.[13] Hirsch

9. Wright, *NTPG*, 58.

10. Hirsch's legacy in contemporary discussions is often focused on his distinction between significance and meaning. It is my contention that Hirsch's term "implications" in its relation to meaning is a far more nuanced and helpful construct for hermeneutics, since he carefully addresses the notion of implications as unconscious or unattended meaning.

11. Packer, *Word of God*, 153; italics in original.

12. Hirsch, *Validity*, 21, 25, 48. He also speaks of meaning as "transcend[ing] . . . the actual contents of consciousness" (49).

13. Ibid., 49–51, 52.

relies on the notion of *type* to explain how this can be so. Meaning, for Hirsch, is a willed type (i.e., the author intends it) as well as a shared type (i.e., the reader can know it). It is a holistic pattern of intention.[14] Meaning as type allows that an author generates aspects of meaning without requiring the author to be aware of all such potential aspects when inscribing meaning. In other words, the type is a principle for generating all parts of meaning.[15] Hirsch provides an extended example of meaning as type:

> Suppose I say, in a casual talk with a friend, "Nothing pleases me so much as the Third Symphony of Beethoven." And my friend asks me, "Does it please you more than a swim in the sea on a hot day?" And I reply, "You take me too literally. I meant that no *work of art* pleases me more than Beethoven's Third." How was my answer possible? How did I know that "a swim in the sea" did not fall under what I meant by "things that please me"? . . . Since I was not thinking either of "a swim in the sea" or "Brueghel's *Hay Gathering*," some principle in my meaning must cause it to exclude the first and include the second. This is possible because I meant a certain *type* of "thing that pleases me" and willed all members belonging to that type, even though very few of those possible members could have been attended to by me. Thus, it is possible to will an et cetera without in the least being aware of all the individual members that belong to it. The acceptability of any given candidate applying for membership in the et cetera depends entirely on the type of whole meaning that I willed.[16]

The recognition of meaning as type or holistic pattern helps us determine valid implications of an author's meaning and distinguish them from non-implications. Hirsch suggests two principles that are important for this validation. First, the *principle of coherence* allows the interpreter to discern an author's implications. If a possible implication is coherent with the whole of meaning or its type, then it may be a valid one.[17] Hirsch uses the image of an iceberg to illustrate the relation of implications to meaning: "The larger part may be submerged, but the submerged part has to be connected with the part that is exposed."[18]

The second principle is the *principle of purpose*. Hirsch contends that at this point we need a principle for structuring implications so as to determine their relative emphases. To give a rather simple example, we

14. Ibid., 48–51, 64–67.
15. Ibid., 64.
16. Ibid., 48–49.
17. Ibid., 54.
18. Ibid., 53.

all know that the following two sentences imply different things because of the difference in emphasis between them.[19]

Do you want to *leave* and have lunch? (Emphasis: whether to have lunch on- or off-site)

Do you want to leave and *have lunch*? (Emphasis: whether to eat or not when off-site)

In order to structure implications in terms of their relative emphases, we must ask about their function in the whole of meaning. Hirsch says that we can understand the function of an implication by attending to the particular purpose of a text. "The unifying and controlling idea in any type of utterance . . . is the idea of purpose."[20]

How does Hirsch's nuanced understanding of implications assist in interpretation? First, it provides a theoretical construct for understanding what I have termed the "edges" of meaning—what the author implied and/or what the author was not primarily attending to, which may still be a part of communicative intention. It is precisely meaning at the edges that is the most difficult aspect of meaning to describe. This circumstance is not surprising, since meaning at the edges is meaning at its most complex. While different theorists often employ varied language to describe the complexity of meaning, it is important to compare conceptual categories, since conceptual overlap may indeed occur, even when terminology does not.[21] The concept of implications provides a

---

19. See Hirsch (*Validity*, 102) for a similar type of example.

20. Hirsch, *Validity*, 99. See 99–100 for the following progression in Hirsch's thinking. Identifying the particular in addition to the general purpose of a text is important for Hirsch, since we can always affirm the truism that a text's purpose is to communicate. More specifically, however, a text or utterance may make a command. But even more specifically, what kind of command is in view? We could subdivide commands into a military order, a parent's demand, or a boss's request, for example. It is to this level that Hirsch means us to go in determining the purposeful idea of a text. Where Hirsch seems to land, in this regard, coincides to some extent with what speech act theorists call "illocutions." Lundin, Thiselton, and Walhout agree: "Questions about hermeneutical 'control' . . . are more specific and tangible when applied to the *functions* of different sorts of acts" (*Responsibility of Hermeneutics*, 110–11; italics mine).

21. For example, Ricoeur's discussion of secondary and potential meanings may have some amount of overlap with Hirsch's concept of implications, even though Hirsch and Ricoeur have rightly been understood to have distinct views of textual meaning, not least in relation to authorial intention. For Ricoeur, surplus of meaning arises from a text's secondary meanings that open a work to several readings. Yet these possible readings "are ruled by the prescriptions of meaning belonging to the margins of potential meanings surrounding the semantic nucleus of the work" (Ricoeur, *Interpretation Theory*, 78). Ricoeur seems to imply that the rules of meaning are derived from a work itself, since they belong to the margins of the work. (Margins are the boundaries of a thing and, therefore, are not

helpful way to understand meaning as both complex and determined by the author.

Second, if we are convinced that understanding implications is crucial for interpretation, then we may draw on Hirsch's dual principles of coherence and purpose for arbitrating between valid and invalid implications. Hirsch's emphasis on the principle of coherence pushes us to focus on the whole of meaning for arbitrating implications. Attention to literary and historical contexts would be at least part of a focus on the whole of meaning. Such holistic ways of reading are always a good move! We will not go wrong by asking, "Does a proposed implication make sense when a text is viewed holistically?" Here is an example. In John 21, we hear the moving story of Jesus and Peter together again after Jesus' death and resurrection. They meet at the shoreline where Peter and some other disciples have been fishing. Jesus provides for a large catch, and then they have breakfast on shore.

> When they had finished breakfast, Jesus said to Simon Peter, "Simon, son of John, do you love[+] me more than these?"
> He said to him, "Yes, Lord; *you know that I love* me more than these?"
> He said to him, "Feed my lambs."
> He said to him a second time, "Simon son of John, do you love[+] me?"
> He said to him, "Yes, Lord; *you know that I love* you*."
> He said to him, "Tend my sheep."
> He said to him the third time, "Simon son of John, do you love* me?"
> Peter was grieved because he said to him the third time, "Do you love* me?" and he said to him, "Lord, you know everything; you know I love* you."
> Jesus said to him, "Feed my sheep." (John 21:15–17 ESV)

The call-and-response of this dialogue centers on the question of Peter's love for Jesus. What do you notice about the dialogue? If you were reading in Greek, you would probably notice that two different words are used for "love" in the passage, *agapō* (+) and *philō* (*). Now there are those who have asserted that John meant to imply something by the alternation of *agapō* and *philō*, in part because there can be distinct differences in their meanings in some contexts.[22] Such a distinction might be read to indicate that Jesus twice asks if Peter loves him with a holy or divine love (*agapō*) and Peter answers that he loves with a brotherly kind of love (*philō*). Yet

---

outside of the thing but in some sense included within it.) If this is the case, then Ricoeur's "potential meanings" share some similarities with Hirsch's "implications," in that they are submeanings of the text that are related to its semantic core and are judged to be valid parts of the overall meaning by some sort of norm prescribed within the text itself.

22. See for example, J. Robertson McQuilkin, *Understanding and Applying the Bible*, rev. ed. (Chicago: Moody, 1992), 112.

if we raise Hirsch's coherence criteria at the passage level, it is difficult to argue for a distinct difference in the way the two terms are used, given the narrator's comment at 21:17 that Peter was grieved because Jesus asked him for the third time whether he loved (*philō*) Jesus.[23] Since Jesus' three questions use either *agapō* or *philō*, it is difficult to maintain that the Gospel writer is promoting a distinction between the two.[24]

If we raise the coherence question for the larger literary context, we might ask whether the larger whole or type supports this possible implication at John 21:15–17? I would contend that the Gospel of John, when read as a whole, does not support the implication that the author meant to distinguish in a significant way between the two terms *agapō* and *philō*. First, these terms are used synonymously across the Gospel.[25] There is simply no evidence that John wants us to hear clear distinctions between them in chapter 21 or elsewhere. The English word "love" is therefore an adequate translation of both terms in John. Second, the threefold questioning of Jesus about Peter's love for him has a much more resonant echo in John's narrative. This threefold enactment of restoration in context probably corresponds with Peter's threefold denial at 18:15–27. The heightened literary quality of this passage, with synonyms abounding, also heightens the poignancy of Peter's needing to reaffirm his love for Jesus in corresponding number to his earlier denials. John, through careful attention to detail, demonstrates Jesus' difficult but powerful reinstatement of Peter, based on Peter's reaffirmed love for Jesus.[26]

The principle of purpose as proposed by Hirsch can also help us arbitrate between possible implications. Determining the purpose of

23. It is also interesting that the point of the supposed differences is not terribly inspiring: Jesus acquiesces to Peter's level of loving in the end, rather like acknowledging that less than full love is acceptable for a disciple. This strikes me as less than what John would want to communicate about discipleship given the whole of his Gospel! For discussion of the lexical issues, see Craig S. Keener, *The Gospel of John: A Commentary* (Peabody, MA: Hendrickson, 2003), 2:1235–36.

24. The alternation of essentially synonymous terms fits the literary flow of the passage, which also nicely highlights the alternation between synonyms for sheep and caring for sheep: "feed my lambs," "tend my sheep," "feed my sheep." This English translation (ESV) does a fine job showing that there are two different words used for caring (translated "tend" and "feed") and sheep (translated "lambs" and "sheep").

25. A thorough study of John's use of the two terms demonstrates this practice. For example, not only does God love⁺ the world (3:16), people love⁺ darkness rather than light (3:19). So *agapō* cannot refer exclusively to a divine kind of love. In addition, we hear that the Father loves* Jesus' followers (16:27). If a clear distinction existed between these two words, we would expect God's love to be described only with *agapō*. Since this is not the case, we can postulate that the terms are used synonymously in John's Gospel.

26. John's emphasis on three denials and three affirmations of Peter's love for Jesus moves us to recognize Hirsch's principle of purpose, since the author seems to intentionally shape 21:15–17 to correspond to Peter's denials.

an utterance or discourse, whether implicit or explicit, will provide a centering point for arbitrating proposed implications. For example, in the book of Judges, there is a refrain that brackets the latter part of the book, so that the entire book ends on this rather ominous note: "In those days there was no king in Israel; everyone did what was right in their own eyes."[27] One purpose of Judges arising from this narrative frame and the stories included in between is to demonstrate the moral and spiritual failure of God's people in the time of the judges, and to attribute it in part to their lack of a king, whether understood as Yahweh or as a human king.[28] With this purpose in mind, the assumption that what various judges and other people do in the narrative is to be viewed as a positive moral example is suspect. This potential implication is shown to be invalid. As I often tell students when we talk about this important Old Testament book, "You do not want to tell your kids to grow up and be just like Samson or Jephthah!"

Hirsch's principles of coherence and purpose are helpful guides for deliberation on implications of which an author is consciously aware, such as the implicit connection between Peter's threefold denial and his threefold restoration by Jesus. But might these principles also help us navigate authorial implications that the author is not attending to directly—those at the very edges of meaning? For there are times when authors seem to be only tacitly aware of what they intend to communicate.[29]

Implications and Echoes, Evocations, Allusions

Authors can mean more than they are fully attending to in any particular utterance. These implications may sit on the edge of an author's awareness. What binds them to meaning or communicative intention is their continuity with the author's broader purposes. Textual echoes, evocations, and allusions fit this type of unattended implication at times. For example, if we understand New Testament writers as saturated in their Scriptures—the Old Testament—we might suspect that there will be occasions when they will echo or evoke an Old Testament text or idea without being fully aware that they have done so.[30] In the end, it is not

27. 17:6 and 21:25; 18:1 and 19:1 include the first half of the refrain: "In those days there was no king in Israel" (NASB).

28. For differing assessments of the question of divine or human kingship, see Daniel I. Block, *Judges, Ruth*, New American Commentary (Nashville: Broadman & Holman, 1999), 57–59; and Dennis T. Olson, "Judges," in *The New Interpreter's Bible* (Nashville: Abingdon 1998), 2:726–27, respectively.

29. Vanhoozer, *Meaning*, 259.

30. This does not negate the fact that New Testament authors are regularly quite conscious of their allusions to the Old Testament.

necessary to determine which echoes or implications fit which category (fully attended to or minimally attended to by the author).[31] What will be important is to determine whether a particular implication is legitimately part of the author's communicative intention.

As Wright contends, "[A theory of reading] must . . . do justice, at the text/author stage, *both* to the fact that the author intended certain things, *and* that the text may well contain in addition other things— echoes, evocations, structures, and the like—which were not present to the author's mind."[32] The concept of implications includes such echoes and evocations, and so once again shows its importance for a theory of interpretation. Interpretation may "highlight features of plot, parallels, characterization, thematic connections, etc., that the author intended, but also (almost inevitably) some or many of which the writer would *not* have been conscious. Such occasions might readily be treated as . . . subconscious workings of the writer's major conscious intentions. They are in any case not problematic for a high view of authorial discourse meaning."[33]

My husband teaches English literature to high school students. Having learned early on that sixteen-year-olds are not always an attentive audience, Tim has made it a habit of reading aloud in class to his students one of his favorite books, *Of Mice and Men*, by John Steinbeck, complete with different "voices" for each of the main characters. On one of his recent readings, Tim noticed a number of allusions to Psalm 23 in Lennie's death scene by the river. Steinbeck describes the valley in which Lennie comes to meet George in the early evening as the sun is going down. After George arrives, Steinbeck writes, "The shadow in the valley was blue and soft." Is Steinbeck alluding to this famous psalm and its reference to "the valley of the shadow of death"?[34] This may very well be the case, given frequent biblical allusions in Steinbeck's work.[35]

---

31. Some echoes, however, may contribute to central ideas of an author in a particular work. For example, though the author of the Gospel of John alludes to (rather than cites from) the exodus narratives in his prologue (1:14–18), his allusions contribute centrally to his communicative intention there.

32. Wright, *NTPG*, 62; italics in original. I would argue that the latter may also be *intended* by the author.

33. Turner, "Theological Hermeneutics," 65–66.

34. Other possible allusions between this scene by Steinbeck and Ps. 23 (KJV) include "the deep green pool of the Salinas River" ("green pastures" and "still waters" in v. 2) and the fast approach of the men coming to "arrest" Lennie ("enemies" in v. 5).

35. For example, *East of Eden* circles around allusions to early parts of Genesis. Notice here that I use a point of information about the empirical author to assist with asking about the implied author (of *Of Mice and Men*). Empirical evidence may be (cautiously) used to assist in sketching the implied author's intentions. Yet such evidence should not be used to trump internal evidence about the implied author.

Yet even if Steinbeck was not consciously or fully attending to Psalm 23, he may have been influenced by it in the construction of this scene. If so, the allusions could be part of his intended meaning. Assembling evidence for these allusions as true implications would involve paying attention to their coherence with the larger whole and their relationship to the author's purposes as he writes this part of his novel.

What about the Bible? How and when do allusions function as part of the overall meaning of a text? Much insightful work has been done in this area in recent years.[36] Particularly helpful is the observation that, by citing a brief part of another text or even alluding to it, an author may be evoking the entire context, message, or story of that other text. One example is the recognition that an important way the Gospel writers communicate the fulfillment of Israel's promised restoration in Jesus is by evoking Isaiah's "new exodus" motif (e.g., Matt. 1–2; Mark 1:1–3). In support of this claim, Rikki Watts tells a compelling story:

> As an Australian student studying in the United States I was fascinated by my lecturers' occasional references to "fourscore and seven years ago" and the uniformly "knowing" response of my American fellow students. Only on learning that the phrase was the first line of Abraham Lincoln's famous Gettysburg address did its significance [become] apparent. By evoking the Founding Fathers' ideology these few words functioned as a hermeneutical indicator, pointing not so much to the text of Lincoln's address *per se* . . . but to the larger interpretation of American history which Lincoln's speech assumed and with which it interacted. This raised the possibility . . . that Mark's use of OT citations might also function in a similar manner.[37]

As we will see in chapter 10, this way of evoking whole stories and ideas by means of allusion makes much sense of how we understand New Testament writers using Old Testament texts.

To sum up where we have been so far in this chapter, we are assisted in the task of interpretation by broadening our understanding of meaning to include implications, those submeanings that an author may not be attending to or fully aware of as he or she writes, yet that fit the overall pattern of meaning the author willed to communicate and shared in the text. This concept helps us understand better the complexity of determinate meaning. Another helpful concept is the speech act construct of perlocutions, and specifically perlocutionary intention.

36. For example, Richard Hays has examined Old Testament allusions in Romans, Galatians, and Corinthians in *Echoes of Scripture in the Letters of Paul* (New Haven: Yale University Press, 1989).

37. Rikki E. Watts, *Isaiah's New Exodus and Mark*, Wissenschaftliche Untersuchungen zum Neuen Testament 2 (Tübingen: Mohr, 1997), 3.

Probing Meaning: Perlocutionary Intention

An important issue for exploring the relationship between meaning and its "fuzzy edges" is how we understand perlocutionary intentions. As you remember, speech-act theory distinguishes a saying (locution) from the force of that saying or what it does (illocution) and the response of a hearer (perlocution) to the locution and its illocution. Now it is fairly clear that the effects of a speaker's communication upon hearers (perlocutions) are not a part of the speaker's speech act. If I say, "Pass the butter, please" (a locution) as a request (the illocution), your act of passing the butter to me does not count as part of my communicative act. So far, so good. Now, in requesting the butter, I want to get you to perform the action of passing the butter to me. This intent can be termed my "perlocutionary intention."

Notice that perlocutionary intention is a mediating concept between what speakers and hearers do in the act of communication, what we have termed the actualized communicative event. A perlocutionary intention is the speaker's intention for hearer response. In this example, my intention is that you pass the butter in response to my request. Is this perlocutionary intention part of speaker meaning? This is an important question, because of the mediating position this concept holds between speakers and hearers. In our definition of meaning in chapter 2, we have defined meaning, in part, as locution plus illocution. What about a speaker's intention for a perlocution? There are a number of factors to consider as we attempt to answer this question.

First, given speech-act categories, it is easy enough to distinguish perlocutionary intentions from both illocutions, which are part of meaning, and perlocutions, which fall outside of communicative meaning. For example, the intention to elicit compliance (desire for butter to be passed) is not the same as the request ("Pass the butter") or the compliance (your act of passing the butter). Speech acts (illocutions), speaker's intentions for hearer response (perlocutionary intentions), and hearer responses (perlocutions) are conceptually distinct from one another. So we should be able to describe the theoretical relationship between illocution and perlocutionary intention.

Second, the particular perlocutionary intent that is most discussed and is most closely connected with utterance meaning is *hearer understanding*. Searle, in fact, considers understanding to be at the center of perlocutionary intention, "The characteristic intended effect of meaning is understanding."[38] The intention for the hearer to understand is almost

---

38. John Searle, *Speech Acts: An Essay in the Philosophy of Language* (Cambridge: Cambridge University Press, 1969), 47.

universally acknowledged as a part of speaker meaning. For most theorists, an illocutionary act is successful if it is understood.

Third, speech-act theorists are generally keen on emphasizing that the heart of a communicative act is its illocution. What I do when I say, "Pass the butter, please," is perform a request. That is the heart of it, with the content of the request being important for a proper understanding of my intention. I readily grant this emphasis. However, it is very difficult to find theorists actually describing the relationship between perlocutionary intent (speaker intention for hearer response) and utterance meaning. They simply do not spend much time probing this relationship.[39]

Alston, who does discuss perlocutionary intentions more than most, states that they are essential for communication but are not a part of communicative meaning per se. Along with other speech-act theorists, Alston understands illocutions to be at the center of communicative meaning. Yet he does grant a place for perlocutionary intentions in the totality of communication. As he puts it, perlocutionary intentions "roughly model sentence meaning."[40] Alston does not go on, however, to define further what this phrase means.

Vanhoozer, drawing on speech-act theory for his theological hermeneutic, comes closest to including perlocutionary intent within meaning. "Meaning . . . refers to the intrinsic action—to the illocution and its intended result—not to its unforeseen consequences."[41] The intended result of an illocution is closely connected to its perlocutionary intention, which Vanhoozer seems to locate within meaning. Yet Vanhoozer is careful to avoid placing perlocutionary intention at the heart of meaning. "Perlocutionary intents fail regularly, but this does not threaten the possibility of communication, for perlocutionary intents pertain not to the act, but to the effects of meaning. If, on the other hand, I fail in my illocutionary intent, then the communicative act itself is defective. . . . Illocutionary intent is thus constitutive of communicative action and of meaning in a way that perlocutionary intent is not."[42]

So where does this leave us in regard to perlocutionary intention and meaning? What is the relationship between the two? It seems to me that we ought not to throw out the baby with the bathwater in this

---

39. The focus of speech-act theorists on defending illocutions versus perlocutions as central to communicative action is probably based on what these particular theorists are countering, namely, a view of meaning that is essentially defined by perlocutionary intent and perlocutions. H. P. Grice is often mentioned as typifying this view: "Grice in effect defines meaning in terms of intending to perform a perlocutionary act, but saying something and meaning it is a matter of intending to perform an illocutionary, not necessarily a perlocutionary, act" (Searle, *Speech Acts*, 44).

40. Alston, *Illocutionary Acts*, 172; see also 169–71.

41. Vanhoozer, *Meaning*, 255.

42. Ibid., 261.

instance. We do not need to say that perlocutionary intention is at the center of meaning to affirm that it is a part of a speaker's meaning. As with our previous discussion of implications, we might suggest that a perlocutionary intention sits at the edges of meaning. Or, to be more precise, perlocutionary intention is part of communicative intention as an extension of meaning.[43]

Why is it important that we understand perlocutionary intention as a part of meaning, extension or otherwise? A central answer has to do with the integrity of the communicative act itself. If we truly believe that words do things as well as say things, it would be premature to cut off the intended "doing" between illocution and perlocutionary intention. If by my words I intend to request something (illocution), it should be clear from the context in which I say the "requesting" words that I am intending a particular response from the hearer to my request.[44] The nature of the discussion about illocutions and perlocutions, which has tended toward an either/or choice regarding meaning, should not keep us from a holistic understanding of the communicative act as intending both illocution and perlocution.[45] Although the perlocution itself is not a part of the communicative intention, the intention to elicit a certain response (i.e., perlocutionary intention) is an extension of meaning. Meaning includes perlocutionary intention as an extension of communicative intention.

Let's conclude our discussion of perlocutionary intention with an everyday example. Imagine that I am on a bike ride with my family. As often happens in Minnesota in the summer, geese have taken over the city and, more to the point, the bike path. I call ahead to Libby, "Watch out for the geese!" My words are intended to warn her about the geese; they get pretty nasty when their space is infringed upon. The illocutionary act of my words is an act of warning. By my warning, I intend to elicit a certain

---

43. Vanhoozer, elsewhere, speaks of "communicative acts having a perlocutionary dimension" (Kevin J. Vanhoozer, "From Speech Acts to Scripture Acts: The Covenant of Discourse and the Discourse of the Covenant," in *After Pentecost: Language and Biblical Interpretation*, Scripture and Hermeneutics Series 2, ed. Craig Bartholomew et al. [Grand Rapids: Zondervan, 2001], 30).

44. Although it is not always the case that we can decipher the exact intended hearer response from the speech act of requesting, the context of the request (verbal and social) will adequately narrow the intended response. For instance, it is possible to conceive of a warning that is not in the end meant to deter someone from an action. A warning could be given in order to have ammunition to throw back in the hearer's face at a later point. In this case, the warning is meant *not* to be heeded, so that the speaker can later say, "See, I told you" or something to that effect. This opposite intention, however, should in most cases be discernable from contextual clues, such as the relationship of the speaker to the hearer and the nature of the danger being warned of.

45. I am indebted for this insight on the integrity of the speech-act event to my colleague Thorsten Moritz.

response by Libby (perlocution). Specifically, I *intend to deter* her from the path of the geese. If Libby *understands* my warning, my illocution has been successful. If Libby *is deterred*, my perlocutionary intention will have been successfully fulfilled. For proper interpretation of my meaning to occur (Austin's "felicitous" or "happy" illocution), Libby needs only to grasp my warning to her. For actualization of the entire communicative event to occur, including meaning's extension to perlocutionary intention, Libby needs to be deterred from entering the path of the geese.

In the end, how are these distinctions important for interpreting the Bible? They are important because, as is so often the case, the writers of Scripture have perlocutionary intentions for their audience beyond understanding what is communicated. Biblical authors certainly want to be understood when they warn and exhort and plead and praise. Yet they also have intentions for their audience that go beyond simply understanding what they are saying and doing with their words. The authors have as extensions of their communicative intentions the shaping of their audience to respond in certain ways. They warn so that their audience will be deterred from harm; they exhort so that their audience will follow the paths they set forth; they praise God—and implicitly invite their audience into worship of God with them.

Probing Meaning and "Beyond": The Movement to Contextualization

So far in this chapter, we have explored two theoretical constructs, implications and perlocutionary intentions, that I believe can help us to understand the complexity of meaning, while still affirming its determinacy. These are concepts that can be applied to human communication generally, both spoken and written. Yet Christians have long affirmed the unique ability of the Bible to speak beyond its original contexts to people in very different eras and cultures. So as we probe the complexities of meaning, it is salutary to ask whether the meaning of Scripture changes when it bridges to new contexts. Does the notion of determinacy still apply to the Bible in the complex ways in which it addresses other contexts?[46]

Sensus Plenior

Traditionally, one way of explaining the apparent differences between Scripture spoken in its original contexts and the ways Scripture ad-

46. The discussion that follows prepares the way for a fuller discussion of contextualization in chaps. 11–12.

dresses new contexts is to speak of *sensus plenior,* or the "fuller sense" of the text in later contexts. This concept has been utilized primarily to explain how the New Testament writers used the Old Testament in terms of prophecy and fulfillment. The New Testament writers were providing the fuller sense of a human author's meaning, which is sometimes associated in this view with the text's divine meaning.[47] Problematic for the *sensus plenior* view as applied to contemporary "fuller meaning" is the lack of any adequate controls for what might be part of this new, fuller sense. For "it is difficult to tell the difference between [the *sensus plenior*] and the projection onto the text of a theological idea or belief acquired by some other means. If one then appeals to the 'literal sense' as the control, has one really learnt anything new from a passage by the *plenior* method?"[48]

"Continuing Meaning"

Rather than appeal to a fuller sense of Scripture to explain the complexity of meaning as it is recontextualized, many contemporary authors who care about the appropriation of the Bible focus from some angle on "continuing meaning." Typically, the goal in using language of this sort is to emphasize the tie between what a text meant to its original hearers in its original context and how the text's meaning speaks beyond the original context. In fact, many of the authors I will be referring to would not be completely comfortable with my last sentence, since it seems to divide meaning into what it meant and what it means. These thinkers want to avoid such a definitive split, since they are interested precisely in emphasizing the continuity between the two.

What is the sense of "continuing meaning"? First, this concept affirms meaning as adapted or transposed to new contexts. For her part, Frances Young claims that our hermeneutical theory must be able to account for our contemporary ways of reading the text, which she terms the "future of the text."[49] Vanhoozer, in a similar vein, speaks of developing "a 'theodramatic' principle for continuing . . . Scripture in new contexts."[50]

47. Not all understand there to be a difference between the human and divine message, however. Kaiser, for example, asserts that "to understand the intention of the human author is to understand the intention of the divine author" (Walter C. Kaiser Jr. and Moisés Silva, *An Introduction to Biblical Hermeneutics* [Grand Rapids: Zondervan, 1994], 41).

48. Wright, *NTPG,* 58–59.

49. Frances Young, "Proverbs 8 in Interpretation (2): Wisdom Personified," in *Reading Texts, Seeking Wisdom: Scripture and Theology,* ed. David F. Ford and Graham Stanton (Grand Rapids: Eerdmans, 2003), 115.

50. Vanhoozer explicitly notes here that he will not say "going beyond" Scripture. His response is directed to (and included at the end of) I. Howard Marshall's proposal for theology (Kevin J. Vanhoozer, "Into the Great 'Beyond': A Theologian's Response to the Marshall

Second, the notion of continuing meaning emphasizes an unbroken tie between the original meaning of Scripture and its "future fulfillments."[51] Wright, for instance, affirms the openness of the text's continued meaning but also argues for testing these "new proposed meanings [by virtue of] their demonstrable *continuity* with the historical meanings."[52]

Yet how can we affirm the newness of continuing meaning (its futurity) while still binding it to the author's communicative intention? I believe we can most adequately address this tension by understanding continuing meaning as an author's "transhistorical intentions." Hirsch introduces this term to express an author's unforeseen intentions for future readers.[53] As Hirsch notes elsewhere, "Different applications do not necessarily lie outside the boundaries of meaning . . . so long as [they belong] to the true extension of meaning, part of what does not change—that is, part of meaning itself."[54] In a similar vein, Vanhoozer speaks of the author's communicative intention as the author's "intended meaning" and refers to its application as the author's "extended meaning."[55]

Meaning and Contextualization

An immediate objection to these formulations will be: Hasn't meaning changed in this application process? Is it really fair to use meaning or intention language for meaning applied to new contexts? Hasn't a profound shift occurred, so that meaning is no longer the author's communicative intent? These are probing and legitimate questions. Without claiming a definitive answer to them, I believe that there are a number of clarifications about the relationship between meaning and "application" that might prove helpful.[56]

First, it is true that at least some authors foresee future readers, and so inevitably some kind of future "application" or "contextualization" of their meaning. Vanhoozer, drawing on Hirsch, notes that the act of

Plan," in I. Howard Marshall, *Beyond the Bible: Moving from Scripture to Theology* [Grand Rapids: Baker Academic, 2004], 88). I use "beyond" in the heading for this section and the chapter title in part to acknowledge the struggle to speak about Scripture and theology, as both Marshall and Vanhoozer attempt to do in the dialogue of the book cited.

51. This is Hirsch's term ("Meaning and Significance Reinterpreted," *Critical Inquiry* 11 [1984]: 210).

52. Wright, *NTPG*, 67; italics mine.

53. E. D. Hirsch, "Transhistorical Intentions and the Persistence of Allegory," *New Literary History* 25 (1994): 555.

54. Hirsch, "Meaning and Significance," 210.

55. Vanhoozer, *Meaning*, 262.

56. Although it has been traditional to speak of "application," in this regard, I prefer the term "contextualization" because the latter emphasizes the importance of attending to the dual contexts of author and reader in this process.

writing enables authors to be able to "communicate at a distance."[57] This means that authors of certain written communication do envision their texts as having ongoing impact and therefore a future audience as well as a present one.

Second, although continuing meaning is in some ways "new" (it is not simply an identical linguistic expression of communicative intention), its tie to original meaning need not be conceived of as a slim one. In fact, we might envision a strong cord binding continuing meaning to original meaning. At least, this ought to be our goal in the contextualization process. There are, in fact, ways to avoid hanging "applicational elephants . . . from interpretive threads."[58] For instance, we can strengthen the connection by doing what I call "macro-contextualization" (attending to larger contextual issues) before contextualizing smaller textual units, such as the sentence or paragraph levels of a text.[59]

Understanding well the distinction between meaning and contextualization can also assist in affirming meaning as stable and unchanging. Contextualization occurs at the intersection of meaning and the reader's context, so, while contextualization is tied to meaning, it is not coterminous with meaning. Therefore, meaning has not necessarily changed when it is contextualized.[60] Meaning contextualized in different settings explains its perceived "newness." But the newness arises from meaning's intersection with a new context, not from meaning itself evolving. In fact, the very stability of meaning is what leads us to sense the importance of a strong connection between meaning and its contextualized expressions.

We may be helped by an analogy from the physical world. Water as a discrete compound has both intrinsic and extrinsic properties. Its intrinsic properties (those inherent in its structure) remain constant, even when it interacts with other elements. For example, the charged nature of water is not altered in different contexts. Yet its extrinsic properties (those arising from interaction with other elements) change as contexts change. Water when heated to a high enough temperature becomes steam. It has been altered extrinsically but not intrinsically—it still consists of a charged structure. We might consider the determinacy of meaning as expressing the intrinsic stability of meaning. Meaning does not change

---

57. Vanhoozer, *Meaning*, 261. Hirsch states that "authors of . . . future-oriented writings intend to make them applicable to . . . unforeseen situations" ("Transhistorical Intentions," 552).

58. Attributed to Howard Hendricks in Jack Kuhatschek, "The Seven Deadly Sins of Bible Study," http://www.zondervan.com/cultures/en-us/use/learn/seven.html (accessed December 15, 2006).

59. See chap. 11 for this discussion.

60. Vanhoozer helpfully speaks of fusing horizons (Gadamer's language) without confusing them (*Meaning*, 263).

fundamentally or intrinsically. In this analogy, continuing meaning is aligned with the extrinsic qualities of meaning. The perceived "newness" of meaning arises from its interaction with other contexts.

Finally, there is a possible assumption accompanying the meaning/ contextualization distinction that needs attention. The assumption goes something like this: Why the need to contextualize meaning for different contexts? Why not simply leave meaning to speak definitively and invariably into new contexts? The problem with this way of formulating meaning is that it presumes that meaning is inherently "uncontextualized" and so able to speak uniformly into all contexts. But as I have proposed in chapter 4, all Scripture is culturally located. So meaning is already contextualized, that is, it speaks initially to a particular time and culture. Paul's meaning to the Corinthian church related to eating idol meat arose within the first-century world of pagan temples and new converts to Christianity. We do not identify normative meaning and then do that non-normative thing called contextualization. Rather we do our best to identify meaning in its original contextualization, which was most certainly understood as normative. Then we attempt to "recontextualize" the message in our situations. This recontextualization is normative for us by virtue of its connection with normative meaning. Meaning remains contextualized and normative in both moves. So it is more precise, in my estimation, to speak of the *recontextualization* of meaning rather than its *contextualization*.[61]

This formulation of meaning and contextualization avoids the critique leveled at certain views of application "that a text can have only one normative meaning but many possible applications, which can never become normative."[62] In my formulation, Scripture's meaning, understood in all its complexity,[63] is normatively addressed to its particular context yet

61. I will, however, continue to use "contextualization" generally in this book given that this is more common nomenclature. For the notion of recontextualizing, see Lundin, Thiselton, and Walhout, *Responsibility of Hermeneutics*, 110.

62. Zimmermann, *Recovering Theological Hermeneutics*, 22. This raises the relationship of Hirsch's term "significance" to contextualization. According to Hirsch, significance is the relationship of meaning to anything else. Significance then is a very broad term that indicates everything that is related though not coterminous with meaning. So a valid application or contextualization of meaning can be labeled significance, as when Cotterell and Turner speak of determining the significance "for the present reader in conformity with [the author's] determined meaning" (Peter Cotterell and Max Turner, *Linguistics and Biblical Interpretation* [London: SPCK, 1989], 52). But significance must also include, by definition, invalid applications of meaning; it must include all such contextual constructions related to meaning, valid and invalid, normative and non-normative. For this reason, I find the term too broad to be of great help as we attempt a more nuanced definition of contextualization. See Hirsch, "Meaning and Significance," for his own nuancing of the concept of significance.

63. Thereby avoiding the definition of meaning as singular that Zimmermann and others critique (see chap. 4).

normatively addresses other contexts as well. The text is able to speak into different cultural contexts without losing its normativity. Thus, if we are serious about contextualizing the biblical message in our settings, we will pursue this as a normative task. This is never a guarantee that I have rightly contextualized the biblical message in practice, but it does mean that we ought to be able to claim normative status theoretically for contextualization on the grounds that the biblical message will speak authoritatively into new contexts. This formulation preserves meaning as distinct from contextualization and prior to it. It also emphasizes the importance of a strong cord of continuity between exegesis—the search for original meaning—and contextualization.

Interpretation and the Complexity of Meaning

In this chapter, we have looked at various aspects of meaning that account for its complexity. The presence of implications in an author's meaning necessitates that we read texts carefully and holistically, attending to their contextual assumptions, so as to ascertain whether possible implications fit the pattern of the whole. Looking for the perlocutionary intentions that are extensions of meaning keeps us true to the fact that the biblical authors wanted to do more than shape readers cognitively—they were interested in holistic life change. And finally by keeping meaning and its contextualization in new situations distinct, yet intimately connected, we can explore the normative stance of the biblical authors for our own contexts, always realizing that this exploration is not a simplistic task but one that requires a wholehearted commitment to the biblical message in its context and sensitivity to our own social location.

6

An Invitation to Active Engagement

The Reader and the Bible

Christians make the initially bizarre gamble that "the strange new world within the Bible" is a more accurate view of the world than our own and that we have to modify our views as a result. This means engaging in dialogue with the Bible.

Robert McAfee Brown, *Unexpected News*

Seldom, very seldom does complete truth belong to any human disclosure; seldom can it happen that something is not a little disguised, or a little mistaken.

Jane Austen, *Emma*

What we see when we think we are looking into the depths of Scripture may sometimes be only the reflection of our own silly faces.

C. S. Lewis, *Reflections on the Psalms*

In the preceding chapters, I have described a hermeneutical model that assumes communication to be a fundamental purpose of Scripture, and so a crucial lens for understanding it. Our focus so far has been primarily on the author/text part of the communicative dialogue. To complete the picture, we will now turn to readers' involvement in biblical communication. What is the role of the reader in this process? How can we take quite seriously locations of different readers without collapsing meaning into a particular person's reading?[1]

We encounter something other than ourselves when we come to the text; we encounter what Robert McAfee Brown describes as "the strange new world of the Bible."[2] We come for dialogue, therefore, rather than monologue, the expression of merely our own perspective. Yet as readers who are finite and less than perfect, we are not always able to discern well or fully the message of the text. From our end of the conversation, we experience, as Jane Austen has intimated, less than full disclosure. We are prone to be mistaken. This chapter addresses the various experiences we have as readers of the Bible, the relationship between meaning and readers, and the ethical issues that arise from reading Scripture on its own terms.

Interpretive Location

Each of us is part of an interpretive tradition. In fact, we are part of a number of traditions that influence how we understand the Bible. For example, I grew up in a Lutheran church and so have as part of my heritage a Lutheran tradition of interpretation.[3] I was also influenced by Reformed theology during my college years through my involvement with InterVarsity Christian Fellowship and great writers like J. I. Packer. Currently, I teach at a Baptist seminary. All these traditions—Lutheran, Reformed, Baptist—influence the way I look at the biblical text. We can refer to these influences as ecclesiological, or church, traditions. "We come to the table as Lutherans, Catholics, Baptists, Pentecostals, and more. Our creeds, confessions, traditions, heroes, and hymns have all provided us with different frameworks from which to read [Scripture], and inevitably lead us to prioritize different aspects of [its] theology and ethics."[4]

1. We will discuss these issues from the angle of contextualizing meaning in chaps. 11–12.

2. Robert McAfee Brown, *Unexpected News: Reading the Bible with Third World Eyes* (Philadelphia: Westminster, 1984), 13. Brown goes on to describe the dialogue between Christians and the Bible as "bringing our questions to [the Bible], hearing its questions to us, examining our answers in its light, and taking its answers very seriously, particularly when they conflict with our own."

3. One particular slice of Lutheranism really.

4. Turner, "Theological Hermeneutics," 57.

I am also influenced in interpretation by my social and cultural location. I was born and raised in the United States and have lived much of that time in the Midwest. I am Caucasian and from a middle-class, white-collar economic and educational sector of society. As a result, I have enjoyed the social advantages and power of being in what has been the majority culture in this country. How does social location affect interpretation? One way my social location has affected how I read the Bible is the rather large blind spot I have inherited and preserved related to wealth. This blind spot has caused me to neglect the pointed biblical emphasis on God's care for and championing of the poor and the frequent warnings about the dangers of wealth.

In addition to my ecclesiological and social location, I am shaped as an interpreter by my personal experiences. My family of origin, my gender, my familial roles as wife and mother, being a musician, my earlier career in a social service field, as well as the events I have experienced in my life thus far—all these and more influence my interpretive vantage point. Becoming a parent for me had profound theological impact, as I was swept up in a love for my children that gave me a new appreciation for God's love.

What I have really been describing about my own interpretive location is what we have already referred to as "worldview"—my entire perspective, shaped by a variety of influences, that impacts the way I read the Bible. Every reader has a worldview, and so every reader comes to Scripture with an "interpretive grid" that predisposes that reader to see and hear certain things in the Bible. We cannot avoid having one. It is like wearing a pair of tinted glasses that color everything we perceive.[5] As Grant Osborne discerns, "Reflection demands mental categories, and these are built upon one's presupposed worldview and by the faith or reading community to which one belongs."[6]

So what is the impact of our worldview on interpretation? First, it means we all have a hermeneutic—an interpretive grid that guides our reading of the Bible. If Osborne is right that reflection demands mental categories, then to think is to have a hermeneutic![7] But isn't having a hermeneutic prior to reading the text a bad thing? Not necessarily. Discussion of this topic tends to emphasize that there can be both advantages and disadvantages that come along with our built-in hermeneutic.

Our built-in hermeneutic is based on our presuppositions about life and Scripture. Now a *presupposition* is any preconception of reality

5. By analogy to our worldview, we have been wearing tinted glasses our entire lives, a situation that significantly limits our awareness of them.

6. Osborne, *Hermeneutical Spiral*, 412.

7. Hart contends that "a 'naked' reading of Scripture . . . is in practice a convenient fiction since even an initial approach to the text is already shaped by all manner of things which we bring to it" ("Christian Approach to the Bible," 191).

that is part of our thinking as we come to interpret the Bible. Presuppositions include what one understands the text to mean from previous readings—sometimes called pre-understandings.[8] And when it comes to presuppositions and interpretation, the consensus is that we need not fear presuppositions. They may be positively related to interpretation; they are only potentially negative.[9] "[Presuppositions] can enable creative and penetrating insight . . . [yet] the same commitments may also lead to eisegesis, selective blindness, and dubious ranking of [textual] elements as central or peripheral."[10]

Presuppositions "gone bad" are what Osborne refers to as *prejudices*. A prejudice is the denigration of a presupposition into an "a priori grid" that then predetermines what the text can or cannot mean.[11] A prejudice, by definition, does not budge even when presented with powerful textual evidence to the contrary. Instead, a prejudice forces the text into alignment with its own position. Prejudices are particularly harmful when they go unnoticed by the interpreter who erroneously assumes freedom from presuppositions. If we come from a perspective that blinds us to our presuppositional vantage point, then "that which we mistakenly think we have escaped from is in reality free to exercise all the more influence over us, and is therefore all the more potentially dangerous."[12]

What then should we *do* with presuppositions? First, we are helped greatly by acknowledging we have them. We all have a reference point from which we read the Bible. It is nothing to apologize for; it is a fact of human finitude. Second, to become increasingly aware and evaluative of our presuppositions is a crucial, and lifelong, task. Trying to discover our presuppositions can be rather like trying to see our own blind spots—very difficult without outside assistance. The Spirit's work in our lives, the influence of the larger Christian community, and the Scriptures themselves when read with a submissive spirit are central correctives to our potential prejudices. We will return to these later in the chapter.

It is the very locatedness of readers—their unavoidable "hermeneutic"—that causes some people to claim that meaning is something readers rather than authors create. For if it is true that none of us is free

8. Osborne, *Hermeneutical Spiral*, 412.

9. Ibid. Thiselton prefers the term "horizon of expectation" to "presupposition" (*New Horizons*, 45). The term provides a helpful way of conceptualizing presuppositions as a grid of expectations that one has when coming to the text.

10. Turner, "Theological Hermeneutics," 57–58. As you may hear, the word "eisegesis" is related to "exegesis." While exegesis is a "drawing out" of the author's meaning, eisegesis refers to imparting one's own meaning into the text.

11. Osborne, *Hermeneutical Spiral*, 412.

12. Hart, *Faith Thinking*, 167.

from presuppositions, is it not necessarily the case that we will always produce rather than simply discover what texts say? Is Gadamer right when he claims "understanding is not merely reproductive but always a productive attitude as well"?[13]

The Relationship between Readers and Meaning

Readers are actively involved in the actualization of meaning.[14] That is, readers are necessary for fulfilling an author's communicative intention, since that intention includes what authors mean for their readers to do in response to their texts.[15] Readers are expected both to understand what is written and to respond in other intended ways. In chapter 4, we have called this the actualized communicative event. The authors of Scripture certainly expected a whole array of responses to their texts, including commitment, obedience, worship, and trust in God. As Green affirms, "Texts require readers for their actualization."[16]

So we are not forced to make a choice between the reader as passive before an overpowering author, and the reader as active participant in *creating* meaning. In a communication model, we can affirm the active nature of reading without capitulating to a more extreme reader-centered model in which readers see and hear only themselves as they come to the text (text as mirror).[17]

Now it is the case that readers often do "create meaning." I am safe in assuming that I frequently do not grasp the normative stance of the text, that is, the author's communicative intention, because my presuppositions act as blinders to what the text really says. When this happens, it is quite accurate to say that I am "creating" meaning. The issue is not whether readers frequently create meaning by reading the text from a perspective that skews what its author intended to communicate. The question is whether this is an adequate proposal of what readers *ought* to do. I would answer a vigorous "no" to the latter question. Although readers often do create something that is not part of communicative intention and call it meaning, this action should not be the goal of reading. The reader's misreading is not a part of the text's meaning.

13. Gadamer, *Truth and Method*, 296.
14. Vanhoozer, *First Theology*, 181.
15. See the discussion of perlocutionary intention in chap. 5.
16. Joel B. Green, "Scripture and Theology: Uniting the Two So Long Divided," in *Two Horizons*, 31.
17. See chap. 3.

We come to the biblical text, which is a reality other than us. We may in our practices collapse the difference between reader and text, but, in theory as well as goal, the text and its meaning remain distinct from us. The text speaks to us an "alien" word. As Thiselton notes, "The key issue . . . is whether a community of readers can be shaped and judged by texts, as it were, 'from outside,' or whether they must remain trapped in their own contextual relativism, hearing no prophetic summons from outside and beyond."[18] The ultimate problem with the idea that readers wholly create meaning is that it does not allow for the frequent and persistent human experience of texts speaking an unexpected word. Our worldviews can be and often are subverted by Scripture. The Bible is able to "dehabitualize" our perceptions.[19]

How do we hold these two ideas together—that readers necessarily read the Bible influenced by a particular hermeneutic *and* that Scripture is able to break through to readers and truly speak? We hold them together by affirming respectful reading habits. One such practice is honoring the distance between the biblical texts and our own world and perspective. This respect means that we ought to expect reading the Bible to be a cross-cultural experience and be ready to learn about those other cultures in which the text was written. Another important reading practice is cultivating a willingness to have our categories and frameworks changed by our encounters with Scripture. Our reading of the text ought not to lull us to sleep in our preconceived ideas. If we are routinely experiencing the Bible as "nonthreatening platitudes" rather than a wake-up call to new ways of thinking, being, and doing, we are probably not reading well.[20]

In the final analysis, it is possible to acknowledge the perspectival nature of all readers and readings, while still affirming the possibility of Scripture "getting through" to readers. In holding these two truths in tension, it is helpful to make a few distinctions. First, we can affirm both the reality of what stands in the text and the subjective nature of our knowledge or appropriation of that reality.[21] Second, without claiming absolute knowledge for our interpretations, we can attain adequate knowledge. "Interpreters may not know everything, but they often know *enough*—enough to understand a text and to respond to it

18. Thiselton, *New Horizons*, 503.
19. Shklovski's term; see Thiselton, *New Horizons*, 34.
20. Brown's phrase in *Unexpected News*, 161.
21. See chap. 4. Clark notes that a "soft foundationalism" is a helpful mediating position between perspectivalism (readers hearing only their own voice in the text) and a modernist obsession with pure objectivity. "Soft foundationalism allows evangelical theology to develop knowledge from its own perspective—its own view of the world centered on the conviction that God is the center of reality. Yet it does not rest content with a self-enclosed perspectivalism. . . . Facts can push through perspectives, critiquing, guiding, and justifying the path to genuine knowledge" (*To Know and Love God*, 162).

appropriately."[22] The goal of understanding the author's communicative intention is a worthy and responsible goal. That we will not fully or perfectly reach it is no reason to give up trying. In fact, we should work diligently to hear as best as we are able the voice of Scripture that often contravenes our own.

The truth of our locatedness in interpretation should, however, encourage humility as we come to the biblical text. Such a humble stance is a good thing, for it keeps us aware that our reading might be a misreading, our interpretation a misinterpretation. This prevents us from "allow[ing] [our] own readings to have a finality bestowed upon them . . . a strategy that effectively subverts [the text's authority] and enthrones our 'objective' readings in its place."[23] A humble stance toward the text is quite appropriate, given our understanding that in Scripture we are ultimately listening for the voice of God. And it is the promise that Scripture is revelation of God that allows for human knowledge of God with conviction and trust without arrogance.

Awareness of our interpretive locatedness allows us to acknowledge that we read the Bible *as Scripture*. As Christians, we need not apologize for our particularly Christian appropriation of the Bible. Since we cannot and do not come with a clean slate to interpretation, it behooves us to acknowledge our intentional stance as Christian readers. This too is an interpretive location, for there are other ways to read the Bible. Jewish readers, for example, interpret the Hebrew Bible, what we call the Old Testament, from and for their Jewish context. One could also read the Bible as a historian, a skeptic, a seeker, or for purposes of literary appreciation. But as Christians, we read the Bible, Old and New Testaments together, as the word of the one creator God who has been fully revealed in Jesus the Messiah and who indwells the church, God's covenant people, by the Holy Spirit. And we believe that this particular point of reference appropriates the Bible on its own terms, for the Bible itself claims to be a testimony to the Triune God's activity and discourse in the world. This is a confessional stance; it certainly impacts our interpretation of the Bible. Learning to acknowledge that we read from an interpretive location frees us to intentionally evaluate and develop a particularly Christian way of reading.[24]

22. Vanhoozer, *Meaning*, 139; italics in original. Vanhoozer distinguishes between adequate interpretive knowledge and the two poles of absolute and anarchic interpretation.

23. Hart, "Christian Approach to the Bible," 195. Vanhoozer speaks of balancing a hermeneutic of humility with a hermeneutic of conviction (*Meaning*, 455–56).

24. This is, in part, what we have been doing throughout the book so far. Some theorists believe that the nature of Scripture requires a special or particular hermeneutic for the Bible. Others, like Vanhoozer, believe that all texts should be read by means of a general hermeneutic, but that this general hermeneutic must be informed by a Christian worldview.

The Ethics of Reading

The topic of ethical Bible reading is a burgeoning one in contemporary academic discussion. Now initially it may seem odd to talk about the ethic of one's hermeneutic. But if Levinas is right that it is impossible for hermeneutics (the human approach to knowing) to be ethically neutral,[25] it will be important to identify ethical ways of approaching the Bible. My concern in this section is to address one particular ethical issue related to the interpretation of Scripture that we have already touched on: the ethical responsibility of reading Scripture on its own terms.

If we view the Bible as a communicative act and not simply an autonomous text disengaged from its author, we are ethically bound to grant the author the privileges due more routinely to all communicators. This means respecting the author's communication through the text as a voice distinct from our own—what we have referred to as "the other."[26] In this ethical stance, "the reader is responsible for [his or] her response to the other and the other's act."[27] An ethic of respect is a difficult one to carry out consistently. We are often tempted to conform the "other" to our own ways of being. Yet the moral imperative, in the midst of this temptation, is to hear Scripture in a way that allows God, through its witness, to examine and shape us, so that we become conformed to the "other." "For those he foreknew, he also predestined to be conformed to the image of His Son."[28]

Part of what it means to approach the Bible on its own terms is allowing the text to speak first in its own context. Hearing the text as other will involve paying close attention to issues of the Bible's genre, language, social world, and literary context, as these would have been understood in its original settings. Our next chapters will take on these four topics in some depth. Our goal in attending to these issues is not to objectify the text but to put ourselves in the position of understanding in the best possible way what the authors of Scripture were communicating, so that we are able to hear their messages well. It is the personal obligation owed to the writers of Scripture.

25. For example, Levinas contends that "[another's] face is a trace of itself, given over to my responsibility" (Emmanuel Levinas, *Otherwise Than Being or Beyond Essence*, trans. Alphonso Lingis [Pittsburgh: Duquesne University Press, 1998], 91). See his extended discussion of knowing in relation to proximity (81–97) and communication (118–21). For a helpful analysis of Levinas's contribution to hermeneutics, see Zimmermann, *Theological Hermeneutics*, 189.

26. See our discussion of Levinas's contribution in this regard in chap. 3.

27. Vanhoozer, *First Theology*, 177.

28. Rom. 8:29a (HCSB); see also 2 Cor. 3:18 and Col. 3:10.

Hearing the Bible on its own terms also requires broadening our appropriation of it. The Bible is meta-cognitive in scope. So our reading of it should allow for the entire range of responses it envisions for readers, cognitive and otherwise. To read only for the cognitive knowledge we can get from the Bible diminishes its value and purposes. Part of allowing Scripture to shape us is submitting to it not only with our minds but also with our affections and actions. Only in this way will we truly and personally know.

In many ways, in this discussion, we are exploring the range of the Spirit's work in interpretation. For as we speak about the personal encounter with the other that occurs in reading Scripture, it is the Holy Spirit as the transcendent other who has inspired the text ("all Scripture is God-breathed") and who continues to speak through what the biblical authors wrote. The Spirit and Scripture is a topic of debate. Specifically, what is the Spirit's role in interpretation? Does the presence of the Spirit in the life of a Christian ensure right interpretation?

First, a fundamental reality: we do not read alone. As Christians we believe that even in our fallible and finite interpretation, God's Spirit somehow works and moves. This is called "illumination" by theologians. We have the promise that the Holy Spirit is with us as we read God's word, just as we have the promise of God's presence in all of life. Yet this does not guarantee that I will never misunderstand or misread Scripture. There is no one-to-one correspondence between personal piety and correct interpretation, although this conviction is sometimes used as a trump card for interpretive correctness ("I prayed and God told me that this passage means . . .").[29] In addition, the Spirit's presence with me as I interpret does not excuse me from the hard work of cross-cultural reading required by the Bible's ancient context.

So what does it mean that the Spirit accompanies us as we approach the biblical text? Fundamentally, I believe this truth should give us great comfort rather than grand arrogance. For, if the Holy Spirit is present with and for us, we can pray, "Help me to see my blind spots. Give me a greater awareness of the ways I am prone to recast your word into my own comfortable ideas." And we can go on to pray something to the effect, "Help me to hear the Scriptures well so that I might hear its message for my setting"—no absolute guarantees, just personal dependence.

---

29. I certainly do not mean to downplay the importance of piety (prayer, moral uprightness, love for others). I simply wish to affirm that piety provides no guarantee of right interpretation. See Stein, *Basic Guide*, chap. 3.

The Implied Reader and Real Readers

We have already seen that the concept of the implied reader assists in developing a theoretical model of communication. I have also found this concept helpful for personal appropriation of Scripture. As we discovered in chapter 2, the implied reader is the one who embodies every right response to the author's communicative intention. To put it another way, the implied reader does exactly what the author wants the reader to do. Essentially, the implied reader is an approximation of the fulfillment of the author's perlocutionary intention.[30] So as real readers, we pursue the goal to take on the role of the implied reader—to do what the author wants us to do in thought, word, and deed. As we read, we shape our responses to match those conceived by the author for the implied reader.

So let's get practical—how do we do this? Well, to become like the implied reader, getting our approach right is half the battle. Let me give an example. My teenage daughter, Kate, loves to read and reread *Chicken Soup for the Teenage Soul*, a book filled with heartwarming stories of people in crisis who in some way experience grace in the middle of their dire circumstances. Now Kate reads this book very much like the implied reader of the book. This is apparent in her responses to the book—she is reassured and encouraged (heart-warmed!) by its stories, very much in line with the book's communicative intention. I, however, read this book against the grain of its intention. For some reason, I am suspicious of the stories. (Did all the rather amazing things reported really happen?) I am also not particularly appreciative of the book's genre. Clearly I do not read *Chicken Soup* as the implied reader.

To read as the implied reader, a real reader should approach the text from a position of trust, ready to be guided by the author's (communicative) intentions. Certainly, readers are not required to read from a position of trust and openness.[31] Yet this kind of approach is required to read as the implied reader. It is my belief that such a trusting stance is characteristic of an evangelical hermeneutic. It is derived from the way the Bible as Scripture invites us to read.

We may try out this interpretive strategy—reading as the implied reader—in Habakkuk. In this Old Testament book, the prophet Habakkuk complains to God about the injustice he sees around him among his own people, the people of Judah in the late seventh century BCE

---

30. See chap. 5 for an extended discussion of perlocutionary intentions.

31. One approach that has gained favor in some quarters of biblical studies is a "hermeneutic of suspicion"—a stance that is suspicious of what particular biblical texts are communicating, since they may represent oppressive ideologies.

(1:1–4). God answers Habakkuk's complaint by assuring him of Judah's impending judgment at the hands of Babylon (1:5–11). This does not exactly reassure Habakkuk, whose follow-up complaint laments the injustice of using a more unrighteous people to judge Judah (1:12–2:1). God's answer is once again an assurance, this time that Babylon too will be judged for its unjust, violent, and idolatrous ways (2:2–20). The book ends with a song of prayer and praise by Habakkuk to God, whose power is matchless and whom the prophet now trusts to come to the aid of his people at the right time (3:1–19).

Habakkuk is a beautiful expression of an individual's honest lament to God and God's surprising and, ultimately, deeply comforting response. How is the implied reader shaped as the book progresses through these complaints and responses? Though we cannot do justice to the full range of responses expected, we can trace one theme woven through Habakkuk—the theme of waiting/trusting—to see how the implied reader construct might be helpful in our reading. The book actually starts with Habakkuk's impatience with God. He is not very good at waiting in trust that God will act:

> How long, LORD, must I call for help, but you do not listen?
> Or cry out to you, "Violence!" but you do not save? (Hab. 1:2; see 1:3–4)

The author begins here to shape the implied reader into one who expects that God will answer, and in so doing shapes an implied reader who waits when God's justice seems to be absent.[32] Habakkuk moves toward trusting God after hearing God's answer that the people of the kingdom of Judah will be punished for their injustice by the fierce Babylonians. Once he has vented his complaint, "Why are you silent while the wicked swallow up those more righteous than themselves?" (1:13), Habakkuk takes on a posture of waiting for God to answer:

> I will stand at my watch
> and station myself on the ramparts;
> I will look to see what he will say to me,
> and what answer I am to give to this complaint. (Hab. 2:1)

The implied reader is encouraged to emulate this position of trusting reception.

A few moments later we hear another signal to the implied reader to trust in God, this time from God's mouth in a parenthetical note amid a

---

32. It is important to note that Habakkuk does not stand in as the implied reader, though some of his responses do. The struggle of Habakkuk to wait and rest in God's providence woven through the book is meant to shape an implied reader who, sometimes in contrast to Habakkuk, fully waits upon God in trust and hope.

lengthy description of those who are unjust in their ways: "But the righteous will live by their faithfulness" (2:4). The faithful, trusting stance of the righteous person is the model for the implied reader to follow. The implied reader hears another facet of this faithful waiting in the final words of God in Habakkuk—the appropriateness of silence in waiting before God. In contrast to lifeless and silent idols (2:18–19), Yahweh, the true God, commands silence by his very presence:

> The LORD is in his holy temple;
>> let all the earth be silent before him. (Hab. 2:20)

After this powerful declaration, which seems to require a breathtaking pause, Habakkuk sings out his prayer that God would act as God had acted in the days of the exodus from Egypt.[33] Yet the song ends with a commitment to waiting, this time filled with reverence, joy, and trust in God:

> I heard and my heart pounded,
>> my lips quivered at the sound;
> decay crept into my bones,
>> and my legs trembled.
> Yet I will wait patiently for the day of calamity
>> to come on the nation invading us.[34]
> Though the fig tree does not bud
>> and there are no grapes on the vines,
> though the olive crop fails
>> and the fields produce no food,
> though there are no sheep in the pen
>> and no cattle in the stalls,
> yet I will rejoice in the LORD,
>> I will be joyful in God my Savior.
> The Sovereign LORD is my strength;
>> he makes my feet like the feet of a deer,
>> he enables me to tread on the heights. (Hab. 3:16–19)

The implied reader is called to fully embrace Habakkuk's final stance of joy and faith in the midst of barrenness and ambiguity. As actual readers of Habakkuk we are invited to be like the implied reader—to take this

33. The allusions throughout 3:2–15 point us back to that foundational event in Israel's history.

34. Other translations render the end of 3:16 as, "Because I must wait quietly for the day of distress / For the people to arise who will invade us" (NASB). These quite different options arise from an ambiguity in the Hebrew text. A good strategy at this point is to consult an exegetical commentary that will guide the English reader through the translational and exegetical issues.

same trusting and joyful reverent position toward our God in the face of life's emptiness and ambiguities.

Here are two final notes about the implied reader and Scripture. First, you may have noticed that during our look at Habakkuk, I referred to "hearing" the text: the implied reader as hearing what the author is communicating. This was intentional. In the ancient world texts would have been read aloud, much of the time in corporate settings. Given the large percentage of people who never learned to read, this practice would have been commonplace.[35] Recently in biblical studies attention has been given to the consequences of this truth for interpretation.[36] It is fairly apparent that the biblical writers "anticipated that their works would be read aloud to their intended readers."[37] By implication, the message and influence of biblical texts may often be received more faithfully as we hear them. In the classroom, I often encourage students doing group work on a text to read it aloud to one another, since the original audience probably would have received it in this fashion.

Second, the implied reader is intentionally constructed as a singular entity—implied reader vs. implied readers. The reason for this singularity is to distinguish the concept from real readers who may or may not follow the pattern of intention of the author for the implied reader. The downside of this singular usage is that it may mislead us into thinking of ourselves as primarily individual readers engaging the text in isolation. Since Western readers are already prone to read the Bible much too individualistically, this result would be unfortunate.[38] So I find it helpful to remind myself that the writers of Scripture were shaping not so much individual readers as faith communities. In fact, we might envision the implied reader as the implied community that the author is addressing and desiring to shape into a community more faithful to God.

"No Reader Is an Island": Readers in Dialogue

Shifting focus from the implied reader to communities of readers raises the issue of actual readers and their intersection with reading

35. "Even private reading was generally performed out loud" (Robert H. Stein, "Is Our Reading the Bible the Same as the Original Audience's Hearing It? A Case Study in the Gospel of Mark," *Journal of the Evangelical Theological Society* 46 [March 2003]: 63–78). See ibid., 68–71, for a wide-ranging discussion of reading texts aloud in the ancient world.

36. See the influential work of Walter J. Ong, *Orality and Literacy: The Technologizing of the Word* (New York: Methuen, 1982). Stein applies the notion of orality to Mark's Gospel, but many of his conclusions may be generalized to the Bible more broadly ("Reading the Bible").

37. Stein, "Reading the Bible," 71.

38. And it would not be the intention of those who developed the implied reader construct!

communities. In reality, we are not lone readers, although in a Western cultural context we often assume that we are. Instead, we read in community by default, since our interpretive location has been formed by all sorts of communities: church communities (both present and historical), our families, and other groups, such as our educational communities.

It is a myth of Western, modernist, and particularly American thinking that we can or should be Lone Ranger readers. "Naive appeals to 'what the Bible says' fail to take seriously the impact of the historical and social location of every act of interpretation. Far from safeguarding or respecting the authority of Scripture, such appeals actually threaten finally to erode it, and to replace it with the authority of particular interpretations."[39] By recognizing that we are not individualistic readers, but instead we represent and integrate various streams of tradition, we will be more likely to understand the nature of reading in community.[40]

Because we are influenced by interpretive communities, we have inherited and absorbed certain ways of understanding the Bible, not all of which are truly biblical. So we have good reason to acknowledge, discern, and evaluate the presuppositions and pre-understandings that we have implicitly appropriated. There is an important place here for critical thinking directed at our own presuppositions and those of the faith community to which we belong, as well as careful reflection upon Scripture itself. Since there are inherent blind spots in all outlooks, our goal should be to discover these as well as we are able and determine how they have influenced our Bible reading.

Of course, discovering our blind spots is not an easy task. The good news is that you usually can see my blind spots better than I can (Jesus alludes to this notion in Matt. 7:3–5). So if I engage you in discussion of Scripture, you may very well detect some of my blind spots. This is a value of reading in community. In fact, by engaging in dialogue with others who do not think exactly as we do, we increase the likelihood of having our own interpretive blind spots clarified. "The ability to hear texts through the ears of other traditions may serve as one of the best exegetical or hermeneutical correctives we can bring to the task."[41] Through

39. Hart, "Christian Approach to the Bible," 184.

40. "Tradition" is one way of talking about the various influences that shape our interpretation. See Gordon D. Fee, *Gospel and Spirit: Issues in New Testament Hermeneutics* (Peabody, MA: Hendrickson, 1991), 67.

41. Fee, *Gospel and Spirit*, 79. One way to listen more widely would be to expand our reading to include Christians from around the world. For an example of how this might be done, see Craig L. Blomberg, "The Globalization of Hermeneutics," *Journal of the Evangelical Theological Society* 38 (1995): 581–93.

dialogue in community, we are in a better position to move toward the communicative intention of the biblical text.[42]

Some Practical Words for Readers

For a while, our local paper published the "Miss Manners" column. Miss Manners not only addressed issues of refined society—social etiquette from A to Z—she also wrote in fine, stylized prose. Her responses to questions always began, "Gentle Reader." Now as much as I rather like that adjective, it is my conviction that readers of Scripture should be described a bit differently. I would suggest something more like "Courageous Reader" or, with an adjective often used to describe Minnesotans, "Hearty Reader." Bible readers, in my experience, need to be hearty and courageous because the task of interpretation is not an easy one, and it requires hard work.

As we have been discovering, interpretation requires readers to be self-reflective as well as other-focused. As one writer has put it, readers of Scripture are to be self-suspicious. We should not suppose that we always "get it right" in our interpretations. In fact, we should expect to be confronted regularly by new, and not always comfortable, truth as we read. As one of my colleagues notes, we need to be ready to hear the iconoclastic messages of the Bible.[43] Scripture's way of regularly confronting us does not mean that we are always to be reevaluating everything we believe, only that we might begin the lifelong task of deliberate theological reflection on our own hermeneutic. In this way we are better able to hear when Scripture counters our perspectives.[44]

42. The value of reading together will always need to be balanced with the experience of reading the text for oneself. Some people have come from settings that have not encouraged people to think for themselves as they read Scripture. At times, something similar happens in my seminary courses, when beginning students are prone to let commentaries do their thinking for them. ("How can I add anything to what this scholar has said?") We will need to balance thinking for ourselves with reading in community. As Green contends, "Our reading must be ecclesially located, theologically fashioned, and critically engaged" (Joel Green, "(Re)turn to Narrative," 23).

43. "Iconoclastic" relates to the destruction of religious images. In this context, it refers to the way Scripture attacks our idolatrous, false images of God. I am drawing here upon a spoken message by Carla Dahl, "The Dangers of Hospitality" (paper presented at Bethel Seminary, St. Paul, MN, 1 March 2005).

44. "Deliberate theological reflection" is Achtemeier's phrase. "If theology is to make sense now about the meaning of Jesus Christ whose career took place then, it has in that moment engaged in a transfer of meaning. It has carried out a hermeneutic. . . . The question is whether that hermeneutic . . . is to be the object of deliberate theological reflection, or whether it is to be assumed and allowed to operate without the benefit of theological

Interpretation of the hearty sort also requires that we be good listeners. I frequently have students in my hermeneutics class who are completing a master's degree in marriage and family therapy. These students are sometimes slightly more nervous than other students about their biblical studies courses. Since their strength areas are related to counseling, they are frequently less confident about their ability to interpret the Bible. I find myself reassuring them. "If you are good at listening to people," I often say, "you will very probably be good at listening to Scripture, since the same kinds of skills are necessary for both." Skills like fostering a nonanxious presence, withholding judgment, asking good follow-up questions, and summarizing what has been said—all of these listening skills will help tremendously when reading and interpreting Scripture.

Listening well to the Bible needs to be coupled with what I have referred to earlier as "guidelines for reading at a distance." Although it is not very popular to speak of rules for interpretation, the guidelines I propose are not really optional for good interpretive practice. As Hart has observed, "We live in a period . . . when the very idea of rules for reading is likely to attract disapprobation. . . . My suggestion here is that some set of constraints has always existed . . . and *must exist* in order for Scripture to function as such within the church."[45] So whether we call them guidelines, rules, or "a series of baseline commitments,"[46] a hermeneutic that takes seriously the communicative nature of Scripture will need to attend carefully to the following:

- Biblical genres
- Language
- Social setting
- Literary context[47]

By following these guidelines in conversation with other readers, we will be much more likely to hear the messages of Scripture well. Subsequent chapters will focus attention on these guidelines.

C. S. Lewis once wrote, "Almost anything can be read into any book if you are determined enough."[48] In this chapter, an invitation has been given to concentrate our determination on listening well as interpreters of God's word. We do this by knowing ourselves and what we bring to

---

clarification" (Paul J. Achtemeier, *An Introduction to the New Hermeneutic* [Philadelphia: Westminster, 1969], 14–15).

45. Hart, "Christian Approach to the Bible," 186–87; italics in original.

46. Green, "(Re)turn to Narrative," 25.

47. See Appendix A for a fuller listing of the exegetical guidelines mentioned here.

48. C. S. Lewis, *Reflections on the Psalms* (London: Geoffrey Bles, 1958), 99.

our reading of the Bible, as well as what might get in the way of hearing the message of the Bible. We listen well by reading the Bible on its own terms, not assuming that we have always understood its message, not imposing our own messages on it. Instead, we take care to hear a biblical text in its own setting, so we might in the end hear it in ours.

Suggestions for Further Reading

Blomberg, Craig L. "The Globalization of Hermeneutics." *Journal of the Evangelical Theological Society* 38 (1995): 581–93.

Fee, Gordon D. *Gospel and Spirit: Issues in New Testament Hermeneutics.* Peabody, MA: Hendrickson, 1991.

Green, Joel B., ed. *Hearing the New Testament.* Grand Rapids: Eerdmans, 1995.

Hart, Trevor. *Faith Thinking: The Dynamics of Christian Theology.* Downers Grove, IL: InterVarsity, 1996.

Lundin, Roger, Anthony C. Thiselton, and Clarence Walhout. *The Responsibility of Hermeneutics.* Grand Rapids: Eerdmans, 1985.

Segovia, Fernando F., and Mary Ann Tolbert, eds. *Reading from This Place.* Minneapolis: Fortress, 1995.

Part 2

Practical Guidance
for Interpreting Scripture
as Communication

7

Genre and Communication

Meaning exists in the interaction of choice and constraint, in genre no less than in language.

Amy J. Devitt, *Writing Genres*

We have much to learn from the question, How does a text mean?

Trevor Hart, "Tradition, Authority, and a Christian Approach to the Bible as Scripture," in *Between Two Horizons*

"Once upon a time. . . ." We all know what's coming with that opening: a fairy tale that will tell of fanciful creatures, talking animals, and magical events. The story will end, "They all lived happily ever after." How do we know all this? How is it that we are not surprised when we encounter a mythical unicorn in a fairy tale? It is because we easily identify and interpret the genre of fairy tale. Hearing that famous first phrase, we immediately identify that we are reading a fairy tale. We then project what we know of fairy tales (their conventions) to interpret rightly the rest of the story. This process happens reflexively and intuitively, since the fairy tale is a part of our Western cultural and literary tradition. Our goal in this chapter is to look carefully at the central genres of the Bible. Given that a fairly wide historical gap exists between the ancient and contemporary worlds, we will want to study these biblical genres in order to understand more fully their unique sets of conventions, that is, how they communicate.

The Importance of Genre

There are three primary biblical genres that will be emphasized in this chapter: poetry, epistle, and narrative. These are three overarching genre categories in Scripture, although together they do not exhaust every one of the Bible's sixty-six books. For example, these categories do not address Hebrew law, apocalyptic literature, or the particularities of such subgenres as prophetic and wisdom literature.[1] Our goal is to get a big-picture view of these overarching genres. Detailed and helpful information on the many specific genre types in Scripture can be found in a number of books on biblical interpretation.[2]

As we follow a communication model in our approach to genre, we will be helped by remembering that one of the primary communicative choices that authors make is their choice of genre. Such genre choice has much to do with the determination of *how* an author communicates, for different genres communicate in distinct ways. While in an epistle an author seeks to persuade through a course of reasoning that is fairly explicit and often linear, narrative authors do their "persuading" most often implicitly, through story and point of view. Poets, in contrast, use sounds and images to somehow speak of the unspeakable and evoke emotions. By paying attention to the genre choice made by an author, we will be in a better position to understand that author's communication.

As we examine the literary conventions of the biblical genres of poetry, epistle, and narrative, we will also reflect on genre as speech act. "Genres are *communicative* practices, . . . speech-acts of a higher order."[3] Biblical genres both say and do things. Another way to express the active nature of genre is to talk about the function of specific genres. A particular genre acts in ways that reflect the literary conventions that circumscribe it.[4] So we will conclude each section of the chapter by re-

1. The latter two major genres are primarily poetic in form. As with these two examples, genre categories frequently overlap with one another. See Osborne, *Hermeneutical Spiral*, 8.

2. For helpful chapter-length treatments of each particular biblical genre, see Stein, *Basic Guide*; Osborne, *Hermeneutical Spiral*; Fee and Stuart, *How to Read the Bible*; and William W. Klein, Craig L. Blomberg, and Robert L. Hubbard Jr., *Introduction to Biblical Interpretation* (Dallas: Word, 1993).

3. Vanhoozer, *Drama of Doctrine*, 283.

4. For an extended discussion of genre theory and pratice in biblical interpretation, see Jeannine K. Brown, "Genre," in *The Bible and Literature*, ed. Jamie Grant and David Firth (Downers Grove, IL: InterVarsity, forthcoming).

flecting on the communicative qualities of the genres of poetry, epistle, and narrative, respectively.

How Does Communication Happen in Poetry?

Our Comfort Level with All Things Poetic

How much poetry do you come in contact with on a daily basis? If we limit poetry to written verse, most of us would probably acknowledge we are not much influenced by poetry. I would venture to guess that many of us do not have an extensive collection of poetry on our bookshelves. But poetry goes beyond written verse. Popular music, rap, songwriting—in these poetry meets the people in American society. Is Bob Dylan the greatest poet of the twentieth century, as my husband suggests? I imagine the answer to this claim will ultimately depend on one's definition of poetry. Yet it is hard to deny that the average person in our culture accesses poetry primarily through "popular" song lyrics.[5]

Even though poetry exists in these forms in our cultural context, I would argue that we are not particularly comfortable with poetic forms of communication. We tend to prefer prose (narratives, technical writing, etc.) to poetry. "Read any good books lately?" usually refers to novels or nonfiction rather than verse. This observation was brought home to me when reading the newspaper quite a while ago, during a U.S.-Persian Gulf crisis of the mid-1990s. After an altercation between U.S. and Iraqi troops, the leaders of both countries gave their press statements. On the front page of the newspaper, there were pictures of Bill Clinton and Saddam Hussein, with their statements in bold print beside their photos. Here is what President Clinton said: "Our objectives are limited but clear: to make Saddam pay a price for the latest act of brutality, reducing his ability to threaten his neighbors and America's interests." The statement sounds like a fairly standard head-of-state commentary. Now listen to Hussein's description: "Iraq is as steadfast as the high mountains, which are unshakeable by the winds of evil, and its sails will not be torn out by the hiss of the snakes."[6] Not only do we receive a very different perspective on the events that occurred, we also get it in essentially "poetic," that is, metaphorical, form.[7]

5. The recent proliferation of poetry slams (an open-mike performance of one's poetry) points to an interest in the poetic that seems to be growing in our culture.

6. *Minneapolis Star Tribune*, 4 September 1996.

7. This is not to say that metaphors occur only in poetry. As with this example, metaphor is often used in prose (nonpoetry). Nevertheless, since metaphor is *characteristic* of poetry, we will discuss it here.

This comparison illustrates the relatively minimal amount of poetic influence in everyday mainstream speech in a Western context. We do use poetic language; it just does not pervade our speech as it does in some cultures (and as it did in Israelite culture). When we do use poetic images, we often do not trust their power to communicate. This is immediately apparent when we recognize that it would not be inconceivable (although it should be) to hear someone say, "It's raining cats and dogs out—literally!" The speaker cannot be affirming the literalness of the metaphor: that there are actual cats and dogs falling from the sky. The import of the statement is that it is raining a lot, and by adding "literally" the speaker wants the hearer to take the use of metaphor not literally, but seriously.[8]

Imagery in Biblical Poetry

Given the ambivalence of mainstream culture toward metaphor, we would do well to pay particular attention to the use of metaphor in the Bible, so as to understand it well and avoid literalistic readings of metaphor.[9] The importance of careful reading of metaphor is really rather obvious. As C. S. Lewis cautions, "People who take [biblical] symbols literally might as well think that when Christ told us to be like doves, He meant that we were to lay eggs."[10]

Understanding metaphors is important for understanding biblical poetry. Although metaphor is used in all genres in the Bible, it is particularly pervasive in poetry. And the use of metaphors or imagery is a very effective form of communication. Metaphors can communicate when literal expressions fall short. You could say, "Life seems to be moving very slowly for me," or you could express this feeling or experience with an

---

8. Although "seriously" is not one of the dictionary definitions of "literally," the latter is often used to refer to the former. This is one reason I find the use of the term "literal" unhelpful; it simply is often ambiguous. The question, Do you take the Bible literally? is a fine example. The speaker probably does not mean, Do you read all parts of the Bible nonmetaphorically? since the use of metaphors in the Bible would call for reading them as metaphors (e.g., "God is our rock" as a metaphor for God as our foundation). Most of the time what is meant seems to be, Do you take the Bible seriously? Or (drawing upon the question of the Reformers in response to medieval allegorizing), Do you apply the literal-grammatical method of reading to the Bible? By all means, let us take the Bible seriously and read it in the way its authors intended it to be read. We do so by interpreting literal language literally and metaphorical language metaphorically.

9. I will use the term "metaphor" rather broadly (as synonymous with poetic imagery) to express the use of a comparison between two dissimilar things that creates unexpected associations in one's mental image of the things compared. Ricoeur refers to metaphor as a "semantic impertinence" to express the effect of the dissimilarity of metaphoric comparison; *Interpretation Theory*, 50.

10. C. S. Lewis, *Mere Christianity* (1952; repr., London: HarperCollins, 2002).

image: "a turtle in the passing lane. . . ."[11] The latter expresses a feeling of stuck-ness even before the hearer explores the metaphor cognitively. Similarly, the metaphor of a weaned child with her mother in Psalm 131 is a powerful way to communicate the believer's stance before God:

> But I have calmed and quieted my soul,
> like a weaned child with its mother;
> like a weaned child is my soul within me. (Ps. 131:2 ESV)

The comparison invites the reader to entertain the possible connotations between the psalmist's soul and a weaned child. In addition, more than cognitive content is communicated by using the metaphor. The metaphor gives an emotive impact beyond the nonmetaphorical description, in part because metaphors are in one sense "mini-stories" that suggest "ways of looking at reality which cannot be reduced to terms of the metaphor itself."[12] This metaphor evokes the picture of a child looking to his mother not for the sustenance she provides him but for the relationship they enjoy.[13]

Metaphors also typically invite greater active participation on the part of readers. In the language of relevance theory, a metaphor "opens up to the addressee a range of weak implicatures and invites some higher degree of exploration on the part of the hearer."[14] Since the hearer or reader must decide which ties to reality are implied in a metaphor and which are not, metaphors challenge readers to greater depths of engagement. In the example above, the reader must actively consider what characteristics of a weaned child apply to the psalmist's soul or person. This does not imply, however, that metaphors are widely open-ended. The social and literary contexts of a text will limit the possible implications of a metaphor.[15] For example, although the image of ashes in the

---

11. One of my favorite metaphors from "Oh My," a song written by my husband, Tim Brown.

12. Wright, *NTPG*, 129–30.

13. To summarize a metaphor, as I have done for purposes of clarification, necessarily involves loss of impact (Sperber and Wilson, *Relevance*, 236). Stiver speaks of the "recognition [behind debates about metaphor] that metaphor is cognitive, that it is often irreducible, and that it is understood—quite apart from the ability to explicitly analyze it" (*Religious Language*, 119). For Stiver's full discussion of metaphor, see *Religious Language*, 112–33.

14. Green, "Context and Communication," 35. Sperber and Wilson note that "[a] good creative metaphor is precisely one in which a variety of contextual effects can be retained and understood as weakly implicated by the speaker. . . . The result is a quite complex picture, for which the hearer has to take a large part of the responsibility but the discovery of which has been triggered by the writer" (*Relevance*, 236–37).

15. Ian Paul provides a helpful discussion of interpretation of metaphor. "The key question is how to discern the contours of the metaphorical predication—how can we

Old Testament can connote death (since commonly after a battle the victors would burn the city of their enemy), the coupling "sackcloth and ashes" points us to another connotation for ashes—mourning or grief. This phrase "paints a vivid [cultural] picture of mourning women and men in torn clothing, lying or kneeling on the ground as they heap ashes and dust upon themselves."[16]

Poetic Devices in Hebrew Poetry

So far, we have been talking about metaphor or imagery in poetry, a feature that characterizes both English and Hebrew poetry. But there are features of Old Testament poetry that are either not prominent in or absent from English poetry and vice versa. For example, while most of us associate rhyme with English poetry, Hebrew poetry does not include a rhyme scheme for ending syllables. In addition, it is not clear whether meter (a standard rhythm) characterizes poetry in the Old Testament, as it does in much English poetry.[17] Hebrew poetry does, however, use some of the sound devices that also characterize English poetry, such as alliteration, assonance, onomatopoeia, and wordplay. As you might suspect, these kinds of sound devices are discernable only in the Hebrew language and not in English translations.[18] Therefore, it is not advisable to draw conclusions about the sound of Hebrew poetry from our English translations.

---

know which aspects of the vehicle fall into the 'is like' and which fall into the 'is not' of the [metaphor]? There is not a short answer; consideration of this must include the study of literary context and forms, questions of structure and rhetorical context, as well as aspects of historical context" (Ian Paul, "Metaphor and Exegesis," in *After Pentecost: Language and Biblical Interpretation*, Scripture and Hermeneutics Series 2, ed. C. Bartholomew, C. Greene, K. Möller [Grand Rapids: Zondervan, 2001], 397).

16. Leland Ryken et al., *Dictionary of Biblical Imagery* (Downers Grove, IL: Inter-Varsity, 1998), 50; Ryken cites 2 Sam. 13:19; Esther 4:1; Isa. 58:5; etc. for examples of its usage. For a categorization of various kinds of imagery used in poetry, such as metaphor, simile, anthropomorphism, personification, and metonymy, see A. Berkeley Mickelsen, "Short Figures of Speech," in *Interpreting the Bible* (Grand Rapids: Eerdmans, 1963), chap. 8.

17. There is debate on this issue. Some argue that meter is present and syllabic (stresses on each syllable), some that it is present and based on stressed syllables (only certain ones stressed), and others that there is little discernable meter in Hebrew poetry. See Osborne's discussion of meter in *Hermeneutical Spiral*, 175.

18. Although translators work to make English translations of biblical poetry as "poetic" as possible by using alliteration and other such sound devices, they cannot reproduce the exact pattern of sound devices without significantly losing the meaning of the poem. When faced with a choice, meaning considerations must be a higher priority than sound in translation.

Sound Devices

Alliteration is the repetition of the same consonant or sound at the beginning of words. One of my favorite English examples comes from a Michael Card song:

> There is a joy in the journey,
> There's a light we can love on the way,
> There is a wonder and wildness to life,
> And freedom for those who obey.[19]

The dual repetition of beginning consonants (j, l, w, f) in each line adds a compelling texture to already powerful ideas. Similar to alliteration, assonance is the repetition of vowel sounds in a group of words with different consonants, as in the repetition of the long-*e* sound in the hymn that begins, "We rest on Thee, our shield and our defender." In the Hebrew text of Numbers 6:24–26, we hear the repetition of the sound *ăh* at the ends of a number of words in this priestly blessing. Assonance may also refer to a repetition of consonants with different vowels.[20]

Onomatopoeia is the combination of meaning and sound in a word, such as the English word "hush," which both means to quiet someone down and sounds like the way we accomplish hushing—"shhhhh." There is a similar word in Hebrew, *has*, that also joins meaning and function.[21] Finally, we have discussed a wordplay from John's Gospel in a previous chapter. We might note that the sound devices we have mentioned here can and do occur in prose (nonpoetry); however, they are much more frequently employed in poetry. An example of wordplay from poetry in the New Testament can be found in Jesus' teaching at Matthew 23:24,[22] where Jesus accuses the scribes and Pharisees of straining a gnat and swallowing a camel. Have you ever wondered why these two particular animals are mentioned, other than their relative size disparity? Jesus' saying is a wordplay, for the terms for a camel (*gamlā'*) and a gnat (*qalmā'*) sound very similar in Aramaic, which was Jesus' mother tongue.[23]

19. Michael Card, "Joy in the Journey," *Joy in the Journey* (Brentwood, TN: Sparrow, 1994) G2-7243-8-51435-2-6, SPD1435.

20. For example: the "mystery of mastery."

21. For this example and others, see G. B. Caird, *The Language and Imagery of the Bible* (Philadelphia: Westminster, 1980), 86.

22. Although the Gospels are historical narrative, they include many kinds of sub-genres, such as parable and poetry, since the Gospel writers record Jesus using a variety of teaching methods.

23. The same wordplay does not occur in English or Greek. Wordplays, as with all sound-based devices, seldom carry over into other languages without losing more meaning than is advisable in the translation (e.g., choosing "mouse" and "moose" to keep the

Structural Devices

Parallelism is a structural feature of Hebrew poetry that deserves our attention, since it is a significant feature of Hebrew poetry and is not characteristic of English poetry. Lines of Hebrew poetry are primarily structured by means of a kind of balancing with neighboring lines. In the convention of Hebrew parallelism, the balanced lines are mutually defining; they are to be understood together rather than as distinctly separate ideas. For example, two (or three) adjacent lines might express a similar idea, with the parallel lines being mutually defining. This is called "synonymous parallelism." This kind of parallelism occurs widely in Old Testament poetry. Proverbs provides a familiar example:

> The fear of the Lord is the beginning of wisdom,
> And the knowledge of the Holy One is understanding. (Prov. 9:10 NASB)

Notice the parallel aspects of the two lines, wisdom paired with understanding and fear of the Lord with knowledge of the Holy One. Together these lines express a unified idea about wisdom.

A group of neighboring lines (usually a pair) that contains balanced yet opposite ideas is called "antithetical parallelism." This kind of parallelism occurs very frequently in Proverbs, where opposing kinds of responses to God and wisdom are often paired. Here is an example:

> The fear of the Lord is the beginning of knowledge;
> Fools despise wisdom and instruction. (Prov. 1:7 NASB)

Knowledge is linked with wisdom and instruction as similar ideas, but the antithesis comes in the pairing of the opposites "fear of the Lord" and foolishness.[24] You may have noticed that both examples of parallelism are drawn from texts that deal with the concept of the fear of the Lord. One value of getting used to noticing parallelism is that it can help us understand terms by their association (in synony-

---

wordplay in English would prioritize form over meaning to an extent that would make most translators shudder!). For the wordplay at Matt. 23:24, see Robert H. Stein, *The Method and Message of Jesus' Teaching*, rev. ed. (Louisville: Westminster John Knox, 1994), 13; William D. Davies and Dale C. Allison, *A Critical and Exegetical Commentary on the Gospel according to Saint Matthew*, International Critical Commentary (Edinburgh: T&T Clark, 1997), 3:293n63.

24. For the biblical concept of a fool, see Ps. 14:1: "Fools say in their hearts, 'There is no God'" (NRSV). A fool in biblical conception is a person who is godless in the way he or she views life.

mous or antithetical pairing) with other ideas. In these two examples, we discover that "the fear of the Lord" is knowledge of the Holy One (that is, right knowledge of God) and the opposite of foolishness (of an anti-God outlook). These two complement each other and reinforce the idea that to fear the Lord is to grow into and live in light of true knowledge of God.

A third kind of parallelism is often identified. For the most part this category is observed when adjacent lines of poetry are not so very parallel after all, as in these lines:

> Come, you children, listen to me;
> I will teach you the fear of the Lord. (Ps. 34:11 NASB)

This feature is called synthetic parallelism. Since the word "synthetic" can be defined as "artificial," you may wonder why this category is used at all. In fact, some have argued that the category should be jettisoned. But there are a few practical reasons for keeping it. One reason is that the lines in question, though not parallel, may be related in some meaningful way. In this case, although there is little balancing between the lines of Psalm 34:11, it is clear in context that these two lines are a pair—they go together. This pairing suggests that it can be helpful to look further at their relationship. In this instance, the second line gives an explanation of the first. A second reason for using the category of synthetic parallelism is that some examples that fall in this category do exhibit some amount of balancing.[25] So classifying lines of poetry as synthetic can be useful as we pay close attention to Hebrew parallelism.

Other devices used to structure Hebrew poetry are *inclusio* (a word borrowed from Latin), chiasm, and acrostics. An inclusio is a "bookend"—a word or phrase that begins and ends a section of poetry. An inclusio ties a section of text together thematically. For example, Psalm 135 begins and ends with the identical refrain, "Praise the Lord."

Chiasm occurs in an ABB'A' pattern used to structure a verse, a passage, or even longer segments of Scripture. As an example at the verse level, in Psalm 137:5–6 (NIV) we read:

---

25. See Proverbs 8:13, for example:

> The fear of the Lord is to hate evil;
> Pride and arrogance and the evil way,
> And the perverted mouth, I hate. (NASB)

Although this is not clearly synonymous, there is a parallelism to the way that the motif of evil progresses through the three lines. Some, in fact, would identify this as a type of synthetic parallelism called progression. For a description and categorization of parallelism, see Appendix C.

> If I forget you, O Jerusalem,   A
>   May my right hand forget its skill.   B
> May my tongue cling to the roof of my mouth,   B′
>   If I do not remember you.   A′

A central feature of chiasm (much like inclusio) is the return at the end to where the text began.

Finally, acrostics use the alphabet to structure a poem. For example, Psalm 119 is structured around twenty-two (the number of letters in the Hebrew alphabet) stanzas of eight lines each. All eight lines of the first stanza begin with the first letter of the Hebrew alphabet, *alef*. Each consecutive stanza moves on to the next letter of the alphabet, so that the psalm ends with its last stanza corresponding to the last letter of the alphabet, *tav*. Acrostics are not only visually and aurally pleasing; they also form a mnemonic device that allows for greater ease in memorization.

As we become familiar with these various structural features in Hebrew poetry, we will be helped by realizing that they are used for the more fundamental purpose of communication. It is rather easy to become immersed in the structural analysis of poetry and miss the intended impact of the way language is structured. As A. Berkeley Mickelsen has warned, "The very essence of poetry is destroyed if we are absorbed in the mechanics of it."[26] The particular value of attending to the mechanics initially, however, comes from our lack of familiarity with the genre of Hebrew poetry. Looking closely at the formal features of parallelism, chiasm, and others acclimates us to what in the genre is foreign to us. Then as we become more used to reading biblical poetry, we will be able to hear and respond to it more organically than technically—as the original audience would have done.

The Communicative Ways of Poetry

We have seen that in Old Testament poetry communication happens to a large extent through use of images (metaphor, understood broadly) as well as various structural and sound devices. So what is the point of using these? Each of these features impacts hearers and readers on an emotive level. Images engage our feelings as well as inspire our thinking. Some images intend to comfort ("The Lord is my shepherd"; Ps. 23:1), others alarm ("Roaring lions tearing their prey open their mouths wide against me"; Ps. 22:13). Metaphors often raise our ire or startle us. In addition, by using sound and form creatively and with care, poets woo us and captivate us. Poetry draws us into a place of responsiveness with

26. A. Berkeley Mickelsen, *Interpreting the Bible* (Grand Rapids: Eerdmans, 1963), 330.

our whole being. Poetry is meta-cognitive; it does more, not less, than communicate on a cognitive level.

As a result, we ought to allow the careful selection of words by the biblical poets without assuming that their particular choice is always only theological. Let me explain. A very common characteristic of poetry is its compactness—it generally uses fewer words than prose, but the words are carefully chosen for their sound, form, and/or metaphorical qualities. Poets select words with great care so that they have aesthetic appeal as well as intended content. For example, if I am writing an English poem that uses a rhyme scheme, I may choose the last word of each line with equal attention to rhyme as well as meaning. The following just does not rhyme, no matter how wonderfully specific it is: "I think that I shall never see / a poem as lovely as a eucalyptus." If words in poetry are chosen for reasons of sound and "feel" as well as meaning, then to study a word in a poem and fasten on a particular, nuanced meaning may be to neglect the author's intentions. The specific word may have been chosen more for its sound than for a possible nuanced aspect of its meaning. David, in his psalm of confession, uses a number of synonyms for the idea of "sin" (over a dozen occurrences of five different words; see Ps. 51:1–5, 9, 13–14). It would be a misreading of the genre of poetry to insist that each distinct synonym is used at particular points to emphasize a specific nuance of the concept of sin.[27] Instead, the author is probably attending to how the various synonyms "fit" in terms of sound and form as well as in terms of general meaning. The richness of the concept of sin in Psalm 51 arises not from specific nuances for each term at particular points but from piling up the various terms used as synonyms to give the effect of the greatness of David's sin.

Finally, at least part of the communicative intention of poetry may well be self-expression.[28] The individual psalms of lament, for instance, often express the psalmist's despair, pain, and anger before God. So it stands to reason that parts of a lament psalm are more an expression of the psalmist's plight before God than a direct communication with a human audience:

27. The evidence from the psalm itself does not support this interpretive move either. Reading the NASB, which uses a different English term for each Hebrew synonym, we can see in English the pattern of usage. The various Hebrew terms often appear in synonymous parallelism with each other: iniquity (*'āôn*) with sin (*ḥaṭṭā't*) (Ps. 51:2, 5, 9); transgressions (*pešaʿ*) with sin (*ḥaṭṭā't*) (51:3, 13); and sin (*ḥaṭṭā't*) with doing evil (*raʿ*) (51:4).

28. See the postscript to chap. 3 for a spectrum of intentionality types ranging from transmissive communication to expressive communication, the latter of which more often characterizes many kinds of poetry. Yet OT prophetic literature, which consists primarily of poetry, has many more transmissive qualities, such as the particularity of audience addressed.

> How long, O LORD? Will you forget me forever?
>   How long will you hide your face from me?
> How long must I bear pain in my soul,
>   and have sorrow in my heart all day long?
> How long shall my enemy be exalted over me? (Ps. 13:1–2 NRSV)

Yet the inclusion of individual lament psalms in the Psalter implies that these personal expressions were valued and used by the wider community of Israel—that they were communicative. In fact, even now they continue to resonate with believers who face overwhelming situations. The laments, even while expressing anger and despair, are set in the context of a stance of trust; they are, after all, addressed to God. They assume the presence of God, even while mourning God's apparent absence. Because of their faith stance, they speak beyond the psalmist's particular self-expression to communicate passionately and powerfully with hearers and readers.

How Does Communication Happen in Epistles?

Although as Western readers we might come to Old Testament poetry with some amount of ambivalence and angst, when we encounter the New Testament letters we feel as if we are in familiar territory. Not only are they in our more comfortable testament,[29] but also we have more genre experience with epistles. After all, we all know how to write and read letters and emails! I have wondered at times if this perceived familiarity has, in fact, lulled us into a complacent reading of the Epistles. We do not have to work as hard to understand them, it seems. This might be why, at least in non-liturgical evangelical settings, there tend to be far more sermons and lessons on Paul than on the Gospels or the Old Testament.[30] We seem to consider the New Testament letters straightforward. Since they teach more directly, we find them easier to interpret.

Yet as we come to the text with respect for the distance between the text and a contemporary world, we will need to remind ourselves that these are *ancient* letters. This invites us to ask questions about the genre of first-century letters. How does communication happen in epistles? Now, communication does happen more explicitly in letters than in

29. We might as well admit it. In fact, while our Bethel New Testament faculty routinely needs to emphasize the distance between modern readers and the New Testament, our Old Testament faculty works against the opposite tendency. They often need to convince their students of the relevance of the Old Testament!

30. This is not necessarily true for non-Western contexts. For example, African cultures are often much more comfortable with biblical narrative than Western churches are.

poetry. This fact may help to explain our comfort level with the former. We, in Western contemporary cultures, like explicit communication! It strikes us as clearer and more "logical." Yet very little communication strives to be fully explicit. A car manual or chemistry textbook might come close, but I suspect we would not want all communication to read as they do. I begin each of my seminary distance (online) courses with an email that introduces the course. Because this is my first communication with students whom I have never met and who know little to nothing about me or the course, I am highly explicit in my email about course objectives, upcoming assignments, and what they can expect from me as their professor. This initial email tends to be long and, I imagine, a bit laborious. But I have found that if I leave much to implication, I inevitably need to clarify the same point for any number of students through follow-up emails. I cannot assume much in these emails, since my students come from many different locations and cultures, and we are just beginning our relationship. Paul and the other New Testament letter writers, in contrast, could assume quite a lot, since most of their writings pick up their communication in relational midstream.[31]

The Genre of Epistle

So how do we hear implicit as well as explicit communication in New Testament letters? First, we are helped by paying attention to genre considerations. Ancient letters, in similar fashion to modern ones, consist of an identification of writer and audience, a greeting, attention to specific issues that the author wants to address, personal news, and a farewell—all very recognizable. The one part of the form of ancient letters we are not used to is a thanksgiving section that was typically included. This section might be rather extensive or simply a prayer for the recipient's good health.[32] Paul, in fact, usually extends the expected thanksgiving section, so that it is quite developed. Knowing these conventions helps us feel the effect of his omission of a thanksgiving in his letter to the Galatians. Paul moves directly from his greeting to the body of the letter: "I am astonished that you are so quickly deserting the one who called you in the grace of Christ and are turning to a different gospel" (1:6 NRSV). The omission, which may not seem so significant to modern readers, would almost certainly have been felt by the Galatian Christians.

31. For example, 1 Cor. is written after Paul spends time in Corinth and founds the church there. It also follows at least one letter Paul has written to the Corinthians (5:9) and a letter they have written to Paul (7:1), as well as personal reports about the church by those who have come from Corinth (1:11).

32. Fee and Stuart, *How to Read the Bible*, 57; Osborne, *Hermeneutical Spiral*, 254.

Reconstructing the Social Setting of the Epistles

A second way to discern implicit as well as explicit communication in epistles is to analyze the fairly substantial shared knowledge assumed by the New Testament letter writers and their audiences. Reading the New Testament letters is rather like listening to one side of a phone conversation without the benefit of hearing what the person on the other end is saying.[33] This situation requires us to reconstruct the conversation's other end. To do this, we will need to pay careful attention to the social setting of a letter, including its historical and cultural backdrop, as well as to the particular settings that existed between author and original audience.

Now you may be wondering why it is necessary to reconstruct the setting into which the text originally spoke. Isn't it better just to take the author's words at face value? The truth is that we always provide a social context for what we read; we do so automatically. For example, Paul's admonitions about practice of the Lord's Supper are given in 1 Corinthians 11:17–34. If we reflexively substitute our way of practicing communion as the backdrop for Paul's exhortations, not only will we miss the power of his words, but we may also misconstrue them altogether. If we envision believers sitting quietly in rows passing the communion elements systematically to each other or walking to the front of the sanctuary to receive a small amount of bread and wine, or juice, we will have read the text with a setting in mind—our own! Yet Paul's words actually inform us of some characteristics of Corinthian practice of the Lord's Supper. Communion in ancient Corinth, we learn, happens in the context of a full meal, and it seems that some are missing out and some are overindulging, so as even to become drunk. This depiction is not much like the contemporary church's practice! By attending to the original backdrop we hear Paul's warning to them more clearly: "Whoever, therefore, eats the bread or drinks the cup of the Lord in an unworthy manner will be guilty of profaning the body and blood of the Lord" (1 Cor. 11:27 ESV). For Paul in this context, unworthy participation has to do with not caring for those who have nothing and so go hungry at the meal (11:22).[34] This interpretation is confirmed by Paul's reference to eating without discerning the body (11:29). Given that in the very next passage, Paul conceptualizes the church as a body (1 Cor. 12), it is likely that here also he is referring to the church as the body, since the central transgression Paul addresses is sinning against one another, and particularly against poorer believers during communion. So the question is not whether to read a text

---

33. Fee and Stuart, *How to Read the Bible*, 58.
34. See Klein, Blomberg, and Hubbard, *Biblical Interpretation*, 353.

with a social context in place.[35] Rather, the question is whether we will do the historical grunt work that will help us hear the text in its original social setting instead of imposing our own setting onto the text without much thought.

So how do we reconstruct the original situation of a letter? The first task is to discern the situation as much as possible from the letter itself. Often important clues to the context are right in the text, as in the example we just examined. I find it helpful to read through the entire letter in one sitting, listening especially for contextual information. Listen with your ear tuned to the setting. You are looking for specifics about the author and audience and their relationship, the date, and the purpose or occasion of the letter. Let me say just a word about the purpose and occasion of a letter. Purpose refers to the broad intentions or reasons for a letter. In Philippians, for instance, Paul writes partly to address disunity and partly to thank the church for their monetary support. These are his purposes. The occasion of a letter refers to the more particular reasons that the author sits down to write it. These reasons bring about, or "occasion," the writing of the letter. The letter to the Philippians is occasioned by Paul's return of Epaphroditus to the Philippian church. He had been sent by the church to help Paul in his imprisonment (1:12–26; 2:25) and probably had reported to Paul about problems of disunity and the like. The occasion of the letter is really included in the broader category of its purpose. But it is often helpful to ask about the specific occasion to get a better sense of the letter's setting.

After attending to the setting of an epistle by reading the letter itself, we can look to broader geographical, political, cultural, and religious information to assist in reconstructing the social context.[36] Part of the religious background will be provided by the overarching story of the Old Testament and its climactic moment in Jesus the Messiah. The New Testament epistles assume this story and often quote or allude to particular Old Testament texts, which we will want to refer to for a better understanding of their message.[37] By drawing on the resources of historical study as well as the text itself and the Old Testament as background, we should usually be able to grasp some information assumed between authors and their audiences. This is necessary preparation for the task of reading for the author's message.

35. As Silva affirms, "the question is not whether we should read between the lines [to reconstruct the setting] but how we should do it" (Silva and Kaiser, *Biblical Hermeneutics*, 127).

36. More help on this topic will be given in chap. 9.

37. For an example of the importance of careful attention to the OT for interpretation, see Thorsten Moritz, *A Profound Mystery: The Use of the Old Testament in Ephesians*, Supplements to Novum Testamentum 85 (Leiden: Brill, 1996).

Although I have argued that we cannot avoid the task of reconstruction as we interpret Scripture, doing so in a balanced fashion is not always easy. The tendencies are either to underconstruct or overconstruct the contextual situation. I have already illustrated underconstructing the social setting with the example of the Lord's Supper from 1 Corinthians. We can also potentially overconstruct the situation, a procedure that has been called "mirror reading." Mirror reading is the determination that each command or argument of a letter is tied to a specific problem being experienced by the audience of the letter. Since we need to use clues from the letter itself in our reconstruction, mirror reading is all too easy to do. Let's take an example from 1 Peter. Some early reconstructions of the setting of 1 Peter concluded that it was written during the time of Nero's persecution of Christians (in 64 CE when he blamed them for the fires in Rome and burned some Christians to death to make his point). Besides the strong emphasis in the letter on Christian suffering under non-Christian persecution, the main evidence given for placing the letter in the time of Nero comes from the statement at 4:12: "Dear friends, do not be surprised at the fiery ordeal that has come on you to test you, as though something strange were happening to you." Yet the term translated "fiery ordeal" in no way necessitates that literal fire be in view.[38] Such slim evidence would be called a mirror reading by most interpreters. Proper historical reconstruction will look for clues that are more pervasive in a letter.

Following the Flow of Thought in an Epistle

We learned that in Hebrew poetry the movement of a poem may be structured through parallel lines and other formal devices. The development of thought in an epistle moves most often by means of ideas and exhortations, along with argumentation and other such supports. The author is at heart trying to persuade his audience of something, whether a particular way of thinking, being, or doing. In the body of a letter, an author will often build a line of reasoning over several successive chapters. After choosing a discrete unit of thought to be studied, an interpreter would be helped to follow the author's "flow of thought" through that section, while also attending to contextual assumptions of author and original audience, which thoroughly influence the given argument.[39]

38. Karen H. Jobes, *1 Peter*, Baker Exegetical Commentary on the New Testament (Grand Rapids: Baker Academic, 2005), 8. In addition, the current consensus in scholarship of 1 Peter is that the persecution being experienced by the audience is "sporadic, personal, and unorganized social ostracism . . . probably reinforced at the local level by the increasing suspicions of Roman officials" (9).

39. The task of determining the author's reasoning has also been termed "arcing" (Fuller, Piper), "tracing the logic" (Schreiner), and "block-diagramming" (Kaiser). See Appendix D

How do you begin this task of following the author's flow of thought? I will illustrate one way of doing so, using a brief part of Galatians: "It was for freedom that Christ set us free; therefore keep standing firm and do not be subject again to a yoke of slavery" (Gal. 5:1 NASB[40]).

The first step is to isolate the individual ideas of the passage. Doing this will help us get a sense of the flow of ideas from start to finish. We do this by identifying clauses, which are word groups that center on a verbal idea. So find the verb that organizes a group of words around it, and place each individual clause on a separate line. Step one applied to Galatians 5:1 would look like this, with three separate clauses identified:

1a   It *was* for freedom that Christ set us free;

1b   therefore *keep standing* firm

1c   and *do not be* subject again to a yoke of slavery.[41]

The second step involves identifying the connecting words between clauses. Connecting words like "and," "therefore," "but," "however," and "for" give us a good idea of the relationships between ideas, so these are important words to highlight. Underline the connecting words between clauses (i.e., the connecting words that begin the clauses you have already isolated).

1a   It was for freedom that Christ set us free;

1b   <u>therefore</u> keep standing firm

1c   <u>and</u> do not be subject again to a yoke of slavery.

The final step is to identify explicitly the relationships among the ideas that you have separated. This identification will often involve drawing on the possible uses of the connecting words you have underlined. Some-

---

for full citations and for further help with this task. It is important to acknowledge that the flow of argument in an epistle is more complex than any single tracing method can capture. The method I sketch out should be understood as a starting point for broader analysis of the author's argument. In addition, not all parts of letters are informed by this kind of analysis, so this task applies to the more argument-oriented sections of letters. One would not, for example, do a logical analysis of Rom. 16, where Paul includes a lengthy section of greetings. Yet this chapter is important for our interpretation of the letter as a whole, because it is part of Paul's strategy for persuading and encouraging his audience.

40. I encourage interpreters working in English to use the NASB or ESV, since these translations keep most closely to the presence and absence of conjunctions and other connecting words in the Greek. See step two.

41. The verbs are italicized. Note that there are two verbs in 1a. Since the second verb, "set free," is part of a relative clause that is necessary to complete "It was for freedom . . . ," I have kept the two together. The point is to have a complete idea on each line.

times, when there is no explicit connecting word between clauses, you will need to infer the relationship by trying out possible connections. In these cases, it is helpful to try out alternate connecting words to see which ones best fit the flow of thought.

1a It was for freedom that Christ set us free;

1b <u>therefore</u> keep standing firm (*result*)

1c <u>and</u> do not be subject again to a yoke of slavery.
    (*negative-positive*)

Since "therefore" identifies an implication or result of what has preceded, 1b is the result of 1a. The "and" that introduces 1c may simply introduce a series between 1b and 1c (this and that). But given that there is a negation in 1c, the "and" seems to make a link in a particular kind of series, a positive and negative construction (this and not that). Our identification of these clausal relationships results in the following description of Galatians 5:1: The result of Christ setting the Galatians free is twofold. Positively, it provides the incentive for standing firm in that freedom. Negatively, it helps to keep them from taking on a former yoke of slavery. The connection of this verse with the overall flow of Paul's thought and its interpretation against its cultural backdrop will be crucial for determining Paul's message to the Galatians.[42]

The Communicative Ways of Epistle

How does communication happen in the genre of epistle? The author of a New Testament letter, drawing upon the shared knowledge between himself and his audience, communicates primarily through persuasion. Paul, for example, wants to convince his audience of certain facets of the truth of what God has done in Jesus the Messiah and how this truth has and ought to continue to shape his audience. The specific topics he addresses in this regard arise from particular problems and issues that his audience is experiencing. His antidote always centers on the gospel and its implications for the ways that the church ought to live in pagan society. Paul uses a variety of rhetorical devices, or means of persuasion, to convince and reshape or "re-form" his audience.[43] A primary

---

42. For a good example of close attention to the flow of the argument of an epistle coupled with careful attention to historical-contextual setting, see N. T. Wright, *The Climax of the Covenant: Christ and the Law in Pauline Theology* (Minneapolis: Fortress, 1992), esp. chap. 7 and his Appendix D.

43. One danger that appears to be especially problematic in interpreting biblical epistles is to limit an author's communicative intentions to cognitive ones. A communi-

device is that of argumentation, providing a line of reasoning to persuade his readers. Following Paul's flow of thought closely (as well as that of other epistle authors) can help us understand both what he is trying to accomplish with his audience and how those same purposes might be accomplished in us.

How Does Communication Happen in Narrative?

As we have seen, it is important to pay attention to implicit as well as explicit communication in epistles. Listening for implicit meaning is all the more crucial in biblical narrative, where the primary action of communication is indirect. A theoretical distinction between the narrative's story and its discourse may assist us in understanding how direct and indirect communication occur in narrative.

Narrative Levels: Story and Discourse

We can distinguish theoretically between story and discourse levels in biblical narrative.[44] The story level is what we are accustomed to noticing in narrative. It includes the story's characters, plot, and settings—who does what, when, and where. In contrast, the discourse level is essentially the implied author's interaction with the implied reader (see chap. 2).[45] On the discourse level, rhetorical devices of various sorts, thematic presentation, and point of view are used to communicate. We might think of the story level as the "what" of the story, while the discourse is "how" the story is told. Most of us have not been guided to think much about how a narrator tells a story. So attention to this level of the narrative often opens up our reading of narratives to new insights.[46] Yet our task is not to attend to the discourse level at the expense of the story level. Rather, we interact with both levels in an integrated fashion, keeping an eye on the ways the narrator tells the story as the narrative progresses.

---

cation model of interpretation that emphasizes meaning as encompassing cognitive and meta-cognitive intentions is a helpful corrective to this tendency.

44. See Mark Allan Powell, *What Is Narrative Criticism?* Guides to Biblical Scholarship (Minneapolis: Fortress, 1990), 23.

45. For the sake of brevity in the rest of this discussion, the implied author will be referenced simply as "author" and the implied reader as "reader."

46. Eco refers to attention to the discourse level as taking "inferential walks," which he defines as going outside of the text "in order to gather intertextual support" for themes, etc. These walks "are not mere whimsical initiatives on the part of the reader" but are foreseen by the text's strategies (*Role of the Reader*, 32).

Discourse Level: Themes

Let's explore further what this discourse level is all about as we ask how narratives communicate. One of the more accessible features of the discourse level consists of the themes the author weaves into the telling of the story. Themes might occur simply through the recurrence of a word or idea in a section of narrative. For example, the New Testament book of Acts has a concerted emphasis on the Holy Spirit, as is clear from the repeated references to the Spirit throughout the narrative. Yet themes do not need continual repetition to be recognized as themes. Strategically placed words or phrases can signal to the reader that the author wants to emphasize an idea. The theme of "God with us" in the person of Jesus occurs only a few times in Matthew, but its strategic placement as an inclusio at the beginning and end of the Gospel guarantees its prominence.[47] In Exodus, we get a double effect related to the theme of God's presence (closely related to God's glory). Not only is this theme woven throughout the narrative (e.g., Exod. 16:7–10; 24:16–17; 29:42–43; 33:14–23), but it is strategically placed at the climactic ending of the book as well, so as to leave no doubt of its importance.[48] Looking for themes is very helpful for discovering the communicative intention in a narrative.[49]

Discourse Level: Sequencing

Various rhetorical devices—formal and compositional devices with communicative purposes—are used by the implied author to shape the narrative in a way that communicates intention. One basic way in which authors shape their narratives is through event sequencing. Now, in the modern era, ways of sequencing historical accounts are almost exclusively tied to chronology. We report events in the sequence in which they occur, and, if we do otherwise, we make the exception clear in our recounting. But the conventions of ancient biography were rather different from ours

47. Matt. 1:23 and 28:20. Eco (*Role of the Reader*, 26) refers to this type of theme placement as strategic versus reiterative placement. Inclusio can occur in narrative as well as in poetry.

48. Both the cloud that leads the people in the wilderness and the tabernacle they are to build are places where God's glory and presence reside. The cloud and tabernacle motifs come together beautifully at the very end of Exodus: "Throughout all their journeys whenever the cloud was taken up from over the tabernacle, the sons of Israel would set out; but if the cloud was not taken up, then they did not set out until the day when it was taken up" (Exod. 40:36–37 NASB).

49. In fact, I sometimes simplify the whole story/discourse distinction to a plot/theme distinction to help students focus on narrative themes, for if they grasp this distinction they will be a long way toward grasping how communication happens in narratives.

in this regard. An author's arrangement of events was often determined by thematic interests as much as chronological ones. This especially helps us understand why there are points at which the four Gospel writers diverge from each other in the order of their narration of Jesus' life. As Graham Stanton explains, "Concern for chronological order was not characteristic of ancient biographical writing. As a stylistic technique, presentation of biographical material *per species* [topically] is much more common."[50] For example, Matthew brings together quite a number of miracle stories in chapters 8–9, some of which are sequenced differently in Mark and Luke. Matthew's point in doing this is thematic—to emphasize in this section the messianic authority of Jesus over sickness, nature, and sin, as he comes to fulfill Israel's hope for restoration (8:17). Paying attention to sequencing often helps us to identify themes the author is communicating. As Thiselton notes regarding narrative, "The structuring of the material convey[s] the message."[51]

Discourse Level: Other Rhetorical Devices

There are many other devices that authors of narratives use to communicate indirectly with readers. I will mention just a few more here, but descriptions of additional structural and composition devices can be found in David Bauer's narrative work on Matthew.[52] Inclusio, as we have already seen, is a "bookending" device that emphasizes a theme by giving it the prominence of first and last position. In the book of Ruth, for instance, the issue of deaths in Naomi's family, and particularly those of her two sons, at the beginning of the narrative (1:3–5) is resolved in the birth of a son to Ruth, Naomi's daughter-in-law. The women of Bethlehem speak for the author when they say, "Naomi has a son" (4:16–17), at the book's conclusion. The loss and restoration of Naomi's progeny "bookends" the entire story.

"Intercalation" is a technical term for what has also been called a "narrative sandwich." Mark, in his Gospel, is particularly fond of this structural device. In an intercalation, the author begins narrating a story, and then interrupts it to include a second event before returning to complete the first. In Mark 5:21–43, the author tells of a synagogue ruler, Jairus, coming to Jesus to beg him to save his daughter (5:21–24). As Jesus begins the journey to Jairus's home, the story is interrupted

---

50. Graham Stanton, *Jesus of Nazareth in New Testament Preaching* (New York: Cambridge University Press, 1974), 121.

51. Thiselton, *New Horizons*, 71.

52. See David R. Bauer, *The Structure of Matthew's Gospel: A Study in Literary Design*, Journal for the Study of the New Testament: Supplement Series 31 (Sheffield: Almond Press, 1988), 13–19.

by a second story of a hemorrhaging woman who comes to Jesus for healing (5:25–34). After she is healed through her faith in Jesus' power, Mark returns to the conclusion of the story of Jairus (5:35–43). This sandwich technique has a purpose—"to encourage the reader to read the two stories in light of each other."[53] In this case, the woman's faith in Jesus is emphasized and helps us to hear the theme of faith in the story of Jairus: "Don't be afraid," Jesus says to Jairus, "just believe."[54]

Repetition is also an intentional device used in biblical narrative. In fact, contemporary readers may chafe at the amount of repetition used in some narrative accounts. Yet often there are compelling reasons for using the technique of repetition. For example, in Exodus, after the rescue from Egypt and the giving of the law, Yahweh gives Moses instructions for building a tabernacle, where Yahweh might live with Israel. The detailed instructions are elaborated in Exodus 25–31. At the end of the book, the tabernacle's construction by the Israelites is narrated at length (Exod. 36–39), much of the text repeating verbatim what was commanded by God (for example, compare 25:10–16 and 37:1–5). Now we might have simply recorded "ditto" if we were narrating the building of the tabernacle. The writer of Exodus thought differently. His use of significant amounts of repetition emphasizes indirectly and effectively[55] what is stated directly by the narrator after all the work had been completed:

> The Israelites had done all the work just as the LORD had commanded Moses. Moses inspected the work and saw that they had done it just as the LORD had commanded. So Moses blessed them. (Exod. 39:42–43 NIV)

It is crucial that Israel "gets it right" in the building of the tabernacle, in contrast to their frequent straying from Yahweh in earlier parts of Exodus (remember the golden calf). At the climactic moment in Exodus 40, their holy God comes to live in the consecrated tabernacle, and not even Moses is able to enter it because of the glorious presence of Yahweh.

53. Ben Witherington III, *The Gospel of Mark: A Socio-Rhetorical Commentary* (Grand Rapids: Eerdmans, 2001), 37.

54. There are approximately seven intercalations in Mark's Gospel. We can see his preference for this structural device in a comparison with Matthew. Matthew "un-sandwiches" some of Mark's intercalations; e.g., the two-part cursing of the fig tree surrounding the temple judgment in Mark 11:12–26 is narrated by Matthew sequentially in 21:12–17 (temple) and 21:18–22 (fig tree).

55. This would likely have been true for an ancient audience at least, although I think contemporary readers ought to learn to appreciate the use and effect of repetition in Scripture. See the dual narration of the story of Peter and Cornelius for another example of repetition, this time highlighting the movement to the Gentile mission in Acts (10–11).

Discourse Level: Point of View

We have already discussed "point of view" at some length in chapter 2. In narrative, point of view is the comprehensive way authors share their perspectives with readers. So point of view would include the discourse-level emphasis on themes, sequencing, and other rhetorical devices. In addition, point of view includes the use of various characters in a narrative either to express the author's perspective or to provide a counterpoint to it. These different possibilities mean that not every statement uttered or action taken in a narrative reflects the author's point of view.[56] This is an extremely helpful realization. For instance, in 1 Kings 18, King Ahab accuses Elijah of being a "troubler of Israel" (18:17 NIV). Elijah returns the characterization: "I have not made trouble for Israel . . . but you and your father's family have" (18:18). Whom are we to believe? The point of view of the author of 1 Kings has been made sufficiently clear, so we do not even vacillate. Ahab's words are certainly not the author's point of view; Elijah speaks here for the implied author.

One of the values of attending to point of view is that it helps the reader clarify the issue of whose voice to trust in a narrative. Through attending to point of view, we can avoid the trap of full identification with biblical characters, unless the author shows us that they provide an entirely reliable voice in the story. So while Jesus' words are to be trusted throughout the Gospels, other characters must be evaluated by their consistency with the author's point of view.[57] The disciples in Matthew, for example, sometimes give the author's perspective (16:16) and other times do not (19:10; 26:9). Knowing that we are to evaluate the actions and words of human characters to test whether they are consistent with and express the author's point of view keeps us from holding up all biblical characters as idealized moral examples.

In addition, point of view assists us in reclaiming the normativity of narrative. It is rather commonplace in some Christian circles to view narratives as merely historical accounts of biblical events. While the biblical narratives are fundamentally historical, they are more than recitations of events. The biblical narrators would assert that their narratives are the right way of understanding the events. Biblical narrative inherently claims normativity. "Worldviews, and the stories which characterize

---

56. One of Stein's guidelines for narrative—attention to authoritative speakers—helpfully anticipates narrative criticism's focus on point of view; *Basic Guide*, 164–65. Narrative criticism emphasizes the omniscience of the implied author as one feature that impacts point of view. Since he or she knows the thoughts as well as words and actions of the characters in the narrative, the implied author is able to provide a framework for analyzing the appropriateness of characters' perspectives and actions.

57. J. Brown, *Disciples*, 128–33.

them, are in principle 'normative,' that is, they claim to make sense of the whole of reality."[58] So we ought not to divide Scripture into didactic, or teaching, material and narrative material. All Scripture claims to be a true rendering of reality, so the biblical narratives are didactic and therefore normative.

Narrative as Normative and Theological in Nature

Recognizing the normativity of narrative through the pervasiveness of its point of view leads us to reestablish narrative as primarily theological in nature. In other words, biblical narratives are primarily about God and God's redemptive activity among humanity, and their authors' claim to reveal God truthfully. This may seem like a truism, but we often focus our attention on the ethical dimensions of narrative rather than on its theological dimension. In other words, it is too easy to ask the question of narratives, What should I be like? rather than, What is God like? or, What is God doing? The ethical question is not inappropriate. Yet, our primary interpretive emphasis should be theological. Our first question ought to be the "God question." As John Goldingay asserts, "The shaping of character is rarely the direct aim of biblical narrative; we are not told stories about Abraham, Moses, Jesus, or Paul chiefly in order that we might let our characters be shaped by theirs. The primary concern of biblical narrative is to expound the gospel, to talk about God and what God has done, rather than to talk about the human characters who appear in God's story."[59] By centering our attention on the theological question, we will be in a better position to hear well the ethical stance of the text.[60]

Our tendency to derive ethics apart from theology in the narratives of Scripture is nowhere more pervasive than in teaching the Bible to our children. We routinely teach Bible stories to children to make an ethical point: "Be like Samson, Ruth, and David. Be like Joseph and share with others just as he distributed food among the Egyptians." The latter point was expressly made in a curriculum I was to teach to the Sunday school class of my three-year-old daughter. What a marvelous lesson for self-centered three-year-olds: share! The problem, of course, is that Joseph also "shares" food with his long-lost family, while in the

---

58. Wright, *NTPG*, 41.

59. John Goldingay, "Biblical Narrative and Systematic Theology," in *Between Two Horizons*, 137. Even in the Gospels where Jesus is the focus of the narratives, the question of what God is now doing in Jesus the Messiah (namely, bringing God's kingdom to his world) is central.

60. "It is not the explicit ethics of the biblical text . . . as much as its theological *ethos* that best provides [ethical] direction" (Vanhoozer, *Drama of Doctrine*, 314).

process not only hiding his identity from them, but also putting his own silver cup in their food bags, so that he can drag them back to Egypt and deceive them a bit longer (Gen. 44). This is not exactly the kind of sharing we want to inculcate in our children! In contrast, if we make our first question the theological question, not only will we teach that God is good even when human beings fail, but we will also provide the right point of view from which to evaluate the human characters of the Bible's narratives.

The Communicative Ways of Narrative

How does biblical narrative communicate? More often than not the author of a narrative communicates indirectly. So as interpreters we are greatly helped by paying attention to such indirect means of communication as the way the story is told and its theological shape. The story communicates in its settings, characters, and plot by means of thematic presentation, sequencing, and other structural cues, as well as authorial point of view. In addition, the narrative's theological stance can be ascertained by keeping to the central question: Who is God revealed to be in this narrative? It is only after wrestling with this question that the secondary ethical question falls into its rightful order: What are God's purposes and plans for the people God has redeemed? Biblical narrative offers a rich resource for Christian theology. By attending to how narratives communicate, we are best able to draw upon this resource in developing a theology that does not ignore the storied nature of salvation history. Finally, it is crucial to remind ourselves that biblical narratives seek to shape communities of faith in all ways—their theology as well as how they embody and practice that theology. Stories do this by displaying a narrative world that readers are drawn to enter and engage in holistic ways.[61]

The Storied Nature of All Genres

Although we have focused in the last section on the way narratives tell their stories, I would like to conclude this chapter by reaffirming that all genres can be described as "storied."[62] "There is no escaping . . . the *narrativity* involved in Scripture."[63] Poetry, epistle, narrative, and

---

61. Vanhoozer speaks of narratives displaying a temporal world (*Drama of Doctrine*, 283).

62. See chap. 3, "Narrative Theology."

63. Green, "(Re)turn to Narrative," 16. As Hart puts it, "Not all texts are 'narrative' in the technical sense. But treated as 'a whole,' Scripture, in all its diversity of types, of-

all other biblical genres show their narrativity by assuming stories, affirming stories, and often subverting stories. Let's take a brief look at each of these functions. First, the biblical authors assume stories. We have explored how important it is in epistles to listen for the assumed context between author and original audience. This shared context is really a shared story, so that an initial interpretive task is to reconstruct this relational story between author and audience. Other genres also assume stories. Proverbial literature, for example, assumes the biblical story of God as creator, who has made the world to function in predictable patterns (e.g., so that the righteous generally prosper).

It is also the case that biblical authors affirm a theological story in their communication—the story of who God is and what God is doing in this world. For example, the Old Testament prophets both assume and affirm the story of God as a covenant-making God, who has covenanted with Israel specifically. So their critique of Israel must be understood in terms of that covenant and its stipulations.

Finally, the biblical writers also subvert stories. They intentionally critique the existing worldviews of their cultures. So theirs is often a countercultural subversion of normalized stories. For example, the book of Ruth speaks to an Israelite audience influenced by its ancient Near Eastern context, an audience that at best kept foreigners at arm's length. In contrast, the story of Ruth shows how God gives refuge to the foreigner and weaves the outsider into the life and story of the people of God (Ruth 2:12; 4:13–22).

Given the storied nature of all genres, we do well to add another question to the one that has occupied us for most of the chapter: How does a particular genre communicate? It will also be helpful for us to think through the question, What stories are assumed, affirmed, or subverted by the text I am studying? [64] The purpose of this question is to determine the continuity (and discontinuity) of any specific biblical text with what has come before in the biblical story and the author's way of participating in that story and in his own place and time. This question necessarily raises the issues of the social, literary, and canonical contexts of the Bible. We will focus on these topics in later chapters. But first we will turn to the task of understanding language as we interpret the Bible.

---

fers a narrative world the reader is invited to indwell, and from within which he or she is now expected to view things" (Hart, "Christian Approach to the Bible," 197). See also Wright, *NTPG*, 65.

64. This question was developed in concert with my colleagues Peter Vogt and Thorsten Moritz, in preparation for a hermeneutics forum for our students, at Bethel Seminary, 2003. This question is all the more pertinent since particular genres are always culturally embedded constructs. Biblical genres occur in specific cultural contexts and so require historical study to gain facility in their interpretation.

Suggestions for Further Reading

Bailey, James, and Lyle Vander Broek. *Literary Forms in the New Testament: A Handbook*. Louisville: Westminster John Knox, 1992.

Brown, Jeannine. "Genre." In *The Bible and Literature*, edited by Jamie Grant and David Firth. Downers Grove, IL: InterVarsity, forthcoming.

Caird, G. B. *The Language and Imagery of the Bible*. Philadelphia: Westminster, 1980.

Fee, Gordon D., and Douglas Stuart. *How to Read the Bible for All Its Worth*. 3rd ed. Grand Rapids: Zondervan, 2003.

Klein, William W., Craig L. Blomberg, and Robert L. Hubbard Jr. *Introduction to Biblical Interpretation*. Dallas: Word, 1993.

Osborne, Grant R. *The Hermeneutical Spiral: A Comprehensive Introduction to Biblical Interpretation*. Downers Grove, IL: InterVarsity, 1991.

Ryken, Leland, and Tremper Longman III, eds. *A Complete Literary Guide to the Bible*. Grand Rapids: Zondervan, 1993.

Sandy, D. Brent, and Ronald Giese, eds. *Cracking Old Testament Codes: A Guide to Interpreting the Literary Genres of the Old Testament*. Nashville: Broadman & Holman, 1995.

8

The Language of the Bible

The biblical authors did not write in a mysterious or coded speech. Under inspiration, they used their daily language in a normal way.

Moisés Silva, *An Introduction to Biblical Hermeneutics*

There is nothing archaic, solemn or mystical about the kind of language used by the inspired authors of the New Testament. It is the Greek of the street. This says a great deal about the nature of God's revelation. Just as God took on the form of common humanity when he revealed himself as the living Word, so his written Word was revealed in language that the person on the street could understand.

Mark Strauss, *Distorting Scripture?*

It was once believed by many that the Greek of the New Testament was a special kind of Greek, given its distinct differences from classical Greek. One assumption was that, unlike regular Greek, the Greek used in the New Testament was a kind of "'Holy Ghost language' created especially for biblical revelation."[1] This perspective was rightfully discarded after a series of discoveries of Greek papyri (writings on papyrus reeds), written about the same time as the New Testament and with the same type of language. Most of these writings were the ordinary stuff of life—bills, letters, and such. They were not intentionally preserved for posterity. Rather, the dry climate of Egypt kept them safe until their discovery. A

---

1. Mark L. Strauss, "Current Issues in the Gender-Language Debate: A Response to Vern Poythress and Wayne Grudem," in *The Challenge of Bible Translation*, ed. Mark L. Strauss, Glen G. Scorgie, and Steven M. Voth (Grand Rapids: Zondervan, 2003), 93.

large store of such writing fragments was discovered beginning in 1897 at the ancient site of Oxyrhynchus. Part of the value of these discoveries was the knowledge that the New Testament was written in "*Koinē*, the common form of Greek, simplified down from the classical standards, which had become widely used throughout the East as a result of the campaigns of Alexander the Great."[2]

In the providence of God, the human authors of Scripture wrote in normal language. This is what Strauss means when he speaks of the language of the street. What difference does this circumstance make for interpretation of the Bible? Well for one, it means we will need to pay attention to the ordinary stuff of word meanings, grammar, and syntax (the relationships between the various grammatical parts of a sentence). It also means that the kinds of issues that befuddle us about human languages more generally will probably be issues when we come to interpret Scripture. In other words, as interpreters we will need to pay attention to linguistics—the study of how language works. And since there are all sorts of ways to understand linguistic issues and the notion of language itself, we will need to think through our fundamental assumptions about language. "How we think about language is a philosophical, and ultimately a religious, question. . . . Because Scripture is a linguistic artifact, perspectives on language will *always already* be involved in biblical interpretation and exegesis."[3]

Since the definition of meaning developed in this book involves an understanding of meaning as communicative intention conveyed through the text's use of shareable language parameters, a careful study of what language is and how it functions in communication is warranted. In this chapter, we will be exploring the linguistic issues of (1) the nature of language and its relationship to human experience; (2) the pragmatics of language (how does it work?); and (3) some practical advice for what to do (and what *not* to do!) with biblical language.

Language: Can We Trust It?

The Gauntlet

Language has become the darling of philosophy in the last one hundred years or so. This linguistic turn is evident in Gadamer's understanding of

2. Stephen Neill and N. T. Wright, *The Interpretation of the New Testament, 1861–1986*, 2nd ed. (Oxford: Oxford University Press, 1988), 159; see 157–59 for a longer discussion.

3. Bartholomew, "Before Babel and after Pentecost," 136; italics in original.

language as "the element in which we live, as fishes live in water."[4] For Gadamer, later Wittgenstein, and others, rather than mastering language, we "are surrounded by it and by the things that are revealed through language."[5] Part of the contextualization of our existence as humans is our "being in language." "Being that can be understood is language," according to Gadamer.[6] This assertion of our linguistic embeddedness is rather like a gauntlet thrown down by twentieth-century philosophy that must be reckoned with. Who has taken up the gauntlet, and what has been their answer to this claim? We will look at two different responses to the claim that language is all-encompassing.

The Challenge Answered

One View: Language as Omnipotent

One response has been to affirm without reservation the notion that human existence is embedded in language and in the process to divinize language.[7] If language is, as it were, the stuff in which "we live and move and have our being," it is not difficult to grant language a measure of omnipotence over human existence. J. Hillis Miller "tips his hat" in this direction when he asserts "the autonomous power of language to do unforeseen things 'independently of any intent or drive or wish or desire that we might have.'"[8] Bartholomew contends that the notion of the omnipotence of language usually leads to either a nihilistic perspective on language (as lacking in meaning) or a magical view of language (as superabundant in meaning).[9]

Yet there are signs that all is not right with nihilistic or magical views of language. Although language is central to our locatedness as human beings, there are indications that it lacks the autonomy claimed for it in this position. A first indication is that it lacks the power to explain human

---

4. Hans-Georg Gadamer, "Reflections on My Philosophical Journey," in *The Philosophy of Hans-Georg Gadamer*, ed. Lewis E. Hahn, Library of Living Philosophers (Chicago: Open Court, 1997), 22. He goes on to say, "We are *in* the words, so to speak" (22). Gadamer also speaks of the "universal mystery of language that is prior to everything else" (*Truth and Method*, 378).

5. Zimmermann, *Theological Hermeneutics*, 168.

6. Gadamer, *Truth and Method*, 474.

7. Bartholomew refers to a "divinization of language" in some postmodern circles ("Before Babel and after Pentecost," 148).

8. J. Hillis Miller, *Speech Acts in Literature* (Stanford, CA: Stanford University Press, 2001), 32. In this context, Miller suggests that Austin's work would be better titled *How to Be Done in by Words*; see Austin, *How to Do Things with Words*.

9. Bartholomew, "Before Babel and after Pentecost," 143. Related to the issue of language's autonomy is the issue of its referentiality. On this, see Clark's evaluation of Wittgenstein (*To Know and Love God*, 376–80).

relationality (and even communication) beyond and prior to language. An infant who has not yet learned a language is still a relational being and interacts relationally with others in significant, though preverbal, ways. A second and more fundamental indication is that such a viewpoint has misconstrued the nature of language, not by affirming its centrality in human experience, but by ignoring its proper place in relation to that which is beyond the human realm. It has ignored God and so, at least in part, it has replaced God with language.

It is possible, however, to acknowledge the "linguisticality of interpretation" without capitulating to the idea that human beings are "imprisoned by language."[10] This is the point at which a theological construal of language is crucial. If God rather than language is omnipotent, then language will need to be understood from within the created order. Such recognition necessitates the secondary nature of language rather than its primacy for human existence.[11]

A Theological View of Language: Created and Secondary

If language is rightly understood as a part of the created order, we can readily acknowledge that "language is one of the frames, perhaps the central one, through which we encounter and understand our world."[12] Yet understanding language as created means that we can withstand the tendency to deify and absolutize language. As Bartholomew states, "the primary importance of God speaking creation into existence for our understanding of language is that language itself must be understood within that 'orderly cosmic arrangement and wholesome stabilization' that results from God's creative activity."[13] When language is understood from a creaturely perspective, we can affirm that language "permit[s] humans to communicate both with God and with one another."[14]

We are not so much fish in the waters of language as we are embedded in the created order, which includes language but is not solely constituted by it. This "secondarity" of language, as Bartholomew calls it,[15] means that we dare not elevate language to a position where it becomes the determining, absolute force behind human relationality. "Language [is]

10. Zimmermann, *Theological Hermeneutics*, 182–83.
11. This is Bartholomew's conclusion ("Before Babel and after Pentecost," 148).
12. Stiver, *Religious Language*, 204.
13. Bartholomew, "Before Babel and after Pentecost," 148. For a brief but helpful biblical theology of language, see ibid., 147–51.
14. Zimmermann, *Theological Hermeneutics*, 174.
15. "It is the very secondarity of human language that is illuminating against the background divinization of language by some postmoderns" (Bartholomew, "Before Babel and after Pentecost," 148).

169

world-disclosing and world-constituting, but not finally world-creating."[16] By this Bartholomew means that human life is not merely a linguistic construct. Human authors may use language to envision new ways of being, but language, apart from its users, does not hold creative sway.

Understanding language as created and so secondary has a number of implications. First, that God has created language implies that language is adequate for the task of communication and theology. Wright affirms that "within the Jewish and Christian worldviews, human speech, as the words spoken by those who are themselves made in the image of the creator, may be seen as in principle not just possibly adequate to the task of speaking of [God] but actually appropriate to it."[17] The reliability of language is built into its design.[18]

Second, the created status of language means that it is trustworthy. A view to the trustworthiness of language has been one of Ricoeur's contributions, whose philosophy "depends on and trusts in words that precede it" as a gift.[19] That we may trust language in our communication with God and others arises from its goodness as a part of creation. "God saw all that he had made, and it was very good" (Gen. 1:31 NIV). It also follows that if language is a good and trustworthy gift, we ought not to treat it lightly, as if it were simply a game to be played. T. S. Eliot captures well the frivolous use of language in *Sweeney Agonistes*:

> I gotta use words when I talk to you
> But if you understand or if you don't
> That's nothing to me and nothing to you
> We all gotta do what we gotta do.[20]

Third, and finally, language as created implies its limits—its finitude. Just as human beings are contextual and finite, so also is language. This limitation really circles back to Bartholomew's notion of the secondary of language. Taking this finitude seriously means acknowledging that language should not be deified. In other words, language ought not to be given sole primacy of place in human experience. It also means that language is capable of misdirection.[21] Although it will not communicate perfectly, nevertheless, as we have already affirmed, it can do so adequately.

So we might sum up our discussion of the nature of language by doing two things. First, we may affirm that language is a good and created gift

---

16. Ibid., 151.
17. Wright, *NTPG*, 130.
18. Zimmermann, *Theological Hermeneutics*, 178.
19. Vanhoozer, *Philosophy of Paul Ricoeur*, 275.
20. As cited in Pratt, *Literary Discourse*, 79.
21. Bartholomew, "Before Babel and after Pentecost," 150.

from God that enables human communication not only to occur but also to be generally successful. Language is adequate for communication. Second, we must always keep in mind that language is finite. Its limits (as well as our own) are apparent whenever misunderstanding happens. The limits of language are also stretched when language is used to describe metaphysical realities. Human attempts to use language theologically will never fully "capture" God.[22] Yet the promise of Scripture as revelation is that God has revealed truth through the finitude and adequacy of human language.

Language: How Does It Work?

Having delved into philosophical issues about what language is, we now move to the more pragmatic concern of how language works. I begin with a warning of sorts for biblical scholars from Bartholomew:

> Often . . . [language's involvement in biblical interpretation] is at an unconscious level, and the result is that biblical scholars sometimes work with naïve, anachronistic, and uninformed views of language. Much of the historical critical paradigm, which has dominated biblical interpretation for the last 150 years or so, has often worked with a naïve and wooden view of literary language.[23]

I begin here because the pattern set by biblical studies almost inevitably charts a course over time for interpretation by the average Christian.

To avoid a naïve and wooden view of language we will need to be true to at least three broad maxims about language: communication happens at the utterance level; language is located in culture; and the use of language in utterance communication is highly flexible.[24] But before discussing these maxims, we will introduce and define a few linguistic terms.

22. Language can only approximate divine reality. This is why philosophers often refer to language used to describe God as metaphorical in nature.

23. Bartholomew, "Before Babel and after Pentecost," 137.

24. These are not particularly novel ideas about language. Yet because there has been a tendency to do things with the biblical languages that we would never do with other languages (and especially our native tongue), these maxims will need to be affirmed and explored. Sometimes an underlying assumption of misuses of Greek and Hebrew is their *idealization*, since they are instruments that God used for communicating his word. This is not a necessary presupposition of a high view of Scripture, however. In addition, as Strauss points out, it is a fallacy to claim that "God created Greek and Hebrew as perfect languages for revelation" (Strauss, "Current Issues in the Gender-Language Debate," 131).

Linguistic Terms

Sense refers to what is expressed in an utterance, whether at the level of a word, sentence, or discourse. Silva defines "sense" as the mental content of an utterance.[25] In 1 Kings 3:16–28—the account of the wise decision of Solomon when confronted with two mothers vying for the same child—the word *melek* (translated in English as "king") is used numerous times. The sense of *melek* in this passage is closely akin to this definition of the English word "king": "a male sovereign or monarch . . . usually by hereditary right, the chief authority over a country and people."[26] Although the Hebrew word has a number of other senses (including those expressed by the English words "captain," "prince," "chief," or "lord"), the context of Solomon's judgment clearly indicates that the author uses *melek* in this part of Kings to refer to a monarch.[27] That is its sense. Often when we speak of the meaning of a word (or utterance), we are interested in ascertaining its sense.[28]

Referent indicates what an utterance points to outside of the language-event itself. It is clear from the context of 1 Kings 3:16–28 that *melek* is used to indicate a particular king, namely Solomon (see 1 Kings 2:45). The extra-linguistic reality to which an utterance points is its referent. In this passage the referent of *melek* is King Solomon, who ruled Israel during the time of the united monarchy. Sometimes when we speak of the meaning of a word or utterance, we are indicating its referent. Since both sense and referent can be a part of what we mean by a word's "meaning," we will do well to keep the distinction between the two in mind.

It is helpful to distinguish two additional terms: *language* and *utterance*. Language is "the (abstract) linguistic system of a particular speech community," while an utterance is a particular, actual speech unit made by an individual.[29] Or as we have defined it in chapter 2, an utterance is a speech act with a context. The value of the distinction between language and utterance arises from an awareness that the rules and conventions of language (what we might think of as dictionary definitions and grammatical conventions) provide the parameters for any particular utterance, but they do not determine the specific meaning of

25. Moisés Silva, *Biblical Words and Their Meaning: An Introduction to Lexical Semantics*, rev. and exp. ed. (Grand Rapids: Zondervan, 1994), 102–3.

26. *The Random House College Dictionary*, rev. ed., s.v. "king."

27. See R. Laird Harris, Gleason L. Archer, and Bruce K. Waltke, *Theological Wordbook of the Old Testament* (Chicago: Moody, 1980), 507–9.

28. As with *melek*, words usually have multiple senses. The context will indicate which of the possible senses are being used in any particular case.

29. Silva, *Biblical Words*, 114–15. The distinction derives from Saussure, who used the French terms, *langue* and *parole*. The latter two terms have become fairly commonplace in linguistic discussion.

an utterance. The "norms of language" (language parameters) provide the possibilities for utterance communication, and so for utterance interpretation. Only by looking at the "norms of the utterance," that is, an author's particular use of language in a specific context, will we be able to arrive at its meaning.[30] As Packer argues, "It is always wrong to think of interpreting any document by combining all possible meanings of each individual word as the dictionaries define it."[31] For instance, the word "boat" has any number of possible specific senses. But when I use it in the sentence, "As the wind died down, the boat came to a standstill," the sense, or intended meaning, has narrowed considerably.

Sentences as well as words only have potential meaning and require a specific usage and context to become utterances. The sentence "She kept her cool" is not yet an utterance because it lacks a context and so a specific meaning. This sentence can hold different meanings if given different settings. In the context of an argument, "She kept her cool" refers to the ability of the subject to maintain her composure. In the context of a hot day, "She kept her cool" might refer to a mother keeping her child from becoming overheated.

A final distinction that can help us as we attend to words in their contexts is the difference between a *word* and a *concept*. A specific word has a lexical domain that includes its various senses, some of which may correspond to differing concepts. A concept, on the other hand, is an idea that may have any number of words or word senses associated with it. For example, the Greek word *sarx* can be used to indicate the concepts of "human body," "body tissue," or "sinful nature," among others. Alternately, the concept of "human body" might be described using different Greek words (e.g., *sarx*, *sōma*, etc.).[32] To use another example, if I want to study kingdom in the Gospels, I am likely interested in the concept of "kingdom" that Jesus and the Gospel writers use. A study of the lexical meaning of *basileia* ("kingdom") gets me only so far in this endeavor.[33] My interest goes beyond the lexical sense to the concept of God's kingdom or reign as announced by Jesus and inaugurated in his ministry, death, and resurrection. A study of a concept should not, however, be confused with a strict lexical study. Studying the concept of kingdom will involve looking at the phrases "kingdom of

30. Stein uses the terminology of "norms of language" and "norms of utterance" in *Basic Guide*, 54–56. See also Hirsch, *Validity*, 69–70.

31. Packer, *Honouring the Written Word of God*, 36.

32. See James Barr, *The Semantics of Biblical Language* (Oxford: Oxford University Press, 1961), 208–11.

33. I do learn in this first step that *basileia* can refer to the act of reigning rather than the territory ruled over, a possible clue for the Gospel's use of the word.

God," "kingdom of heaven(s)," and "eternal life,"[34] and the parameters of their usage in the Gospels.

As may be apparent, it is often easier for English Bible exegetes to study biblical concepts than it is to do strict lexical study. The former can be done with less attention to particular words in Greek or Hebrew. My study of the concept of the kingdom in the Gospels allows me to study any number of lexical combinations, without having to isolate the sense of any particular Greek word. Knowing the difference between lexical and conceptual analysis can also help us avoid loading individual words with more conceptual weight than they are meant to handle.[35]

Three Maxims about Language

Communication occurs at the utterance level.

The first maxim that is crucial for understanding language is that communication does not occur at the level of individual words, but at the level of sentences and discourses, that is, at the level of utterances.[36] This means that communication cannot be divorced from literary context. A text should not be atomized by dividing it into its smallest pieces. A word alone rarely communicates a complete thought. (Single word exclamations like "Ouch!" are the exception.) Words take on particular meaning in the context of the complete utterance of which they are a part. Therefore, understanding an utterance is not done by simply adding together possible meanings of the individual words in an utterance. This truth is most obvious in the case of idioms, such as, "Don't let the cat out of the bag!" The mere computation of individual words' meanings will not help you arrive at the meaning, "Don't tell the secret." An utterance means something different than the mere computation of its possible word meanings.

Here are two utterances. They are almost exact in their linguistic makeup. Other than the presence of the indefinite article in the second, they are identical. Yet their meanings are quite distinct from each other, more different than would seem reasonable if computation was the way we determined meaning:

34. The latter is John's essentially synonymous way of expressing the already/not yet of the kingdom.

35. For a helpful example, see Kenneth Berding, "Confusing Word and Concept in 'Spiritual Gifts': Have We Forgotten James Barr's Exhortations?" *Journal of the Evangelical Theological Society* 43 (March 2000): 37–51.

36. Conceiving of an utterance ultimately at the book level will help us hear biblical authors on their own terms. See chap. 10.

At a time like this, few words will do.
At a time like this, a few words will do.

What is the difference in utterance meanings? The first statement implies that there is little of help that can be said in the particular circumstances (implying, "keep your words to a minimum"). The second states that, in the particular situation, one is required to say only a few words (implying, "you need not say all that much"). You might imagine the first statement being expressed in a time of loss and grief. The second could be uttered when someone is getting up to give an ad hoc speech. The first may be used to warn; the second to reassure. And the difference between the utterance meanings will not be discovered by an in-depth word study of "a"! Instead, we infer the meaning of the utterance from the dynamic interplay of individual words with the whole of the utterance in its context.

According to James Barr, "Theological thought of the type found in the New Testament has its characteristic linguistic expression not in the word individually but in the word-combination or sentence."[37] Barr's contribution to biblical studies in this observation, and his work on semantics generally, provided a linguistic paradigm shift in biblical studies. In the biblical theology movement of the mid-twentieth century, there was concerted attention to individual words, attributing whole concepts as supposedly embedded in words.[38] Barr's critique of reading entire theological concepts into individual words, while frequently ignoring the contexts of word usage, was decisive. With the publication of *The Semantics of Biblical Language* in 1961, Barr essentially ushered modern linguistics into biblical studies. After Barr, it is no longer possible to argue that theology is communicated on the level of individual words. Instead, we must attend to the whole utterance to understand the author's linguistic and theological meaning.

Does primary attention to the utterance level make a difference for interpretation? A significant difference arises at the level of basic methodology.

37. Barr, *Semantics*, 233. Long before Barr, Schleiermacher had made the same point really: "The proposition as a unit is also taken as being the smallest thing that can be understood or misunderstood" (Schleiermacher, *Hermeneutics and Criticism*, 28). Beyond the sentence level, Ricoeur emphasizes the importance of the larger whole: "A work of discourse is more than a linear sequence of sentences. It is a cumulative, holistic process" (Paul Ricoeur, *Interpretation Theory: Discourse and the Surplus of Meaning* [Fort Worth, TX: Texas Christian University Press, 1976], 76).

38. This is illustrated in the proliferation of many-volumed theological dictionaries that have extensive entries on single words. For example, there are almost sixty pages devoted to the "faith" word-group (*pisteuō*) in *Theological Dictionary of the New Testament*, ed. G. Kittel and G. Friedrich, trans. G. W. Bromiley, 10 vols. (Grand Rapids: Eerdmans, 1964–76). The original German publication began in 1949.

Instead of placing the study of individual words ("word study" or "lexical analysis") as our first and primary task, the focus of exegesis will be on what has been termed "discourse analysis." It will still be necessary to attend to meanings of individual words, especially when studying the Bible in its original languages.[39] Yet priority should be given to how words function together to form a coherent discourse. If a particular nuance of a word, though possible within the norms of language, contradicts the sense of the whole utterance in its original setting, that nuance will have to be rejected as part of the particular utterance meaning. We determine the lexical sense that best coheres with the context, regardless of other possible semantic choices. For example, the Hebrew word *rōm* can be translated with any of these English equivalents: "(be) high," "exalted," "overbearing," "boastful," "haughty," "tall," or "uplifted."[40] Yet most of them are ruled out by context in Psalm 131:1: "My heart is not proud, O LORD, my eyes are not [*rōm*]." "Overbearing," "exalted," "boastful," "tall," and "uplifted" simply do not fit what eyes do (e.g., they do not boast). The two remaining possibilities appear in various English translations: "haughty" (NIV, NASB, HCSB, NLT, TNIV) and "raised too high" (NRSV, ESV). The context has assisted in narrowing the norms of language toward the norms of the utterance.

If you are an English language exegete, the good news is that it is much easier to attend to whole discourses in the Bible, and so pay attention to context, than it is to trace Greek or Hebrew words, trying to determine their precise usage. Good exegesis is much more about listening carefully to the whole movement of a discourse, rather than isolating individual words for study. As I frequently tell students: It's better to be a good English exegete than a poor Greek or Hebrew one.[41] Now admittedly, this English exegesis involves relying on translators who have determined the

39. Since studying English words will not help us determine the range of meaning of a word in Hebrew or Greek.

40. William Lee Holladay, *Concise Hebrew and Aramaic Lexicon of the Old Testament* (Leiden: Brill, 1988), 335. English equivalents are not strictly identical to the lexical senses of a word, however, since a number of English equivalents may adequately reflect a single sense of a Hebrew or Greek term.

41. It is even better to be a good exegete who has studied the original languages! I would strongly encourage those interested in studying the Bible to learn the original languages. There is much to be gained exegetically by studying Greek and Hebrew, though not always what is typically expected. The original languages will not be the "magic key" to unlocking deeper meanings of Scripture. "The value of studying the biblical languages does not reside in its potential for displaying exegetical razzle-dazzle" (Moisés Silva, *Has the Church Misread the Bible? The History of Interpretation in the Light of Current Issues*, Foundations of Contemporary Interpretation 1 [Grand Rapids: Zondervan, 1987], 13). Rather, gaining facility in the original languages will allow you to do significant work for yourself and from a "broader base of information" (ibid.). You will not be immediately reliant on secondary sources, such as translations and commentaries; you will be able to do preliminary linguistic work on your own.

best way to translate words within the Bible's discourses into English. Yet if you have to rely on others for knowledge of original languages, you could not be in better hands than those of translators. The English translations we have are very good; they have been done by teams of scholars who care very much about accuracy of translation.[42]

Language is located in culture.

Our second maxim guarantees that understanding a particular language requires a large amount of cultural information. In fact, the location of all language within particular cultural contexts means that communication cannot be divorced from historical context. Our review of the insights of relevance theory in chapter 2 has affirmed this central notion about language. Authors assume that their readers share a certain amount of background contextual information, and their communication relies on this shared cultural context to be meaningful.

The culturally located character of language has significant implications for biblical interpretation. First, to study a language is to cross a cultural boundary. Beginning Greek and Hebrew students often feel the foreignness of the biblical text precisely as they delve into learning its languages (I know I did). Different language norms (grammar) and structure (syntax), as well as different alphabets and vocabulary, encourage this feeling of distance. Study of the original languages of the Bible must be wedded with careful historical study of their social settings. Any study of Hebrew, for instance, that attends carefully to word meanings, grammar, syntax, and other textual features but ignores historical-contextual issues is not doing all the work required in interpretation.

Now, this link between language and culture does not mean that we understand a culture primarily through its language. This is a fallacy that has been discredited by Barr and others. It has been claimed that Hebrew thought was distinct from Greek thought, based on key differences between the two languages. Silva sums up the supposed comparison nicely: Greek "is static, contemplative, abstract, intellectualized, divisive . . . [while Hebrew] is dynamic, active, concrete, imaginative, stressing the totality of [humanity] and [its] religion."[43] Barr decisively demonstrated

---

42. I want to emphasize this point precisely because of recent debates over English translations that tend to idolize certain translations (or translation theories) and demonize others. I am convinced that some of the issues raised in this debate, such as the issue of gender-inclusive/gender-specific translation, need a more concerted focus on linguistics. In the end, however, we ought to realize that we are spoiled by the sheer number of carefully prepared English translations, all of which strive to convey the original meaning of the Bible as accurately as possible into contemporary English idiom.

43. Silva, *Biblical Words*, 18. Silva describes this viewpoint but does not adhere to it.

that the linguistic evidence used to support this claim was weak. He also disentangled the constructs of language and thought, disavowing any neat correspondence between how a people speak and how they think.[44] For example, it had been frequently asserted that because the Hebrew language has little in the way of abstract vocabulary, the Hebrew people thought consistently in concrete terms.[45] This kind of direct correspondence is just not sustainable. As Barr argues, it is simply wrongheaded to assume that particular characteristics of a people group correspond to "patterns in the linguistic structure when analysed itself. And even if it may be possible to see such relations occasionally in particulars, this does not entitle us to begin by taking as an obviously valid instrument of investigation the idea that a language is a full expression of the national character."[46]

The relationship between language and culture rightly construed does, however, point to the referentiality of language. Contrary to the view that language used in literature is self-referential (is only about itself), we can affirm that language, in ordinary speech as well as in literature, regularly refers to realities outside of itself. This is certainly the case for the Bible. When encountering the character of Herod in the Gospels, a reader will know some things about him from the text itself, including that he is the king of Israel at the time of Jesus' birth (Matt. 2:1). Yet the designation of "Herod" refers the reader to a particular person in history. The character points to an extratextual reality. And the reader will be helped by knowing more about that person, such as that Herod the Great was not an ethnic Jew, but was put as king over Israel by his good friends in Rome. Such information is not irrelevant for interpretation, since the collusion between Herod and Rome will help us read Herod not so much as a representative of Judaism, but as an emissary of Rome.[47] Careful attention to the language used in Scripture requires that we pay attention to cultural context to help us further define the biblical referents and the author's contextual assumptions.

The use of language in utterance communication is highly flexible in nature.

Our final maxim emphasizes that languages, including biblical ones, are quite flexible. It is not uncommon for beginning language students to fixate on the "rules" of a language. Often when I am introducing a new grammatical category in beginning Greek, my students ask, Does

44. Ibid., 19.
45. Barr, *Semantics*, 44.
46. Ibid., 41.
47. We could say that the author expects the competent reader to have such knowledge. See Mark Allan Powell, "Expected and Unexpected Readings of Matthew: What the Reader Knows," *Asbury Theological Journal* 48 (1993): 31–51.

that happen all the time (i.e., Is it an absolute rule)? I usually have to say "No," since there are many rules in Greek that can be stretched or broken by Greek writers. This is why one of my New Testament colleagues gives the following proviso on the first day of beginning Greek: "I am going to lie to you frequently in this class!" He means, for example, that after introducing the rule that the Greek genitive noun should be translated "of [noun]," the class will run into all sorts of examples where this is not the case. The establishment of such rules is essential for beginners in a language. What is equally essential is that we grow to understand most of these rules as generalities, or flexible linguistic parameters, as we become more conversant with a language.

There are fewer hard and fast rules than we might like for particular usages in any language, biblical languages included. What becomes important, then, is to pay attention to the clues provided by an author's utterance. Yes, a specific word or grammatical structure can mean any of a number of options, but how does the author seem to use it here? We need to ask how it fits the context and the author's style, for different authors exhibit different stylistic tendencies.[48] The author of 1 Peter, for instance, uses relative clauses very frequently (more so than some epistle writers) and tends to use structural embedding of clauses within other clauses.[49] So as we study language use in Scripture, we need to be aware of the flexibility that allows individual authors to use language and grammar in distinctive ways for their communicative purposes.

As we attend to various levels of linguistic flexibility, it will help us to be aware of the distinction between *technical* and *nontechnical terminology*. Most language use falls into the latter category. But biblical writers will at times use language technically, which means they will use a word more uniformly by elevating it to a full-blown concept.[50] For instance, the word translated "gospel" has a technical meaning for the authors of the New Testament. The lexical sense of *euangelion* ("gospel") is "good news." The New Testament writers, however, use this term in a technical sense to refer to the content of the good news that has happened in the advent of Jesus. Since it is a technical term for many New Testament writers, they use the term to convey not only its lexical sense but also the more particular conceptual content of the gospel of God.[51] In the New

---

48. Jeanrond defines style as the phenomenon of an author's selection (Werner G. Jeanrond, *Text and Interpretation as Categories of Theological Thinking*, trans. T. Wilson [Dublin: Gill and Macmillan, 1988], 95).

49. The former is apparent in English translation; the latter is not.

50. Silva defines technical terms as "words that serve as cultural tokens" (*Biblical Words*, 68).

51. Silva notes that with technical terms "we are less dependent on the context when we wish to grasp the meaning of the word" (*Biblical Words*, 77). Of course, we will need

Testament, *euangelion* refers to the arrival of God's kingdom or reign in the person of Jesus the Messiah, whose resurrection has decisively demonstrated God's power over all other powers. The announcement of this good news is meant to compel both Jews and Gentiles to respond to God's reign through Jesus in repentance and allegiance.[52]

Another way of attending to the flexible nature of language is to allow for the fact that different authors may use the same term with different senses. This is really a commonplace allowance, but when it comes to biblical language, we tend to force a certain rigidity on the Bible that we would never expect of ourselves or others in communication. It is simply the case that not every occurrence of a word in the Bible will necessarily carry the same sense.[53] It has been observed time and again that Paul and James say different (some people claim even contradictory) things about "faith" (*pistis*):

> So faith by itself, if it has no works, is dead. But someone will say, "You have faith and I have works." Show me your faith apart from your works, and I by my works will show you my faith. You believe that God is one; you do well. Even the demons believe—and shudder. Do you want to be shown, you senseless person, that faith apart from works is barren? (James 2:17–20 NRSV)

> For if Abraham was justified by works, he has something to boast about, but not before God. For what does the Scripture say? "Abraham believed God, and it was reckoned to him as righteousness." Now to one who works, wages are not reckoned as a gift but as something due. But to one who without works trusts him who justifies the ungodly, such faith is reckoned as righteousness. (Rom. 4:2–5 NRSV)

It is clear, however, that Paul and James are using the term "faith" with different senses. James draws on the sense of *pistis* as affirmation of

---

to focus on the contexts of *euangelion* for a definition of its technical meaning in the New Testament in the first place.

52. Wright provides a definition of the concept of the gospel that gives the context of Jewish expectations about a future reign of God. "The idea of 'good news' [gospel] had two principal meanings for first-century Jews. First, with roots in Isaiah, it meant the news of YHWH's long-awaited victory over evil and rescue of his people. Second, it was used in the Roman world for the accession, or birthday, of the emperor. Since for Jesus and Paul the announcement of God's inbreaking kingdom was both the fulfilment of prophecy and a challenge to the world's present rulers, 'gospel' became an important shorthand for both the message of Jesus himself and the apostolic message about him. Paul saw this message as itself the vehicle of God's saving power (Rom. 1:16; 1 Thess. 2:13)" (N. T. Wright, *Paul for Everyone: Galatians and Thessalonians*, 2nd ed. [Louisville: Westminster John Knox, 2004], 167–68).

53. This is even the case for technical terms. A technical term used by one author may not be a technical term for another author.

Christian truth (which even demons exhibit).[54] This sense of "faith" needs to be accompanied by works to become a living faith (James 2:17). Paul, in contrast, uses *pistis* in its sense of "trust" (a very common way the term is used in the New Testament, as in Rom. 4:2–5). This wholehearted reliance on God is antithetical to a perspective that relies on its own "works" before God.[55]

Finally, we should avoid assuming that a biblical author cannot use the same word with different senses. There is no rule that stipulates that I cannot use the same term differently within even the same written work. Authors may have tendencies, but these tendencies are not straitjackets. Now if it can be determined that an author uses a word as a technical term, we can be almost certain that that term means the same thing in all cases in that author's writing, and maybe even those of a number of biblical authors. This may be the case with the phrase "fear of the Lord" in Old Testament wisdom literature, which might be summed up as knowing who we are in relation to God. To fear the Lord is to revere God as God alone and to acknowledge that we are not the gods of our own life and destiny.

Most of the language in the Bible is nontechnical terminology, however, and this means we must allow for stylistic and contextual variations in word usage. For example, it has been argued that Matthew's use of *ethnē* ("nations" or "Gentiles") in the "Great Commission" (28:19) must refer to the evangelization of the Gentiles only, excluding the Jews, since Matthew seems to use *ethnē* in this sense throughout the rest of his Gospel (i.e., *ethnē* is a technical term in Matthew).[56] Even if it could be demonstrated that each of the other occurrences of *ethnē* refers to "Gentiles" (non-Jews) and not "nations," we must allow in theory for Matthew to draw on another, frequently used sense of the word ("nations"), if he so chooses. Contextual evidence will be the conclusive factor. In fact, the universality of the final judgment scene of Matthew 25:31–46 argues for Jewish inclusion in "all the nations" at 25:32 (*panta ta ethnē*), and the identical phrase occurs at 28:19. These variations argue against viewing *ethnē* as a (fixed) technical term in Matthew. So we are not compelled to read *ethnē* as "Gentiles" at 28:19. Matthew seems instead to be referring once again to all "nations" (Jews included) as the recipients of the ministry of disciple-making.

54. This is part of the range of meaning of *pistis*; *A Greek-English Lexicon of the New Testament*, ed. F. W. Danker, 3rd ed. (Chicago: University of Chicago Press, 2000), 820.

55. As might be apparent, Paul and James are also using the term "works" (*erga*) in different senses in these passages! See Stein, *Difficult Passages*, 243–49.

56. See Carson for discussion of this viewpoint and his arguments against *ta ethnē* as a technical term in Matthew (D. A. Carson, *Exegetical Fallacies*, 2nd ed. [Grand Rapids: Baker Academic, 1996], 47–48).

In the final analysis, being true to the maxim that language use is highly flexible involves being on guard against artificial ways of interpreting biblical language. The less familiar we are with a language, the more likely we are to treat it artificially. One way of working against this tendency with the biblical languages is to remind ourselves that communication is a matter of doing as well as saying, as speech-act theory reminds us. If we give attention to the illocutionary actions of authors in what they say, we may be more careful to interpret language in a way that honors its flexibility.

For example, in our everyday use of language we might use what grammatically is one type of illocution to communicate a quite different illocution. When a supervisor *requests* that an employee come to her office, she may very well be doing more than *asking* if the employee will do so. Context and tone of voice may indicate that this is an illocution that expects compliance rather than a freely made decision!

To use a biblical example, the language in 1 Peter 3:14, "if you should suffer on account of righteousness," is a translation of a Greek optative verb (also at 3:17). Now in its grammatical definition, an optative is used to express a remote possibility. Some have taken this to indicate that the author of 1 Peter speaks to an audience that is not (yet) experiencing suffering or persecution.[57] On the grammatical surface, it would seem that the optative requires this reading (also 3:17). Yet the consensus of commentators affirms that the Petrine audience *is* experiencing persecution from their pagan neighbors and possibly from local officials.[58] How does this square with the use of the optative at 3:14 and 3:17? It may be that the optative, whose grammar expresses remote possibility, is being used for vivid rhetorical purposes to express that the recipients ought not to presume too readily that their suffering derives from good behavior. Instead, they should ensure that their actions are exemplary, so that any suffering they experience truly comes because of good behavior.[59] It is quite possible that the "iffy-ness" of the notion of suffering for righteousness stems not from its remote possibility in their situation but from the author's deep desire to have them examine (and reexamine!) their behavior to ensure that the suffering they do experience never arises from doing evil. If this is the case, then the point of the optative is more about doing something (admonishing to ensure exemplary behavior) than simply saying something (suffering

57. Daniel B. Wallace, *Greek beyond the Basics: An Exegetical Syntax of the New Testament* (Grand Rapids: Zondervan, 1996), 484.

58. See, for instance, Paul J. Achtemeier, *1 Peter*, Hermeneia (Minneapolis: Fortress, 1996), 28–35.

59. This notion is, in fact, prominent across 1 Peter (see 2:12–13; 2:20; 3:13–14; 3:16; 4:14–16; 4:19).

has not yet begun).[60] "For it is better, *if* God should will it so, that you suffer for doing what is right rather than for doing what is wrong" (3:17 NASB). Allowing for this kind of possibility is one way we might honor the flexibility of language use in the Bible.

Can We Be Trusted with Language?

In the beginning of this chapter, we asked the question, Can language be trusted? After we have discussed the tendencies within philosophy and theology to either divinize or atomize language, another set of questions seems appropriate: Can *we* be trusted with language? How might we pursue ways of interpretation that respect what language is and what it is not? How might we avoid abusing language in our efforts to understand what the biblical writers mean in their language use?

Linguistic Pitfalls to Avoid[61]

Don't infer the meaning of a word from its etymology.

Etymology refers to the origins of the form of a word. The English word "nice," for example, comes from the Latin *nescius*, meaning ignorant. The problem with using etymology for word definition is that the meaning of a word in a particular utterance is determined by the usage of that term at the time of writing. Today, we do not use the word "nice" to call someone ignorant unless we desire to be completely obscure.[62] If we want to communicate effectively, we will use the word as it is defined in current parlance.

Now drawing on a word's etymology can provide insight in the case of some biblical names. For example, Naomi asks to be called Mara ("bitter") instead of Naomi ("sweet" or "pleasant") given her dire circumstances (Ruth 1:20). Hearing the contrast offered by etymology guides the reader. The author of Ruth makes at least part of this connection clear by referring to bitterness in 1:20 (see also 1:13). In addition, etymology may be all we have to determine the usage of a rare word. In Matthew 6:11, Jesus tells his followers to pray for their "daily" (*epiousion*) bread.

60. Presumably, the audience of 1 Peter does not need to be told that they are or are not suffering under persecution. This would be something they would be intimately aware of!

61. A number of these are adapted from Silva's discussion: "Let's Be Logical," in *Biblical Hermeneutics*, 46–64. For other helpful discussions and examples, see Carson, *Exegetical Fallacies*, chap. 1; and Silva, *Biblical Words*.

62. "The meaning of the Latin word from which the derivation has taken place is no guide at all to the sense of ['nice'] in modern usage" (Barr, *Semantics*, 107).

The Greek word *epiousion* is used nowhere else in the Bible or other extant writings of the time.[63] One of the few recourses for determining the possibilities of its meaning is etymology.[64] Given that the word comes from the combination of a preposition and a root indicating existence (*epi* + *ousa*), many scholars and translators have landed on "daily" as a possible English equivalent. But not many of them would bet their last dollar on this choice.

Etymology in most cases gives us a general approximation at best and, in the end, may not represent current usage at all. Silva illustrates this truth nicely with a mock conversation between Harry and Mike.

> "Say, Mike, I heard some interesting gossip at the convention last week."
>
> "Oh, really? Who was being christened?"
>
> "Nobody was being christened. Why do you ask?"
>
> "Come on, Harry! The basic meaning of the word 'gossip' has to do with godparenting."
>
> "Who cares? I was just talking about the rumors I heard last week."
>
> "That's what you think. Words preserve their core meanings, so it's impossible to understand your statement without some reference to christening."
>
> "Take my word for it, Mike: I did not intend to say anything at all about christenings or godparents."
>
> "But you can't just make language mean what you want it to. Seems like you would have more respect for the essence of language. I'm rather disappointed in you."[65]

Don't infer the meaning of a word from its later usage.

An anachronistic reading draws upon a later meaning of a word and imports it into its biblical usage. For example, a key theme in John's Gospel is testimony or witness, expressed by the Greek word *martys* and its various verb and noun forms. We derive the English word "martyr" from *martys*,

---

63. "Extant" refers to documents to which we currently have access via preservation or discovery.

64. Another recourse is to look at the ways in which the word was discussed or referred to in the writings of the early church. Jerome (342–420 CE) draws upon a noncanonical Aramaic gospel (currently nonextant) to define *epiousion* (via Aramaic translation equivalent) as bread "for tomorrow" (Joachim Jeremias, *The Lord's Prayer*, trans. John Reumann [Philadelphia: Fortress, 1964], 23–24).

65. Moisés Silva, *God, Language and Scripture: Reading the Bible in Light of General Linguistics*, Foundations of Contemporary Interpretation 4 (Grand Rapids: Zondervan, 1990), 87–88. He follows up: "Such a conversation sounds ludicrous, and indeed none of us goes around injecting historical ideas of that sort into statements made by our friends. When it comes to literature, however, especially older literature, this method of interpretation becomes the order of the day."

which in later Greek usage comes to connote martyrdom. In the Gospel of John, however, this word does not include the later connotation of dying for the witness one gives, so we should not import such a connotation into its use there.[66] As we have affirmed in our definition of meaning in chapter 2, an author's communicative intention will align with the shareable parameters of language. This alignment implies that a word cannot be interpreted to mean what it could not have meant at the time of writing.[67]

Anachronistic reading is most tempting when teaching or preaching on the Bible, because it makes for great illustrative material. A frequently heard example arises from Paul's statement, "God loves a *cheerful* giver" (2 Cor. 9:7). Say a preacher tells the congregation that the word Paul uses is actually *hilaron*, from which we get the English word "hilarious." The preacher leaves the impression that Paul is referring to a hilarious giver. You might notice a couple of problems. The first is anachronism—defining a New Testament term by a contemporary one. The second is the bilingual nature of the anachronism: an English word that is etymologically derived from a Greek word is used in turn to define that ancient Greek term! As Carson ironically notes in his discussion of this particular example (which must be all too common), "Perhaps we should play a laugh-track record while the offering plate is being circulated."[68]

A more subtle form of this type of anachronism occurs when an English word is so tightly associated with a word used in the Bible that it comes to essentially define that word. The use of "peace" to define the well-known Hebrew word *shalom* is a case in point. *Shalom* may be adequately translated as peace in some cases, but there are many other cases where its close connections to justice and covenant terminology imply something beyond or other than the meaning indicated by the English word, peace.[69] So we will want to be careful not to define words in their biblical usage by our understanding of related terms in English. The context of a particular usage will be definitive for determining its meaning.

Don't read all possible meanings of a word into a specific usage.

This particular pitfall is what Barr calls "illegitimate totality transfer."[70] It essentially collapses the norms of language (all possible meanings of a

---

66. Carson (*Exegetical Fallacies*, 35–36) in his discussion of this term notes that the connotation of dying for one's testimony is clearly a part of the meaning of *martys* by the time of the martyrdom of Polycarp (mid-second century CE).

67. Adaptation of Fee and Stuart's aphorism: "a text cannot mean what it never could have meant to its author or his or her readers" (*How to Read the Bible*, 74).

68. Carson, *Exegetical Fallacies*, 33.

69. See Isa. 48:18; 60:17; and Ezek. 34:25; 37:26, respectively, for justice and covenant connections to *shalom*.

70. Barr, *Semantics*, 222.

word) into the norms of utterance (the specific meaning intended in an utterance). For example, *ruach* is a Hebrew word that may be translated into English depending on context as "air in motion," "blowing," "wind," "what is empty or transitory," "spirit," or "mind."[71] Yet *ruach* does not mean all of these things in any one occurrence. When the Lord makes an east wind (*ruach*) to blow across Egypt to bring in locusts (Exod. 10:13), it is not the case that a mind or a spirit is in view; it is a wind that is indicated. Context narrows the possibilities of the norms of language to arrive at the norms of the utterance.

It is usually helpful when exploring these linguistic categories (like illegitimate totality transfer) to think through an example in our own language, since we rarely fall into these same pitfalls when we are fluent in a language. (A little Greek or Hebrew *is* a scary thing!) If we look up the word "head" in an English dictionary, we will find the following possible senses and more:

- The upper or anterior division of the body that contains the brain, the chief sense organs, and the mouth
- The seat of the intellect (as in two heads are better than one)
- Natural aptitude or talent (as in a good head for figures)
- The obverse of a coin (heads, I win)
- The source of a stream
- Director, leader (headmaster)
- The oval part of a printed musical note
- A ship's toilet
- The foam or scum that rises on a fermenting or effervescing liquid
- Culminating point of action (events came to a head)

It is obvious that we are not meant to import all, most, or even a number of these senses into a single occurrence of "head." Take, for example, the sentence, We hiked all day to get to the head of the river. We will quickly and intuitively choose the appropriate, specific sense for "head" by attending to context. We ought to bring the same rubric to our understanding of how words work in the Bible.

Don't overemphasize fine points of grammar.

We have spent quite a bit of time addressing how words do and do not work, and thus how we should or should not treat them. This is

71. Holladay, *Concise Hebrew and Aramaic Lexicon*, 334.

necessary because of the way in which words have been isolated and misused in the past. Yet it is also very possible to misuse grammar in biblical languages. To borrow Wittgenstein's image, grammatical categories may be so overloaded that we end up with a "whole cloud of philosophy condensed into a drop of grammar."[72] Since any discussion of grammar presumes some knowledge of original languages, one general example will suffice.

A classic illustration of overloading Greek grammar involves the aorist verb tense.[73] Although grammar books describe the aorist tense as the undefined Greek tense, it was common until recently to further describe the aorist as the punctiliar tense. As a result, it became rather commonplace to assume that when the aorist tense was used, it indicated a single point of action. For example, Paul in 1 Corinthians 5:7 ("Christ our Passover lamb was sacrificed") uses the aorist tense for the verb "sacrifice." Following the path of aorist as single point, some have emphasized that Paul here means that this sacrifice was a once-for-all event.[74] Yet Paul could not have been saying this through the tense of the verb, since the aorist by definition simply does not specify the kind of verbal action. The action remains undefined. For those digital natives among us, we could use the example of a computer's default settings—those settings that are the automatic, "first blush" settings. The aorist is the default tense—the one that on its own (outside of contextual indicators) does not signal a particular kind of action. Recent linguistic discussion has a helpful pair of terms for this: "marked" and "unmarked." The aorist is an unmarked tense. We might say that it does not signal its importance to the reader. As readers, we want to pay attention to marked linguistic signs—those that are not the defaults. Marked linguistic signs communicate particular intentionality.[75]

Conclusion

As we conclude this chapter on language, I want to reemphasize a few crucial points. First of all, in the beginning God created language

---

72. Ludwig Wittgenstein, *Philosophical Investigations*, trans. G. E. M. Anscombe, vol. 2 (Oxford: Basil Blackwell, 1968), xi: 222. For a good parody of how commentaries easily slip into this kind of over-interpretation mode, see Silva, *God, Language and Scripture*, 11–13.

73. For a number of examples of misuse, see Frank Stagg, "The Abused Aorist," *Journal of Biblical Literature* 91 (1972): 222–31. See also Carson's more brief but helpful discussion in *Exegetical Fallacies*, 69–75.

74. Carson refers to this example (*Exegetical Fallacies*, 70).

75. Pratt refers to unmarked signs as "the standard or expected member of a paradigm" (*Literary Discourse*, 55n3). English exegetes can turn to biblical commentaries as a resource for grammatical issues.

and pronounced it good. Human sinfulness has tainted all of creation, including the human ability to understand and use language in ways that avoid misunderstanding and miscommunication. Yet God in great wisdom chose to use human language as a vehicle of his perfect truth. We can affirm that Scripture is truth and still acknowledge that "it remains a divine mystery how an imperfect vehicle (language) can communicate inerrant truth."[76] Second, studying the Bible is a rich experience, an experience that does not diminish in its richness the more it is studied. Yet the richness of the Scriptures is not found for the most part on the level of individual words. Isolated words do not communicate truth. Words are woven together into whole discourses. And it is at the level of discourses (sentences and beyond) that we hear the message of Scripture for us. Finally, we honor Scripture by treating its authors' use of language with respect. We do this by paying attention to the ways language works and does not work. And, as we will see in the following chapters, we honor the words of Scripture by hearing them in relation to their broader contexts.

Suggestions for Further Reading

Barr, James. *The Semantics of Biblical Language*. Oxford: Oxford University Press, 1961.

Bartholomew, Craig G., Colin Greene, and Karl Möller, eds. *After Pentecost: Language and Biblical Interpretation*. Scripture and Hermeneutics Series 2. Grand Rapids: Zondervan, 2001.

Carson, D. A. *Exegetical Fallacies*. 2nd ed. Grand Rapids: Baker Academic, 1996.

Silva, Moisés. *Biblical Words and Their Meaning: An Introduction to Lexical Semantics*. Rev. and exp. ed. Grand Rapids: Zondervan, 1994.

———. *God, Language and Scripture: Reading the Bible in Light of General Linguistics*. Foundations of Contemporary Interpretation 4. Grand Rapids: Zondervan, 1990.

Silva, Moisés, and Walter Kaiser Jr. *An Introduction to Biblical Hermeneutics: The Search for Meaning*. Grand Rapids: Zondervan, 1994.

Strauss, Mark L., Glen G. Scorgie, and Steven M. Voth, eds. *The Challenge of Bible Translation: Communicating God's Word to the World: Essays in Honor of Ronald F. Youngblood*. Grand Rapids: Zondervan, 2003.

---

76. Strauss, "Current Issues in the Gender-Language Debate," 131.

9

The Social World of the Bible

To yank Jesus out of his Jewish background and universalize him sells short Christian theology (if one takes the incarnation seriously, surely one should take seriously the time and place it happened, and the people who paid attention to it originally), sells short Christian history (if the church were not itself concerned with history, why did they bother to write historical documents and preserve them), and sells short human interaction (if the church is to engage in mission to the world, it might start with a better knowledge of the world from which it originally sprang).

Amy-Jill Levine, "Putting Jesus Where He Belongs"

I grew up in a home and church where I was steeped in Scripture. Coming to seminary as a student, I expected my learning to center on studying the Bible, with a special emphasis on reading the Bible in its original languages, something I had looked forward to for quite a while. I was not disappointed. At seminary, I not only learned more about the Bible and began a lifelong study of Greek and Hebrew, but I was also surprised that I was expected to learn quite a lot about the historical settings in which the Bible was written. I was expected to be a historian of sorts!

Why is this the case? Isn't it enough to learn to read carefully the words of the biblical text, especially if we are fortunate enough to have the time and teaching to learn them in their original languages? Why would we need to become historians of the ancient world? Turner's pointed answer to the first of these questions is, "We cannot arbitrarily restrict the presuppositional pool to the content of biblical texts and to facts about Greek language . . . bracketing out all the rest of our knowledge of the contemporary Greco-Roman and Jewish history and culture in which the New Testament texts are embedded."[1] And Wright answers the second question about the need to be budding historians in his characteristically memorable way: "There is an innate laziness which affects us all: the sense of 'd'you mean I've got to learn all that stuff about first-century Judaism just to get the simple gospel message?' Answer: Yes. If God chose to become a first-century Jew you might have thought finding out about first-century Jews would be something a believer in God would want to do!"[2] If this is true for the New Testament, most readers' experiences would indicate that an even wider gap exists between our world and that of the Old Testament.

We have already introduced the idea that the gaps between our world and the ancient world are wide enough to require our focused attention. During a stay in England, I got used to hearing a phrase that nicely sums up what we as interpreters are required to do. Whether getting on and off trains or crossing over areas of the street under construction, I would read the safety sign "mind the gap." We need to "mind the gap" as well—by paying attention to the gap between our own cultural knowledge and the knowledge necessary to understand the Bible in its own context.

In fact, "the further one stands from the original situation . . . the more discipline one needs to bridge the gaps."[3] It takes discipline and plain old hard work. Why do it then? Why spend the time and energy bridging the historical and cultural gaps between the modern world and the text? Because, as relevance theory has emphasized, meaning is predicated on contextual assumptions shared between author and original recipients. In fact, as the definition of meaning in chapter 2 emphasizes, communicative intention can be discerned only in light of the text's background conceptual assumptions. So a respectful reading of the text requires that we explore these assumptions related to social setting. In order to read the text on its own terms, we will want to learn about the original contexts of the Bible. For "the honest and fair reading

1. Turner, "Theological Hermeneutics," 69. Turner's comment that even Greek language is a "behind-the-text" issue (i.e., that it presumes all sorts of first-century cultural knowledge) argues against learning the Greek language for Bible study without learning about the cultures partnered with that language.

2. N. T. Wright, *IVP Academic Alert* 8, no. 3 (Autumn 1999): 2.

3. K. C. Hanson and Douglas E. Oakman, *Palestine in the Time of Jesus: Social Structures and Conflicts* (Minneapolis: Fortress, 1998), 4.

of an ancient text requires hard work, demanding from us every ounce of skill and knowledge we can muster."[4]

Tired out yet by the specter of all this hard work? The good news is that we have significant help in this work of understanding the historical contexts of the Bible. In fact, one of the strengths of today's biblical studies is its focus on historical reconstruction of the cultures in which the Bible was written. A wealth of pertinent information is available, some of it packaged very helpfully for Bible students not called to be full-time historians.

Types of Context

As we consider the task of understanding the social world of the Bible, it will help us to identify various levels of social context.[5] We start with the broadest context, what we might term the "world context." The world context is information and experience shared by humanity generally. For instance, metaphors of light and darkness work across cultural boundaries because of their universal applicability. We readily understand that light provides the best conditions for going in the right direction, and that moving about in the dark is often confusing. So we intuitively understand the logic of the psalmist: "Your word is a lamp to my feet and a light for my path" (Ps. 119:105). At this level of social context, we are least aware of gaps between our own context and that of the text.

The next level of social context we can identify is that of the "cultural context": a particular society's ways of understanding and living. It is at this level that we often sense the foreignness of the world of the Bible from our own world. This category is quite extensive, given that it covers the entire spectrum of political, social, and religious beliefs and practices of a given society. Given the breadth of the category, it can be helpful to envision this level as consisting of multiple domains. A "domain" is the particular cultural topic addressed by or assumed in a biblical text that requires exploration. For example, the retaining of

4. Wayne A. Meeks, "Why Study the New Testament?" *New Testament Studies* 51 (April 2005): 166.

5. I use "social world" (or social context) as an overarching term to indicate historical, cultural, religious, political, geographical, and relational contexts of a written text. Parts of the categorization that follows are derived from contemporary linguistic theory, specifically the following contexts or "models": world model, domain/application model, user model, and dynamic model. For these general categories, see Kristina Jokinen, "Goal Formulation Based on Communicative Principles," in *Proceedings of the Sixteenth International Conference on Computational Linguistics* (Copenhagen, Denmark: Center for Sprogteknologi, 1996), 600; see also 598–603.

professional mourners when a loved one died was part of the practice of Hebrew mourning (e.g., Amos 5:16).[6] The domain of mourning fits within religious and cultural practices of ancient Israel and can help our reading of any number of biblical passages (e.g., Mark 5:38–40). Since becoming an expert in all areas of the social world of the Bible is unrealistic for most people, understanding particular domains as they arise in our study of Scripture is a more accessible goal. Osborne lists and describes the following categories that are pertinent to biblical study: geography, politics, economics, military/war, religious customs, and cultural practices, which include family customs, material customs (such as home and dress), everyday customs, athletics and recreation, music, and art.[7] We might think of a domain as a particular area within one of these wider-ranging categories. Bible commentaries will usually discuss contextual domains that are directly applicable to the passage they are addressing.

A third type of context is tied specifically to the original recipients of a biblical book—the "audience context." With this phrase we are envisioning the common experiences and specific knowledge of the text's original audience. This concept is more narrowly focused than the general cultural understanding and practices that an audience would certainly have been schooled in. It involves particularities of a certain time period and possibly of a local community (as with some of the New Testament epistles that were written to particular local churches). For instance, the original audience of Malachi, which was the people of Judah after the return from Babylonian exile, would have been familiar with the abuses of the Levitical priesthood at the time of Malachi's prophetic ministry. Although we as later readers hear about some of these abuses from the text itself (Mal. 1:6–8, 12–14; 2:1–9), the original audience would have had a clearer understanding of them through their own experience at the temple and in their cultural networks.[8] Asking the question, How would the original audience have understood this text? is helpful precisely because it focuses attention on this category of their social context (along with the preceding levels of context).

Finally, we can identify the level of "dynamic context." In one sense, all context is dynamic, because culture is dynamic, always shifting and changing. Dynamic context as used here, however, refers specifically to the evolving relationship between the author of a text and the intended

6. Other aspects of mourning in the Jewish context included the way those in mourning dressed and adorned themselves and what foods were acceptable to eat (see Ezek. 24:22).

7. Osborne, *Hermeneutical Spiral*, 129–34.

8. For additional information on priestly and Levitical irregularities during the time after the exile, see Neh. 13.

audience. It is the shared knowledge developed through their ongoing conversation. This category is more helpful for some biblical books than for others. A number of New Testament epistles are based on an ongoing conversation between author and recipients. The longer the relationship, the greater the number of contextual factors that developed and therefore are assumed between the two. This is one reason why the correspondence between Paul and the church in Corinth assumes so much shared context. The two New Testament letters to the Corinthians are part of an already-developed stream of communication and relationship between Paul and the Corinthian church.

Sources for Social-World Analysis

After getting a feel for the range and levels of social context that might apply when studying a biblical text, we will want to explore various sources for acquiring pertinent contextual information. These include the Bible itself, as well as a variety of extrabiblical primary and secondary sources.[9] As we examine a whole variety of sources from these categories, we should remind ourselves that the question of what counts as a relevant contextual assumption in any particular communication will help to focus our historical work.[10] For example, although it would be ideal to have a wide-ranging knowledge of life in ancient Israel at the time of the Babylonian exile to understand the book of Lamentations, we can prioritize the information we will need to gather initially by asking what background-contextual assumptions are most directly pertinent for understanding this book that laments the fall of Jerusalem.

The Bible as Source for Social World Analysis

The Bible itself often provides important contextual information. Reading very carefully the biblical book under study is a good first step toward reconstructing the social world of the text, since authors often refer or allude to the situations they are addressing. We can observe such references, for instance, in the book of Ezra. The author indicates that the events he narrates occur at the time of Persian rule (Ezra 1:1; 4:6) after the Babylonian captivity (2:1). The author assists the reader by historically locating the story of the rebuilding of the temple. In

9. Texts from the time period being studied are referred to as "primary sources." Written sources from a later time that draw upon, interpret, and discuss primary sources are called "secondary sources."

10. This is one contribution of relevance theory to interpretation.

addition, crucial information about the social world of a text may be provided by other parts of Scripture, specifically those that are temporally prior to the book being studied. In Ezra, the author mentions the book or law of Moses as a point of reference for the reader (3:2; 6:18; see also 7:6). By doing so, he explains the activity of the people as they rebuild the temple and reinstitute its sacrifices against the backdrop of God's covenant with Israel and the stipulations for sacrifices found in the Old Testament law. This signals that to understand Ezra the reader will need to be familiar with the covenant as described in the first books of the Old Testament.

As we move to study the social world of the New Testament, the Old Testament itself will be a crucial background source. Not only are Old Testament texts cited extensively in the New Testament, but the larger contours of the story of God's covenant relationship with Israel are also assumed and evoked in the New Testament writings. For instance, the genealogy that introduces the Gospel of Matthew rehearses the story of the people of God from Abraham on, and without knowledge of this story Matthew's reader will miss some of the significance of his introduction. So knowledge of the Old Testament is both crucial in its own right and informative for a proper understanding of the New Testament, as it tells of the advent of Jesus the Messiah and the ways in which he fulfills the promise of the Old Testament.

Extrabiblical Sources

After spending time studying the Bible itself to illuminate the social world in and to which it was written, we can also gain important information from other sources contemporary with the Bible. We will examine the relevance of these sources for interpreting both the Old and New Testaments.[11]

The Ancient Near Eastern World

The social backdrop for the Old Testament is the world of the ancient Near East. As is widely known, there are written records from peoples besides the Hebrews who lived in the Mediterranean world in the centuries prior to the common era. Texts from Egyptians, Mesopotamians, and other ancient peoples written in this period of time provide information about beliefs and practices of these groups of people in the ancient

11. For thorough bibliographic information on primary and secondary sources for both testaments, see David R. Bauer, *An Annotated Guide to Biblical Resources for Ministry* (Peabody, MA: Hendrickson, 2003); and Frederick W. Danker, *Multipurpose Tools for Bible Study*, rev. ed. (Minneapolis: Fortress, 2003).

Near East. By comparing and contrasting these writings with the Old Testament, we gain information that can help us in interpretation.[12] In addition, archaeological sources, such as inscriptions, artifacts, and excavation sites provide further information about the thinking and behavior of various groups of people.

Let's take an example. In a Mesopotamian creation account, the Babylonian *Enuma Elish*, creation occurs because of a conflict between the gods, with the heavens and earth being formed out of the body of a slain god. In this account, humanity is created as a sort of afterthought in order to serve the gods. Knowing that this was one ancient way of understanding how the world and humanity came into existence, we are in a better position to understand the biblical account of creation in Genesis 1, which seems to be intentionally shaped to counter such a cosmology.[13] We can note that attempts to explain the origin of the world and humanity in the ancient Near East were inherently theological. We can also see that it was important to account for the creation of humanity by providing their purpose (e.g., to attend to the needs of the gods). Theological and anthropological emphases are also present in Genesis 1 and are apparent in a number of ways. First, the chapter is thoroughly theological, although the account differs dramatically from its ancient Near Eastern counterparts. In Genesis 1, creation is a result of the biblical God's creative activity by his word (1:3), not a haphazard result of divine warfare. "In the beginning, God created the heavens and the earth" (1:1). As a way of expressing its anthropological emphasis, the creation of humanity comes at the pinnacle moment of the Genesis creation account. Humanity is the climax of the creation, created distinctly in the image of God (1:27). The Genesis account counters its contemporary cultural worldview by providing a different explanation of what creation and humanity are all about.

The Jewish World of the First Century

There are two social "worlds" that we will need to attend to as we move to interpretation of the New Testament in the first century CE: the

12. For access to primary sources, consult Kenton L. Sparks, *Ancient Texts for the Study of the Hebrew Bible: A Guide to the Background Literature* (Peabody, MA: Hendrickson, 2005).

13. The comparisons drawn here stand whether the author of Genesis knew the *Enuma Elish* itself or other creation traditions more generally. Wenham argues that the "author of Gen. 1 . . . shows that he is aware of other cosmologies and that he wrote not in dependence on them so much as in deliberate rejection of them" (Gordon J. Wenham, *Genesis*, Word Biblical Commentary [Waco: Word, 1987], 9). If this is correct, then the information gleaned from the ancient Near Eastern creation traditions is relevant as part of the assumed context of the author and his audience.

Jewish world and the Greco-Roman world. Now, these are not so much two distinct worlds in the first century as they are intertwining cultural settings for the rise of early Christianity. In spite of the interweaving of these cultural streams, it is helpful for our discussion to separate them in theory. We begin with the Jewish backdrop to the New Testament.

A significant number of Jewish writings have survived from what is termed the "intertestamental" or "second-temple" period (from about the fourth century BCE to the first century CE). We can categorize these writings into four groupings: (1) Jewish Apocrypha and Pseudepigrapha, (2) Philo and Josephus, (3) the Dead Sea Scrolls, and (4) rabbinic literature.[14]

The collection of the Jewish Apocrypha consists of the books that are included in the Catholic and Anglican Bibles but that are not a part of most Protestant Bibles. The Apocrypha includes narratives such as 1 and 2 Maccabees and Tobit; the apocalyptic 2 Esdras; as well as wisdom books like Sirach.[15] The Jewish Pseudepigrapha is a catchall category for much of the Jewish literature outside the Apocrypha that is not represented in the already-listed categories. The name "Pseudepigrapha" indicates that many of the books in this group borrow the names of past Jewish heroes for their titles. The Assumption of Moses, 1 and 2 Enoch, the Testament of Job, and the Psalms of Solomon are just a few of the Jewish pseud-epigraphic writings. While the ideas and perspectives represented by the Apocrypha and Pseudepigrapha are by no means uniform, these writings are helpful for interpretation of the New Testament, because they contribute to a sketch of Jewish thought leading up to the first century CE. As Bruce Metzger has noted, "The importance of the intertestamental apocryphal and pseudepigraphic literature lies in the information that it supplies concerning the development of Jewish life and thought just prior to the beginning of the Christian era."[16]

The writings of two Jews of the first century are particularly influential given the sheer amount of their material that is extant. Philo, a Jew from Alexandria, Egypt, who wrote in the early part of the first century CE, provides a portrait of the belief system of a Jew influenced by and trying to influence the Greek culture in which he lives.[17] For

14. More precisely, this source provides access to oral traditions later recorded in rabbinic literature.

15. Narrative is the largest genre category in the Apocrypha: 1 and 2 Macc., Tob., Jdt., Add. Dan. (Pr. Azar., Sg. Three, Sus., Bel), and Add. Esth. Its wisdom literature consists of Wis., Bar. (which includes Ep. Jer.), and Sir. (also called Ecclus.). 2 Esd. is the single example of apocalyptic literature in the Apocrypha.

16. Bruce M. Metzger, *The New Testament: Its Background, Growth, and Content*, 3rd ed. (New York: Abingdon, 2003), 48.

17. Greek influence is referred to as "hellenization." Philo is often referred to as a hellenized Jew.

example, Philo attempts a compelling rationale of Jewish food laws for his Greek neighbors, who are put off by the stringent and seemingly odd dietary requirements of the Jewish people. Josephus, a Jewish historian writing in the latter part of the first century CE, provides a history of the Jewish people and a chronicle of the Jewish war of 67–70 CE.[18] His intended audience is the authorities in the Roman empire. Part of his purpose is to show the Jews in a positive light to his Roman audience.

In the mid-twentieth century, a major discovery was made in the area of the Dead Sea in Palestine. In 1947 Bedouin (shepherds) discovered a cave containing two-thousand-year-old manuscripts. This find was the first of a number of such discoveries in subsequent years. These manuscripts, the Dead Sea Scrolls, can be divided into three groups. One group of manuscripts and fragments are Old Testament biblical books; another consists of books from the Apocrypha and Pseudepigrapha; and the third group is made up of sectarian writings from the Qumran community, which lived at the Dead Sea site from about 150 BCE to 70 CE. Even though the Qumran community was a sectarian group, and thus not always representative of first-century Jewish belief more broadly, the Dead Sea Scrolls have been important for our understanding of the New Testament. "In Qumran, as in the early church, we have the opportunity to observe how a Jewish sect distinguished itself from the rest of Israel, crafted rites of passage into the community, organized into a community that could sustain itself and provide for the relief of all its members, theorized about the struggles of attaining virtue and pleasing God in this life, drew inspiration from a variety of texts . . . and read their own story through the lens of sacred Scripture."[19]

A final set of writings that assist in understanding the Jewish setting of the New Testament is the rabbinic material recorded in the Mishnah and Talmud. Even though the earliest of these, the Mishnah, was not written down until the end of the second century CE, some of the traditions it records and interprets go back to the first century or earlier. One of the difficulties in drawing on rabbinic material to aid in New Testament interpretation is precisely our inability at some points to determine whether a tradition goes back to the first century and so whether it is relevant for New Testament interpretation. Yet discerning which rabbinic traditions were likely to have circulated in oral form within first-century

18. Flavius Josephus, *The Jewish War* and *Antiquities of the Jews*. These are Josephus's two major extant works that illuminate the Jewish setting up to and through the first century.

19. David A. deSilva, *An Introduction to the New Testament: Context, Methods, and Ministry Formation* (Downers Grove, IL: InterVarsity, 2004), 88.

Judaism is quite helpful in providing background information for New Testament interpretation.[20]

One of the strengths of current biblical and second-temple research is the picture of Judaism that emerges. Rather than viewing first-century Judaism as a monolithic entity, recent research has affirmed the variegated nature of Judaism at the time of the writing of the New Testament. Some even speak of the "Judaisms" of the first century. While we should not lose sight of the core tenets that unified first-century Jewish belief,[21] we can benefit from the more nuanced sketch of recent scholarship that emphasizes the distinct forms of Jewish thought and practice among various groups such as the Pharisees, the Essenes (to which the community at Qumran was in some way related), and the Sadducees, as well as the Jewish understandings represented in the literature already discussed above.[22]

All in all, attention to these four categories of primary sources for understanding first-century Judaism provides significant assistance for New Testament interpretation. Yet the large amount of material available makes mastering these primary sources a daunting task. That is the reason why the growing number of summary materials on first-century Judaism will be of significant interest to the serious Bible student.[23]

The Greco-Roman World of the First Century

The reasons for studying the Jewish backdrop when interpreting the New Testament may seem obvious. The first Christians were Jews, and so understanding Jewish thought and practice at the advent of Jesus, the Messiah, makes a lot of sense. But why study the world of the Greeks and Romans to understand better the New Testament? Is this really necessary or helpful?

The answer is an unqualified "yes." We have already seen that biblical Judaism did not exist in a vacuum. It lived in interaction with its broader culture. This is why understanding Old Testament Israelite faith in the light of ancient Near Eastern culture is so crucial. This also means that the contours of first-century Jewish belief and practice existed in an organic interplay with the wider Greco-Roman culture of the Mediter-

20. For help in this process of discerning the dating and relevance of rabbinic materials, see David Instone-Brewer, *Traditions of the Rabbis from the Era of the New Testament* (Grand Rapids: Eerdmans, 2004).

21. Wright (*NTPG*, 247) identifies twin pillars of Jewish belief in the first century as monotheism (there is only one god) and election (Israel is God's covenant people).

22. There are a number of websites that provide primary source material. A simple search for "Josephus," "Philo," or "Apocrypha" will turn up numerous sites containing full texts in English translation.

23. See Bauer, *Biblical Resources*, 163–78; Danker, *Multipurpose Tools*, 203–23.

ranean world. As Warren Carter has commented on the Gospel of Matthew particularly: "We are reading a story in which the main character is crucified, a distinctly Roman form of imperial control and execution used to remove troublesome members of the empire."[24] This observation alone should be enough to demonstrate that we need to take the Greco-Roman backdrop of the New Testament quite seriously.

First, a word of explanation: Attention to the Greco-Roman social world takes account of the Greek and Roman influences upon the whole of the Mediterranean world, including Jewish society, in the centuries leading up to the rise of Christianity. The Greeks ruled the ancient Mediterranean world for almost 300 years. Alexander the Great conquered Judea in 331 BCE. Then in 63 BCE, Rome gained control of Judea, so that Roman occupation of Judea and Galilee sets the backdrop for the New Testament. Though Rome's influence was a primary one, particularly through exertion of its political and military power, the Greek influence was not insignificant in the first century. First, the Greek language had become the lingua franca of the Mediterranean world by the time of the first century, so that any local people whose livelihood required them to interact with Romans or other nonnatives would need to know enough Greek to communicate adequately (e.g., tradespeople, political figures). Second, Greek culture had made its mark in most parts of the Roman Empire, so that many of the major cities of the Mediterranean were significantly hellenized. Even the Jews of Judea, many of whom had resisted hellenization initially, were not immune to Greek influence. This can be seen in the presence of Greek theaters, gymnasiums, and horse tracks (hippodromes) in Judean cities in this time period.

Primary sources that illuminate the worldview and practices of the Greco-Roman world include extant Greek and Roman literary, historical, and philosophical works.[25] For instance, it is important for interpreting the household instructions of the New Testament (Eph. 5–6; Col. 3–4; 1 Pet. 2–3) to know how they are patterned after and also diverge from the Greco-Roman household codes from Aristotle to first-century moralists.[26] In addition to Greco-Roman literature, discoveries of Greek papyri that record transactions of ordinary life, such as letters and legal documents, also give indication of first-century practices. Again, the

24. Warren Carter, *Matthew and Empire: Initial Explorations* (Harrisburg, PA: Trinity Press International, 2001), 4.

25. As with Jewish primary texts, websites are a helpful resource for accessing Greco-Roman texts. Consult the Perseus website (http://www.perseus.tufts.edu/) for Greco-Roman literature from A to Z (or from Aristotle to Xenophon!).

26. See Jeannine K. Brown, "Silent Wives, Verbal Believers: Ethical and Hermeneutical Considerations in 1 Peter 3:1–6 and Its Context," *Word and World* 24 (Fall 2004): 395–403.

large amount of primary source material is a blessing for our understanding of the cultural backdrop of the New Testament, but it is also a difficulty, given that most of us do not aspire to become Greco-Roman historians! Consequently, Bible students will benefit from interaction with the secondary literature that provides composite sketches of the Greco-Roman world.[27]

Getting Started: Some Guidelines

Reading the Primary Sources

Even though the sheer amount of primary material from the time when the Bible was written makes for a daunting reading list, the value of accessing and reading this material makes it worth the effort. Whether accessing ancient Near Eastern material or Jewish and Greco-Roman writings, readers may benefit from some important guidelines for reading ancient primary sources.

First, keep in mind that your goal is to get a better understanding of the worldview of the author(s) of the text you are reading. This is a big task, but the more reading you do in the primary sources, the better you will get at it. Look for the authors' assumptions about and perspectives on a whole range of topics, including their political and social thinking and activities, their understanding of education and religious life, and the way they draw upon the past (e.g., via antecedent sources and philosophies).[28] Be ready to hear presuppositions quite different from your own as you read. Whenever you read something that strikes you as odd, assume that the idea in question actually makes sense within the worldview of the writer.

Second, realize that you are probably hearing one voice among many. In other words, do not presume that a single author represents *the* ancient (monolithic) perspective on the subject at hand. Worldviews were as complex and diverse in the ancient world as they are in our own! It may well be that there is some amount of uniformity on some subjects.

---

27. For example, Bruce J. Malina, *The New Testament World: Insights from Cultural Anthropology*, 3rd ed. (Louisville: Westminster John Knox, 2001); and James S. Jeffers, *The Greco-Roman World of the New Testament Era* (Downers Grove, IL: InterVarsity, 1999). We have focused our attention on textual evidence for reconstructing the social context of the Bible. Another source is material evidence uncovered by archaeology. This evidence includes material artifacts (e.g., pottery and remains of houses, temples, etc.) and inscriptions. For an introduction to the topic of biblical archaeology, see John D. Currid, *Doing Archaeology in the Land of the Bible: A Basic Guide* (Grand Rapids: Baker Academic, 1999).

28. For example, how do Jewish sources, such as the Pseudepigrapha, use the Old Testament in their writings?

It is just as likely, however, that there were multiple ways of looking at something, of which your author only expresses one vantage point. For example, while polytheism was the overwhelmingly predominant religious perspective in the Greco-Roman world, there seem to have been some philosophers who expressed a kind of monotheism in their philosophic deliberations.[29]

Third, assume that an ancient writer, like his or her modern counterpart, writes from a particular vantage point for a particular reason, and that these purposes influence how the text was written. For example, Josephus is a very helpful source for reconstructing Jewish life in the first century. Yet we will want to be cautious in assuming that Josephus provides an unbiased historical account, given that his intended audience was the Roman authorities. Indeed, he consistently seems to downplay Jewish nationalism, in order to show his Roman audience that the Jews were not such a volatile populace as might have been presumed following the Jewish rebellion of 67–70 CE. In this way, we will want to assess the historical value of what we read in the extrabiblical primary sources.

Fourth, we should evaluate the relevance of sources for the interpretive issue at hand. The issue of whether an ancient extrabiblical source is pertinent for the study of a specific biblical text is not always immediately straightforward. The viewpoint expressed in a particular extrabiblical text may not be one that was widely held. If this is the case, we ought to be careful in assuming that the original audience of the biblical book necessarily held that perspective. For example, although records indicate that at Qumran there was an expectation for two messianic figures (a Messiah of Israel and a Messiah of Aaron),[30] there is no other extant textual evidence for this dual expectation. It is not likely, then, that most first-century Jews were expecting two messiahs. This evidence from the Dead Sea Scrolls, however, does provide evidence for understanding the variegated nature of messianic expectation in the first century. In other words, there were a number of existing scenarios for Messiah within Jewish expectation at this time in history, so that when Jesus appears on the scene, the relevant question is not only, Is this the Messiah? but also, Which kind of Messiah is this? The Gospels are very interested in answering the latter as well as the former question.

29. E.g., "The Epistles of Heraclitus," trans. David R. Worley, in *The Cynic Epistles*, ed. Abraham J. Malherbe, Society of Biblical Literature Sources for Biblical Study 12 (Atlanta: Scholars Press, 1977), sec. 4, p. 191. Heraclitus writes, "Where is God? Locked up in the temples? . . . Don't you know that God is not made by hands, that he has not from the beginning had a pedestal, and that he does not have a single enclosure but that the whole world . . . is his temple?"

30. See I QS 9:10–11; CD 12:22–23.

It is also important to determine the relevance of general categories of sources for historical reconstruction. This is quite important in New Testament study, where the interplay of Jewish and Greco-Roman contexts will often need to be evaluated. For instance, is Paul best understood against his Jewish or his Greco-Roman backdrop? In most cases, the answer lies not in an either/or approach but in a judgment of the relative weight of these contexts for particular interpretive questions. In general, the Jewish sources (the Old Testament and Jewish extrabiblical literature) are highly significant for the New Testament writers in their theological discussions, since in their theological formation they draw upon the story of Israel and how Jesus the Messiah has brought that story to a climactic point in his life, death, and resurrection. Yet Greco-Roman sources provide important information about the broader moral discourse going on in the first century,[31] with which the New Testament regularly interacts. Paying attention to Greco-Roman moralists often proves quite important for understanding New Testament ethical discussion.

For example, in 1 Peter 4:15, the author warns his readers to avoid evil behavior that will necessarily bring about suffering: "But let none of you suffer as a murderer, a thief, an evildoer, or as a busybody in other people's matters" (NKJV). The sense of the final of these four terms, translated "busybody," has often puzzled commentators, not the least because it seems too innocuous to fit with the first three terms. Is the author referring to one who is inappropriately involved in the general affairs of others (as in most translations); or is one who breaks the law, specifically an "embezzler," the intended sense of the word, *allotriepiskopos*? (Yes, it is a mouthful!) The Greek word occurs nowhere else in the Bible or in the extant literature of the day until the fourth century CE. Yet the components of this compound word suggest that *allotriepiskopos* may refer to one who meddles in the affairs of others. By consulting Greco-Roman moral discourse, we find that meddling is a well-known concept in the Greco-Roman world.[32] If *allotriepiskopos* does refer to such a person, then what becomes clear from Greco-Roman moral discourse is that "meddling" is a serious offense. From a study of various Greco-Roman writings, the concept of meddling can be described as interfering with or performing activities outside of one's assigned sphere. It is aligned at times with such serious offenses as adultery. So this concept does fit

31. Greco-Roman sources also illuminated political issues of the day, which often directly impacted New Testament authors.

32. Greek authors use a number of related compound words to describe such a person and their activity (e.g., *polypragmosunē, periergos*). For more on this concept, see Jeannine K. Brown, "Just a Busybody? A Look at the Greco-Roman Topos of Meddling for Defining *allotriepiskopos* in 1 Peter 4:15," *Journal of Biblical Literature* 150 (Fall 2006): 527–46.

with the seriousness of murder, theft, and evildoing in 1 Peter 4:15. This fourth term is a good fit after all.

Finally, the issue of the dating of texts is a crucial one for using primary sources appropriately. It may seem obvious, but it bears repeating that if a source was written after ("postdates") the biblical book being interpreted, its usefulness for sketching the backdrop of the book diminishes significantly. This question of dating really comes back to the relevance issue. For example, Jewish second-temple literature that draws upon the Old Testament will not be directly helpful for interpreting the Old Testament.[33] It may be the case, however, that sources that only slightly postdate the biblical book in question provide a window into the general worldview of that era. Writers of the early church, for instance, may assist modern New Testament interpreters, since they sit so very close to the first century themselves.[34]

Taking Advantage of the Secondary Sources

In all likelihood, if you are just getting started in the study of the social contexts of the Bible, you will begin with secondary rather than primary sources. These are a great place to start, especially given the wealth of such materials currently being produced by biblical scholarship. Some of the types of resources available include Bible dictionaries, encyclopedias, and atlases; Bible commentaries; and books devoted to specific social-contextual issues.

Bible Dictionaries and Encyclopedias

Bible dictionaries and encyclopedias provide significant attention to the social world of the Bible. The individual entries, discussing such topics as "temple," "Hezekiah," and "denarius," are listed in alphabetical order. So if you are studying the letter to Philemon, in which Paul encourages Philemon to accept back his runaway slave, Onesimus, an entry on slavery in the first-century world will provide helpful background information for understanding the social dynamics assumed in Paul's letter.

Bible Atlases

A Bible atlas contains maps of the Mediterranean world, and Israel/Palestine specifically, for all biblical time periods. Gaining familiarity

---

33. Yet the Old Testament may be tremendously helpful for understanding the second-temple writing in question.

34. These writers from the early church are often called the early church fathers. "Patristics" (built on the Greek word for fathers) is the general term used to refer to the study of the early church writers. As we have already discussed, the issue of dating is also significant in the use of rabbinic material to illuminate the first-century Jewish world.

with the geographical terrain assumed and referenced in Scripture can provide important interpretive information. For example, we hear in the first verse of the book of Amos that the prophet Amos is from Tekoa. Later in the book, we hear Amos's prophetic words regarding places such as Samaria (4:1), Bethel (4:4), and Gilgal (4:4). If we consult a Bible atlas, we will see that Tekoa is in the southern kingdom of Judah, while Samaria, Bethel, and Gilgal are in the northern kingdom of Israel. Using this information, we will quickly grasp the nature of Amaziah's words to Amos, "Get out, you seer! Go back to the land of Judah" (7:12 NIV). Amos is an outsider, coming to Israel to prophesy a message of judgment. Amaziah, an Israelite priest, tells Amos to go home with his message of doom.

Commentaries: Introductory Section

Although the bulk of a commentary consists of verse-by-verse analysis of a book of the Bible, the introductory section of a commentary provides quite pointed contextual information. Typically the introduction discusses the book's author, audience, date, purpose, occasion, and provenance (location of its writing).

In addition to the introductory section of traditional commentaries, there is a newer genre of commentary that attends exclusively to background issues. These background commentaries combine the usefulness of a Bible dictionary with the easy access of a commentary. The background information is provided on a passage-by-passage basis. The reader consults the background commentary for the particular passage being studied by turning to, for instance, John 4, the story of Jesus and the woman at the well. Pertinent background information is provided by the commentator, such as the ostracism the woman seems to be experiencing in her village, the importance of Mount Gerizim in Samaritan worship, and particular messianic expectations among Samaritans.[35]

Books Devoted to Social-Contextual Issues

Given current concerted attention to social-contextual study of the Bible, there are many book-length treatments of various social world issues. Academic presses produce individual books on topics ranging from ancient Egypt to families in the ancient world to the identity and role of the Pharisees in the first century. There are also significant numbers of books that provide helpful and nuanced overviews of particular eras

35. See Craig S. Keener, *The InterVarsity Press Bible Background Commentary: New Testament* (Downers Grove, IL: InterVarsity, 1993), 272–74. There are companion volumes for the Old Testament as well. See also the Zondervan Illustrated Bible Backgrounds Commentary series.

and areas of the ancient world by drawing on the work of historians. For example, you can access books that focus on the Jewish backdrop of the New Testament or a history of the ancient Near East for illuminating the Old Testament.[36]

Some Cautions

Helped along by these primary and secondary resources, anyone can learn about the social world of the Bible. Yet a few cautions are in order as we study the social worlds of Scripture.

Underconstructing the Setting

First, there is the danger of underconstructing the social setting. We have already introduced this danger in chapter 7 when discussing biblical epistles. When we ignore or minimize the importance of the original context, our default position will be to fill in the textual backdrop with our own social context. In other words, we will assume that things in the biblical context are just like they are in our own. So there is no way to attain a reading of a biblical text without a context. Instead, when we underconstruct the original context we superimpose our own social context on Scripture. And this is not how to go about reading the Bible on its own terms.

When my husband and I were traveling in Europe a number of years ago, we witnessed a fascinating miscommunication. We were having lunch in a quaint restaurant in Innsbruck, Austria, having just arrived that day from a week in Italy. On our way into Innsbruck, we had seen the vista of fresh water cascading down the side of a steep and craggy mountainside. Now at lunch we overheard an Italian woman ask about the kinds of water that were for sale in the restaurant. Since we had consistently purchased bottled water during our stay in Italy, we understood her request. The waitress responded to the woman's question by saying that they served tap water. The Italian woman asked how that was spelled, clearly assuming that "tap water" was a brand of bottled water. The waitress simply reiterated that they served tap water. The Italian woman then queried explicitly about bottled water, noting that she had never heard of that particular brand (Tap Water). The dialogue went on for a bit longer, and we never did hear a resolution to it. It seems that, with both the language barrier and the cultural gap, this woman was not

36. See Bauer (*Biblical Resources*) and Danker (*Multipurpose Tools*) for suggested resources in this regard.

able to overcome the natural tendency to superimpose her own frame of reference on the waitress's words and meaning. This was essentially a case of underconstructing!

We can easily do the same when we come to the biblical text. An example is Amos 4:4: "Go to Bethel and sin." If we underconstruct the context, we will be prone to misunderstand what the prophet Amos means by these words. But if we understand that Bethel is one of the centers of worship in the northern country of Israel, we will be led to hear this statement as ironic. How can one go to a place of worship and sin? Asking this question forces us to look at the literary context of Amos. We discover that God is not pleased with the Israelites' sacrifices at worship, because they are not pursuing justice and mercy in their daily lives (Amos 4:1–2; 5:7–13, 21–24). So God speaks through Amos and ironically "invites" Israel to sin in their very act of worship, for that is in essence what they are doing. Their worship is not pleasing to God as long as their interactions with one another are tainted by injustice.[37]

Overconstructing the Setting

The opposite danger is to overconstruct the text's social setting. By overemphasizing the social context of a biblical text, the reader can cause the text itself to lose its distinctiveness. One example of overconstructing the social setting is the mirror-reading we discussed in chapter 7, in which each exhortation or argument in a biblical epistle is presumed to reflect a related problem being experienced by the letter's audience. Overconstructing the social setting can also occur in nonepistle texts. For example, the assumption that, when the Old Testament writers refer to the myths of their pagan neighbors (see the discussion of Gen. 1 above), these authors necessarily "buy into" the same mythological worldview, is another way of overconstructing the relationship between the text and its setting. While the Old Testament writers make reference to "Leviathan," a mythological sea creature that also appears in ancient Ugaritic texts, this does not necessarily imply that they share the same mythological assumptions as their Ugaritic neighbors. It is significant that the emphasis of relevant Old Testament texts is often on Yahweh's victory over Leviathan and the chaotic powers it represents (e.g., Ps. 74:14; Isa. 27:1). In this case, mythology is used in the service of monotheistic theology. It is important for interpretation to strike a balance between understanding

---

37. One way that Caucasian readers are prone to underconstruct the biblical context is to simply assume that biblical characters are "white." For a discussion of this tendency with regard to the Ethiopian eunuch, see Clarice J. Martin, "A Chamberlain's Journey and the Challenge of Interpretation for Liberation," *Semeia* 47 (1989): 105–35.

the social context of a biblical text and hearing the distinctive message of that text, which may be a critique of its social context.

Overgeneralizing about the Social Context

This final tendency is all too easy to fall into, since as we study the Bible we are students of cultural contexts other than our own. While the complexity of social, cultural, political, and religious factors that influence our own world is obvious to us, it is more difficult to see the same kinds of complexities in cultures that we are just beginning to study, including, and especially, ancient ones. Accordingly, the tendency to simplify is correspondingly greater. As we attempt to reconstruct aspects of an ancient culture, we will need to be careful not to assume that all people of that culture shared identical perspectives on all issues. Any time we assert, "All Israelites thought or did this," or "All first-century people believed this," we are in danger of overgeneralizing. The topic of women in the ancient world has often suffered from overgeneralization. Whether studying the rights, roles, and activities of women in ancient Israel or in first-century Jewish, Greek, or Roman society, we should be suspicious of all-or-nothing kinds of statements like, "No women were allowed to read or study the Law in Judaism," or "All Roman women had equal rights and status with men."[38] Both of these assertions suffer from overstatement in addition to overgeneralization. We will want to remind ourselves that disagreement over all sorts of topics abounded in the ancient world, and that reality is more complex than such simplistic statements allow. Avoiding overgeneralization will involve reading more widely in the primary sources and choosing balanced treatments of topics in secondary sources.

The Impact of Social World Analysis on Interpretation: An Example

In this chapter, I have argued for the importance of studying the social world of the Bible for adequate interpretation of it. We have discussed the various levels of the social world to be studied, the primary and secondary sources that guide us in our study, and some methodological pointers and cautions to help us as we read primary texts and do social world analysis. To conclude our discussion and illustrate what

---

38. The first statement may find partial support from rabbinic sources, but given that not all rabbinic materials reflect first-century realities, and not all rabbis in these sources agree with each other, we will want to be careful about applying this without much qualification to New Testament backgrounds.

the process of doing social world analysis might look like, let's explore the Jewish sect of the Pharisees and hear what we learn for interpretation of the Gospels.

What do we know about the Pharisees? If you would ask the average even semi-biblically informed person this question, you would probably hear a reply such as, all Pharisees were legalists. If ever there were a classic case of overgeneralization, this would fit the bill. Yet a careful look at the sources for information about Pharisees in the first century does not support such an overgeneralization. Instead, as we might now suspect, the picture is more complex. Our goal will be to see what we can learn about the Pharisees from primary and secondary sources, and then apply it to the study of the New Testament.[39]

Outside the New Testament, two primary sources provide us with information about the Pharisees: Josephus and rabbinic material. Neither seems interested in portraying what we might call the better qualities of the Pharisees.[40] But even in these sources, we hear things about Pharisees that do not fit the mold of myopic legalists. In fact, what we do learn about the Pharisees from Josephus and the Talmud, as well as the New Testament itself, might surprise us.

But first, we will want to understand the relation of the Torah, or law, to Judaism more broadly. As we look at the Old Testament, we see that the Torah was never intended to provide a way for Israel to earn God's approval (one aspect of the popular definition of legalism). God gave the law so that Israel would know how to live in the covenant relationship God had already established with them through Abraham and reaffirmed in their redemption from Egypt. Law was understood within the context of covenant. First-century Judaism was no more prone to legalism than any other religion, including twenty-first-century Christianity!

Second, the sources do not indicate that there was only one kind of Pharisee, so we ought to be cautious of overgeneralization. The Talmud acknowledges various types of Pharisees, one of which is termed a "born Pharisee," who is worthy of the name "Pharisee," in contrast to Pharisees who are ostentatious with their good works or lovers of reward, for example.[41] Contributing to this broader and richer picture of the Pharisees, the New Testament indicates that not all Pharisees

39. You will see references to a range of types of secondary sources in subsequent footnotes.

40. Remember that we should take the time to evaluate the vantage point of the primary sources we consult.

41. *Avot of Rabbi Nathan*, 45. It is quite possible that this Talmudic tradition postdates the first century CE. Nevertheless, the general notion that first-century Pharisaism is not monolithic but varied in its expressions does fit well with the picture we glean from other sources of the time. So the rabbinic material is illustrative vs. definitive in this case.

rejected the message of Jesus as Messiah. In John, we hear of Nicodemus, a Pharisee sympathetic to Jesus and his cause (John 3, 19). In Acts, we also hear of Pharisees who believed the message of Jesus (Acts 15:5).

Third, a common thread about the Pharisees from the primary sources (including the New Testament) indicates that their main concern was right interpretation of the Torah. For example, Josephus mentions that the Pharisees supposedly surpassed other Jews in their knowledge of the Law.[42] As Steve Mason concludes after looking at the evidence, "[The Pharisees] were a lay, not priestly, association who were thought to be expert in the laws; . . . they promoted their special living tradition in addition to the biblical laws; they were interested in issues of ritual purity and tithing."[43] This last part sounds familiar. The Pharisees were interested in ritual purity issues. In fact, the impetus for this interest in ritual purity was their desire to see the purity codes that applied to temple worship lived out in everyday life. I sometimes liken them in this regard to Bible camp counselors, who give that famous pep-talk on the last night of camp: "Let's not lose all that we've experienced with God here at camp; let's live with God every day, not just in the mountaintop experiences." The Pharisees wanted to live out the rigor and piety of what was experienced at temple all year long.[44]

Does this reconstructed snapshot of the Pharisees help us interpret the Gospels? Let's look at Matthew in particular to see what we might learn. Matthew is the Gospel that most frequently shows the Pharisees in conflict with Jesus. In particular, it is the Pharisees from the area of Galilee where Jesus spends much of his ministry who are most often at odds with Jesus (Matt. 8–16). This makes sense. Since these Galilean Pharisees were the local experts in interpreting the law, they would have been those most likely to come into direct conflict with Jesus, who was teaching, among other things, an alternative way of interpreting the Torah, in line with the Old Testament prophetic tradition, and in light of the arrival of the kingdom of God. Jesus and the Pharisees would not have been the only Jewish teachers in strong disagreement on this issue of Torah interpretation in the first-century context. Various Jewish groups vied for interpretive authority in relation to the Torah. It is what the Mishnah calls "making a fence around the Torah," that is, interpreting it in keeping with tradition. There was no single way of doing this in

42. *Life*, 38. For Josephus on the Pharisees, see also *Ant*. 6.8.2; 13.5.9; and 13.10.6.

43. Steve Mason, "Pharisees," in *Dictionary of New Testament Background*, ed. Craig A. Evans and Stanley E. Porter (Downers Grove, IL: InterVarsity, 2000), 786.

44. The Pharisee movement "encompassed nonpriests, who attempted to live out the holiness code of the temple in everyday life" (Hanson and Oakman, *Palestine in the Time of Jesus*, 147–48).

first-century Judaism. As Markus Bockmuehl notes, the clash between Jesus and the Pharisees involved "different ways of building that protective hermeneutical fence."[45]

So if the point of contention between Jesus and the Pharisees is interpretation of the law (and not primarily legalism as popularly defined), what is Jesus' critique of the Pharisees? If we look again to Matthew, we see that Jesus begins his critique by affirming that the Pharisees have a right to interpret the Law (23:2). But Jesus in Matthew has two issues with their perspective on the law. First, they themselves do not keep the law consistently (15:1–3; 23:2–3); in fact, at times their oral traditions result in disobedience to central commands of the Torah. For example, the tradition of the elders, about devoting to God what one would have dedicated to one's parents, can stand in the way of fulfilling the command to honor one's father and mother (15:3–6). Second, according to Jesus in Matthew, the Pharisees do not view the law through the right interpretive lens or center. In their interpretation, purity concerns outweigh more fundamental concerns, which Jesus defines as love (5:43–48; 7:12; 22:37–40), mercy (9:12–13; 12:7), justice, and faithfulness (23:23).[46] An important text in this regard occurs where Jesus speaks as follows:

> Woe to you, scribes and Pharisees, hypocrites! For you tithe mint and dill and cummin, and have neglected the weightier provisions of the law: justice and mercy and faithfulness; but these are the things you should have done without neglecting the others. (Matt. 23:23 NASB)

Notice that Jesus' critique is *not* that they have attended to the more minute demands of the law (another aspect of the popular definition of legalism). Rather, they have neglected the weightier matters of the Torah. Jesus' remedy is to put love, mercy, and justice at the center without neglecting the rest of the law.

This brief example is meant to illustrate that careful attention to the social world of the Bible helps us interpret the text more faithfully. By reconstructing the setting in which the text was written, we are more likely to hear the message of the text as it was intended. Another crucial factor to attend to as we read Scripture is its literary context. This topic will be our focus in chapter 10.

45. Markus Bockmuehl, *Jewish Law in Gentile Churches: Halakha and the Beginning of Christian Public Ethics* (Grand Rapids: Baker Academic, 2000), 4.
46. See Klyne Snodgrass, "Matthew and the Law," in *Treasures New and Old: Recent Contributions to Matthean Studies*, Society of Biblical Literature Symposium Series 1, ed. David R. Bauer and Mark Allan Powell (Atlanta: Scholars Press, 1996), 99–127.

Suggestions for Further Reading

Bauer, David R. *An Annotated Guide to Biblical Resources for Ministry*. Peabody, MA: Hendrickson, 2003.

Currid, John D. *Doing Archaeology in the Land of the Bible: A Basic Guide*. Grand Rapids: Baker Academic, 1999.

Danker, Frederick W. *Multipurpose Tools for Bible Study*. Rev. ed. Minneapolis: Fortress, 2003.

Hanson, Kenneth C., and Douglas E. Oakman. *Palestine in the Time of Jesus: Social Structures and Conflicts*. Minneapolis: Fortress, 1998.

Malina, Bruce J. *The New Testament World: Insights from Cultural Anthropology*. 3rd ed. Louisville: Westminster John Knox, 2001.

Sparks, Kenton L. *Ancient Texts for the Study of the Hebrew Bible: A Guide to the Background Literature*. Peabody, MA: Hendrickson, 2005.

Walton, John H. *Ancient Near Eastern Thought and the Old Testament: Introducing the Conceptual World of the Hebrew Bible*. Grand Rapids: Baker Academic, 2006.

10

Literary Context, Intertextuality, and Canon

After the fragmentation of previous years, there is still much to be learned by analyzing the [biblical books] as wholes. . . .

> Janice Capel Anderson, "Matthew," in *Treasures New and Old*

Oh you rascals—you are not instructed or versed in the Gospel, and you pick out verses from it without regard to their own context, and wrest them according to your own desire. It is like breaking off a flower from its roots and trying to plant it in a garden. But that is not the way: you must plant it with the roots and soil in which it is embedded. And similarly we must leave the Word of God its own proper nature.

> Huldrych Zwingli, *Of the Clarity and Certainty or Power of the Word of God* (1522 CE)

The Importance of Studying Literary Context

Words derive their meaning from their usage in literary context. How do we go about discerning the meaning of the word "buckle," for instance? We can look up the word in a dictionary and list any number of definitions or synonyms for buckle, but in the end we cannot know what the word means apart from the way it is used in a specific context. In fact, the verb "buckle" can mean quite contradictory things: to fasten together (as in buckling a seatbelt) or to fall apart (as in buckling under pressure). Only by hearing the word used in a context do we get a sense of its usage in any particular utterance.

In chapter 8, we talked about some dangers in the analysis of words apart from their use in particular contexts. The danger holds not only for individual words but also for sentences and ideas disengaged from context. We can, as Zwingli charges, extract Bible verses from their contexts and do with them as we will. But such an approach does not show a proper respect for the text as communicative act. It does not approach Scripture on its own terms.

If we want to come to the Bible on its own terms, we will pay attention to the literary context of any specific word, sentence, and even passage. None of these stand alone to communicate meaning. So it is not just a matter of hearing individual words in their contexts, although this is crucial. As Silva notes, "We do not normally convey meaning by single propositions, but by propositions that form part of a larger whole."[1] Even full-length passages or discourses take their meaning from the biblical book of which they are a part.

One of the most well-known chapters in the Bible, 1 Corinthians 13, is a beautiful, inspiring hymn to love. It is often used as a stand-alone text for weddings. Yet the literary context of 1 Corinthians 11–14 provides an added dimension to a reading of chapter 13, since it indicates that Paul is addressing problems arising from the corporate worship of the Corinthian church. Paul's assessment is that they are using the gifts that the Spirit has provided without the requisite of love. This results in arrogance and one-upmanship rather than in unity and the building up of the church. Using the analogy of a body, Paul argues that, since it is the Spirit who assigns gifts, all gifts are valuable and boasting therefore has no place alongside the gifts (1 Cor. 12; see especially 12:27–31). As Paul turns to extol the centrality of love in the practice of the gifts of the Spirit, his words are directed toward Corinthian worship gone astray.

In this context, 1 Corinthians 13 takes on a rather pointed critique: "If I speak in the tongues of mortals and of angels, but do not have love, I am a noisy gong or a clanging cymbal" (1 Cor. 13:1 NRSV). Since the Corinthians seem to be touting the gift of tongues as the greatest of gifts, Paul's opening words in chapter 13 function as an indictment of their behavior in worship. In the very practice of what they deem the most

1. Silva, *God, Language and Scripture*, 124.

important gift, they are simply producing noise if the gift of tongues is not accompanied by love.[2]

I hope it is becoming clear that we ought to read books of the Bible as wholes, since that is how their authors would have intended that they be read. This means that an author's utterance level ultimately extends to the whole of a biblical book. The method of reading select passages here and there, which is rather common in the Christian tradition, can lead to misreading if the literary context is ignored. "When we receive a letter from a friend, do we read the middle paragraph today, the last sentence next week, the introductory section two months from now? Unfortunately, many Christians use precisely that 'method' in their reading of [biblical] letters."[3] Attention to the literary context of the whole book avoids the problems that come from ignoring literary context.

Problems of Ignoring Whole-Book Context

Ignoring the literary context of a Bible verse or passage may lead to what is called "proof-texting." Hart defines proof-texting and its effects: "the smallest atoms of the text are torn away from their textual . . . contexts and reassembled within some other framework of interpretation, often in order to demonstrate a point that is anything but natural to them." Hart balances this by adding that it is possible to focus on a Bible verse or passage without doing harm to the integrity of the author's thought in context. "[Avoiding proof-texting] does not mean, of course, that individual sentences or phrases from Scripture may not function or be used in isolation, but simply that the implications and possible dangers of such use must always be fully considered."[4]

The latter warning is crucial. We must always be aware of the danger of misinterpreting an author's message when focusing on only part of a text. This does not mean we must avoid studying a single passage in depth, as is often done in preaching and teaching. We should, however, be careful to attend to the literary context of the passage in question, so that we are not ignoring its crucial role in understanding the meaning of the passage.

There is never a shortage of examples of isolating passages from their literary context. In worship settings, for instance, we tend to use Scrip-

2. The critique of the Corinthians resonates in other parts of 1 Cor. 13, as when the words used as negative corollaries to love are used earlier by Paul to describe the Corinthians themselves, e.g., "love is not arrogant" (*phusioō*; 13:4). Paul has already called the church arrogant (*phusioō*) at 4:18–19 and 5:2.

3. Silva, *God, Language and Scripture*, 125.

4. Hart, "Christian Approach to the Bible," 199.

ture selectively. This is particularly common in our use of the Psalms. Parts of lament psalms that emphasize praise to God are much more likely to be read aloud in corporate worship, while the rest of the psalm that deals with either lament or warning is left to the side. It is easy to use the first half of Psalm 95 in a worship context ("O come, let us sing for joy to the Lord, let us shout joyfully to the Rock of our salvation" [95:1 NIV]) and to leave out the latter verses that give a warning against hard-heartedness (95:8–11). Even in churches that follow prescribed readings in a lectionary for Scripture reading and preaching, the assigned passages are by necessity selective, and the text is sometimes treated in a more piecemeal fashion.[5] After illustrating the tendency to "sanitize" the text by excising certain difficult elements (a tendency we all have, whatever our church context), Mark Throntveit invites the reader to hear the text holistically even when it raises difficult issues: "Why not immerse yourself in the text as it came to us, whole and unexpurgated? Wrestle with God's wrath and Jesus' cursing the fig tree. Discover a God who 'hates' evil. Rejoice with Elijah's triumph over Ba'al on Mt. Carmel or the repentance of Manasseh."[6]

It is not only with the "harder" parts of Scripture that we tend toward proof-texting. It is often the case that the more well-known the passage, the easier it is to proof-text it. A single verse that fits this description is Philippians 4:13: "I can do all things through Him who strengthens me." While this verse probably has been used to claim strength for any number of endeavors, in the immediate context Paul is interested in one particular Christian attitude—contentment (4:10–19).

> I know how to get along with humble means, and I also know how to live in prosperity; in any and every circumstance I have learned the secret of being filled and going hungry, both of having abundance and suffering need. I can do all things through Him who strengthens me. (Phil. 4:12–13 NASB)

The problem with proof-texting this verse is not that it can never be legitimately applied to other Christian activities.[7] Rather, something is lost when the verse is extracted from its context. In this case, the strength that Paul claims to receive from the Lord for learning contentment

5. For an example from 2 Sam. 7, see Mark A. Throntveit, "Face to Face: Should I Preach from a Lectionary? Why?" *Word and World* 24 (Fall 2004): 443, 446. See the counterpoint to Throntveit's perspective in the same volume by Arland J. Hultgren, "Face to Face: Should I Preach from a Lectionary? Yes!" (442, 444).

6. Throntveit, "Face to Face," 446.

7. Such a generalization, however, would need to be defended from the context of Philippians itself.

may be sorely needed in our own settings. For a culture that revels in "having it all," those people with plenty are often no closer to learning contentment than those who struggle to get by. By pulling Philippians 4:13 out of its literary context, we miss the invitation to learn contentment by relying on the Lord's strength—an invitation that is thoroughly countercultural.

Finally, the tendency toward proof-texting is nowhere as common as in topical Bible study. Part of this stems from the procedure typically followed in topic-oriented studies. It is all too common for a topic study to begin with a conclusion about the topic and then proceed to amass verses, although seldom full passages, to support the predetermined conclusion. The tendency then is to assume a certain way of reading the chosen verses rather than hearing each text well in its literary context. Yet this kind of procedure is not a requirement for topical study. It is quite possible to do a topical study using a much more inductive approach.[8] This will involve trying to find larger portions of a biblical book that expressly deal with the topic at hand. It will also be important to study the literary context of each verse or passage used to ensure that the author's message is heard and maintained.[9] By allowing the ideas of the text to emerge inductively, rather than looking for texts that fit our preset ideas, we will be much more likely to honor the author's intentions on the whole-book level.

Attending to the Whole-Book Context

A good place to begin as we focus on the whole-book context is with the realization that study of Scripture has often been done in opposite fashion. In fact, the early years of modern biblical scholarship are typified by an atomistic method. In methodologies such as source criticism, form criticism, and even early redaction criticism, the text was most often studied in its smaller parts.[10] Sometimes the assumption that the text should be studied at the level of the whole book was undermined by questions of a book's integrity.[11] It is to biblical studies that Anderson's

8. An inductive approach is typified by study of component parts of a passage, discourse, or book to determine the meaning of the whole. In this method, study moves primarily from the parts to the whole rather than from the whole to the parts. Extrapolating the meaning of the parts from the whole is called deduction.

9. Cf. Appendix E for additional guidelines for pursuing topical or thematic study of Scripture.

10. See Appendix B for a review of what these various methods are about.

11. Integrity is the issue of whether a book was originally one book or a composite of a number of texts. In some of the New Testament letters, it has been argued that multiple

comment, which begins this chapter, is directed: "After the fragmentation of previous years, there is still much to be learned by analyzing the [biblical books] as wholes."[12]

As we have seen in our discussion of proof-texting, atomization has been a tendency not only of biblical scholarship. In the practicing of teaching and preaching in the church, focused attention on whole books has often been lacking. So it will take conscious effort to overcome the tendency to isolate individual verses or passages from their literary contexts.

What we want to cultivate is a big-picture mentality when reading Scripture. This may be easier for global thinkers than for those who are more analytical in their makeup. Yet no matter what our personal inclinations, attention to literary context will help us hear the biblical authors more clearly. When my daughter Kate was a preschooler, she loved to hear stories about Jesus. She would routinely say, "Tell me a story about Jesus, Mom." I would recall a story from the Gospels and tell her about the time Jesus healed the leper, or talked to the disciples about how important children are, or raised Lazarus back to life. Eventually, it seemed to me that I had told her all the stories of Jesus from the Gospels, many more than once. But she continued to ask for a story about Jesus. So one day, I decided to put my conviction about emphasis on larger sections of narratives to the test: could attention to literary context actually work with a five-year-old? I began telling Kate about one of the big stories about Jesus in the Bible—the one that Matthew told. And I told her that Matthew wanted at one point in his story to tell us about the miracles of Jesus and how important it is to follow him. So Matthew told a whole lot of stories about Jesus healing people, first a leper, then a centurion's servant, and then Peter's mother-in-law. I ended up telling each of the stories from Matthew 8–9 sequentially, so that Kate could get the feel for a whole section of the gospel narrative. At the end, I asked Kate why she thought Matthew told all these stories about Jesus healing people, forgiving sins, and calming the sea. She did not hesitate; "So that we know that Jesus is powerful," was her response. Not a bad summary, I thought. Even a child can get a sense of the big picture of a narrative when it is sketched out for her.

Structural Clues for Seeing the Whole

As a first step to attending to the whole of a biblical book, it is helpful to pay attention to its structure. Studying a book's structure assists in

letters were combined to produce the present form. Analysis was then focused on the individual letters that were prior to the final form.

12. Janice Capel Anderson, "Matthew: Sermon and Story," in *Treasures New and Old*, 247n32.

discerning the movement of a biblical book, in part because it clarifies the relationships between sections of the book. By emphasizing the importance of structure, I am not arguing that all biblical authors had a specific outline in mind when writing, and that our goal is to reproduce such an outline. In fact, in one sense, applying a detailed outline to a biblical book is an artificial process. Yet because authors deliberately shape the direction of their writing, asking questions about structure will help us discern that movement or sequence more clearly. In the end, if we get a better sense of the whole of a book, even through a somewhat artificial outline, we will be in a better position to understand the relationships of the parts of the book to the whole.

In the church context of my youth, Romans 9–11 seemed to be considered parenthetical to the rest of Romans. Even though I was fairly familiar with the Bible by the time I was a young adult, I remember being surprised by the content of Romans 9–11, thinking I had not been exposed to it as a coherent argument. So is this section of Romans tangential to Paul's wider argument? Or is it the climax of his earlier chapters? Or is the climax still to come in chapters 14–15, where the issue of Jew/Gentile relations comes to practical fruition? Attending to the structure of Romans will lead us to make a preliminary determination about this. A thorough study of the book may result in a reassessment of our proposed outline. Yet the very act of outlining—of attending to structural issues—pushes us to ask questions about what is primary and what is secondary in the flow of Paul's argument. And these questions are important for interpretation. As Schleiermacher noted, misunderstanding occurs "if I take as the main thought what is only a secondary thought."[13]

Some of the structural features that help us to see what authors are up to as they write include formulaic markers, chiasm,[14] inclusio, climactic moments, alternation, and contrast.[15] We might call these macrostylistic features, since they are used in the broad scope of a biblical book to shape its movement. We have already described some of these structural

13. Schleiermacher, *Hermeneutics and Criticism*, 28.

14. For some reason, chiasm (an ABBA pattern) gets overapplied to biblical texts. In other words, it is the case that chiasm is seen in passages and books where it likely is not present! For such an overapplication, see John Breck, *The Shape of Biblical Language: Chiasmus in the Scriptures and Beyond* (Crestwood, NY: St. Vladimir's Seminary Press, 1994). Breck's conclusion is wildly overextended: "To return to the question posed at the onset of this study, How are we to read the Bible? The evidence indicates that we should read it 'chiastically,' according to the same principles of concentric parallelism by which it was composed" (350). See Stein's warning about overapplying chiasm in "Reading the Bible," 73–74.

15. For more categories with helpful examples from biblical narrative, see Bauer, *Structure*, 13–19.

features when discussing biblical genres. An author may use any number of these features in writing. Attending to them can help us discern the organizational pattern of a particular book and so illuminate the author's movement of thought. In the Gospel of Luke, for instance, the author begins his narrative by alternating accounts of the conceptions and births of John the Baptist and Jesus (Luke 1–2). By doing this, the author encourages the reader to compare and contrast John and Jesus. Through the similarities in the accounts, God's restoration of Israel is shown to be set in motion by these miraculous births. The differences illustrate that Jesus is greater than John in both function and identity.

Thematic Clues for Seeing the Whole

Identifying themes can also be helpful as we attend to the whole of a book. By asking what themes the author is developing, we will tend to "major on the majors." In other words, we will ideally focus in interpretation where the author was focusing in writing. Themes may also give the reader clues about the structure of the book by delineating book sections.

Looking for themes may be as simple as listening for repeated words, phrases, or ideas. Yet careful attention to these repetitions will be one of the signposts on the way toward the biblical author's message. We will, however, want to distinguish between various purposes of repetition. Words or phrases may be repeated because they signal a theme. Or the repetition may be more stylistic or ornamental in nature, since effective writing often involves repetition. Therefore, we ought to analyze the importance of any particular set of repetitions for their semantic weight or meaning value. We will want to focus particularly on those "repetitions that might be significant for getting at the meaning, structure, or persuasive strategy of the passage within the larger work. . . . [Identifying themes] can lead to some surprising insights into the ways that something as simple as verbal repetition contributes to the larger rhetorical and ideological goals of the author."[16]

As we have seen in chapter 7, themes may emerge in more than one way in a book. Frequently, a theme will emerge clearly by consistent repetition throughout a book, as with the theme of disobedience in the books of 1 and 2 Kings. Near the beginning of the narration about most kings of Israel and Judah, we hear a statement about their conduct before God. "He did evil in the eyes of the Lord" is a frequent indictment of various kings.[17] It is much more prevalent than the converse statement,

---

16. deSilva, *New Testament*, 908.
17. E.g., 1 Kings 11:6; 15:26; 21:25; 22:52; 2 Kings 3:2; 8:18; 13:11; 14:24; 15:24.

"He did what was right in the eyes of the Lord." The former marker emphasizes the theme of royal disobedience, which in turn is closely tied to the theme of idolatry in the books of 1 and 2 Kings.

Themes may also be specific or unique to a certain part of a book—a kind of thematic clustering. New Testament letters often move along by virtue of different, but related, themes, given that authors of letters frequently move through their material topically. For example, Paul in 1 Corinthians highlights the theme of resurrection in chapter 15, so that every part of 1 Corinthians 15 deals with resurrection in one way or another.

A theme may also appear at the beginning and the end of a book as "bookends" to it. This device, as we have noted, is called an inclusio.[18] The book of Ecclesiastes has such an inclusio. Other than the book's heading (Eccles. 1:1) and final conclusion (12:9–14), the book begins and ends with the statement: "'Vanity of vanities,' says the preacher, 'all is vanity!'" (Eccles. 1:2; 12:8 NASB). This idea is reinforced by the frequent repetition of the vanity of labor, pleasure, and riches. Inclusio can also be used by authors to delineate a section of a book. For example, the middle section of Mark (8:22–10:52) focuses on sacrificial discipleship and the difficulties that Jesus' disciples have in understanding such self-denial. This section is "bookended" by two narratives of blind men receiving their sight (Mark 8:22–26; 10:46–52). While these men receive their physical sight from Jesus, the disciples continue to be "blind" to the way of the cross that Jesus travels and that he expects them to follow as well.

Finally, themes are often interwoven with other communicative strategies that emphasize their thematic status. For example, in John's Gospel, themes are combined with particular Jewish festival settings to emphasize some aspects of Jesus' identity in relation to his followers. For instance, the setting of John 6 is the Jewish Passover, in which unleavened bread plays an important role (see Exod. 12:1–20). The Passover becomes the setting for Jesus' feeding of the five thousand (John 6:1–15), his claim to be the bread of life (6:35; see 6:32–33), and the dialogue that surrounds this claim (6:25–59). Thus, the motif of bread, the Passover setting, and the controversy around Jesus' claim to be the bread of life all work together to highlight Jesus' identity and role as the sustenance of his people (see John 6:53–58).

Other Literary-Contextual Issues

Attending to the whole-book context raises other important issues. For example, genre is discerned at the whole-book level. We are not able

18. See chap. 7 for this rhetorical feature.

to identify the genre of a whole book by simply appealing to one section or part of the book. The overarching genre emerges only at the book level. We should not conclude, for instance, that the book of Chronicles is either a genealogy or a poetic book, even though genealogy takes up the first nine chapters of 1 Chronicles, and a lengthy psalm of David appears in 1 Chronicles 16. Instead, we need to determine the genre category that describes the book most broadly, in this case, historical narrative. In one sense, the question of the macrogenre of a book is a speech-act inquiry.[19] We are asking what the author intends to do at the whole-book level. The choice of genre is fundamental to the fulfillment of these authorial purposes. And determining the genre chosen will help the interpreter understand the specific parts of the work and their relationship to the whole. Once we understand Chronicles as a narrative and treat it as such, the purposes of the various subgenres within that narrative, like genealogy and poetry, will become clearer.

Another aspect of the biblical text that requires careful attention to literary context is what we might call "authorial attitude." This language comes from relevance theory. According to relevance theory, the question of the author's attitude toward what is spoken is a crucial one for interpretation.[20] Now in many cases, we assume a writer's attitude toward what he or she has written to be rather straightforward: the author is communicating what he or she believes to be right, true, important, or helpful. Yet this is not always the case. There are times when the author does not "hold to" what he or she explicitly says and readily expects the reader to figure this out.[21] To figure this out, the reader must pay attention to the literary context of the utterance in question.

Take the opening line of Jane Austen's *Pride and Prejudice*: "It is a truth universally acknowledged that a single man in possession of a fortune must be in want of a wife."[22] With no previous context, the reader must make a preliminary decision about the narrator's attitude toward this utterance. Yet given a proper genre expectation (that of novel), most readers are quick to assume that the opening line is ironic. Why? Because the statement violates what we know to be true, namely, that not all rich men need a wife.[23] Given this experiential incongruity, we not

19. For an introduction to speech-act theory, see chap. 2.

20. For relevance theory, other important interpretive questions are (1) What is a speaker saying? (2) What is a speaker implying? and (3) What is the intended context? See Green, "Context and Communication," 23.

21. As in the cases of irony, hyperbole, and jokes.

22. See Pratt for the example and its relation to relevance principles (*Literary Discourse*, 16–17).

23. Proper attention to historical context will be important for this as well, since the use of "want" in English during the early nineteenth century indicates one's need, not one's desire.

only balk at this truth claim, but we also resist the additional claim that all people acknowledge the original claim! Even if it were true that all rich men were in need of matrimony, it is far less likely that all people everywhere would agree with this statement. By using overstatement, Austen clues the reader into her ironic stance. The preliminary decision that the opening statement is ironic is confirmed time and again in the early chapters of *Pride and Prejudice*, where various comic characters hold similarly illogical views. So contextual features as well as extra-linguistic factors (such as the reader's knowledge of what is and is not universally acknowledged and what single rich men need) signal the irony of the opening line.

Determining speaker attitude is also important as we read the Bible. Irony, for example, is used effectively across the Bible. We find a beautiful example in Ruth:

> So [Ruth] departed and went and gleaned in the field after the reapers; and she happened to come to the portion of the field belonging to Boaz, who was of the family of Elimelech. (Ruth 2:3 NASB)

Recalling that Elimelech was Naomi's husband (1:2–3), the fact that her daughter-in-law, Ruth, just "happens" to show up at that particular field provides a signal of possible irony. The language is quite striking really: something like "it happened that she happened upon. . . ."[24] The reader, who has already heard of the great misfortune of Naomi from God's hand (1:21), may suspect that, while Ruth had no intention in choosing that particular field, God did. By the end of the story, it is quite clear that God has orchestrated the connection between Ruth and Boaz (4:14). So if the writer's attitude toward the statement at 2:3 is incongruous with the authorial point of view clearly indicated elsewhere, then the reader is right to attribute irony to this statement. In Ruth, as in Old Testament narrative generally, there is no "it just so happened" from God's perspective.[25]

Skills for Addressing the Whole-Book Context

We have already discussed literary context from a variety of angles. We will conclude our discussion by getting practical. Here are a few

24. In Hebrew, this phrase consists of two different forms of the same root (*qārāh*). Bush renders the phrase "as it happened she came upon" and states that it indicates a lack of intention on Ruth's part (Frederic W. Bush, *Ruth/Esther*, Word Biblical Commentary [Dallas: Word, 1996], 104).

25. Ibid., 106.

exegetical skills that are especially helpful for studying literary context, especially books as wholes.

First, the skill of *outlining* a book is a good one to cultivate. Although I have already mentioned that we need to be careful in attributing detailed outlines to the biblical authors, this does not mean that outlining books of the Bible is not a helpful heuristic tool. In outlining, we look for natural breaks in the flow of thought. These, in turn, help us to understand the movement of the book as a whole. We might begin by reading through the book a few times, identifying major and minor shifts in topic, focus, or theme. In addition to shifts in subject matter, some clues that signal section changes are audience change, change of personal pronouns (e.g., "we" to "you" in Eph. 1:12–13), and "seams" or transitions. In narrative, we could also look for changes of setting, climactic points, and shifts in focal characters. Do not be afraid if your assessment of section breaks disagrees with either the paragraphing in your translation or with chapter and verse divisions. Chapter and verse markings were not part of the Bible's original documents; they were added later in the process of dissemination and use.

Another crucial skill for exegesis is *summarizing*—that is, reading a section of text and condensing its main ideas into a few words. One reason summarizing is such an important skill is that it allows you to keep a mental log of the ideas of an author in a larger section of text. I may not be able to keep the entire text of Philippians 3 in my head at once, but I am able to attend to brief summaries of the seven to eight paragraphs of Philippians 3:2–4:1. These can help me follow Paul's train of thought in this section of Philippians, which could be summarized as follows: Paul warns against those who place confidence in human (ethnic, religious) identity markers (3:2–4a), conceding that if anyone could do so it would be himself (3:4b–6). Yet Paul has treated all that was gain to him to be loss for the purpose of knowing Christ and attaining resurrection (3:7–11). Not that Paul has already "arrived" at this goal, but he continues to strive for it (3:12–14), and he encourages all believers to do the same (3:15–16). The Philippian believers should follow the examples of Paul and all those who live rightly rather than those who are focused on their own desires. In this way, believers show that they are citizens of God's reign, awaiting resurrection (3:17–4:1).

Summarizing is also an important skill when it comes to studying a single passage in greater depth. In this case, we might provide a bit more detail in our summary of a single passage than we would when summarizing a number of passages in the outlining process. For example, Philippians 3:7–11 might be summarized as follows: Paul considers all things loss for the purposes of knowing Christ, completely identifying with Christ, and attaining final resurrection. By developing a summary of a passage, we force ourselves to determine which ideas are central and which are secondary. And as we reread and continue to study the passage, we will want to be ready to refine our summary, since summaries (our approximation of the author's key ideas) are always works in progress.

Third, *identifying themes* is an important exegetical skill related to literary context. Looking for repeated words, phrases, and even sentences will help us identify an author's themes. (Concordances are helpful tools for this type of theme identification and verification.) In addition, a theme may be emphasized through use of a contrasting idea. Psalm 1, for instance, highlights the "way" of the righteous person (Ps. 1:1–2, 6) by indicating its opposite. The way of the righteous individual is antithetical to walking "in the counsel of the wicked," standing "in the way of sinners," or sitting "in the seat of mockers" (Ps. 1:1 NIV).

Even when there is little verbal repetition, thematic *ideas* may recur in a text. For example, Luke develops the theme of the restoration of Israel in his initial chapters, even though the language used to express this theme of restoration is quite varied. We see the theme early on at 1:16, when the angel prophesies that John the Baptist "will turn many of the people of Israel to the Lord their God." The angel speaking later to Mary states that Jesus will be given "the throne of his ancestor David" (Luke 1:32 NRSV). With David's name the context of restoration is evoked. According to Jewish hopes in the Old Testament and in some second-temple writings, one from the line of David would be enthroned over Israel at the time of restoration (see other Davidic references at 1:27, 69; 2:4, 11). The theme of restoration is also apparent in Zechariah's prophetic hymn (1:68–69), where God's visitation and redemption of Israel are mentioned, and where the Abrahamic covenant is said to be fulfilled in the ministries of first John and then Jesus.

Finally, *identifying the function* of a particular text in relation to its literary context is important for addressing the whole-book context. It is possible to spend considerable energy and skills determining connections of text to literary context, but to leave the crucial question of function unaddressed. How does the specific passage being studied function in relation to the whole of the book?[26] By asking about function, we honor the way that utterances not only say things but also do things, for function is really a speech-act question. For example, Luke 4:16–30, Luke's narration of Jesus' preaching and rejection in Nazareth, certainly captures themes that are addressed elsewhere in Luke, including the Spirit, ministry to those who are marginalized, and Gentile inclusion. Yet it is Luke's emphasis on this story through his expansion and care-

26. Or the prior question of its function in relation to its immediate context.

ful placement that allows us to hear its great significance in the story line of the third Gospel. Luke makes this account of Jesus' reading from Isaiah's picture of kingdom restoration his lead story for the ministry of Jesus (4:14 begins the part of the Gospel devoted to Jesus' ministry).[27] By making it the lead story, Luke shows that it functions to define Jesus' ministry in Luke's Gospel. By asking the function question, we move closer to communicative intention.

The Canonical Context and Intertextuality

We have been focusing on the biblical book level as we have discussed literary context. In fact, our discussion of biblical interpretation has focused primarily on the level of individual books of the Bible. This emphasis has been intentional, since it is at the book level that we hear the individual authors of Scripture speaking.[28] As Richard Hays warns: "We must let the individual voices [of the biblical authors] speak if we are to allow the New Testament to articulate a word that may contravene our own values and desires. Otherwise, we are likely to succumb to the temptation of flipping to some comforting cross-reference to neutralize the force of any particularly challenging passage we may encounter."[29]

Yet hearing well the individual biblical authors in their literary contexts is not the final task for those who hold to the Bible as Scripture. We will want to attend to the canonical context of the Bible as well. The Christian canon refers to the sixty-six books that comprise the Old and New Testaments (for Protestant Christians). It is at the canonical level that a particularly Christian interpretation of Scripture emerges. But what does reading in canonical context mean? And what might it look like in practice?

Intertextuality: Other Texts Assumed in the Text

Before answering more directly the question of canonical interpretation, it might be helpful to describe the phenomenon of intertextuality more broadly. Intertextuality is the notion that texts are mutually interdependent. "Each and every text forms part of a network of texts from which it derives

27. Recall our discussion (chap. 7, sec. 3) of the value of thematic versus purely chronological placement in Greco-Roman biography.

28. This is true even of authors of multiple books, like Paul. While it may be helpful to hear how Galatians might inform our understanding of Romans, we should be careful not to make Galatians determinative for the meaning of Romans.

29. Richard B. Hays, *The Moral Vision of the New Testament: A Contemporary Introduction to New Testament Ethics* (San Francisco: HarperSanFrancisco, 1996), 188.

its meaning."[30] Intertextuality can thus include a canonical reading of the Bible. It can also refer to the ways that individual biblical books assume and refer to other earlier biblical and nonbiblical texts. Let's begin with the latter category before moving to the issue of canonical context.[31]

Exodus assumes some knowledge of the story of Genesis (e.g., Exod. 1:1, 8). Acts assumes knowledge of the Gospel of Luke (Acts 1:1). Matthew quotes Isaiah (e.g., Matt. 15:7–9) and alludes to the Psalms (e.g., Ps. 73:1 in Matt. 5:8). Jude refers to the Jewish pseudepigraphic book of Enoch. Revelation invokes the imagery of Daniel and Ezekiel. This is the phenomenon of intertextuality. We will want to look carefully at prior texts that inform a biblical text, so that we understand the author's purposes in assuming, citing, or alluding to other texts. This is distinct from the cross-referencing Hays refers to when he warns of neutralizing the text. Cross-referencing systems in various translations do not necessarily distinguish between texts that are used and assumed by a biblical author and other texts that could not have been known by that author because they postdate the time of writing. For example, we should not assume that Paul knows Revelation as he writes 1 Thessalonians, since the latter predates Revelation by a number of decades.

Let's illustrate how attention to intertextuality may assist in interpretation. In 1 Samuel 1 we read the poignant story of Hannah, unable to have children, who prays intensely for a child while worshiping at Shiloh with her husband. She asks the Lord to remember her by giving her a son. After she is blessed by Eli, she returns home. "They rose early in the morning and worshiped before the LORD; then they went back to their house at Ramah. And Elkanah knew Hannah his wife, and the LORD remembered her" (1 Sam. 1:19 ESV). The verb "remembered" is only used with the Lord as subject at these two points in Samuel (1:11, 19), but the reader of Samuel may recall its use in earlier parts of the Old Testament. When the Lord "remembers" in Genesis and Exodus, this activity is often tied to God's covenant with Israel (see *zākar* in Gen. 8:1; 19:29; Exod. 2:24). If the writer of Samuel is invoking this association, then the reader should hear covenantal overtones in the story of Hannah and the birth of her son, Samuel.[32]

---

30. Kristen Nielsen, *Intertextuality and Hebrew Bible*, Supplements to Vetus Testamentum 80 (Leiden: Brill, 2000), 17.

31. To keep the two levels distinct, I will hereafter use "intertextuality" to refer to what an author does with antecedent texts (e.g., assumes them, cites them, alludes to them) and "canonical context" to refer to the relationship of the books in the Christian Bible given their canonical connection.

32. "'Remembered' [*zākar*] suggests the initiation of a major new activity by the covenant-making God" (Robert D. Bergen, *1, 2 Samuel*, New American Commentary [Nashville: Broadman & Holman, 1996], 70).

Yet how do we go about determining if a prior text is being alluded to in the text at hand? Mark Powell identifies three criteria for determining the legitimacy of possible intertextual dependence. First, availability refers to the plausibility of the author's (and readers') knowledge of the alluded text. We have already mentioned the importance of this criterion. Powell's second criterion is the degree of repetition—the extent to which the features of the alluded text are repeated in the text at hand. The greater the degree of repetition, the more likely is the allusion. Third, thematic coherence refers to the strength of relationship between the potential allusion's effect and the overall sense of the text at hand. Adequate coherence provides support for the author's use of the potential allusion.[33] The greater the satisfaction of these three criteria, the more likely is the intertextual connection.

A major area of intertextuality in the Bible is the use of the Old Testament in the New Testament. It will come as no surprise that New Testament authors make consistent use of the Old Testament in their writings. It has become a rather commonplace argument that New Testament authors tend to ignore Old Testament literary contexts when citing or alluding to texts. The accusation has often been that New Testament authors routinely proof-text. A careful look at the data, however, may provide reasons for reconsideration. Recent work done in this area has suggested that New Testament authors may be much more attuned to the contexts of their Old Testament sources than previously argued.[34] In addition, it will help us to realize that New Testament authors draw upon the Old Testament for varied purposes. A look at these purposes will keep us from overgeneralizing about their intentions in their use of the Old Testament.

Before exploring these varied purposes, we should remind ourselves that when the Old Testament is referred to in the New Testament, it is not simply a textual phenomenon, but also a story phenomenon. That is, by citing an Old Testament text that speaks to part of the central story line of Israel, that text may evoke the story itself. Lindbeck comments that "it was the whole of [Israel's story] which [the early Christians] appropriated."[35] The Old Testament text then might be used by a New Testament writer to accomplish one or more of the following purposes:

- To support a part of the author's argument, as in the use of Psalm 34:12–16 in 1 Peter 3:8–12

33. Mark Allan Powell, *Chasing the Eastern Star: Adventures in Biblical Reader-Response Criticism* (Louisville: Westminster John Knox, 2001), 101–2.

34. E.g., Richard Beaton, *Isaiah's Christ in Matthew's Gospel* (Cambridge: Cambridge University Press, 2002). Peter Enns covers the topic of the use of the Old Testament in the New in a thoroughgoing way in *Inspiration and Incarnation: Evangelicals and the Problem of the Old Testament* (Grand Rapids: Baker Academic, 2005), 113–65.

35. Lindbeck, "Story-Shaped Church," 43.

- To show the fulfillment of an Old Testament promise in a New Testament event, as in the promise of Yahweh's return to his people announced by his messenger as now fulfilled in Jesus, the Messiah, announced by John the Baptist (Isa. 40:3 in Mark 1:2–3)
- To evoke key parts of Israel's story (i.e., significant salvation-history themes), as in Matthew's use of a genealogy to begin his Gospel; the genealogy in effect retells the story of Israel from Abraham to Jesus (Matt. 1:2–17)
- To provide an analogy or "event connection" between the Old and New Testaments, as in Paul's reference to the fate of Old Testament believers in the wilderness as a warning for what could happen to the Corinthians if they persist in their idolatry (Exod. 32:6 in 1 Cor. 10:1–11)[36]
- To provide an illustration, as in Jesus' comparison of hypocrites among his contemporaries with hypocrites in Isaiah's time (Isa. 29:13 in Matt. 15:3–9)
- To stress continuity between some aspect of the new covenant and the Old Testament, as in the use of the examples of David (Ps. 32:1–2) and Abraham (Gen. 15:6) in Romans 4

In the end, the topic of the use of the Old Testament in the New Testament is really one that bridges intertextuality and canonical reading, since it begs the larger question of the relationship between the Old and New Testaments.

Canonical Interpretation

We need to acknowledge that when we follow the New Testament in assuming that the Old Testament, or Hebrew Bible, is intimately connected to the events that occurred around the person of Jesus of Nazareth, we are making a confessional move, related to our religious beliefs. Since the Hebrew Bible has functioned and continues to function as Scripture within Judaism, the assumption that the Old and New Testaments fit together into a single story is the expression of a theological conviction.[37] To call the sixty-six canonical books "Scripture" is to confess a particularly Christian way of reading the whole. Yet, as we have

36. As Lindbeck notes, "It was not only the favorable parts [of the Old Testament] that [early Christians] applied to themselves. All the wickedness of the Israelites in the wilderness could be theirs" as well ("Story-Shaped Church," 43).

37. For a helpful resource on the topic of a Christian reading of the Old Testament, see Christopher J. H. Wright, *Knowing Jesus through the Old Testament* (Downers Grove, IL: InterVarsity, 1995).

emphasized in chapter 6, we need not apologize for coming to the Bible with a confessional, theological stance. "The Bible is an overwhelmingly religious book, and the requirement to read it in strictly nonreligious terms is unreasonable."[38] All people who read the Bible, even those who come from a nonreligious perspective, read from some particular stance, rather than from some supposedly objective location.

What we are confessing when we read the Christian Scriptures canonically is that they are best read this way—that the texts themselves point to a way of reading with Old and New Testaments conjoined. "Christians are precisely those who confess the Messiah of the Jews to be also the Lord of the church, and they can never sever the bond with Israel and its Scriptures without suffering the loss of their own identity. But these same [Hebrew] Scriptures are, nonetheless, transformed in our reading of them as part now of a different 'whole'—namely, Christian Scripture."[39] While we can defend this position as persuasive, we should never assume that everyone who reads the Bible holds this position, or that any other way of reading the Bible is illogical or indefensible.

The unity of Scripture is a foundational assumption behind a Christian canonical interpretation. By assuming a canon, that is, the normative stance of the Christian Bible, we presume its essential unity. While allowing for each author's distinctive purposes and message, the Christian affirmation is that the diversity of the sixty-six books fits within a broader theological and narrative unity. All of Scripture together points to a coherent picture of God's redemptive work in creation and humanity. The Old Testament is not at odds with the New Testament in this picture. And Matthew's message about Jesus' work does not contradict Paul's message, even though they communicate their messages through different genres and often by using different language.

So what does it mean to read the Bible canonically? First, reading canonically does not mean that we ride roughshod over the particularities of individual biblical books. Specific biblical authors will communicate in ways that reflect unique theological emphases and specific historical audiences. We must honor these distinctions before seeking the resonances between their varied testimonies. Much of this book has focused on how we might hear individual biblical authors well.

Yet if we read the Bible as Scripture, we will not end our interpretive endeavors there. Reading canonically means that we will listen for the overarching biblical story as we read the biblical text. We will engage in biblical theology—the theology of the whole Bible—not only the theology

38. Al Wolters, "Confessional Criticism and the Night Visions of Zechariah," in *Renewing Biblical Interpretation*, 110.
39. Hart, "Christian Approach to the Bible," 199.

of Isaiah or the theology of John.[40] After carefully attending to the messages of the individual books of the Bible, we will be drawn into reflection on the theological vision that emerges from the whole of Scripture. The theological vision will take the shape of story, time and time again. "A canonical interpretation is one that reads individual passages and books as elements within the divine drama of redemption."[41] For even as we take hold of a biblical theme like the mercy of God, we will see this theme concretely enacted throughout the biblical story in Yahweh's redemption of Israel from slavery, which has its mirror image and fulfillment in the redemption of Israel through the death of Jesus the Messiah. And just as Israel's redemption was part of God's larger purpose to redeem all the nations, so in Jesus that purpose finds its full expression in Jesus' death on behalf of the whole world (1 John 2:2).

A key question that will assist us in the task of canonical interpretation is, How does the text I am studying draw upon and contribute to the overarching story of God's redemptive activity in and through his covenant people on behalf of creation and all humanity? Since stories are designed to draw us into the world they create, we will not conclude the task of interpretation at the canonical level until we engage the biblical story ourselves and enter into the covenant that God, through Christ, makes with fallen humanity. For as Vanhoozer helpfully notes, it is God's action of covenanting that most clearly emerges at the canonical level of Scripture. "What God does with Scripture is covenant with humanity by testifying to Jesus Christ . . . and by bringing about the reader's mutual indwelling with Christ . . . through the Spirit's rendering Scripture efficacious."[42] It is this impact of Scripture upon contemporary readers that we will explore in our final chapters on contextualization.

Suggestions for Further Reading

Alter, Robert. *The Art of Biblical Narrative*. New York: Basic Books, 1981.

Clark, David K. *To Know and Love God*. Wheaton: Crossway Books, 2003.

40. Osborne defines biblical theology as "that branch of theological inquiry concerned with tracing themes through the diverse sections of the Bible (such as the wisdom writings or the epistles of Paul) and then with seeking the unifying themes that draw the Bible together" (*Hermeneutical Spiral*, 263). I would want to add that the unifying biblical themes fit into a larger unifying biblical story. See Lindbeck for the theme of the people of God examined through the lens of story or narrative theology ("Story-Shaped Church," 46).

41. Vanhoozer, *Drama of Doctrine*, 149.

42. Vanhoozer, *First Theology*, 203.

Fowl, Stephen E., ed. *The Theological Interpretation of Scripture: Classic and Contemporary Readings*. Blackwell Readings in Modern Theology. Cambridge, MA: Blackwell, 1997.

Hays, Richard B. *Echoes of Scripture in the Letters of Paul*. New Haven: Yale University Press, 1989.

Powell, Mark Allan. *What Is Narrative Criticism?* Guides to Biblical Scholarship. Minneapolis: Fortress, 1990.

Vanhoozer, Kevin J. *First Theology: God, Scripture and Hermeneutics*. Downers Grove, IL: InterVarsity, 2002.

Wright, Christopher J. H. *Knowing Jesus through the Old Testament*. Downers Grove, IL: InterVarsity, 1995.

11

Conceptualizing
Contextualization

We do not invite the text into a transformation of its original meaning,
into a new application geared toward our thought forms; rather, the text
invites us into a transformation of allegiances and commitments, which
will manifest itself in behaviors appropriate to our social worlds.

Joel Green, "Practicing the Gospel in a Post-Critical World"

In Christian circles, the descriptor "biblical" gets applied to a lot of
things. We want our thinking to be biblical. In debates on various ethical topics, we often hear both sides claim that they hold to the biblical
view on the topic. We stress the importance of biblically based preaching
and teaching in our churches. The adjective "biblical" is even applied to
merchandise. In a quick search on the Internet, I found for sale biblical action figures, biblical jewelry, and even a Song of Solomon biblical
perfume! So who gets to say what deserves to be called "biblical"? If we
sprinkle in a few words from the Bible, do they make our product or
our lifestyle or our theology "biblical"?[1]

How do we go about evaluating what constitutes biblical thinking
and living? This is the fundamental question of contextualization. Con-

---

1. The accounts of Jesus' temptation by the devil (Matt. 4; Luke 4) remind us that
simply referring to a Bible verse does not guarantee a biblical mindset.

textualizing the message of Scripture for our own settings is not simply an add-on at the end of the exegetical process. It is integrally related to a careful study of the biblical text in its own context, so that we might hear it rightly in our own. Contextualization is about taking the message of Scripture so seriously that it shapes and directs all that we think and do. The goal is the enactment of a truly biblical worldview.

Contextualization: What Is It?

In chapter 1, we defined contextualization as the task of bringing a biblical author's meaning to bear in other times and cultures, or hearing Scripture's meaning speak in new contexts. At the end of chapter 5, we returned to the topic of contextualization. There I suggested that we might think of contextualization as recontextualizing the message of Scripture into our setting, given that the messages of the biblical authors were already contextualized for their audiences.[2] So we can speak of the original contextualization of Scripture and the recontextualization of it for our settings. These final two chapters will look more closely at the process of recontextualizing Scripture.

Where You Begin Makes a Difference

How I understand contextualization is very much dependent upon my assumptions about Scripture. If I understand Scripture to be a flawed testimony of God's redemptive work, then I will not feel the necessity of recontextualizing those elements that I deem mistaken. If I believe God to have authored the Bible with little or no involvement on the part of the human authors, I will find little reason to recontextualize at all. The words spoken to the original audience will be words spoken to me without a need for any kind of transferal of meaning.[3]

My conviction is that the Bible is fully divine and fully human. In other words, I hold what might be called an "incarnational" view of Scripture.[4] I believe that God inspired Scripture in such a way that the human authors' own styles and distinctive voices are quite discernable,

2. As relevance theory points out, all communication is contextualized.

3. This hermeneutic is actually difficult to sustain in practice, since a whole variety of biblical utterances tend to be ignored in the process, e.g., "If a man has a stubborn and rebellious son . . . all the men of his town shall stone him to death" (Deut. 21:18, 21); or "And do not call anyone on earth 'father,' for you have one Father, and he is in heaven. Nor are you to be called 'teacher,' for you have one Teacher, the Christ" (Matt. 23:9–10 NIV).

4. In other words, the nature of Scripture as both human and divine is analogous to the incarnation proper, which affirms that God became human in Jesus Christ. "The

233

while still ensuring that what God wanted to communicate was communicated. Scripture is divine communication or divine discourse.[5] Yet it fully bears the human handprint of its human authors. We will explore this wonderful paradox, especially the Bible's humanity, in our final chapter. Here, I would simply point out two ramifications for contextualization, if Scripture is indeed divine discourse.

First, because the analogy of incarnation allows us to affirm that Scripture is truly God's word to us, we can approach the Bible with a hermeneutic of engagement. We can expect God to speak as we open the Bible. We can come ready to hear from God and be engaged by God. Walter Brueggemann speaks of this engagement as the proper work of the text.[6] This means our response to Scripture will encompass more than just our head. A hermeneutic of engagement will involve a readiness to respond with all we are to the call of God to us through Scripture.

Second, understanding the Bible as divine discourse also encourages us to come to the Bible from a stance of trust. Although it is common to encounter the phrase "hermeneutics of suspicion" in current conversations, Scripture as God's word puts the priority on trusting that we will hear God's voice as we read the biblical text. This does not mean that we cannot ask honest and tough questions of the text. It does not mean that we must leave doubts at the door. It does mean that our basic stance as we approach the Bible is one of trust rather than suspicion.[7]

The Fluidity between Exegesis and Contextualization

Before we turn to conceptualizing the task of contextualization, we ought to acknowledge the fluidity of the entire interpretive process. In fact, calling contextualization a task is a bit simplistic—as if we can follow the exegetical guidelines we have been discussing and then turn to the final, discrete task of contextualizing our exegetical results. More true to experience would be Gadamer's aphorism that "understanding is application." Our understanding of the meaning of a biblical text and our realization of the proper response to it are more organically con-

---

incarnation itself is a kind of translation (of God into humanity), and hence the ultimate paradigm for contextualization" (Vanhoozer, *Drama of Doctrine*, 322). See chap. 12.

5. This is Wolterstorff's terminology in *Divine Discourse*.

6. "Our scientific, objective, historical-critical ways find it difficult to let the text do its proper work without demanding that it do some other work, perhaps more palatable to our rationality" (Walter Brueggemann, *Interpretation and Obedience: From Faithful Reading to Faithful Living* [Minneapolis: Fortress, 1991], 63).

7. Marshall refers to "believing criticism" in contrast to skepticism (*Beyond the Bible*, 20). Sometimes the phrase "hermeneutics of suspicion" is appropriately used to express a stance of suspicion toward our own ways of reading. In other words, we can rightly be self-critical in the interpretive process.

nected than a two-step method allows. This fact becomes clear upon listening to the average sermon on Ephesians 6:5–8, which provides household instructions to Christian slaves. It is fascinating to me how the message of the text can move almost imperceptibly from a word to first-century Christian slaves to obey their masters to an exhortation for proper conduct in the workplace for modern employees. Using analogy, the preacher has transferred the message of the text to the contemporary setting, often without explicitly acknowledging the transfer. My point here is not to argue that this move is inappropriate.[8] I use this example to illustrate how naturally and often intuitively we move between exegesis and contextualization.

That the tasks of exegesis and contextualization overlap is also suggested by multiple movements between the two during the interpretive process. We do not tend to progress in a singular, linear fashion between meaning and contextualization. Instead, it happens more often than not that we move back and forth between preliminary conclusions regarding meaning and possible ways to recontextualize that message in our own settings. Given this fluidity between exegesis and contextualization, we will need to be careful not to oversystematize the relationship between the two. Nevertheless, for the sake of clarifying what it is we do in contextualization, we will allow for the separation of contextualization from exegesis in our theoretical discussion, while remaining aware of the fluidity between the "then" and the "now" of the interpretive process.

The Complexity of Exegesis and Contextualization

The relationship between exegesis and contextualization is complex, as well as fluid. Not only do we need to consider the movement between the text's original setting and our own settings, we will also want to attend to the movement between a specific text and the canonical level of Scripture. The model that was proposed at the end of chapter 2 visualized the movement between original and contemporary settings—the author's text and the reader. Yet it did this with a particular passage in mind (1 Cor. 8). When we add the movement from individual texts (whether passages or whole books) to the canonical context, we might visualize the aggregate of interpretive issues on a dual axis (see figure 11.1).[9]

8. Although in evaluating the appropriateness of this move we will want to examine the strength of the analogy between first-century slavery as Paul addresses it (a household phenomenon) and modern workplace relationships.

9. This figure grows out of my interaction with the fourfold task of New Testament ethics developed by Hays. He delineates the four tasks as follows: (1) the descriptive task is the exegesis of specific texts; (2) the synthetic task is the synthesizing of various texts

Figure 11.1: Contextualization as Movement

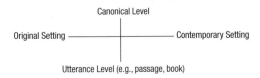

In exegesis and contextualization, not only do we repeatedly traverse the horizontal line between settings, but we also want to ask interpretive questions that draw together the varied voices of the biblical authors to discern the normative stance of Scripture more broadly on issues facing the church in society.

These axes raise crucial yet rather complex questions. For example, how do we honor the distinct voices of individual texts, while remaining committed to a canonical reading? How do we remain faithful to the normative stance of the biblical authors while at the same time reading for ourselves and our own settings? Wright illustrates part of this complexity: "We . . . read the text, examining it in all its historical otherness to ourselves as well as all its transtemporal relatedness to ourselves, and being aware of the complex relation that exists between those two things."[10]

The dual-axis figure not only illustrates the complexity of the interpretive and contextualization process, it may also assist us as we seek to dialogue constructively with others. The figure can clarify the junctures at which interpretive disagreement might happen. It may be that your dialogue partner disagrees with you on the interpretation of a particular text (the utterance level). If so, productive discussion can ensue on exegetical issues such as genre, language, and social and literary contexts.

Some interpretive issues, however, have to do with the interpretive task at the canonical level—the synthesis of any number of texts on a particular theme, topic, or part of the biblical story line. It seems to me that one part of the disagreement regarding women in ministry that remains least

---

on an ethical theme at the canonical level; (3) the hermeneutical task is the transfer of the message from then to now; and (4) the pragmatic task is the church's obedience in living out the text. The vertical axis of the figure shows the relationship between (1) and (2). The horizontal axis illustrates his (3). See Hays, *Moral Vision*, 3–7.

10. Wright, *NTPG*, 67. Bauckham argues for the complexity of contextualization based on the relationship of tradition to Scripture: "Tradition is the process by which the Gospel takes particular form in the various times and places of the church's history . . . [therefore] a much more complex process of contextualization needs to be envisaged" (Richard Bauckham, "Tradition in Relation to Scripture and Reason," in *Scripture, Tradition, and Reason: A Study in the Criteria of Christian Doctrine*, ed. R. Bauckham and B. Drewery [Edinburgh: T&T Clark, 1988], 130).

discussed sits at the canonical level. Whatever one's viewpoint on this issue, some texts are weighted more heavily than others—certain texts form the focal lens through which to evaluate the issue. Is 1 Timothy 2:8–15 such a primary text? Or should Galatians 3:26–29 take precedence? How about 1 Corinthians 11, in which Paul exhorts women to be veiled as they prophesy? If, as we have discussed in chapter 7, narrative texts communicate normatively, then how do narrative texts, such as Acts 18:18–28 (Priscilla correcting Apollos), fit in? Or Jesus' interaction with women in the Gospel narratives? And how does our interpretation of Genesis 1–3 influence our understanding of the issue? If we know that our disagreements may not be only, or even primarily, at the utterance level of particular texts, we will be better able to discuss our points of disagreement with clarity and ideally with charity.

Finally, it is possible to agree with someone on both utterance and canonical levels regarding an issue and still disagree about how the message of the Bible in its setting should impact our own context. Let's take the issue of divorce. It is quite possible that two Christians might agree that, while divorce is not God's ideal, Scripture does allow for divorce in cases of adultery (Matt. 19:9) and desertion by an unbelieving spouse (1 Cor. 7:15).[11] Although agreeing on both the utterance and canonical levels, they may disagree as to how this should be enacted in contemporary culture. One may hold that, since there are only two exceptions envisioned in Scripture, only these two exceptions are valid ones for Christians today. Another may consider that, since the biblical texts allow for divorce in circumstances where the marriage covenant has been transgressed by one party, we should leave open the possibility for other such circumstances today, for example, when spousal abuse is present.[12] In all the examples we have been looking at, it is by clarifying the nature of a disagreement that more productive dialogue can occur.

I offer a final note on contextualization in contemporary settings: All the clear thinking and theological deliberation in the world will fall short if we do not, in the end, live out what we discern to be the normative stance of Scripture. I appreciate that Hays includes in his model of exegesis and contextualization the final pragmatic task—faithfully living

11. This is by no means the only view of meaning at the utterance and canonical levels on this topic. Some Christians understand Scripture to prohibit divorce in all cases, i.e., Matt. 19 and 1 Cor. 7 do not allow for exceptions.

12. Robert H. Stein, "Divorce," in *The Dictionary of Jesus and the Gospels*, ed. J. Green, S. McKnight, and I. H. Marshall (Downers Grove, IL: InterVarsity, 1992), 192–99. These views do not exhaust the possibilities regarding the contextualization of Scripture to this issue today. For a helpful discussion of the range of viewpoints in evangelical ethical deliberation, see Craig Blomberg, "Marriage, Divorce, Remarriage, and Celibacy: An Exegesis of Matthew 19:3–12," *Trinity Journal* 11 (1990): 161–96.

out the message of the text.[13] Brueggemann also, in his summary of the exegetical and contextualization process, places the emphasis on obedience. "Interpretive obedience is an act of imaginative construal to show how the non-negotiable intentions of Yahweh are to be discerned and practiced in our situation, which is so very different from the situations in which those intentions were initially articulated."[14]

Two Pictures of Contextualization

Now I must tell you that I love lists—just love them. They are so wonderfully linear. If I can follow a checklist to complete a task, I am in my element. So if I believed a checklist would solve all our contextualization problems, I would be the first to sign up. But a simple list will not do justice to the complexity and fluidity of exegesis and contextualization as we have been describing them. So we will need to look for other ways of understanding the interpretive process, as we focus on the way recontextualization happens in this process.

Recent evangelical proposals for contextualization that allow for its growth out of, and integrity with, exegesis fall fairly well into two categories. The first envisions the interpretive process and more specifically contextualization as a back-and-forth *movement* between the text and readers. In the process of exegesis and contextualization, we repeatedly move between the text and our own contexts as we attempt to hear God's word for us today. This fits the way we have already conceptualized the exegetical task in chapter 2. Interpretation, contextualization included, involves multiple movements between the world of the text and our own world.[15]

Another set of proposals fits what we might call contextualization as *participation*. In this construal, contextualization occurs at the intersection of textual meaning and the contemporary context. Contemporary readers bring their contexts with them as they enter the textual world, so contextualization is a discernment of the overlap of the two worlds of text and reader. In this construal of interpretation, as in the first, contextualization is an integral part of the interpretive process. I believe that the participation construal is an equally helpful way to conceptualize contextualization and interpretation more broadly. Both contextualization as movement and contextualization as participation take the complexity of contextualization seriously. In addition, the one provides

13. Hays, *Moral Vision*, 7.
14. Brueggemann, *Interpretation and Obedience*, 1.
15. The final movement in the interpretive model proposed in chap. 2—discerning the normative stance of the text—addresses the contextualization process.

a helpful balance to the other. We will take a look in turn at both ways of conceiving contextualization.

Contextualization as a Movement

Conceptualizing contextualization, and interpretation more broadly, as a series of movements between biblical text and reader is essentially envisioning hermeneutics as a spiral. Hart describes this as "a progressive hermeneutical spiral in which [the] oscillation [between Scripture and tradition/reader] moves understanding forward through a constant return to the reading of Scripture itself."[16] The model of interpretation proposed in chapter 2 was weighted toward exegesis, although the third of its movements addressed contextualization (i.e., discerning the normative stance of the text and standing in for the implied reader). Yet we could also construct an interactive representation that focuses more deliberately upon contextualization, in order to illustrate what happens when we read Scripture from and for our own contexts (see figure 11.2).[17]

Notice that this figure makes more explicit than the model of chapter 2 the various influences on the reader as well as the reader's context, since the focus of this figure is on Scripture recontextualized in a new context. I expect, however, I have not covered every issue that arises from readers and texts in the interpretive process. As with the model of chapter 2, I am also in no way attempting to illustrate a particular order of movement or to legislate the number of movements back and forth between text and reader. Any number of return movements will occur as the reader moves from preliminary or provisional ideas to confirmation or revision of those interpretations. This is not a fully linear process, even though the figure is essentially linear for the sake of visual simplicity. The purpose of this figure is merely to visualize the kinds of movements that may and often do happen in the interpretive process with a focus on the contextualization aspect of that process.

The "tasks" delineated in relation to the world of the text are based on the guidelines for interpretation provided in our earlier chapters, such

---

16. Hart, "Christian Approach to the Bible," 191. Two other proponents of contextualization as movement (or spiral) are Osborne, *Hermeneutical Spiral*, 324–25; and Daniel M. Doriani, *Putting the Truth to Work: The Theory and Practice of Biblical Application* (Phillipsburg, NJ: P&R Publishing, 2001), 74. Doriani contends that contextualization (which he calls "application") is neither separate from nor coterminous with exegesis. Instead, there is a blurry boundary between the two (26–27).

17. The visual depiction in chap. 2 and the one given here are not meant to provide two alternatives, but two ways of viewing the interpretive process, one giving more weight to exegesis and the other to contextualization.

Figure 11.2: Contextualization as Movement

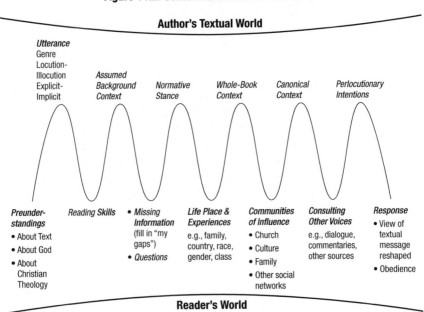

Author's Textual World

Utterance
Genre
Locution-
Illocution
Explicit-
Implicit

Assumed Background Context

Normative Stance

Whole-Book Context

Canonical Context

Perlocutionary Intentions

Preunder-standings
• About Text
• About God
• About Christian Theology

Reading Skills

• *Missing Information* (fill in "my gaps")
• *Questions*

Life Place & Experiences
e.g., family, country, race, gender, class

Communities of Influence
• Church
• Culture
• Family
• Other social networks

Consulting Other Voices
e.g., dialogue, commentaries, other sources

Response
• View of textual message reshaped
• Obedience

Reader's World

as paying attention to the whole-book context. Accordingly, I would consider these textual tasks *prescriptive* (that is, I think that you should do them!). Alternately, the contribution of the world of the reader does not arise out of any set of guidelines. Rather, it is *descriptive* of the kinds of things readers bring to the interpretive process (a whole range of experiences, skills, questions, and understandings).

One of the strengths of visualizing contextualization within interpretation as a series of movements between text and reader is that it does justice to the distance between the two. Movement between text and reader implies a gap of at least some distance between them. In chapter 1, we compared biblical interpretation to visiting a foreign country—reading the Bible as a cross-cultural experience. There is great value in this construal of interpretation. Our natural tendency to domesticate the text—to make it say what we would like it to say—is minimized when we take seriously the distance between our settings and the biblical world. In fact, as Green notes: "Precisely in the juxtapositions of the worlds, that of the text and our own, lies the potential for our values, commitments, and behaviors to be unmasked for what they are, *ours*."[18]

18. Green, "(Re)turn to Narrative," 27; italics in original.

Figure 11.3: Contextualization as Participation

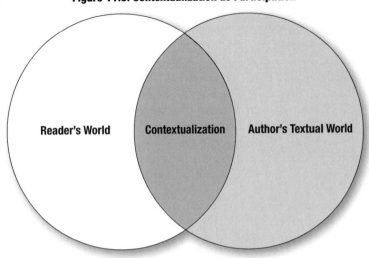

Contextualization as Participation

Yet it is inadequate to emphasize only the distance of the text from the reader in the process of contextualization. It is also crucial to hear the resonances between the two worlds of author and reader—to engage the text with the assumption of some amount of continuity with our own. This is one of the strengths of construing interpretation and particularly contextualization as participation. Participation emphasizes that we are invited to hear Scripture as familiar as well as foreign. There is a balancing between the two that is not only helpful but crucial.

The picture projected by the notion of contextualization as participation is one of overlap between the author's textual world and the reader's world (see figure 11.3). In fact, Brueggemann suggests that in the intersection of these two worlds a third is created, what he calls the "third world of evangelical imagination."[19] In this construal of contextualization, when the reader enters the world of the text, she necessarily brings her own world to the interpretive task. It is the third world projected from the first two that becomes the focus of contextualization—the text as paradigmatic for the interpreter's setting. In fact, some scholars refer to this way of contextualizing as a paradigmatic model. Christopher Wright, for example, calls for interpreters of the Old Testament "to go back to the

19. Brueggemann, *Interpretation and Obedience*, 12. He goes on to note that "evangelical imagination" might be construed by some as an oxymoron (20)! See discussion of the role of the imagination in interpretation in chap. 12.

hard given reality of the text of the Bible itself and imaginatively to live with Israel in their world . . . before returning to the equally hard given reality of our own world, to discover imaginatively how that paradigm challenges our ethical response there."[20] Notice that, while Wright refers to a back-and-forth movement between text and reader, he also describes an imaginative construal that occurs in both worlds and functions as a bridge between them.

The overlap between the textual world and the reader's world in this figure fits a Christian reading of Scripture, since contemporary Christian communities understand themselves to stand in continuity with the people of God to whom the Bible was written. As Green contends, "We are the family of God to whom these biblical books are addressed, historically and canonically, and . . . our theological imaginations find their horizons here, in the narrative of Scripture."[21] James McClendon stresses this interpretive continuity in his assertion that "the present Christian community [is] the primitive community and eschatological community."[22]

Now it is quite possible to set these two visual representations as opposing systems of contextualization. I think it is more helpful to see them as complementary ways of visualizing the complex interpretive process as it relates to contextualization. Allowing both of these images to help us define contextualization resonates with Ricoeur's interpretive notion of a second naïveté. Ricoeur describes a person's growing self-awareness as an interpreter of the Bible in this way: The interpreter begins with an assumption that the text speaks directly and immediately to him (the first naïveté). At some point, the interpreter is confronted with a new awareness of the distance between the text and his world. This is a rather disorienting experience, as he comes to grips with the significant gaps between these two worlds. The second naïveté refers to the interpreter's reappropriation of the Bible as familiar and accessible, but without a loss of awareness of its distance. Hart aptly expresses the movement to the second naïveté: "The world of the biblical writers 'becomes' our world in some identifiable sense. Or, put differently, we discover that it was our world all along."[23] The two pictures of contextualization we have sketched

20. Christopher J. H. Wright, *Old Testament Ethics for the People of God* (Downers Grove, IL: InterVarsity, 2004), 71. The question in a paradigmatic model for Old Testament texts becomes, "If this is what God required of [the people of Israel], what, in our different context, does God require of us?" (469).

21. Green, "Practicing the Gospel," 394. For Green, the narrative of Scripture refers more to the narrative quality of all Scripture rather than to the genre of biblical narrative more narrowly.

22. James W. McClendon Jr., *Systematic Theology*, 2nd ed. (Nashville: Abingdon, 2002), 31.

23. Hart, "Christian Approach to the Bible," 197.

provide the point and counterpoint of this progression. Interpretation as a movement between the two worlds is necessary so that we do not forget our historical distance from the world of the Bible. Interpretation as participation mirrors our second naïveté. It is a crucial reminder that we belong to the people of God addressed in and by Scripture.

The Interrelationship of Exegesis and Contextualization in Practice

Not only do these two ways of understanding contextualization do justice to the complexity and fluidity of the interpretive process, they also have practical results that avoid some of the problems that have often accompanied contextualization, or application. Because these models highlight the integration of exegesis and contextualization, they should make it more difficult to do contextualization at odds with good exegetical habits. Here are just two examples of how exegesis should inform our contextualization in the areas of genre and literary context.[24]

Genre-Sensitive Contextualization

As we have emphasized, early in the exegetical process one must clarify the genre of the biblical text being studied (see chap. 7). There is a reason why most books on exegesis deal with genre toward the beginning. We need to know what we are reading to interpret it properly. Yet concerted effort to identify and grasp the conventions of a literary genre will not help us if we lose sight of genre issues in the move to contextualization. This is rather easy to do, especially in cases of genres that are more indirect in the way they go about communicating their messages.

When I was teaching an introductory Bible class to college students a few years ago, I had the students keep a reading journal. They were to write their reflections as they read Scripture. A number of students got stuck in Genesis when they arrived at the less-than-pristine parts. I started to read entries like, "I can't believe the Bible has incest in it," in response to Lot and his daughters in Genesis 19:30–38. The students who wrote these types of comments were shocked by the human sin, conflict, and even violence that they read about in the early sections of Scripture. What was their struggle? They were under the impression that if a book narrates evil actions, the book itself is suspect. This impression betrays inexperience of the way narrative as a genre works. Narrative

---

24. In chap. 12 we will address contextualization that attends to the original culture in and to which the message was written.

authors are quite good, in reality, at letting their readers know what actions they condone, or encourage, and which ones they disapprove of.[25] The author of Genesis makes it clear that after sin enters the created order, human relations go awry. The evil that is described, however, is not prescribed—it is not to be emulated. Figuring this out is part of understanding the narrative genre of Genesis. If we do not take the time to address the genre and its conventions, we will be prone to misunderstanding and miscontextualization. My students had the impulse to emulate what they read in biblical narratives. I suspect that is the way they had been taught to apply biblical narratives, probably with a bit of sanitizing done by well-meaning parents and Sunday school teachers. When they came to the end of Genesis 19, however, the nonsanitized text caught them by surprise as they could not bring themselves to emulate the actions of these less-than-ideal characters. They rightly had to think through a new way to contextualize the text, which was more sensitive to its genre.

This is just one example of the importance of keeping genre considerations at front and center when we move to contextualize the biblical message. As another example, we could reflect on ways in which Bible teaching or preaching is done. While the biblical authors freely used nonprose forms to communicate in Scripture, Christian preaching and teaching have most often focused on a prose exposition of the text in question. As Grant Lovejoy explains: "Literary form and theological content cannot be as easily separated. . . . For much of Christian history, preachers have ignored the literary forms of Scripture when it came to developing the sermon. . . . Yet in doing that we have often lost important dimensions of the biblical message."[26] One of the more memorable sermons I have experienced was a first-person retelling of the story of John 4 from the perspective of the woman at the well, which focused on John's thematic interests, with social-contextual information interspersed. As the speaker developed the story, I experienced the impact of John's message about Jesus as the one who quenches our spiritual thirst.[27] In communicating God's word in ways that fit the variety of genres used

25. As Wenham argues, "it is most important to distinguish the implied author's ethical stance from that of the characters within the story. In recounting the nation's past its storytellers have a didactic purpose, but that certainly does not mean that they approved of all they described" (Gordon J. Wenham, *Story as Torah: Reading the Old Testament Ethically*, Old Testament Studies [Edinburgh: T&T Clark, 2000], 151).

26. Grant Lovejoy, "Shaping Sermons by the Literary Form of the Text," in *Biblical Hermeneutics: A Comprehensive Introduction to Interpreting Scripture*, ed. B. Corley, S. Lemke, and G. Lovejoy (Nashville: Broadman & Holman, 1996), 319; see also 318–39.

27. Kristine Causton, "The Water Man" (sermon at Christ Community Church, 17 August 2003). The preacher provided a creative and helpful visual reminder by drinking regularly from a bottle of water during the sermon.

in Scripture, it can be helpful to ask the question, How may the sermon do what the text says and does?[28]

Macro-contextualization

In chapter 10, we saw that when we isolate a verse or even a passage from its larger literary context, we are prone to misinterpret it. Yet even if we are careful to study a passage with its literary context in mind, it is possible to jettison the wider context when it comes to contextualization, especially if we view contextualization as a discrete phase, rather than as integrally tied to exegesis. Part of the problem is in our conditioning. Most of us have been trained to think that whatever unit of Scripture we select to study must have at least one point of application. Yet the smaller the unit we choose, the less likely it is that the author intended an isolated application from it. This is rather obvious in some cases, as with this example: "People swear by someone greater than themselves, and the oath confirms what is said and puts an end to all argument" (Heb. 6:16). Now if we were to isolate this statement by the author of the letter to the Hebrews, we might be tempted to apply the verse to the purpose of human oaths, or even how oaths should be made. But attention to context will confirm that this verse provides the example for what the author will say in the following verses about the oath God made to Abraham, in which believers in Jesus now participate (Heb. 6:13–20). The author's purpose is not at all to exhort his audience regarding human oaths, but to encourage them that their hope is as secure as the unbreakable oath of God. Focusing questions of contextualization on larger literary units, what we might call "macro-contextualization," before zooming in on smaller units of discourse helps us remain true to authors and their purposes as we contextualize their messages.

It is not just on the verse level that we lose sight of macro-contextualization. We may even go astray in contextualization at the chapter level by ignoring the literary context. This is particularly easy to do in narrative, since isolating a chapter from the rest of the text is not likely to have been what the author wanted to have happen to the story! Take Genesis 40, the narration of Joseph's interaction with the royal baker and cupbearer while in prison. Given that this account sits midway through the extended story of Joseph that concludes Genesis (Gen. 37–50), we should not treat Genesis 40 as a separate story. If we do, we will struggle to find a self-contained application for the chapter, especially since the chapter ends without bringing even the substory of Joseph's prison term to a resolution. (It's a cliff-hanger!) The chapter concludes with the state-

---

28. Lovejoy, "Shaping Sermons," 324.

ment that the cupbearer forgets Joseph's interpretation of his dream when he is released from prison. An isolated application that focuses on, for instance, a warning against asking favors of pagans will rightly smack of artificiality. Genesis 40 simply was not meant to be contextualized apart from its literary context.

So if we commit ourselves not only to good exegetical habits, like faithfulness to literary context, but also to carrying these habits through our contextualization, how might this impact a reading of Genesis 40? How might we allow macro-contextualization to help us here? Since Genesis 40 is part of the larger story of Joseph, we may assume it shares a common theme with the whole story. In spite of human attempts to harm Joseph, God sustains his life and makes him prosper in order to preserve Israel and God's promise through Israel. Genesis 40 shares this theme as it sets up (but does not complete) another dire circumstance in Joseph's life that God redeems. A macro-contextualization of Genesis 40, then, will circle around God's redemptive activity among his people developed in this part of the story, as well as a call to participate in and trust God's redemptive plans in spite of difficult circumstances.

So, in sum, we will want to let the good exegetical habits we are developing, such as attention to literary context, infuse our contextualization as well. If we are struggling to apply a text in our own setting, perhaps we need to pull back and attend to the larger literary context. There is no reason to "fish" for a point of application. The biblical authors had ample interest in impacting their audiences. And Scripture has a great history of effectively doing so! Our goal is not to dream up points of contextualization from the smallest parts of the text. It is to read the Bible well—to read it on its own terms. If we do this consistently in the interpretive process, we will learn to contextualize with the big-picture perspective always in mind.

The Pattern of Contextualization: Two Questions

I have already shared my conviction that what we need as we contextualize is not a detailed checklist, but ways of conceptualizing contextualization as integrally connected to exegesis. Now, a good number of hermeneutics books provide information on contextualization in the form of a list of guidelines, and I have found these guidelines to be helpful in my own thinking about contextualization. Yet two observations have led me to be cautious in providing my own list for contextualization. First, many earlier discussions and their accompanying guidelines have centered on what David Clark has called a "principlizing" approach to contextualization. While not without its merits, principlizing as an overarching method has its share of problems.[29] Second, the complexity of some recently proposed guidelines has caused me to wonder whether guidelines get interpreters to the heart of contextualization. Don't misunderstand me. I have just argued that contextualization is a fairly complex task. I become cautious when that complexity becomes systematized into a schema that gets applied in a uniform manner to all texts, whatever their variations.

Let me give you a couple of examples, both from books that I have appreciated, and from which I have learned much. Daniel Doriani, in *Putting the Truth to Work*, introduces a grid for understanding the various ways texts can be applied. He delineates seven means by which texts generate application and four crucial questions to be asked.[30] Doriani speaks of the intersection of the seven means and four questions as providing the possibility of twenty-eight areas for exploration when applying texts. Although Doriani's seven categories and four questions provide helpful ways to think more clearly about the breadth of the contextualization process, it is unwieldy to identify which of the twenty-eight potential areas for application might fit a particular text and how they might do so.

In *Slaves, Women, and Homosexuals: Exploring the Hermeneutics of Cultural Analysis*, William Webb puts forth a redemptive-movement hermeneutic based on eighteen criteria for determining whether particular components of a biblical text or teaching are culturally relative or transculturally binding.[31] A selection of Webb's eighteen criteria include seed ideas, basis in original creation, basis in new creation, opposition to original culture, basis in theological analogy, and appeal to the Old Testament. While appreciating the breadth of Webb's work, and finding myself in agreement on the validity of any number of the criteria he suggests, I find that the system he proposes is almost overwhelming for the average person reading the Bible.[32] Is this level of systematiza-

---

29. Clark, *To Know and Love God*, 91. See chap. 12 for further discussion.

30. The seven means, or ways, in which texts generate application are rules, ideals, doctrine, redemptive acts, exemplary acts, images and symbols, and songs and prayers. The four questions have to do with duty, character, goals, and discernment. See Doriani, *Putting Truth to Work*, 82, 98.

31. This is Webb's language (68). He does acknowledge, however, that "even transcultural elements in Scripture have a cultural component" (William J. Webb, *Slaves, Women, and Homosexuals: Exploring the Hermeneutics of Cultural Analysis* [Downers Grove, IL: InterVarsity, 2001], 24). See my concerns raised in chap. 12 about dividing Scripture into these two categories.

32. This is not a substantive argument against his proposal. For my interaction with Webb's proposal beyond its systematization of contextualization, see chap. 12. Webb's central point about a redemptive-movement hermeneutic is rather less complicated and might be briefly summed up with this question: On a particular ethical issue, which direction do the biblical writers move in relation to their own cultural context? This question helps us to hear what the biblical authors intend to effect in their readers.

tion a prerequisite for contextualization that aims to take seriously the complexity of its relationship to original meaning? Or are there some central categories that help us get started down the right track in contextualization, and from which we can then evaluate and utilize the helpful insights of various contextualizing systems?

I believe there are two important questions that provide an evaluative starting point for contextualization. So, instead of providing a list of guidelines for contextualizing a biblical text, I will conclude this chapter with two questions that might guide our contextualizing efforts. These questions should be familiar, since they are based on Hirsch's two principles for discerning whether a possible implication is truly tied to an author's communicative intention.[33] Given that contextualization asks how the author's intention can be discerned for a future audience, the application of Hirsch's two principles of *coherence* and *purpose* to contextualization is quite appropriate.

Coherence

As we have discerned earlier, coherence is the first of Hirsch's relevant principles. Specifically, Hirsch argues that any possible implication must fit with the whole pattern of meaning. If we apply the principle of coherence to the task of contextualization, we will ask if there is adequate coherence—a significant sense of fit—between the original meaning in its context and its recontextualization for another setting.[34] For Hirsch, it is important that the potential implication (in this case, the recontextualization) coheres with the pattern of meaning understood holistically. This means, for instance, that a recontextualization ought to fit with the text understood in its literary context, in other words, macro-contextualization. Recontextualizing in a way that coheres with original meaning also involves asking how the biblical text is paradigmatic for our setting. As we do this, it may be that we seek the closest analogy between the normative stance of the original meaning and the cultural context into which the text is being recontextualized, in order to see if there is adequate fit between the two. Whatever the specific means of contextualization, the central focus initially is related to the level of coherence between meaning and the proposed contextualization.

33. See chap. 5, sec. 1, "Probing Meaning: Implications."
34. For the distinction and connection between original meaning and contextualization, see chap. 5, sec. 3, "Probing Meaning and 'Beyond': The Movement to Contextualization."

Purpose

Hirsch's second relevant principle, which follows closely from the first, is the principle of purpose. In fact, this principle provides a key criterion for determining the coherence of any proposed contextualization. The question to be asked is, Does the possible recontextualization fit the purposes of the author's original meaning? The purposes of the text viewed broadly include both the author's illocutionary purposes in relation to locution and the perlocutionary intentions.[35] That is, the biblical author's purposes encompass what the author does in what is said, as well as what the author hopes to accomplish in his audience. So we could speak of "purpose-guided contextualization" to indicate allowing the purpose of a text to guide our recontextualizing of it.

Let's illustrate purpose-guided contextualization with an example from Leviticus 19:19, a verse that is seldom contextualized directly by contemporary readers.[36] As part of a series of three commands about separation, we hear the following words: "You shall not . . . wear a garment upon you of two kinds of material mixed together" (NASB). The illocution is a command, specifically a command forbidding the mixing of material worn on the body (the locution). The perlocutionary intent is obedience, but we will want to ask more pointedly about the purpose of the obedience, the goal of obedience to wearing a garment of single material rather than mixed materials. This is also a question of intention, and so we are rightly interested in such a question when we seek to hear the communicative intention of the text. The answer is clear in the literary context, where we hear the command: "You shall be holy, for I the LORD your God am holy" (19:2).[37] God's forbidding the Israelites to wear two kinds of material in one garment required them to physically illustrate and participate in their unique call to be holy, that is, set apart for the Lord. Even their clothing is a reminder of and, even more, a participation in the holiness that is to mark them as belonging distinctly to Yahweh, in witness to the other nations.

35. See chaps. 2 and 5 for more on speech-act theory applied to biblical texts. There I have argued that perlocutionary intentions are an extension of meaning.

36. The argument that this verse is part of the old ceremonial covenant and so not applicable to Christians is not an unusual one. However, recent scholarship in both the Old and New Testaments has become less comfortable with easy distinctions between moral and civil/ceremonial law, since this distinction is hardly tenable from a careful reading of the Old Testament. In addition, this conclusion would nullify much of Leviticus for Christians, which would essentially question its inclusion in the Christian canon! For more on the issue of recontextualizing Old Testament biblical law, see Peter T. Vogt, *Interpreting the Pentateuch: An Exegetical Handbook* (Grand Rapids: Kregel, forthcoming).

37. Note that it is important to allow the broader literary context to shape interpretation, and hence contextualization.

By hearing the whole pattern of intention, including the intended effect (i.e., perlocutionary intention) of what is said and done in the speech-act, we have a better sense of how this command, in all its cultural particularity, might speak paradigmatically to our contemporary context. How ought we to be marked out as belonging solely to the Lord now, in the context of the new covenant? What kinds of cultural participation are at cross-purposes with single and wholehearted allegiance to God in our context? Asking such questions of purpose will help us put Leviticus 19:19 into effect in ways appropriate to a different context, without ignoring the command as irrelevant or obsolete for us. As Powell notes, "We yield to the intent of Scripture by allowing [its] goal to be fulfilled in us."[38]

Conclusion

Contextualization is a crucial part of the exegetical process. One concern people raise about studying the Bible with close attention to its original context and meaning is that we will never find time to ask the contextualization question: So what does the text mean for us today? Yet it has been my experience that when I study a biblical text carefully, with attention to its original setting, literary context, and communicative intention, its message is more powerfully unleashed in my own life and contemporary setting. It is as if the message cannot be imprisoned in the past; it resonates powerfully with current situations, attitudes, and life contexts. This result should not surprise us, if we believe that Scripture in concert with the Spirit has the power to change us and to change our world.

To conclude this chapter, allow me to imaginatively review contextualization within the interpretive process from a personal vantage point. The task of contextualization occurs at the intersection of the world of the text and my world. As I enter the world of the text on its own terms, the task of exegesis, I begin to intuit the connections between the text and my own life, Christian community, and world. I continue to study the text, moving back and forth between the world of the text and my world. I seek to study it holistically and against its social context, to hear the author's message to the original audience, but not in a dispassionate way, as if I am a scientist studying a specimen. Instead, I listen to the text, in all its otherness, as if my life depends on it. I am passionate about discovering what the author's message might mean for my own contexts, for me and for us these many years later. I listen to hear from God, who

---

38. Mark Allan Powell, *Loving Jesus* (Minneapolis: Fortress, 2004), 67. Powell is speaking to a different biblical text, but his conclusion is helpful more generally.

has authored Scripture as much as its human authors did. I listen in continuity with the people of God in all other times and places. I read and listen, aware of both the distance and nearness of the Bible. This distance and nearness arise from the incarnational nature of Scripture, which we will explore in the final chapter.

Suggestions for Further Reading (for Chapters 11 and 12)

Brueggemann, Walter. *Interpretation and Obedience: From Faithful Reading to Faithful Living*. Minneapolis: Fortress, 1991.

Doriani, Daniel M. *Putting the Truth to Work: The Theory and Practice of Biblical Application*. Phillipsburg, NJ: P&R Publishing, 2001.

Enns, Peter. *Inspiration and Incarnation: Evangelicals and the Problem of the Old Testament*. Grand Rapids: Baker Academic, 2005.

Fee, Gordon D. *Listening to the Spirit in the Text*. Grand Rapids: Eerdmans, 2000.

Green, Joel B., and Max Turner, eds. *Between Two Horizons: Spanning New Testament Studies and Systematic Theology*. Grand Rapids: Eerdmans, 2000.

Hays, Richard B. *The Moral Vision of the New Testament: A Contemporary Introduction to New Testament Ethics*. San Francisco: HarperSanFrancisco, 1996.

Marshall, I. Howard. *Beyond the Bible: Moving from Scripture to Theology*. Grand Rapids: Baker Academic, 2004.

McKnight, Edgar V. *Reading the Bible Today: A Twenty-First Century Appreciation of Scripture*. Macon, GA: Smyth & Helwys, 2003.

Vanhoozer, Kevin J. *The Drama of Doctrine: A Canonical-Linguistic Approach to Christian Theology*. Louisville: Westminster John Knox, 2005.

Webb, William J. *Slaves, Women, and Homosexuals: Exploring the Hermeneutics of Cultural Analysis*. Downers Grove, IL: InterVarsity, 2001.

Wenham, Gordon J. *Story as Torah: Reading the Old Testament Ethically*. Old Testament Studies. Edinburgh: T&T Clark, 2000.

Wolterstorff, Nicholas. *Divine Discourse: Philosophical Reflections on the Claim that God Speaks*. Cambridge: Cambridge University Press, 1995.

Wright, Christopher J. H. *Old Testament Ethics for the People of God*. Downers Grove, IL: InterVarsity, 2004.

12

Contextualization

Understanding Scripture Incarnationally

> If we desire absolutes that are detached from history, we are not following the model of the incarnation. God makes himself known to us in history, and any theological hermeneutics must begin here. . . . God discloses himself never "purely" but incarnationally, so that the scripture follows the very principles of the incarnation in its human and divine elements. The text is both human and divine.
>
> Jens Zimmermann, *Recovering Theological Hermeneutics*

> The human marks of the Bible are *everywhere, thoroughly integrated* into the nature of Scripture itself. Ignoring these marks or explaining them away takes at least as much energy as listening to them and learning from them.
>
> Peter Enns, *Inspiration and Incarnation*

I have a confession to make: I have a favorite doctrine. Now it is probably not exactly respectable, especially as a seminary professor, to show a preference for one Christian doctrine over another. But try as I might, I have not been able to overcome this deficiency. I have a favorite doctrine; it is the doctrine of the incarnation. As I have reflected on the paradoxical act of God becoming a human being in Jesus, it has struck me that God's activity throughout salvation history is of an incarnational sort. God's desire to live among his people is manifested in the tabernacle and then the temple. The climactic point is certainly the incarnation of God in Jesus (see John 1:14–18), but the precursors are already present in Old Testament history.[1]

The Bible can also be understood as part of God's incarnational work. Somehow it too exhibits this paradoxical mixture of the divine and human, but human in its best and originally intended sense.[2] The incarnation proper becomes an analogy for the Bible in its divine and human identity.[3] The Bible itself points us in this direction by its explicit and implicit testimony. On the explicit front, we could cite 2 Peter 1:

> We also have the prophetic message as something completely reliable, and you will do well to pay attention to it, as to a light shining in a dark place, until the day dawns and the morning star rises in your hearts. Above all, you must understand that no prophecy of Scripture came about by the prophet's own interpretation of things. For prophecy never had its origin in the human will, but prophets, though human, spoke from God as they were carried along by the Holy Spirit. (2 Pet. 1:19–21)[4]

Biblical prophecy is explicitly affirmed as humans speaking from God. We could extrapolate from this connection that Scripture more generally has the quality of humans speaking from God through the Spirit. This rings of incarnation.

The implicit testimony of the Bible for its humanity is the human handprint left on the text. This comes across in the unique themes of various biblical authors and their individual writing styles. We can see it most clearly, I suppose, in texts that provide multiple accounts of essentially the same issue or event. The four Gospels are a case in point: one story of Jesus, but four different ways of telling the story, each with unique

1. See N. T. Wright, *The Challenge of Jesus: Rediscovering Who Jesus Was and Is* (Downers Grove, IL: InterVarsity, 1999), 111–20.

2. Just as we may affirm Jesus' full humanity without sin or fault (the paradigm of restored humanity), we can hold to the full humanity of Scripture without being required to deem it fallible.

3. Enns, *Inspiration and Incarnation*, 18. As Wright concedes, "I know that the analogy between the Bible and the person of Jesus is not exact, and that some have seen serious problems with it; I believe that provided it is seen *as an analogy*, not as a precise two-way identity, it remains helpful." N. T. Wright, *The Last Word* (New York: HarperSanFrancisco, 2005), 130; italics in original.

4. Although in this passage the author refers more particularly to prophetic testimony in Scripture, it would seem to be fair to extrapolate to Scripture broadly conceived, especially as the immediate context points to the testimony recorded in the Gospels about Jesus' transfiguration as likely part of what is in mind (2 Pet. 1:16–18).

authorial interests woven into the telling (e.g., the pronounced theme of repentance in Luke). We could also compare Kings and Chronicles to hear the unique emphases of each, given their clear topical overlap. The point is not that these comparisons undermine the nature of Scripture as divine discourse. They do not. What they do, however, is demonstrate that the human particularities of the biblical authors were not obscured in the inspiration process.

We see this as well in the linguistic and stylistic differences that accentuate the Bible's human authorship. Why is it that almost every first-year Greek class jumps into the New Testament in the Johannine literature? It is because the Gospel of John and the Johannine epistles are some of the easiest reading in the New Testament. The sentence structure is generally less complex, and the vocabulary less diverse than in other New Testament books. But only the most malevolent Greek teachers would have their beginning students read the letter to the Hebrews! The amount of vocabulary to learn can be overwhelming, and the Greek grammar is much more complicated.

Yet we can also point to evidence for the Bible as more than just a compilation of human books. Not only do we have the historical testimony of the church that God speaks through Scripture, we can also look to the coherence of the biblical story across the Bible as an implicit demonstration that it is held together by more than human experience and ingenuity. On the level of the overarching biblical story, there is a coherence of divine plot and purpose.

Taking Our Cues from the Incarnational Nature of Scripture

If understanding Scripture as incarnational fits the biblical testimony, we might still ask whether such an understanding makes a difference in interpretation and contextualization. I am convinced that it does make a difference, and in helpful ways. Explaining how it does will be our focus in this final chapter. After brief attention to two overarching effects of an incarnational understanding of Scripture, we will go into more detail by explaining the following description of the Bible: culturally located divine discourse for the shaping of the Christian community.

One effect of giving full credence to the *human quality of the Bible* is that we will not be prone to bypass the human author. "Sure, Amos said that, but God really meant. . . ." We have no access to God's meaning apart from the meaning of the human author. Instead, we will affirm that what Amos meant, God also meant. This is what Vanhoozer calls "divine appropriation of the illocutions [and locutions] of the human authors."[5] If we acknowledge that in Scripture we are participating in more but not less than human communication, we will honor the particularities of the human authors that we have been describing.

Yet by also committing ourselves to the *divine quality of the Bible*, we will not feel free to cast off parts of the Bible that do not suit our ideas and purposes. "All Scripture is God-breathed and profitable. . . ." Even parts of Scripture that lack one-to-one correspondence with our own settings will nevertheless prove profitable if we attend to their recontextualization for us. For example, I will listen for the resonances between Deuteronomy and my nonagrarian setting so that I can profit from its message:

> When you are harvesting in your field and you overlook a sheaf, do not go back to get it. Leave it for the alien, the fatherless and the widow, so that the LORD your God may bless you in all the work of your hands. (Deut. 24:19 NIV)

If I assume that I can ignore this passage because I do not have a field and will not be harvesting any time soon, I miss the text's purpose to promote care for those who are most vulnerable. In contextualizing, I must not try to somehow divide Scripture into what is human and what is divine. As Edgar McKnight puts it, "The matter is not one of deciding which words are human and which contain a divine message. They are all human. They grow out of specific physical, historical, and social environments. They are subject to all of the characteristics of other literature. But, more importantly, they are a means of revealing God and of helping men and women to know God's reality and will."[6]

The Bible as Culturally Located Divine Discourse for the Shaping of the Christian Community

An incarnational model of Scripture affirms that the Bible is culturally located divine discourse for the shaping of the Christian community. We will discuss each part of this affirmation in an effort to understand how the incarnational nature of Scripture impacts the reading and contextualization process. To emphasize Scripture as from God, we will be speaking of the Bible as divine discourse.[7] Yet because of the assump-

5. Vanhoozer (*First Theology*, 194) clarifies that God's appropriation of the author's illocutions happens "particularly at the generic [genre] level but not exclusively there."

6. Edgar V. McKnight, *Reading the Bible Today: A Twenty-First Century Appreciation of Scripture* (Macon, GA: Smyth & Helwys, 2003), 5.

7. This is Wolterstorff's language in *Divine Discourse*.

tion that it is divine discourse via appropriation of the human discourse of the Bible, we will add the adjective "culturally located." "Culturally located divine discourse" takes seriously the fact that all human discourse is culturally located, although not necessarily culturally bound or culturally relative.[8] Finally, after discussing the first two descriptors, divine discourse and culturally located, I will address the overarching purpose of the Christian Scriptures: to shape the Christian community into the pattern of restored humanity.

The Bible as Divine Discourse

What difference does it make to read and interpret the Bible with the conviction that it is divine discourse? First, if it is divine discourse, we can assume the unity of the Bible, although without muting the diversity of the voices of its individual human authors. The Bible's unity is both a presupposition that follows from recognizing its divine origin and a conclusion that comes from reading Scripture. It is my conviction that the Bible demonstrates its unity and coherence, particularly as its overarching story emerges in a canonical reading.[9] We could liken the Bible to an orchestra in which the distinctiveness of each individual instrument playing its separate part does nothing to mar the unity of the performance of a musical score. Instead, whatever points of perceived dissonance occur along the way find their resolution without losing their distinctiveness in the final form of the performance. As Hart puts it, "The move to a canonical reading does not entail blending the various voices into a mulch of identical texture."[10]

Since a canonical reading involves attending to the broad range of the biblical story, we can affirm the unity of the Bible without demanding uniformity from every biblical author. For example, while it has not been uncommon to set Paul and Matthew at odds over the place of obedience and law-keeping in the Christian life, we are helped in interpretation by a canonical glance at covenantal assumptions from the Old Testament. Just as obedience was understood in the framework of covenant faithfulness in the Old Testament,[11] so Matthew does not propose obedience as a way to earn salvation (which Paul is opposed to, goes the standard

8. The latter two terms have traditionally been used to describe parts of the Bible that do not have one-to-one situational correspondence with contemporary contexts. I am not particularly enamored with them for a number of reasons and so prefer "culturally located." More on this below.

9. See chap. 10 for more on canonical reading of the Bible.

10. Hart, "Christian Approach to the Bible," 200.

11. Amy-Jill Levine, "Putting Jesus Where He Belongs: The Man from Nazareth in His Jewish World," *Perspectives in Religious Studies* 27 (Summer 2000): 171. "[First-century

reply). Instead, Matthew expects that Jesus' followers, having experienced the inauguration of the coming kingdom in Jesus himself, will exhibit covenant faithfulness to an even greater extent than the Pharisees—those most known for their covenant obedience (see Matt. 5:20). Neither Matthew nor Paul envisions Christian obedience as a human work that earns salvation. Both seem to view obedience in covenantal terms as the result of already-received grace and power in the life of the believing community.[12]

Second, reading the Bible as divine discourse means we will expect the Bible to impact readers. We can affirm the cultural locatedness of the biblical text without downplaying its power to speak into new contexts, because it is the Holy Spirit who empowers its message. "The role of the Spirit is to enable us to take the biblical texts in the sense they were intended, and to apply or follow that sense in the way we live."[13] The empowered message will be likely to "hit home" in both familiar and unexpected ways. Often it will reaffirm its truth when we need to be encouraged. Yet it may also come to us as a surprisingly new and fresh word from God. In his early twenties, my husband did a lot of reading from various world religions in his search for truth. Although not a Christian, Tim read the Bible regularly. One day while reading in the third chapter of John's Gospel, he came across these words: "And this is the judgment, that the light has come into the world, and people loved darkness rather than light because their deeds were evil. For all who do evil hate the light and do not come to the light, so that their deeds may not be exposed" (John 3:19–20 NRSV). The truth of what was written struck him in palpable fashion. He thought, "Running and hiding from the light—that describes me and almost everyone I know." The Spirit spoke to Tim through John's message to confirm it and apply it with a power he was not expecting. "Reading the Bible as Scripture . . . is above all a matter of being in the presence and open to the handling of the One who, in some sense, is the final 'author' of its message."[14]

The Bible as Culturally Located Divine Discourse

In an incarnational understanding of Scripture a conviction of the Bible as divine discourse will be balanced with an emphasis on its human quality, as first written from and for particular cultural contexts. I am

---

Jews] followed the Torah (better translated 'instruction' than 'Law') because that was what G-d wanted; it was part of their responsibility under the covenant with Moses."

12. For Paul on this, particularly in relation to the Spirit's work in the believer, see Gal. 5:16–26.

13. Vanhoozer, *First Theology*, 228.

14. Hart, "Christian Approach to the Bible," 204.

referring to this quality as Scripture's "cultural locatedness." This language seems to me to be more helpful than "culturally relative" or "culturally bound." In some evangelical discussions of contextualization, individual Scriptures have been categorized as either transcultural or culturally bound. The point of the distinction is to identify biblical texts that describe cultural practices that have no direct application in the interpreter's cultural setting (e.g., women wearing head coverings in worship).[15] These "culturally bound" practices then require cultural adjustment to make them applicable to the interpreter's setting.

There are problems in accepting such a division, however. First, the distinction assumes the possibility of disengaging the meaning of the text from its form.[16] Yet this assumption has received pointed critique in recent years. Form is not just a conveyer of meaning. Rather, meaning is embedded to such a degree in the formal aspects of language, genre, and culture that meaning embraces form. Paul, in 1 Corinthians 11, is actually saying something about the appropriateness of head coverings for women when they pray and prophesy. In fact, that is his primary communicative concern. The cultural practice of women covering their heads is not just a form, with Paul's meaning being something more universal. Paul's meaning is tied up with the issue of head coverings! How we go about hearing the connections that emerge from Paul's meaning regarding head coverings for our own contexts must first honor the integrity of his meaning as spoken to and contextualized in his own setting.

In fact, an appeal to a distinction between form and meaning sounds a lot like the husk/kernel distinction made by liberal Protestant hermeneutics of over one hundred years ago. In that model, the interpretive goal was to remove the unnecessary husk from the essential kernel. For example, in interpreting Jesus' notion of the kingdom of God, some interpreters felt free to remove the husk of the Jewish eschatological expectation of God's intervention in human history from what they deemed to be the theological kernel of the fatherhood of God and the brotherhood of humanity. Yet by removing any kind of eschatological expectation from Jesus' teaching on the kingdom, these interpreters divorced Jesus from the very Jewish context in which his teaching about the kingdom made sense. Form and meaning are not so easily separated.

Second, the distinction is problematic because it assumes that some or most Scriptures are transcultural, while some are not. Yet if by "transcultural" we mean timeless, abstracted truth, we have not taken seriously

15. This is not directly applicable in Western contexts but may potentially have a more direct message in certain Middle Eastern cultures. The aligning of the purposes of veiling in both contexts would be the determining factor.

16. For an example of this distinction and how it is used in application, see Larkin, *Hermeneutics and Culture*, 354.

the cultural location of all books of the Bible.[17] By insisting that Scripture comes to us as timeless, abstracted truth, we lose sight of the historical particularity of its origins. We lose sight of its incarnational nature. Zimmermann powerfully describes this attitude as "allergic to the historical embodiment of knowledge." He goes on to say that "knowledge derived from the world of history with all its flux and contingency makes us uneasy, and it is no wonder that a scientific rather than a biblical paradigm of knowledge continues to inform the cries of modern evangelicals for absolute truth and certainty. An incarnational hermeneutics, however, must take its orientation from the fact that God entered history without compromising transcendence."[18]

So it seems unwise to create a dichotomy between parts of the Bible that are timeless or transcultural and those that are culturally bound. It seems more helpful to acknowledge that all Scripture is culturally located. Osborne describes this quality as "the circumstantial nature of Scripture—the fact that it was written to specific situations."[19] This does not, however, limit the message of Scripture only to its original cultural context. The incarnational balance ought to be preserved by affirming that all Scriptures are culturally located, *and* all Scriptures are able to speak beyond their cultural location. "The union between the human and divine in the inspiration of Scripture is one in which neither side of the equation is diminished. Scripture's historical particularity is truly a scandal, but no less so than the incarnation of Christ himself."[20]

The Temporal Movement of the Bible

If the Scriptures are culturally located, then it follows that they also are temporally located, that is, they have historical location. "The radical consequence of the incarnation is that human knowledge of God cannot be ahistorical."[21] We should expect, then, to see temporal movement within the biblical text. There is good reason that the phrase "salvation history" is used to describe the revelation of God in Scripture. God has revealed himself in history, and so the temporal flow of Scripture matters. The cultural particulars we see all along the way in the biblical story are

17. If "transcultural" indicates that the Bible can speak beyond its cultural location, then we ought to affirm all Scripture as transcultural, but this is precisely not done when the distinction is made between transcultural and culturally bound texts. It is the distinction I am arguing against, not the language per se, since terms can often be defined and used differently. As Vanhoozer notes, "to affirm Scripture as transcultural is not to say that it is *acultural* or *supracultural*. The language of Scripture would be unintelligible if not for its inculturation" (*Drama of Doctrine*, 314).

18. Zimmermann, *Recovering Theological Hermeneutics*, 163–64.

19. Osborne, *Hermeneutical Spiral*, 326.

20. Green, "Context and Communication," 38.

21. Zimmermann, *Recovering Theological Hermeneutics*, 45.

not just husks to be removed to get at culturally abstracted, ahistorical truths, or kernels. Instead, the cultural particulars provide the settings into which God spoke and acted. In order to hear God in Scripture, we need to give full due to those specific settings in which it was given.

In chapter 2, we described contributions of narrative theology to a communicative model of interpretation, in its emphasis upon the narrative quality of all Scripture. Narrative theology stresses the Bible's historical-temporal movement by calling theology to reengage the biblical story. Goldingay, for example, asks theology to take seriously the Old Testament story in all its historical temporality.

> *Old Testament faith centrally concerns the way in which God related to Israel over time.* It relates the story of the way Yahweh did certain things, such as create the world, make promises to Israel's ancestors, deliver their descendants from Egypt, bring them into a sealed relationship at Sinai, persevere with them in chastisement and mercy in the wilderness, bring them into their own land, persevere with them in chastisement and mercy through another period of unfaithfulness in the land itself, agree to their having human kings and make a commitment to a line of kings, interact with them over centuries of inclination to rebellion until they were reduced to a shadow of their former self, cleanse their land, and begin a process of renewal there.[22]

Old Testament texts may be found anywhere along this historical continuum. Where they are found ought to make a difference in our interpretation.

What then does it look like in interpretation to pay attention to the historical unfolding of God's work with his creation and people? First, it will mean giving careful consideration to *progressive revelation*. Progressive revelation is the idea that God's revelation in the Bible becomes clearer over time—it unfolds progressively. Christian interpretation necessarily adheres to progressive revelation in its understanding that Jesus fully reveals God to humanity (see John 1:18). There are other areas of revelation that also seem to fit this pattern of unfolding. For instance, a clearer conception of the afterlife, focused on resurrection, develops in later parts of the Old Testament. By the time of the New Testament, the notion of resurrection is quite well developed.

Second, listening to texts from the temporal vantage point in which they were given will help us to keep in proper relationship the theological motifs that weave through the biblical story. The Torah (or law), understood as good and perfect (e.g., Ps. 119:137–144), fits well within the temporal framework of God's covenant actions toward Israel. We hear the order of the story in Exodus: Israel is redeemed from slavery in Egypt

---

22. Goldingay, "Biblical Narrative," 130; italics mine.

(Exod. 14–15). Then Yahweh reaffirms the covenant with Israel, promising to be their God (Exod. 19). It is only after Yahweh has redeemed and covenanted with them that they are given the Torah (Exod. 20–23). Attention to this historical movement will keep us from viewing the law as a means for Israel to somehow earn a place in covenant with Yahweh, a common misconception that circulates among some Christian groups. Instead, we will understand Torah as a part of the covenant that spells out how Israel was to live in restored relationship with their God.

Timeless Principles or Enculturated Truth?

If Scripture is culturally located, it also follows that the truth contained therein is enculturated truth. It is truth spoken already to a cultural context, tailor-made especially for that situation. "Culture . . . becomes the providentially controlled matrix out of which [God's] revelation comes to us."[23] As such, Scripture's "communicative aims are at the same time both constrained and mobilized by the contexts within which they were generated."[24] The reality that biblical truth is enculturated does not diminish its truthfulness—it is no less truth for being enculturated or storied.[25] It does mean, however, that there is a necessary recontextualization that occurs when we allow Scripture to address our own contexts. How does this recontextualization happen?

We have already discussed one rather common method of contextualization, which begins with determining whether a biblical text is transcultural and culturally bound. If a text is thought to be culturally bound, the next step is to discover the principle underlying what is culturally bound and to apply that principle to the new context. As Jack Kuhatschek explains, "Look beneath the surface [of a passage] for a general principle."[26] The idea in this method is to extract the transcultural principle from the culturally bound form. I have already mentioned my hesitation with assuming the validity of the distinction between these two types of texts. My second concern with this principlizing procedure as an overarching contextualization method is that it has as its goal timeless, abstracted truth.[27]

23. Conn, "Normativity," 200.

24. Green, "Practicing the Gospel," 396.

25. Moritz helpfully speaks of "storied knowledge" in distinction to principles disembodied from story (Moritz, "Critical but Real," 184). My emphasis on enculturated truth assumes the importance of knowledge as "storied."

26. Jack Kuhatschek, *Taking the Guesswork Out of Applying the Bible* (Downers Grove, IL: InterVarsity, 1990), 52.

27. Johann Philipp Gabler, the "father" of the modern disconnection between historical study of the Bible and biblical theology, had as his goal to arrive at "timeless and universal principles of the Bible" (Green, "Practicing the Gospel," 389). In pursuing principlizing as our primary method of contextualization, have we internalized a particularly modern methodology originally meant to domesticate and deconfessionalize the Bible?

In fact, even if we are able to extract a principle from a passage that has no direct corollary to our setting, we would surely want to affirm that it is Scripture itself in all its cultural particularity that is inspired and authoritative. It is not the principle we extract that earns that description. It would be all too easy to venerate the principle in place of the text, if we have been taught that ahistorical, timeless truths are what we are after. But Scripture itself is God's word, not our attempts to "principlize" it.[28] It would be highly ironic if those who claim to believe the very best about the Bible (its authority, infallibility, inerrancy) actually downplayed the importance of Scripture by preferring the timeless truths they extract from it. As Vanhoozer warns, "It is dangerous to think that a set of deculturalized principles is a more accurate indication of God's will than its canonical expression."[29]

In addition, we do not somehow avoid the "problem" of culture by principlizing, because we ourselves are enculturated. We are influenced by our own settings and cultures, and so we do not qualify as experts on discerning timeless principles. We will be quite prone to see our own ideals underlying the biblical text. As Clark notes, "In principlizing, the biblical content is carried, if you will, from one context to another in the container of abstract, transcultural principles. But principlizing obscures the fact that any articulation of the allegedly transcultural principles still reflects the culture of the [interpreter]."[30]

Wright contends that reading the Bible to discern abstract truths may actually sit at odds with an incarnational understanding of Scripture.

> At no point can we abstract Paul's ideas from [his] setting; and this, within an incarnational religion such as Christianity, has almost always been and is undoubtedly a strength, not a weakness. To suppose that one must boil off doctrinal abstractions from the particularities of the letters in order to gain material that can be usable in different situations is at best a half-truth; it always runs the risk of implying that the "ideas" are the reality, and that the community in which they are embodied and embedded (Paul's community on the one hand, ours on the other) is a secondary matter.[31]

Wright points to another way of contextualizing that avoids making principlizing our primary method in his reference to the two "communities" of the interpretive process—the biblical world and our own. In the previous chapter, we suggested that one productive way of visualizing

28. Clark, *To Know and Love God*, 94. In this regard, see the critique by both Conn ("Normativity," 197) and Vanhoozer ("Great 'Beyond,'" 92).

29. Vanhoozer, "Great 'Beyond,'" 92.

30. Clark, *To Know and Love God*, 112.

31. N. T. Wright, "The Letter to the Galatians: Exegesis and Theology," in *Between Two Horizons*, 230.

contextualization is as participation, focused on the intersection of our world with the biblical world. In this model the interpreter is invited to enter the biblical world and hear the resonance or overlap between the normative stance of the text and our own context.[32] As we will see in a moment, this way of thinking about contextualization does not bypass completely what happens in principlizing. Nevertheless, contextualization as participation does take the primary methodological focus away from principlization.

Contextualization as participation invites us to explore how a biblical text is paradigmatic for our own contexts. As we bring our own contexts into the evaluative light of the biblical world, we experience resonance between the two worlds. The overlap between the world of the text and our world suggests certain recontextualizations. These can then be tested and refined by asking the questions of coherence and purpose we have introduced in the previous chapter. Does a proposed recontextualization cohere with the original message? And specifically, does it fit the author's purposes for the original message?

In this kind of paradigmatic exploration, we will be drawn to use our imagination to envision points of overlap between the world of the text and our world. Just as in exegesis, a disciplined imagination is required in contextualization.[33] "Creativity" and "imagination" are not dirty words in interpretation or contextualization.[34] Using one's imagination does not presuppose that the reader is thereby creating meaning. Imaginative skill is necessary all along the interpretive process, from envisioning how the words of the biblical text would have been heard by the original audience to discerning how the text's normative stance ought to impinge upon and impact the contemporary world. We engage our imaginations not simply for the sake of creativity itself but to envision how the text's message might be enacted in our own context. Contextualization calls

32. Conn, "Normativity," 188. Conn argues that "the heart of the hermeneutical task . . . does not lie simply in the effort to find the biblical principles that emerge out of the historical meaning of each passage. . . . Our hermeneutical task is to see how [the Bible] applies to each of us in the cultural context and social setting we occupy in God's redemptive history. We are involved in looking for the place where the horizons of the text and the interpreter intersect or engage" (188).

33. Gorman speaks of exegetical method as "disciplined investigation and imagination" (Michael J. Gorman, *Elements of Biblical Exegesis: A Basic Guide for Students and Ministers* [Peabody, MA: Hendrickson, 2001], 141).

34. I am indebted to Mary Hinkle for her stimulating presentation reviewing the relative lack of the attention to interpretive imagination in exegesis textbooks, as well as for the particular citations from Gorman and Fee (Mary E. Hinkle, "Whither Imagination? Comparing Exegesis Textbooks" [paper presented at the annual meeting of the Upper Midwest Region of the Society of Biblical Literature, St. Paul, MN, 2 April 2005], 1).

for "a lively imagination and the hard work of thinking, as well as the skill of having done the exegesis well."[35]

Principlizing as a Tool within Purpose-Guided Contextualization

We have looked at some disadvantages of principlizing as an overarching method of contextualization. So it might come as a surprise to hear that principlizing is not at odds with contextualization that takes seriously the cultural and temporal locatedness of the Bible. In fact, principlizing can be quite helpful as one tool within a broader purpose-guided method of contextualization.[36] In my estimation, as long as we do not elevate this one tool among others to a place where it becomes our only method for contextualization, principlizing can assist the contextualization process.[37] As Clark notes, "Some kind of principlizing is necessary to evangelical theology. . . . But using this model only—seeing all theology as principlizing the Bible—is inadequate."[38]

A comparison of principlizing and purpose-guided contextualization demonstrates how the latter functions more adequately as an overarching method than the former, for a number of reasons. First, principlizing tends toward abstraction, with the result often being ahistorical truth abstracted from its cultural context. Hence some advocates of principliz-

35. Gordon D. Fee, *New Testament Exegesis*, 2nd ed. (Louisville: Westminster John Knox, 1993), 60. Fee is particularly focusing on preaching in his discussion, with the goal of making the biblical point "a living word for a present-day congregation" (60). For a call for the restoration of Christian imagination in a postmodern context, see Garrett Green, *Theology, Hermeneutics, and Imagination: Interpretation at the End of Modernity* (Cambridge: Cambridge University Press, 2000), 13–22.

36. For Christopher Wright, principles fit within a paradigmatic method of contextualizing. "To use a paradigm you do have to look for and articulate the principles the paradigm embodies and then see how they can be reconcretized in some other context" (*Old Testament Ethics*, 70).

37. Principlizing is really about bringing the conceptual tools of generalizing and particularizing to bear in the contextualization project. We consistently use these dual conceptual tools as we process the world around us. For example, as children we seek to discern where in the scheme of things certain specifics fit. So if I would say to my daughters when they were preschoolers, "No treats until after dinner," I could expect to hear a reply to the effect, "Fruit snacks aren't treats, are they, Mom?" By particularizing fruit snacks to a category outside of "treats," they hoped that they might get something sweet before dinner! As they have gotten older, the subjects change a bit, but the skills are still being refined. "Can we go to the mall today?" "No, not today." "Does that mean we can't go shopping at all, or just not at the mall?" Here generalization and particularization are at work.

38. Clark, *To Know and Love God*, 94. He argues for "a culturally nuanced, 'soft' principlizing approach by admitting that all formulations of principles are culturally embedded" (95). Vanhoozer speaks of incorporating the proposition "into a larger model of truth and interpretation" (Kevin J. Vanhoozer, "Lost in Interpretation? Truth, Scripture, and Hermeneutics," *Journal of the Evangelical Theological Society* 48 [March 2005]: 102).

ing also emphasize necessary caution when doing this task.[39] Asking the purpose question of a text, on the other hand, invites the interpreter to keep the original setting in focus, since it is precisely reflection on the original setting that will illuminate the purpose question. The purpose question begs contextual questions. The purpose for the original setting can then be understood as paradigmatic for the interpreter's setting.

I recently asked some students to contextualize Exodus 40, where Moses completes the final stages of the tabernacle as instructed, after which God's presence comes upon the completed tabernacle.[40] What I found interesting in our subsequent class discussion was that the first impulse of many students was to detect a principle in the text, which they then applied to our own contexts. One of the first principles suggested was that of obedience: as Moses obeyed in every detail of the tabernacle completion, so we should obey in the little things of life. By enacting a kind of contextualization that began with and focused on principlizing, students discerned an ethically focused abstraction. In contrast, if we were to ask about the purposes of Exodus 40, we would be more likely to stay in the cultural specificity of the story, and so hear Moses' obedience serving the theological purposes of God's coming to dwell with Israel (Exod. 40:34–38), after their obedience in crafting the tabernacle exactly as instructed (Exod. 25–31, 35–40)—even after their idolatrous worship of the golden calf (Exod. 32).[41] The culminating moment of Exodus illustrates the author's purpose: to reveal a God who goes to great lengths to live in covenant relationship with a sinful, idolatrous people.

A second advantage of purpose-guided contextualization over principlizing is that, while principlizing can theoretically be applied to any amount of text, asking about the purposes of a text tends to expand our vista to acknowledge the larger literary context. This expansion happens because asking the purpose question turns interpreters toward the author, who purposes something by the text. And once the author is on "our radar screen," we are less likely to isolate a small bit of text from the wider context that makes sense of it. It is easy enough to draw an

39. Kaiser, who proposes following a ladder of abstraction from an Old Testament command that is situationally located to its application in another context, also warns of the "enormous possibilities for abuse of such a system of interpretation that lays heavy emphasis on a ladder of abstraction, analogy, and the search for undergirding principle" (Walter C. Kaiser Jr., *Toward Rediscovering the Old Testament* [Grand Rapids: Zondervan, 1987], 164).

40. We must be careful to heed the earlier warning to avoid isolating any chapter of a narrative from its literary context. I was able to ask students to reflect on the contextualization of Exod. 40 because of work we had done on Exodus prior to this.

41. We have noted in our discussion of biblical narrative that we should routinely ask the theological question before the ethical one, since a focus on the theological purposes of a text will help us rightly hear its ethical thrust. See chap. 7.

abstract principle from a single sentence, but as soon as we acknowledge an author who communicated that sentence, we are drawn to ask how that sentence functions in the author's wider discourse. The question of purpose invites the specific question, Whose purpose? This is an author-focused question. A purpose-guided approach to Exodus 40 encourages us to think about the author and so also the wider context.

A third benefit of purpose-guided contextualization is that it will encourage us to recognize the differences between the world of the text and our world. Principlizing uses abstraction to move beyond cultural particularities in a text that do not seem to transfer to other cultural contexts. But if we use this kind of abstraction as our first and primary way of contextualizing, we risk smoothing over cultural and temporal distinctions that deserve our careful attention. As much as Exodus 40 should significantly impact us, we should also recognize where in the flow of salvation-history this text sits. It is interesting to me that one response that invariably comes up when discussing this text is a kind of longing for such obvious manifestations of God's presence. When God's glory comes upon the tabernacle in the cloud, it is an amazing moment, to be sure. Yet given that we read this text after the coming of Jesus the Messiah, after the time when God's presence has come to us in the person of Jesus (John 1:14–18), is it the case that Israel in the tabernacle had more palpable experiences of God than we do? Or as the church, are we promised the presence of Jesus in our midst by the Spirit in a way that would have caused any faithful Israelite to long for our days?

Finally, principlizing often remains on the cognitive level of the text, since a principle is a cognitively focused construct. Purpose-guided contextualization, in contrast, can help us envision a whole range of responses appropriate to any given text. There is a holistic cast to the question, What were the author's purposes in this text? that enables us to expand contextualization to include both cognitive and noncognitive responses. For example, if in Exodus 40 a key purpose of the author is to reveal a God who goes to great lengths to live in covenant relationship with a sinful, idolatrous people, we might ask what that revelation is to accomplish in the readers. Certainly to believe and affirm the truth of that revelation is important. How we *think* is rightly impacted by this text. Yet asking the purpose question also pushes us to wonder about how we might respond in other ways to this text. If God goes to such lengths to live with an imperfect people, we might be drawn into *new ways of experiencing* this amazingly relational God. We also will hear the text's call to obedience within its proper covenantal framework. It makes all the sense in the world to *respond in obedience* to a God who goes to such lengths to live among his people.

This multifaceted way of contextualizing fits with an incarnational understanding of the Bible, since one of the ultimate purposes of Scripture is to shape the believing community into all God intends it to be. We will explore this aspect of an incarnational perspective on Scripture in the final portion of this chapter.

The Bible as Culturally Located Divine Discourse for the Shaping of the Christian Community

Incarnation is first of all an action—the action of God dwelling with his people. In a sense, this is what God did with Israel in the Old Testament: God "tabernacled" with them. Incarnation is what God has done definitively in Christ, "the Word became flesh." There is no disjunction between speech and action in the work of God. In the beginning God spoke, and creation came into being. So it should not be at all surprising that Scripture too may be conceived as God's speech-acts.[42] Allow me to remind you of the definition of meaning introduced in chapter 2: the complex pattern of what an author intends to communicate with his or her audience for purposes of engagement, which is inscribed in the text and conveyed through use of both shareable language parameters and background-contextual assumptions. Our definition emphasizes that communicative intentions are for *purposes of engagement*. Biblical authors do things as they say things, and they intend for their audiences to respond by doing things as well!

On the big-picture level, what is it that Scripture does? As Vanhoozer has suggested, on the level of the whole canon, one of the primary ways God acts is by covenanting.[43] Through Scripture, God invites fallen humanity into restored relationship. Along with this purpose, God intends to shape that community into full restoration. In fact, we might envision the shaping of the people of God into the christological pattern of restored humanity as God's perlocutionary intention at the canonical level of the Bible.[44] Scripture functions to do this shaping work among communities of believers as they actively respond to the shaping work of God. As the biblical writers instruct, command, warn, assure, and testify, we hear the speech-acts of God to instruct, command, warn, assure, and testify. These illocutions are part of the larger perlocutionary

42. As we have seen in the discussion of speech-act theory in chap. 2, to speak is to act.

43. Vanhoozer includes with covenanting "instructing the believing community [and] testifying to Christ" (*First Theology*, 195).

44. "The ultimate purpose of the divine canonical discourse is to form a new people, the vanguard of a new creation. This is the 'perlocutionary' purpose of Scripture, its intended effect" (Vanhoozer, *Drama of Doctrine*, 182).

project of shaping a people who receive and embody the salvation of God in Christ. I am speaking here of salvation conceived broadly in its "profound[ly] biblical sense of God's purposes that began with creation and that will be consummated at Christ's coming—namely creating a people for his name, who will live in close relationship with him and will bear his likeness, and thus be for his glory."[45]

Contextualization is something that not only impacts our minds but also shapes all we are, as individuals and as communities of faith. Given this shaping effect, we will want to attend to the performative concerns of Scripture in contextualization as described in chapter 2. At that point in our discussion, meaning was conceived as an author's communicative intention for purposes of engagement with readers. Revisiting the conceptual work of that chapter, we are assisted by the contributions of speech-act theory and the construct of the implied reader.

The connection between speech-act theory and Scripture's shaping influence is a natural one. As we have just discussed, we can envision the Bible at its canonical level in terms of divine locutions, illocutions, and perlocutionary intentions. How might these conceptual categories assist us in the contextualization process of specific biblical texts? One contribution of speech-act theory is its attention to the intentions of an author for reader enactment. In other words, authors, including God as author, have intentions for how readers respond to their messages. These intended effects, the author's perlocutionary intentions, are an extension of meaning.[46] This construct encourages us in our quest to contextualize its message to ask the question of the intended effect of any particular text.[47] If a particular locution, that is, a set of words, does not bring about an effect in a new setting that is consistent with the intended effect for the original audience, we may need to hear a recontextualized locution for the new setting.[48]

Now the notion that the words of Scripture may need recontextualizing is bound to make nervous anyone who takes the Bible seriously. So let me clarify what I mean by recontextualizing biblical locutions. Since meaning consists of not only locutions but also illocutions and perlocutionary intentions, we will need to include each of these categories in interpretation. If a locution that brought about a particular effect in the original audience enacts a quite different effect in another setting, we will not honor the author's communicative intentions by merely replicating

45. Gordon D. Fee, *Listening to the Spirit in the Text* (Grand Rapids: Eerdmans, 2000), 26.

46. See chap. 5.

47. We have seen in chap. 11 that this fits the criterion of purpose raised by Hirsch.

48. We already looked at the example of Lev. 19:19 in chap. 11, where this was essentially the case.

the locution in the new setting. In fact, mere reproduction of an utterance from one context into a different context may very well produce a meaning that is foreign to an author's communicative intention.[49] As a result, we will want to consider carefully how a locution originally uttered in one context might be "transferred" into another setting in order to be true to communicative intention.[50] As Enns affirms, "Our task in biblical interpretation is to communicate the one, unchanging gospel . . . in such a way that respects and even *expects* that message to be articulated differently in different contexts."[51] This seems to fit Vanhoozer's notion of a pattern of judgments. He speaks of "learn[ing] not simply to parse the verbs or to process the information, but to render the same kinds of judgments as those embedded in the canon in new contexts and with different concepts."[52]

A frequently used example is the New Testament command to greet fellow believers with a kiss (e.g., Rom. 16:16). Not much of that kind of greeting occurs in the Christian communities I am familiar with (the Minnesotan kind, at least!). Since the intended effect of the exhortation is the enacting of a warm greeting among those who share the bond of Christ, it is fair to ask whether this intended effect is accomplished by the act of kissing in one's own cultural context. In some contemporary cultures, the answer is yes, so that the intention of Paul's exhortation is heard well with the original locution-illocution pairing. In some contemporary cultures, a kiss "may not make people feel welcomed at all" and may instead work against the goal of community building.[53] As we

---

49. This is an insight from relevance theory. For example, if I say "Put a lid on it" to my daughter as she puts a food container in the refrigerator, I intend an activity on her part that will keep our leftovers fresh. Those words in a different context (without any physical lids present) will likely convey an entirely different meaning!

50. To state the obvious: since the original locution of a biblical text is in Hebrew, Aramaic, or Greek, the first transferal will be translation (a linguistic-interpretive transferal). See Vanhoozer's distinction between *ipse* and *idem* "sameness" for another way of expressing this notion of transferal (*Drama of Doctrine*, 314).

51. Enns, *Inspiration and Incarnation*, 170–71.

52. Vanhoozer, "Great 'Beyond,'" 93.

53. Wayne Grudem, "Should We Move Beyond the New Testament to a Better Ethic?" *Journal of the Evangelical Theological Society* 47 (June 2004): 338. Given his flexibility with locution here, it is not clear to me why Grudem disavows the intended effect of a biblical text as a helpful category for discerning appropriate contextualization. In the very same paragraph in which he affirms asking about the intent of the "holy kiss," he argues against the use of the same category in relation to the command for wives to be subject to their husbands: "[The intent category] implies that we can disobey New Testament commands [such as wives being subject to their husbands] if we decide that the purpose specified in the command will no longer be fulfilled" (338). The very same accusation (disobedience to a New Testament command) could be leveled at his transferal of the command to greet fellow believers with a kiss into a warm greeting! The entire point of asking about intent is that there are times when an original locution no longer fulfills its

saw in chapter 11, asking the purpose question—Hirsch's second principle—helps us to discern how we might recontextualize biblical texts in other contexts.[54] This kind of purpose-guided contextualization takes seriously the importance of authors' perlocutionary intentions.

And the concept of perlocutionary intentions can help us navigate at least some of the issues in the current debate in evangelical circles over the appropriateness of applying a redemptive-movement hermeneutic in contextualization.[55] A fundamental critique of Webb's proposal for a redemptive-movement hermeneutic is that it elevates an ethic that is "beyond" the New Testament, rather than honoring the New Testament ethic.[56] This critique, put in speech-act language, assumes that a New Testament ethic consists solely of locutions (and possibly illocutions), rather than extending to the perlocutionary intentions of particular texts as well. If the whole meaning of a textual utterance, including its intended effects, is in view, then the resulting ethic or contextualization is not one that sits beyond the New Testament, but within the intention parameters of its authors.[57] In fact, Webb's response to this critique is that it misinterprets his proposal. According to Webb, when he uses the phrase "going beyond," he is consistently referring to going beyond an understanding of the Bible as "isolated words" to understanding its meaning in its original context.[58] In speech-act terminology, Webb's

purpose in a new context. This means that "disobeying" a locution does not necessitate "disobeying" the author's message. See Webb's discussion of this example, *Slaves, Women, and Homosexuals*, 105–6.

54. I am convinced that asking the purpose question will also frame the contemporary debate about the roles of women in different terms. Hearing the locutions of the New Testament authors on this issue against the backdrop of the first-century context is crucial in this regard. Yet I do not believe that the New Testament writers were uniformly "egalitarians" (an anachronism, in any event), though the New Testament authors seem consistently more "egalitarian" than their Greco-Roman cultural counterparts. The latter observation is an important one in the debate, as Webb points out (*Slaves, Women, and Homosexuals*, 76–77).

55. Proposed by Webb in *Slaves, Women, and Homosexuals*.

56. See, for example, Grudem, "Better Ethic?" 299–346.

57. The same critique has been leveled against Marshall's contextualization model by Vanhoozer in *Beyond the Bible*, which includes both Marshall's proposal and two responses, one by Vanhoozer. In my estimation, the critique that Marshall elevates an extrabiblical ethic over that of the New Testament is justified at some points (see Vanhoozer, "Great 'Beyond,'" 85–86). In addition, Marshall's work on Jesus seems to suffer from inadequate attention to the narratival and so temporal character of the Gospels (63–69). Reading each Gospel holistically with a sense of its temporal movement offers a better understanding of the category of "liminality," which is important to Marshall's formulation of contextualization.

58. William J. Webb, "A Redemptive-Movement Hermeneutic: Encouraging Dialogue among Four Evangelical Views," *Journal of the Evangelical Theological Society* 48 (June 2005): 336.

proposed hermeneutic seeks to attend to the perlocutionary intention as well as locution-illocution, rather than focusing solely on textual locution.[59]

Finally, we may return to the implied reader construct introduced in chapter 2 and illustrated further in chapter 6. Since the implied reader is the hypothetical reader who fulfills all the intentions of the author, the implied reader will not only understand the author's message but also will be shaped by the author's communicative intention. The implied reader construct can help us to reenvision the exegetical task in a more holistic way, what Green refers to as the task of conversion rather than merely application.[60] Clearly, the biblical authors were interested in converting their readers to a theological perspective and a life vocation. And conversion is not a "halfway deal."

Consideration of the implied reader moves us toward active participation in the world of the text, since it moves us to appropriate the author's normative stance holistically. As we read a text with appropriation in mind, we might reflect on the following question: "What sort of world, what sort of community, and what sort of person is this text constructing?"[61] This is, in essence, the question of discerning the implied reader of a text. In the final analysis, the task of contextualization involves not only answering such questions but also living out the answers in response to God's work in our lives, in the church, and in the world.

Conclusion

As real readers, who live in a world both near and distant from the ancient texts of Scripture, we are invited to take our cues from its incarnational nature. The reality is that we sit at a distance from the text, separated by thousands of years, by cultures, by languages, by the span of history. This distance should give us pause. It means we should seek

59. In addition, Webb's redemptive-movement hermeneutic recognizes the importance of attention to the social setting of the text for interpretation, though this is by no means unique to his proposal. In particular, asking the question of where along a spectrum of views a biblical teaching or command sits helps us to hear the intended effect of that teaching in its original context. We are then better able to hear right ways of recontextualizing the original message in our own settings. A weakness of Webb's proposal, in my estimation, is its elaborate systematization, without a clear sense of primary questions or issues that might assist in contextualization. I believe that the intent criterion he describes (criterion four of eighteen) is a primary lens through which to view contextualization, given its overlap with communicative intention. Webb's intent criterion aligns with my notion of purpose-guided contextualization.

60. Green, "Practicing the Gospel," 397.

61. Ibid.

to avoid any sort of simplistic approach to the text and its meaning. Humility ought to be the order of the day.

> The ultimate aim of exegesis . . . is to produce in our lives and the lives of others true Spirituality, in which God's people live in faithful fellowship both with one another and with the eternal and living God and thus in keeping with God's own purposes in the world. In order to do this effectively . . . true "Spirituality" must *precede* exegesis as well as be the final result of it. We must begin as we would conclude, standing under the text, not over it with all of our scholarly arrogance intact.[62]

Yet there is also a nearness, a participation between text and reader, given that we live in the flow of human history that connects then and now. And more particularly, we live as the people of God, the same audience in a very real sense that was addressed by God and God's word at many specific points and locations within biblical history. We experience this nearness, this engagement of horizons, because Scripture is not only a human testimony but is also God's testimony—it is "God-breathed." Scripture's nearness, I believe, invites us to live with conviction—to trust that we are on the path to knowing God and living as a faithful community in this world as we read the Bible to be shaped by it. That is the grand intention of Scripture. In the end, conviction *and* humility are proper attitudes that reflect the incarnational nature of the Bible.[63]

Reading the Bible to be fully shaped by it is a worthy goal, and one that fits the incarnational and communicative nature of Scripture. I believe the biblical writers would be disconcerted, to say the least, to think that what they had written might be used to shape only our thinking.[64] In other words, there is no biblical justification for the notion that if we just get our theology right, we have done justice to the contextualization task. There is no true theology divorced from ethics. To read the Bible on its own terms will mean reading to be shaped in our thinking, being, and doing. No part of who we are individually or as church communities ought to be left untouched by Scripture. As Jesus reckoned the shaping influence of his Bible:

> "Love the Lord your God with all your heart and with all your soul and with all your mind." This is the first and greatest commandment. And the second is like it: "Love your neighbor as yourself." All the Law and the prophets hang on these two commandments. (Matt. 22:37–40 NIV)

62. Gordon D. Fee, *To What End Exegesis? Essays Textual, Exegetical, and Theological* (Grand Rapids: Eerdmans, 2001), 280.

63. Vanhoozer, *Is There a Meaning?* 455–56.

64. This dichotomy is, of course, a fallacy. How we think inevitably affects our identity and our behavior. In this sense, theology is ultimately the most practical of inquiries.

I love that the mind is included in Jesus' assessment of the Scripture's central thrust.[65] To love God with our minds is a crucial challenge of the biblical message. Yet "all that we are" matters to God. And so all that we are matters in exegesis and contextualization. We bring our whole person to the task of reading the Bible. And we are called to respond to Scripture with our whole person, so that our lives, both individually and communally, are fully shaped by the God who speaks to us through the Bible.

65. This in itself is an example of recontextualization, since the *Shema* (Deut. 6:5) speaks of loving God with heart, soul, and strength. Jesus includes loving God with one's mind as well. This appropriately expresses what is already implicit in the terms translated "heart" and "soul" from the Hebrew text.

Exegesis Guidelines

A Christian reading of the Bible as Scripture must be one conducted within certain identifiable constraints.

Trevor Hart, "Tradition, Authority, and a Christian Approach to the Bible as Scripture," in *Between Two Horizons*

The following nine guidelines take seriously the issues raised in chapters 7 through 10 about genre, language, and social and literary contexts. In addition, they begin and end with concerted attention to how we might raise our own consciousness of the presuppositions we bring to the biblical text. It should be noted that these guidelines have been developed for students who study the Bible in English translation. Attention to original language work that precedes English study involves determining the text (textual criticism) and translating the text.[1]

1. Reflect on presuppositions that impact interpretation of a passage.

a. Read through the passage briefly. Note your level of familiarity with the passage.

---

1. The nine guidelines in broad strokes have been developed in conjunction with my Bethel colleagues Peter Vogt and Thorsten Moritz. The details that develop each guideline and the illustrations of them from Ephesians are my own.

    b. Jot down any particular interpretations of this passage that you have heard before (in sermons, teachings, books, etc.) that influence your current reading of it.

    c. Are there any other biblical passages that come to mind that you would be likely to use as an interpretive lens for this text?

    d. Jot down any terms or ideas that seem "foreign" to you, that you might be likely to fill in with contemporary definitions or your own ideas.

    e. As you move through the following guidelines, try to hear the passage and its message on its own terms as much as possible. Ask for God's guidance in this process.

2. Identify social-world context: the sociohistorical, political, and religious contexts.

    a. Identify the author, audience, date, and purpose of the biblical book being studied. Some of this information can be deduced from a careful reading of the book itself. At times, it is necessary and helpful to consult secondary sources: e.g., Old Testament and New Testament introductions, Bible dictionaries or encyclopedias, and the introductory section of commentaries.[2]

    Example: For a study of Ephesians, it would be important to identify that the letter is quite likely a circular letter written for a variety of churches, not only or primarily for Ephesus. The evidence for this is the omission of "at Ephesus" in the earlier manuscripts, as well as the general nature of Paul's comments at 1:15; 3:2; and 4:21. This would account for the more general nature of the letter.

    b. Note any historical, cultural, or religious issues that need to be investigated to better understand the particular text you are studying. In addition, pay attention to any citations or allusions to Old Testament texts in your passage and how they function in the New Testament passage (the issue of intertextuality; see 5d below).

    Example: To understand Ephesians 2:11–22, it would be important to be familiar with the Old Testament covenants and the related rite of circumcision, background to the images of cornerstone and temple, and the allusion to Isaiah 57:19.

---

2. Other than parts of the introductory section, commentaries should not be consulted until a preliminary analysis of the text has been completed. This helps the exegete to avoid undue reliance on commentaries.

3. Identify genre: the literary category of the writing being studied.

a. Identify the literary form or forms in the text.
Example: If you are studying a Gospel text, note if the text is strictly narrative or if it includes other kinds of material, such as parable or genealogy.

b. Consult secondary sources (e.g., Fee and Stuart; Osborne) to learn about the tendencies of these forms and the principles for interpreting them.
Example: For a study of Ephesians, it would be important to know the basic parts of an ancient letter (epistle) and to recognize the necessity of identifying the purpose of a Pauline letter as well as analyzing the argument of the letter.

4. Identify the text and literary context: the text to be interpreted and its literary surroundings.

a. The whole book
  i. Read through the entire biblical book a few times to get an overview.
  ii. Outline the book by looking for its natural divisions. (Hint: Look for major sections, "seams," and subject changes.)
  iii. Provide your own "title" (i.e., short summary) for each section.
  iv. Notice the major themes of the book.
  v. Determine the stated or implicit purpose(s) of the book.
  Example: The regulation of conduct within households (Eph. 5:21–6:9) naturally divides into the relationships between wives and husbands (5:22–33), children and parents (6:1–4), and slaves and masters (6:5–9), introduced by a general statement concerning mutual submission in 5:21.

b. The larger section: Note how the passage fits into its larger section by tracing the themes, subject matter, and/or argument within the major section in which your passage appears.
  Example: Ephesians 2:11–22 falls within the first of two major sections in Ephesians. 1:3–3:21 is an extended benediction and prayer, focusing on God's eternal purpose in Christ to unite into one body Gentiles and Jews. 2:11–22 fits within this section by emphasizing the change that has occurred for Gentiles who now have been enfolded into God's chosen people.

c. The immediate context: Note how the passages/verses that immediately precede and follow the passage help in understanding the passage in question.

Example: Ephesians 2:11–22 is immediately preceded by Paul's contrast between what the Gentiles were before Christ and the grace and mercy they have received from God in Christ. 2:11–22 continues to emphasize this contrast. In the passage immediately following it (3:1–13), Paul speaks of his ministry to the Gentiles: preaching the gospel and sharing the mystery of their inclusion into the people of God.

d. At this point, reassess the boundaries of your passage to ensure that you are dealing with the entire thought unit.

5. Carefully study the text using appropriate methods and tools.

Do a detailed analysis of the passage by:

a. Outlining the passage: Divide the text into its natural sections and give a short title to each section summarizing its main idea.
b. Mapping the passage:
   i. Identifying and connecting repeated words/phrases/ideas.
   ii. Identifying comparisons and contrasts.
   iii. Studying the relationships of ideas through the passage.
      • If your text is a narrative, pay attention to the flow of the plot and such issues as the setting, dialogue, and climax of the narrative.
      • If your text is poetic, look for repetition between lines (parallelism) and metaphorical (figurative) language.
      • If your text is an epistle, pay close attention to the relationships between clauses or ideas.
c. Identifying the key ideas of the passage: "Stand back" from your detailed analysis to identify a number of the key ideas of the text. Put these in full-sentence form.
d. Identifying any biblical texts that are cited or clearly alluded to in the passage you are studying. (Often a New Testament writer will draw upon Old Testament texts.)
   i. Note the context of the cited text as well as the biblical-theological themes or meta-stories that are present in that text.
   ii. Reflect on the connection between these features of the text cited and its use in the passage under consideration. Try to determine the reason for the writer's use of the cited text. Here are some possibilities: Is it used

- To support a part of the argument?
- To evoke a part of Israel's story?
- To provide an analogy?
- To stress continuity between some aspect of the New Testament and the Old Testament?

  e. Researching key words and phrases. (Knowledge of original languages is important for proper lexical study.)

    i. Choose words to study that are ambiguous, thematic (i.e., repeated in your passage and throughout the book), and/or theologically important.

    ii. Trace how the author uses the word or phrase in the book as a whole as well as in other books by the same author. (This will entail using a concordance and other word study references.)

  f. Consulting exegetical commentaries for comparison with your results and for additional insights.

6. Summarize the key ideas of the text.

Attempt to capture in one sentence the *main ideas* of the passage. It is often helpful to cast this sentence in past-tense, third-person language (i.e., author-oriented language: e.g., Paul was teaching that . . .). A summary sentence will stress the main idea(s) and will demonstrate how secondary points of the passage support this main idea. The goal is to produce a *disciplined, interpretive paraphrase.*[3]

Example: A summary of Ephesians 2:11–22 might read: Paul was reminding his Gentile audience that, even though they had formerly been alienated from God, they were now reconciled with God and God's people, Israel, through Christ and, as a result, part of the living temple in which God's Spirit dwells.

7. Integrate conclusions with larger biblical-theological story.

  a. Revisit any biblical texts that are cited or clearly alluded to in the passage you are studying (cf. guideline 5d).

  b. Ask how the cited (prior) text fits with the overarching story of God's work in humanity and creation.

3. I owe the language and suggestion of a "disciplined interpretive paraphrase" to Garwood Anderson, who has developed this concept for an assignment with his exegetical students at Asbury Theological Seminary, Orlando, Florida.

c. Ask how the author in the passage you are studying builds on and contributes to the overarching biblical-theological story.
Example: In Ephesians 2:17, Paul references part of Isaiah 57:19. Since the Isaiah text is about Israel's restoration, Paul seems to be evoking the story of God's returning his people from near and far to show that in Christ this has now happened. In the process, he expands the referent of those "far away" from scattered Israel (from exile) to the Gentiles explicitly. In addition, Paul shows how the story of God's presence with his people has come to a restorative climax in Jesus, so that the new covenant people of God are now the locus of God's dwelling place.

8. Delineate relevant implications for today.

a. Preaching/teaching application: Recast your summary sentence (cf. guideline 6) into a "sermon idea" (using present tense, audience-oriented language).
b. Theological application
  i. Ask the questions: What does the text teach about God, God's nature, work, and intentions? What does the text teach about humanity, its condition, purpose, future?
  ii. What does Scripture have to say about the same topic elsewhere?
c. Personal application: Ask God to change the way you think and live through what you have studied.
Example: Ephesians 2:11–22 is an important passage for understanding the biblical theology of the people of God. Specifically, we hear how the church is that people, Jew and Gentile, who have been brought together by the work of Jesus the Messiah to be the physical manifestation of God's Spirit.

9. Rethink presuppositions: Are we being transformed?

a. Review your notes on guideline 1 above (reflect on presuppositions). Have your initial ideas about the passage changed at all? If so, how and why?
b. Has interaction with other interpreters (e.g., commentators) impacted the way you understand this passage? If so, how and why?
c. Has studying this passage closely and prayerfully brought transformation in terms of thinking, being, and/or doing?

Appendix B

Historical Criticism

Historical Criticism

Historical criticism is analysis of the Bible that focuses upon what has been called "behind the text" issues, such as the traditions, sources, and oral forms that were used by the biblical authors as they wrote. Historical criticism has also traditionally focused on determination of the original context of biblical books, including issues regarding authorship, dating, and audience as well as more general historical study of the time periods in which the biblical text was written.[1] We can identify three fairly distinct movements within historical criticism: source, form, and redaction criticisms.

---

1. For helpful overviews of historical criticism in both testaments, with attention to its presuppositional tendency toward skepticism, see Duane A. Garrett, "Historical Criticism of the Old Testament," and Craig L. Blomberg, "Historical Criticism of the New Testament," in *Foundations for Biblical Interpretation: A Complete Library of Tools and Resources*, ed. D. Dockery, K. Matthews, and R. Sloan (Nashville: Broadman & Holman, 1994), 187–204, 414–33.

Source Criticism

Source criticism, which arose as a discrete inquiry during the nineteenth century, focuses on delineating and describing the sources that underlie the final form of the Bible. For example, in the synoptic Gospels (Matthew, Mark, and Luke), the amount of overlap between the various accounts has led scholars to suggest a literary relationship between them. Determining which gospel(s) were used as sources for the others is the task of source critics. Source criticism has been most extensively applied to biblical narrative (Old Testament narratives; Gospels), but has also been used in other genres, such as in New Testament epistles.

Form Criticism

The goal of form criticism, which experienced its heyday in the early part of the twentieth century, has been twofold. First, the form critic seeks to identify the various oral forms that gave rise to certain books of the Bible. Second, these forms are then analyzed to determine the ways in which Israel or the church used the forms in their life and worship. For example, form criticism has been applied to Old Testament poetic genres like psalms and prophetic literature, since most of these books contain material that circulated orally before being committed to writing. Two central assumptions of form criticism are that oral traditions tend to be passed on in predictable patterns, and that these patterns provide insight into the *context* and *purpose* of the telling of the tradition.

Redaction Criticism

Redaction criticism builds on the work of source criticism and has developed primarily in relation to Gospel studies in the mid-twentieth century. Redaction refers to the editing of source material by biblical authors. The first goal of redaction criticism is to identify an individual author's literary and theological contribution to the shaping of the traditional material inherited. For example, a redaction critic would be interested in Luke's unique emphases discernable by comparing what Luke adds to his source material from Mark.[2] The second goal of redaction criticism is to hypothesize what an author's unique emphases say about the author's audience.

2. Most redaction criticism is built on the assumption of Markan priority, that is, that Mark's Gospel was written first and that Matthew and Luke used Mark in the composition of their Gospels.

Resources on Historical Criticism and Other Biblical Studies Methodologies

Green, Joel B., ed. *Hearing the New Testament*. Grand Rapids: Eerdmans, 1995.

McKenzie, Steven L., and Stephen R. Haynes, eds. *To Each Its Own Meaning: An Introduction to Biblical Criticisms and Their Application*. Louisville: Westminster John Knox, 1993.

Parallelism in Hebrew Poetry

The basic unit of the Hebrew poem is the line (sometimes called the "colon"). There is usually a balancing between combinations of lines, called "parallelism." Parallel lines are mutually defining. The *most frequent* combination consists of two lines, i.e., "two-line verse" (e.g., Ps. 100:4a, b), but also occurring are three (or more) parallel lines, such as a "three-line verse" (e.g., Ps. 100:1–2) or a single nonparallel line (e.g., Ps. 100:3a). Once parallel lines have been identified, the relationship between sets of parallel lines can be determined. The following are some of the most common relationships between parallel lines in Hebrew poetry (with each line labeled A and B).

1. Synonymous Parallelism

A is essentially parallel in meaning to B with a shift in nuance between the two. Together A and B express a unified idea (e.g., Ps. 20:1).

2. Antithetical Parallelism

A is a contrast to B (e.g., Ps. 20:7).

3. Synthetic Parallelism

A is more loosely related to B in one of the following ways:

a. Statement/Reason (e.g., Ps. 28:6)
   B gives reason for A (often connected by "because" or "for")
b. Statement/Question or Question/Statement (e.g., Pss. 6:5; 119:9)
   A or B is a question
c. Statement/Refrain (e.g., Ps. 136:1–26)
   Refrain (B) is repeated throughout the psalm section
d. Progression (e.g., Isa. 40:9; Ps. 1:3)
   B extends or develops the thought of A
e. Specification or Explanation (e.g., Pss. 18:24; 72:9)
   B explains or makes more specific the thought of A
f. Statement/Result (e.g., Ps. 81:12)
   B provides the result or purpose of A (often connected by "to" or "that")

Appendix D

Epistles

Following an Author's Flow of Thought

Basic Guidelines

1. Use either the NASB or ESV version as your preliminary translation, since these translations tend to follow closely the connecting words that link clauses. We will see that conjunctions and other connecting words help us hear connections between ideas in a passage.
2. Divide the passage into clauses. Think of a clause as a group of words with a verbal idea holding them together. Try to keep just one verbal idea in each clause (although you may combine relative clauses with their preceding clause).[1]
3. Once you have placed each distinct clause on a separate line, identify and underline the connecting words that begin each clause. Some clauses will have no beginning connecting words.
4. Moving from clause to clause through the passage, identify relationships between clauses by examining the connecting words as well as trying to hear the implicit connections between clausal

---

1. I do this because relative clauses (beginning with "who," "whom," or "which") routinely provide an explanation for a single word in the previous clause. So, almost by default, a relative clause separated from its previous clause will be an explanation of that previous clause.

ideas when no conjunction or connecting word is present. See the Logical Connections chart below for assistance identifying English conjunctions and their usages.

5. Keep the analysis of the entire passage on one page if possible, so that in the end you can visualize the entire argument of a passage, while also seeing the details of the analysis.

Short Example from Galatians 5:1

1a It was for freedom that Christ set us free;
1b <u>therefore</u> keep standing firm (*result*)
1c <u>and</u> do not be subject again to a yoke of slavery. (*negative-positive*)

Logical Connections: The most common types of logical relationships between ideas or clauses in English are listed below. They are typically identified by the connecting word that introduces the second clause or thought.

and, or	additional idea[2]
if-then	two clauses connected together with a conditional idea
question-answer	two clauses connected together: need to rephrase into a statement
but	contrast
but, and	positive/negative: restatement of idea with its negation ("not")
even though, even if, although, however, nevertheless	concessive (a type of contrast)
moreover	greater/more important idea
in order that, that, for the purpose of	purpose
so that, that, as a result	result
because, since, for	reason
therefore, then, so	implication
by, by means of, with	means (i.e., *the way* something is done)
for, in that, that is	explanation
when, then, while, after, before	temporal idea (relating to time)
just as, as, even as	comparison
to restate, again	restatement

2. The conjunction "and" sometimes connects two clauses whose relationship can be more closely defined than an additional idea. For example, there may be an implicit cause-effect between two clauses connected by "and," as in the following two clauses: I ate an entire box of chocolates, and I was depressed.

Examples of These Procedures in Other Sources

Cotterell, Peter, and Max Turner. "Sentence and Sentence Clusters." In *Linguistics and Biblical Interpretation*, 188–229. Downers Grove, IL: InterVarsity, 1989.

Guthrie, G. H., and J. S. Duvall. "How to Do Semantic Diagramming." In *Biblical Greek Exegesis*, 39–53. Grand Rapids: Zondervan, 1998.

Kaiser, Walter C. "Syntactical Analysis" and "Illustrations of Syntactical and Homiletical Analysis." In *Toward an Exegetical Theology*, 165–81. Grand Rapids: Baker Academic, 1981.

Osborne, Grant. *The Hermeneutical Spiral*. Downers Grove, IL: InterVarsity, 1991. See esp. 27–40.

Piper, John. *Biblical Exegesis: Discovering the Original Meaning of Scripture Texts*. Minneapolis: Desiring God Ministries, 1999.

Schreiner, Thomas R. "Tracing the Argument." In *Interpreting the Pauline Epistles*, 97–126. Grand Rapids: Baker Academic, 1990.

How to Go about Topical Studies

Contrary to popular thought, a topical study is actually more difficult and time-intensive than an inductive study of single passages or texts. If we take seriously the need to listen well to every text we draw upon, we will need to read and study carefully around any number of biblical passages in a topical study. Topical study also presumes that we have a fairly good sense of the whole of Scripture, so that we know which books or passages deal with a specific topic. Given this proviso, there are some guidelines for topical study that can help us as we seek to read and study Scripture on its own terms.

1. Determine *if* Scripture speaks to the proposed idea or topic.
2. Determine *how* Scripture speaks to the proposed idea or topic (i.e., directly or indirectly).
3. Are there key texts that address the topic as their primary point?
   a. If so, choose such a text for your focal text. A concordance search can be helpful in this process.
   b. Study the text carefully to hear the main idea. What does this main idea contribute to the topic being studied?
   c. You may find it helpful to choose a few secondary texts to illustrate ideas from the primary text.

4. If there are no key texts (with their primary point about the topic), choose a few texts that deal with the topic as a secondary issue (or indirectly). Study the passages and their contexts carefully.
5. If choosing a broad biblical topic, such as faith, consider studying one author's take on that topic rather than selecting verses from across Scripture.
6. In the end, recognize the value of *not* finding what you were looking for. It's easy to assume the biblical "answer" when coming into a topical study rather than coming to learn what Scripture truly says about a particular topic. So listen for the biblical message carefully.

Bibliography

Achtemeier, Paul J. *An Introduction to the New Hermeneutic*. Philadelphia: Westminster, 1969.

———. *1 Peter*. Hermeneia. Minneapolis: Fortress, 1996.

Alston, William P. *Illocutionary Acts and Sentence Meaning*. Ithaca, NY: Cornell University Press, 2000.

Austin, J. L. *How to Do Things with Words*. 2nd ed. Cambridge, MA: Harvard University Press, 1975.

Barr, James. *The Semantics of Biblical Language*. Oxford: Oxford University Press, 1961.

Bartholomew, Craig. "Before Babel and after Pentecost: Language, Literature and Biblical Interpretation." In *After Pentecost: Language and Biblical Interpretation*, edited by C. Bartholomew, C. Greene, and K. Möller. Scripture and Hermeneutics Series 2. Grand Rapids: Zondervan, 2001.

Bartholomew, Craig G., Colin Greene, and Karl Möller, eds. *After Pentecost: Language and Biblical Interpretation*. Scripture and Hermeneutics Series 2. Grand Rapids: Zondervan, 2001.

———. eds. *Renewing Biblical Interpretation*. Scripture and Hermeneutics Series 1. Grand Rapids: Zondervan, 2000.

Bauckham, Richard. "Tradition in Relation to Scripture and Reason." In *Scripture, Tradition, and Reason: A Study in the Criteria of Christian Doctrine*, edited by R. Bauckham and B. Drewery. Edinburgh: T&T Clark, 1988.

Bauer, David R. *An Annotated Guide to Biblical Resources for Ministry*. Peabody, MA: Hendrickson, 2003.

———. *The Structure of Matthew's Gospel: A Study in Literary Design*. Journal for the Study of the New Testament: Supplement Series 31. Sheffield: Almond Press, 1988.

Bauer, David R., and Mark Allan Powell, eds. *Treasures New and Old: Recent Contributions to Matthean Studies*. Society of Biblical Literature Symposium Series 1. Atlanta: Scholars Press, 1996.

Beaton, Richard. *Isaiah's Christ in Matthew's Gospel*. Cambridge: Cambridge University Press, 2002.

Berding, Kenneth. "Confusing Word and Concept in 'Spiritual Gifts': Have We Forgotten James Barr's Exhortations?" *Journal of the Evangelical Theological Society* 43 (March 2000): 37–51.

Bergen, Robert D. *1, 2 Samuel*. New American Commentary. Nashville: Broadman & Holman, 1996.

Block, Daniel I. *Judges, Ruth*. New American Commentary. Nashville: Broadman & Holman, 1999.

Blomberg, Craig L. "The Globalization of Hermeneutics." *Journal of the Evangelical Theological Society* 38 (1995): 581–93.

———. "Historical Criticism of the New Testament." In *Foundations for Biblical Interpretation: A Complete Library of Tools and Resources*, edited by D. Dockery, K. Matthews, and R. Sloan. Nashville: Broadman & Holman, 1994.

———. "Marriage, Divorce, Remarriage, and Celibacy: An Exegesis of Matthew 19:3–12." *Trinity Journal* 11 (1990): 161–96.

Bockmuehl, Markus. *Jewish Law in Gentile Churches: Halakha and the Beginning of Christian Public Ethics*. Grand Rapids: Baker Academic, 2000.

Booth, Wayne. *The Rhetoric of Fiction*. 2nd ed. Chicago: University of Chicago Press, 1983.

Breck, John. *The Shape of Biblical Language: Chiasmus in the Scriptures and Beyond*. Crestwood, NY: St. Vladimir's Seminary Press, 1994.

Brett, Mark. "Motives and Intentions in Genesis 1." *Journal of Theological Studies* 42 (1991): 1–16.

Briggs, Richard S. *Words in Action: Speech Act Theory and Biblical Interpretation—Toward a Hermeneutic of Self-Involvement*. New York: T&T Clark, 2001.

Brown, Jeannine K. *The Disciples in Narrative Perspective: The Portrayal and Function of the Matthean Disciples*. Academia Biblica 9. Atlanta: Society of Biblical Literature, 2002.

———. "Genre." In *The Bible and Literature*, edited by Jamie Grant and David Firth. Downers Grove, IL: InterVarsity, forthcoming.

———. "Just a Busybody? A Look at the Greco-Roman Topos of Meddling for Defining *allotriepiskopos* in 1 Peter 4:15." *Journal of Biblical Literature* 150 (Fall 2006): 527–46.

———. "Silent Wives, Verbal Believers: Ethical and Hermeneutical Considerations in 1 Peter 3:1–6 and Its Context." *Word and World* 24 (Fall 2004): 395–403.

Brueggemann, Walter. *Interpretation and Obedience: From Faithful Reading to Faithful Living*. Minneapolis: Fortress, 1991.

Bultmann, Rudolf. "Is Exegesis without Presuppositions Possible?" In *Existence and Faith*, translated by Schubert M. Ogden. London: Hodder and Stoughton, 1960.

Bush, Frederic W. *Ruth/Esther*. Word Biblical Commentary. Dallas: Word, 1996.

Caird, G. B. *The Language and Imagery of the Bible*. Philadelphia: Westminster, 1980.

Capel Anderson, Janice. "Matthew: Sermon and Story." In *Treasures New and Old: Recent Contributions to Matthean Studies*, edited by David R. Bauer and Mark Allan Powell. Society of Biblical Literature Symposium 1. Atlanta: Scholars Press, 1996.

Carson, D. A. *Exegetical Fallacies*. 2nd ed. Grand Rapids: Baker Academic, 1996.

Carter, Warren. *Matthew and Empire: Initial Explorations*. Harrisburg, PA: Trinity Press International, 2001.

Clark, David K. *To Know and Love God*. Wheaton: Crossway Books, 2003.

Conn, Harvie M. "Normativity, Relevance, and Relativism." In *Inerrancy and Hermeneutic: A Tradition, a Challenge, a Debate*. Grand Rapids: Baker Academic, 1988.

Cotterell, Peter, and Max Turner. *Linguistics and Biblical Interpretation*. London: SPCK, 1989.

Currid, John D. *Doing Archaeology in the Land of the Bible: A Basic Guide*. Grand Rapids: Baker Academic, 1999.

Dahl, Carla. "The Dangers of Hospitality." Paper presented at Bethel Seminary, St. Paul, MN, 1 March 2005.

Danker, Frederick W. *Multipurpose Tools for Bible Study*. Rev. ed. Minneapolis: Fortress, 2003.

Davies, William D., and Dale C. Allison. *A Critical and Exegetical Commentary on the Gospel according to Saint Matthew*. Vol. 3. International Critical Commentary. Edinburgh: T&T Clark, 1997.

deSilva, David A. *An Introduction to the New Testament: Context, Methods, and Ministry Formation*. Downers Grove, IL: InterVarsity, 2004.

Dilthey, Wilhelm. *Hermeneutics and the Study of History*. Vol. 4, *Selected Works*, edited by R. Makkreel and F. Rodi. Princeton, NJ: Princeton University Press, 1996.

Doriani, Daniel M. *Putting the Truth to Work: The Theory and Practice of Biblical Application*. Phillipsburg, NJ: P&R Publishing, 2001.

Eco, Umberto. *The Role of the Reader: Explorations in the Semiotics of Texts*. Bloomington, IN: Indiana University Press, 1979.

Eliot, T. S. "Tradition and the Individual Talent." In *Selected Essays*. London: Faber & Faber, 1932.

Enns, Peter. *Inspiration and Incarnation: Evangelicals and the Problem of the Old Testament*. Grand Rapids: Baker Academic, 2005.

"The Epistles of Heraclitus." Translated by David R. Worley. In *The Cynic Epistles*. Edited by Abraham J. Malherbe. Society of Biblical Literature Sources for Biblical Study 12. Atlanta: Scholars Press, 1977.

Fee, Gordon D. *The First Epistle to the Corinthians*. New International Commentary on the New Testament. Grand Rapids: Eerdmans, 1987.

———. *Gospel and Spirit: Issues in New Testament Hermeneutics*. Peabody, MA: Hendrickson, 1991.

———. *Listening to the Spirit in the Text*. Grand Rapids: Eerdmans, 2000.

———. *New Testament Exegesis*. 2nd ed. Louisville: Westminster John Knox, 1993.

———. *To What End Exegesis? Essays Textual, Exegetical, and Theological*. Grand Rapids: Eerdmans, 2001.

Fee, Gordon D., and Douglas Stuart. *How to Read the Bible for All Its Worth*. 3rd ed. Grand Rapids: Zondervan, 2003.

Fish, Stanley. *Is There a Text in This Class? The Authority of Interpretive Communities*. Cambridge, MA: Harvard University Press, 1980.

Fowler, Robert M. "Who Is 'the Reader' in Reader Response Criticism?" *Semeia* 31 (1985): 14.

Gadamer, Hans-Georg. "Reflections on My Philosophical Journey." In *The Philosophy of Hans-Georg Gadamer*, edited by Lewis E. Hahn. Library of Living Philosophers. Chicago: Open Court, 1997.

————. *Truth and Method*. Translated by Joel Weinsheimer and Donald G. Marshall. 2nd ed. New York: Continuum, 2004.

Garland, David E. *1 Corinthians*. Baker Exegetical Commentary on the New Testament. Grand Rapids: Baker Academic, 2003.

Garrett, Duane A. "Historical Criticism of the Old Testament." In *Foundations for Biblical Interpretation: A Complete Library of Tools and Resources*, edited by D. Dockery, K. Matthews, and R. Sloan. Nashville: Broadman & Holman, 1994.

Goldingay, John. "Biblical Narrative and Systematic Theology." In *Between Two Horizons: Spanning New Testament Studies and Systematic Theology*, edited by Joel B. Green and Max Turner. Grand Rapids: Eerdmans, 2000.

Gorman, Michael J. *Elements of Biblical Exegesis: A Basic Guide for Students and Ministers*. Peabody, MA: Hendrickson, 2001.

Green, Garrett. *Theology, Hermeneutics, and Imagination: Interpretation at the End of Modernity*. Cambridge: Cambridge University Press, 2000.

Green, Gene. "Context and Communication." Paper presented at the linguistics section of the annual meeting of the Society of Biblical Literature, Toronto, Ontario, 25 November 2002.

Green, Joel B. "Practicing the Gospel in a Post-Critical World: The Promise of Theological Hermeneutics." *Journal of the Evangelical Theological Society* 47 (September 2004): 392.

————. "The (Re)turn to Narrative." In *Narrative Reading, Narrative Preaching*, edited by Joel B. Green and Michael Pasquarello III. Grand Rapids: Baker Academic, 2003.

————. "Scripture and Theology: Uniting the Two So Long Divided." In *Between Two Horizons: Spanning New Testament Studies and Systematic Theology*, edited by Joel B. Green and Max Turner. Grand Rapids: Eerdmans, 2000.

Green, Joel B., and Max Turner, eds. *Between Two Horizons: Spanning New Testament Studies and Systematic Theology*. Grand Rapids: Eerdmans, 2000.

Grudem, Wayne. "Should We Move Beyond the New Testament to a Better Ethic?" *Journal of the Evangelical Theological Society* 47 (June 2004): 338.

Gunn, David M., and Danna Nolan Fewell. *Narrative in the Hebrew Bible*. Oxford Bible Series. Oxford: Oxford University Press, 1993.

Gutt, Ernst-August. *Relevance Theory: A Guide to Successful Communication in Translation*. New York: United Bible Societies and Summer Institute of Linguistics, 1992.

Hanson, Kenneth C., and Douglas E. Oakman. *Palestine in the Time of Jesus: Social Structures and Conflicts*. Minneapolis: Fortress, 1998.

Hart, Trevor. *Faith Thinking: The Dynamics of Christian Theology*. Downers Grove, IL: InterVarsity, 1996.

———. "Tradition, Authority, and a Christian Approach to the Bible as Scripture." In *Between Two Horizons: Spanning New Testament Studies and Systematic Theology*, edited by Joel B. Green and Max Turner. Grand Rapids: Eerdmans, 2000.

Hays, Richard. *Echoes of Scripture in the Letters of Paul*. New Haven: Yale University Press, 1989.

———. *The Moral Vision of the New Testament: A Contemporary Introduction to New Testament Ethics*. San Francisco: HarperSanFrancisco, 1996.

Hazlitt, William. "On Reading Old Books." In *The Plain Speaker*. London: Henry Colburn, 1826.

Heidegger, Martin. *Being and Time*. Translated by J. Macquarrie and E. Robinson. Oxford: Blackwell, 1978.

Hinkle, Mary E. "Whither Imagination? Comparing Exegesis Textbooks." Paper presented at the annual meeting of the Upper Midwest Region of the Society of Biblical Literature, St. Paul, MN, 2 April 2005.

Hirsch, E. D. "Meaning and Significance Reinterpreted." *Critical Inquiry* 11 (1984): 210.

———. "Transhistorical Intentions and the Persistence of Allegory." *New Literary History* 25 (1994): 555.

———. *Validity in Interpretation*. New Haven: Yale University Press, 1967.

Holladay, William Lee. *Concise Hebrew and Aramaic Lexicon of the Old Testament*. Leiden: Brill, 1988.

Hultgren, Arland J. "Face to Face: Should I Preach from a Lectionary? Yes!" *Word and World* 24 (Fall 2004): 442, 444.

Instone-Brewer, David. *Traditions of the Rabbis from the Era of the New Testament*. Grand Rapids: Eerdmans, 2004.

Jeanrond, Werner G. *Text and Interpretation as Categories of Theological Thinking*. Translated by T. Wilson. Dublin: Gill and Macmillan, 1988.

Jeffers, James S. *The Greco-Roman World of the New Testament Era*. Downers Grove, IL: InterVarsity, 1999.

Jeremias, Joachim. *The Lord's Prayer*. Translated by John Reumann. Philadelphia: Fortress, 1964.

Jobes, Karen H. *1 Peter*. Baker Exegetical Commentary on the New Testament. Grand Rapids: Baker Academic, 2005.

Jokinen, Kristina. "Goal Formulation Based on Communicative Principles." In *Proceedings of the Sixteenth International Conference on Computational Linguistics*. Copenhagen, Denmark: Center for Sprogteknologi, 1996.

Kaiser, Walter C., Jr. *Toward Rediscovering the Old Testament*. Grand Rapids: Zondervan, 1987.

Kaiser, Walter, Jr., and Moisés Silva. *An Introduction to Biblical Hermeneutics: The Search for Meaning*. Grand Rapids: Zondervan, 1994.

Keener, Craig S. *The Gospel of John: A Commentary*. Vol. 2. Peabody, MA: Hendrickson, 2003.

———. *The InterVarsity Press Bible Background Commentary: New Testament*. Downers Grove, IL: InterVarsity, 1993.

Kittel, G., and G. Friedrich, eds. *Theological Dictionary of the New Testament*. Translated by G. W. Bromiley. 10 vols. Grand Rapids: Eerdmans, 1964–76.

Klein, William W., Craig L. Blomberg, and Robert L. Hubbard Jr. *Introduction to Biblical Interpretation*. Dallas: Word, 1993.

Kuhatschek, Jack. *Taking the Guesswork Out of Applying the Bible*. Downers Grove, IL: InterVarsity, 1990.

Laird Harris, R., Gleason L. Archer, and Bruce K. Waltke, *Theological Wordbook of the Old Testament*. Chicago: Moody, 1980.

Larkin, William J., Jr. *Biblical Theology of Hermeneutics and Culture: Interpreting and Applying the Authoritative Word in a Relativistic Age*. Grand Rapids: Baker Academic, 1988.

Leith, Dick, and George Myerson. *The Power of Address: Explorations in Rhetoric*. London: Routledge, 1989.

Levinas, Emmanuel. *Otherwise Than Being or Beyond Essence*. Translated by Alphonso Lingis. Pittsburgh: Duquesne University Press, 1998.

———. *Totality and Infinity*. Translated by Alphonso Lingis. Pittsburgh: Duquesne University Press, 1969.

Levine, Amy-Jill. "Putting Jesus Where He Belongs: The Man from Nazareth in His Jewish World." *Perspectives in Religious Studies* 27 (Summer 2000): 171.

Lewis, C. S. *Mere Christianity*. 1952. Reprint, London: HarperCollins, 2002.

———. *Reflections on the Psalms*. London: Geoffrey Bles, 1958.

Lindbeck, George. "The Story-Shaped Church: Critical Exegesis and Theological Interpretation." In *The Theological Interpretation of Scrip-*

ture: Classic and Contemporary Readings, edited by Stephen E. Fowl. Blackwell Readings in Modern Theology. Cambridge, MA: Blackwell, 1997.

Lovejoy, Grant. "Shaping Sermons by the Literary Form of the Text." In *Biblical Hermeneutics: A Comprehensive Introduction to Interpreting Scripture,* edited by B. Corley, S. Lemke, and G. Lovejoy. Nashville: Broadman & Holman, 1996.

Lundin, Roger, Anthony C. Thiselton, and Clarence Walhout. *The Responsibility of Hermeneutics.* Grand Rapids: Eerdmans, 1985.

Malina, Bruce J. *The New Testament World: Insights from Cultural Anthropology.* 3rd ed. Louisville: Westminster John Knox, 2001.

Marshall, I. Howard. *Beyond the Bible: Moving from Scripture to Theology.* Grand Rapids: Baker Academic, 2004.

Martin, Clarice J. "A Chamberlain's Journey and the Challenge of Interpretation for Liberation." *Semeia* 47 (1989): 105–35.

Mason, S. "Pharisees." In *Dictionary of New Testament Background,* edited by Craig A. Evans and Stanley E. Porter. Downers Grove, IL: InterVarsity, 2000.

McAfee Brown, Robert. *Unexpected News: Reading the Bible with Third World Eyes.* Philadelphia: Westminster, 1984.

McClendon, James W., Jr. *Systematic Theology.* 2nd ed. Nashville: Abingdon, 2002.

McKnight, Edgar V. *Reading the Bible Today: A Twenty-First Century Appreciation of Scripture.* Macon, GA: Smyth & Helwys, 2003.

Meeks, Wayne A. "Why Study the New Testament?" *New Testament Studies* 51 (April 2005): 166.

Metzger, Bruce M. *The New Testament: Its Background, Growth, and Content.* 3rd ed. New York: Abingdon, 2003.

Mickelsen, A. Berkeley. *Interpreting the Bible.* Grand Rapids: Eerdmans, 1963.

Miller, J. Hillis. *Speech Acts in Literature.* Stanford, CA: Stanford University Press, 2001.

Moritz, Thorsten. "Critical but Real: Reflecting on N. T. Wright's Tools for the Task." In *Renewing Biblical Interpretation,* edited by C. Bartholomew, C. Greene, and K. Möller, 172–97. Scripture and Hermeneutics Series 1. Grand Rapids: Zondervan, 2000.

———. *A Profound Mystery: The Use of the Old Testament in Ephesians.* Supplements to Novum Testamentum 85. Leiden: Brill, 1996.

Neill, Stephen, and N. T. Wright. *The Interpretation of the New Testament, 1861–1986.* 2nd ed. Oxford: Oxford University Press, 1988.

Nielsen, Kristen. *Intertextuality and Hebrew Bible*. Supplements to Vetus Testamentum 80. Leiden: Brill, 2000.

Olson, Dennis T. "Judges." In *The New Interpreter's Bible*. Vol. 2. Nashville: Abingdon, 1998.

Ong, Walter J. *Orality and Literacy: The Technologizing of the Word*. New York: Methuen, 1982.

Osborne, Grant R. *The Hermeneutical Spiral: A Comprehensive Introduction to Biblical Interpretation*. Downers Grove, IL: InterVarsity, 1991.

Packer, J. I. *Honouring the Written Word of God: The Collected Shorter Writings of J. I. Packer*. Carlisle: Paternoster, 1999.

Paul, Ian. "Metaphor and Exegesis." In *After Pentecost: Language and Biblical Interpretation*, edited by C. Bartholomew, C. Greene, and K. Möller. Scripture and Hermeneutics Series 2. Grand Rapids: Zondervan, 2001.

Penner, Myron B. "Christianity and the Postmodern Turn: Some Preliminary Considerations." In *Christianity and the Postmodern Turn: Six Views*, edited by Myron B. Penner. Grand Rapids: Brazos, 2005.

Powell, Mark Allan. *Chasing the Eastern Star: Adventures in Biblical Reader-Response Criticism*. Louisville: Westminster John Knox, 2001.

———. "Expected and Unexpected Readings of Matthew: What the Reader Knows." *Asbury Theological Journal* 48 (1993): 31–51.

———. *Loving Jesus*. Minneapolis: Fortress, 2004.

———. *What Is Narrative Criticism?* Guides to Biblical Scholarship. Minneapolis: Fortress, 1990.

Pratt, Mary Louise. *Toward a Speech Act Theory of Literary Discourse*. Bloomington, IN: Indiana University Press, 1977.

Reinhartz, Adele. *Befriending the Beloved Disciple: A Jewish Reading of the Gospel of John*. New York: Continuum, 2001.

Ricoeur, Paul. *Interpretation Theory: Discourse and the Surplus of Meaning*. Fort Worth: Texas Christian University Press, 1976.

———. *Time and Narrative*. Translated by Kathleen Blamey and David Pellauer. Chicago: University of Chicago Press, 1984.

Robertson McQuilkin, J. *Understanding and Applying the Bible*. Rev. ed. Chicago: Moody, 1992.

Ryken, Leland, et al. *Dictionary of Biblical Imagery*. Downers Grove, IL: InterVarsity, 1998.

Schleiermacher, Friedrich. *Hermeneutics and Criticism and Other Writings*. Edited and translated by Andrew Bowie. Cambridge Texts in the History of Philosophy. Cambridge: Cambridge University Press, 1998.

Searle, John. *Speech Acts: An Essay in the Philosophy of Language*. Cambridge: Cambridge University Press, 1969.

Silva, Moisés. *Biblical Words and Their Meaning: An Introduction to Lexical Semantics*. Rev. ed. Grand Rapids: Zondervan, 1994.

———. *God, Language and Scripture: Reading the Bible in Light of General Linguistics*. Foundations of Contemporary Interpretation 4. Grand Rapids: Zondervan, 1990.

———. *Has the Church Misread the Bible? The History of Interpretation in the Light of Current Issues*. Foundations of Contemporary Interpretation 1. Grand Rapids: Zondervan, 1987.

Skinner, Quentin. "Motives, Intentions and the Interpretation of Texts." *New Literary History* 3 (Winter 1971): 393–408.

Snodgrass, Klyne. "Matthew and the Law." In *Treasures New and Old: Recent Contributions to Matthean Studies*, edited by David R. Bauer and Mark Allan Powell. Society of Biblical Literature Symposium Series 1. Atlanta: Scholars Press, 1996.

Sparks, Kenton L. *Ancient Texts for the Study of the Hebrew Bible: A Guide to the Background Literature*. Peabody, MA: Hendrickson, 2005.

Sperber, Dan, and Deirdre Wilson. *Relevance: Communication and Cognition*. Cambridge, MA: Harvard University Press, 1986.

Stagg, Frank. "The Abused Aorist." *Journal of Biblical Literature* 91 (1972): 222–31.

Stanton, Graham. *Jesus of Nazareth in New Testament Preaching*. New York: Cambridge University Press, 1974.

Stark, Rodney. *The Rise of Christianity: A Sociologist Reconsiders History*. Princeton, NJ: Princeton University Press, 1996.

Stein, Robert H. *A Basic Guide to Interpreting the Bible: Playing by the Rules*. Grand Rapids: Baker Academic, 1994.

———. *Difficult Passages in the New Testament: Interpreting Puzzling Texts in the Gospels and Epistles*. Grand Rapids: Baker Academic, 1990.

———. "Divorce." In *The Dictionary of Jesus and the Gospels*, edited by J. Green, S. McKnight, and I. H. Marshall. Downers Grove, IL: InterVarsity, 1992.

———. "Is Our Reading the Bible the Same as the Original Audience's Hearing It? A Case Study in the Gospel of Mark." *Journal of the Evangelical Theological Society* 46 (March 2003): 63–78.

———. *The Method and Message of Jesus' Teaching*. Rev. ed. Louisville: Westminster John Knox, 1994.

Steiner, George. *Real Presences: Is There Anything in What We Say?* London: Faber & Faber, 1989.

Steinmetz, David C. "The Superiority of Pre-Critical Exegesis." In *The Theological Interpretation of Scripture: Classic and Contemporary Readings*, edited by Stephen E. Fowl. Blackwell Readings in Modern Theology. Cambridge, MA: Blackwell, 1997.

Sternberg, Meir. *The Poetics of Biblical Narrative: Ideological Literature and the Drama of Reading*. Bloomington, IN: Indiana University Press, 1987.

Stiver, Dan R. *The Philosophy of Religious Language: Sign, Symbol, and Story*. Malden, MA: Blackwell, 1996.

Strauss, Mark. "Current Issues in the Gender-Language Debate: A Response to Vern Poythress and Wayne Grudem." In *The Challenge of Bible Translation*, edited by M. Strauss, G. Scorgie, and S. Voth. Grand Rapids: Zondervan, 2003.

Strauss, Mark L., Glen G. Scorgie, and Steven M.Voth, eds. *The Challenge of Bible Translation: Communicating God's Word to the World: Essays in Honor of Ronald F. Youngblood*. Grand Rapids: Zondervan, 2003.

Sugirtharajah, R. S. "Critics, Tools, and the Global Arena." In *Reading the Bible in the Global Village: Helsinki*, edited by Heikki Raisanen et al., 49–60. Atlanta: Society of Biblical Literature, 2000.

Thiselton, Anthony C. "'Behind' and 'In Front Of' the Text: Language, Reference and Indeterminacy." In *After Pentecost: Language and Biblical Interpretation*, edited by C. Bartholomew, C. Greene, and K. Möller. Scripture and Hermeneutics Series 2. Grand Rapids: Zondervan, 2001.

———. *New Horizons in Hermeneutics: The Theory and Practice of Transforming Biblical Reading*. Grand Rapids: Zondervan, 1992.

———. *The Two Horizons: New Testament Hermeneutics and Philosophical Description with Special Reference to Heidegger, Bultmann, Gadamer, and Wittgenstein*. Grand Rapids: Eerdmans, 1980.

Throntveit, Mark A. "Face to Face: Should I Preach from a Lectionary? Why?" *Word and World* 24 (Fall 2004): 443, 446.

Tolbert, Mary Ann. *Sowing the Gospel: Mark's World in Literary-Historical Perspective*. Minneapolis: Fortress, 1989.

Turner, Max. "Theological Hermeneutics." In *Between Two Horizons: Spanning New Testament Studies and Systematic Theology*, edited by Joel B. Green and Max Turner. Grand Rapids: Eerdmans, 2000.

Vanhoozer, Kevin J. *Biblical Narrative in the Philosophy of Paul Ricoeur*. Cambridge: Cambridge University Press, 1990.

———. *The Drama of Doctrine: A Canonical-Linguistic Approach to Christian Theology*. Louisville: Westminster John Knox, 2005.

―――. *First Theology: God, Scripture and Hermeneutics*. Downers Grove, IL: InterVarsity, 2002.

―――. "From Speech Acts to Scripture Acts: The Covenant of Discourse and the Discourse of the Covenant." In *After Pentecost: Language and Biblical Interpretation*, edited by C. Bartholomew, C. Greene, and K. Möller. Scripture and Hermeneutics Series 2. Grand Rapids: Zondervan, 2001.

―――. "Into the Great 'Beyond': A Theologian's Response to the Marshall Plan." In *Beyond the Bible: Moving from Scripture to Theology*, by I. Howard Marshall. Grand Rapids: Baker Academic, 2004.

―――. *Is There a Meaning in This Text? The Bible, the Reader, and the Morality of Literary Knowledge*. Grand Rapids: Zondervan, 1998.

―――. "Lost in Interpretation? Truth, Scripture, and Hermeneutics." *Journal of the Evangelical Theological Society* 48 (March 2005): 102.

Vogt, Peter T. *Interpreting the Pentateuch: An Exegetical Handbook*. Grand Rapids: Kregel, forthcoming.

Wallace, Daniel B. *Greek beyond the Basics: An Exegetical Syntax of the New Testament*. Grand Rapids: Zondervan, 1996.

Watts, Rikki E. *Isaiah's New Exodus and Mark*. Wissenschaftliche Untersuchungen zum Neuen Testament 2. Tübingen: Mohr, 1997.

Webb, William J. "A Redemptive-Movement Hermeneutic: Encouraging Dialogue among Four Evangelical Views." *Journal of the Evangelical Theological Society* 48 (June 2005): 336.

―――. *Slaves, Women, and Homosexuals: Exploring the Hermeneutics of Cultural Analysis*. Downers Grove, IL: InterVarsity, 2001.

Wenham, Gordon J. *Genesis*. Word Biblical Commentary. Waco: Word, 1987.

―――. *Story as Torah: Reading the Old Testament Ethically*. Old Testament Studies. Edinburgh: T&T Clark, 2000.

Wilkinson, Loren. "Hermeneutics and the Postmodern Reaction against 'Truth.'" In *The Act of Bible Reading: A Multidisciplinary Approach to Biblical Interpretation*, edited by Elmer Dyck. Downers Grove, IL: InterVarsity, 1996.

Wimsatt, W. K., and Monroe C. Beardsley. "The Intentional Fallacy." In *On Literary Intention*, edited by David Newton-de Molina, 1–13. Edinburgh: University Press, 1976.

Witherington, Ben, III. *The Gospel of Mark: A Socio-Rhetorical Commentary*. Grand Rapids: Eerdmans, 2001.

Wittgenstein, Ludwig. *Philosophical Investigations*. Translated by G. E. M. Anscombe. Vol. 2. Oxford: Basil Blackwell, 1968.

Wolters, Al. "Confessional Criticism and the Night Visions of Zechariah." In *Renewing Biblical Interpretation*, edited by C. Bartholomew, C. Greene, and K. Möller. Scripture and Hermeneutics Series 1. Grand Rapids: Zondervan, 2000.

Wolterstorff, Nicholas. *Divine Discourse: Philosophical Reflections on the Claim that God Speaks*. Cambridge: Cambridge University Press, 1995.

Wright, Christopher J. H. *Knowing Jesus through the Old Testament*. Downers Grove, IL: InterVarsity, 1995.

———. *Old Testament Ethics for the People of God*. Downers Grove, IL: InterVarsity, 2004.

Wright, N. T. *The Challenge of Jesus: Rediscovering Who Jesus Was and Is*. Downers Grove, IL: InterVarsity, 1999.

———. *The Climax of the Covenant: Christ and the Law in Pauline Theology*. Minneapolis: Fortress, 1992.

———. *IVP Academic Alert* 8, no. 3 (Autumn 1999): 2.

———. *The Last Word*. New York: HarperSanFrancisco, 2005.

———. "The Letter to the Galatians: Exegesis and Theology." In *Between Two Horizons: Spanning New Testament Studies and Systematic Theology*, edited by Joel B. Green and Max Turner. Grand Rapids: Eerdmans, 2000.

———. *The New Testament and the People of God*. Minneapolis: Fortress, 1992.

———. *Paul for Everyone: Galatians and Thessalonians*. 2nd ed. Louisville: Westminster John Knox, 2004.

Young, Frances. "Proverbs 8 in Interpretation (2): Wisdom Personified." In *Reading Texts, Seeking Wisdom: Scripture and Theology*, edited by David F. Ford and Graham Stanton. Grand Rapids: Eerdmans, 2003.

Zimmermann, Jens. *Recovering Theological Hermeneutics: An Incarnational-Trinitarian Theory of Interpretation*. Grand Rapid: Baker Academic, 2004.

Subject Index

abstraction, 264–65, 266
Achtemeier, Paul J., 134n44
acrostics, 147, 148
actualization of meaning, 124
actualized communicative event, 97–98
Alexander the Great, 167, 199
alliteration, 144, 145
allusion, 108–10
Alston, William P., 32, 33n7, 84n12, 97n39, 112
alternation, 218
ambiguity in meaning, 90–94
anachronistic reading, 184–85
ancient Near East, 194–95
antithetical parallelism, 146–47, 284
aorist tense, 187
apocalyptic literature, 24, 140
Apocrypha, 196, 197
application, 26n13, 116, 118, 234, 239n16, 247, 280
archaeology, 195, 200n27
arcing, 154n39
argumentation, 156–57
Aristotle, 199
assonance, 144, 145
assumed context, 35, 36–38. *See also* background-contextual assumptions
atlases, 203–4
atomistic method, 216–17
audience context, 192

Austen, Jane, 121, 221–22
Austin, J. L., 32–33, 98, 114
author, 14–15, 22, 27–28
  and ambiguity, 91–93
  background-contextual assumptions, 48, 49
  banishment of, 28
  in history of hermeneutics, 57–60
  as irrelevant, 63
  and meaning, 22–23, 80–82
  and speech-act theory, 35
  world of, 240
authorial attitude, 221
authorial discourse, 13
authorial intention, 22–23, 27, 39, 60–61, 69, 70–72, 92, 181
authoritative speakers, 161n56

background-contextual assumptions, 48, 49, 50, 53–54
Baptist tradition, 121
Barr, James, 177–78, 185
Bartholomew, Craig, 168, 169–70
Bauckham, Richard, 236n10
Bauer, David, 159
Beardsley, Monroe, 62
belief system, 29–30
believing criticism, 234n7
Bible
  as canon, 235–37

304

Scripture Index